DATE DUE

THE FANATICS

A BEHAVIOURAL APPROACH TO POLITICAL VIOLENCE

THE FANATICS

A BEHAVIOURAL APPROACH
TO POLITICAL VIOLENCE

by

MAXWELL TAYLOR

BRASSEY'S (UK)

A Member of the Maxwell Macmillan Group

LONDON · OXFORD · WASHINGTON · NEW YORK · SYDNEY

23383210
DLC

8-31-92

Copyright © 1991 Brassey's (UK)

First edition 1991

UK editorial offices: Brassey's, 50 Fetter Lane, London EC4A 1AA
orders: Brassey's, Headington Hill Hall, Oxford OX3 0BW

USA editorial offices: Brassey's, 8000 Westpark Drive, First Floor, Virginia 22101
orders: Macmillan, Front & Brown Streets, Riverside NJ 08075

Library of Congress Cataloging-in-Publication Data
Taylor, Maxwell, 1945–
The fanatics: a behavioural approach to political violence /
Maxwell Taylor. — 1st ed.
p. cm.
Includes bibliographical references and index.
1. Violence. 2. Fanaticism. 3. Ideology. I. Title.
HM281.T345 1991 303.6—dc20 91-12088

British Library Cataloguing in Publication Data
Taylor, Maxwell 1945–
The fanatics: a behavioural approach to political violence.
1. Politics. Violence
I. Title
322.42

ISBN 0–08–036274–5

Printed in Great Britain by B.P.C.C. Wheatons Ltd., Exeter

Contents

Glossary

(terms referred to in the Glossary are indicated in **bold** type).

Aggression. Any form of behaviour directed towards the goal of harming or injuring another human being. In this work a contrast is made between the use of the term aggression and **violence** (see **Violence**).

Authoritarian. A personality state showing patterns of submissive obedience to authority, punitive rejection of other groups, and a tendency to see the world in black-and-white terms.

Aversive. An undesirable or unpleasant state. **Aversive** is used when referring to unpleasant states to which the individual is exposed, or to refer to forms of learning. **Aversive** learning refers to the elimination of an undesirable response through association with punishment.

Behaviour. Those activities of an individual that can be observed by another, or by instruments designed for the purpose. Verbal reports are a form of behaviour (see **Phenomenology** for a contrasting approach).

Behaviour Chains. Behaviour linked to other behaviour through sequences of learning, often involving **discriminative stimuli**.

Behavioural Contingency. A threefold description of a **response**, a description of an outcome, and the identification of circumstances of some form in the presence of which a **response** will produce that outcome.

Behavioural Control. The regulation of behaviour through previous learning. Significant factors in the **control** of behaviour are the past history of **reinforcement** and **environmental** qualities such as **discriminative stimuli**.

Behavioural Rules. A **behavioural rule** is a verbal description of the relationship between **behaviour** and the **consequences of**

behaviour, especially **reinforcement**. **Behavioural Rules** are also a description of the **contingencies** (both future and past) that may control behaviour. Amongst other things, **behavioural rules** mediate between distant outcomes and immediate **behaviour**.

Chains, Behaviour. See **Behaviour Chains**.

Consequences of Behaviour. The events that terminate, or coincide with the end of, a sequence of **behaviour**. The most significant consequence in the control of behaviour is **reinforcement**.

Contingency. A description of the relationship between **reinforcement** and **behaviour**.

Control, Behavioural. See **Behavioural Control**.

Discriminative Stimulus. The circumstances or associated events that set the occasion for a **response** to be **reinforced**.

Environment. The physical situation and surroundings in which **behaviour** takes place. In some circumstances, it can also embrace passage of time as a variable.

Fanatic, Fanaticism. Behaviour which is excessive and inappropriately enthusiastic and/or inappropriately concerned with something, implying a focused and highly personalised interpretation of the world. In a political sense, behaviour which is strongly influenced and controlled by **ideology**, where the influence of **ideology** is such that it excludes or attenuates other social, political or personal forces that might be expected to control and influence **behaviour**.

Ideology. The organisation of beliefs and attitudes – religious, political or philosophical in nature – that are more or less institutionalised or shared with others, and which derive from external authority. In behavioural terms, it is a common, public and broadly agreed set of externally derived **behavioural rules** which influence, in some measure, an individual and which help to regulate and control behaviour in social and political contexts.

Imminence. The impending attainment of the **millenarian** event. In the sense used in this book, the imminent event is not just eventually to be attained, but is soon to happen. As such, it is a critical element in the development of political **violence** (see **Millenarian**).

Mentalistic. Making reference to explanations of **behaviour** in terms of mental events.

Messianism, Messianic. Related to the attainment of **Messianic** promises of a new perfect state of being, where the Messiah is the promised deliverer (see **Millenarian**).

Militancy. Combative or aggressive qualities associated with **ideology**.

Millenarian. Looking forward to the promised better future, related to the Biblical prophesy of Christ's return to earth to reign for 1000 years. More generally used as a generic term in both secular and religious contexts to describe the attainment of future perfect states of being. 'Symptoms' of millenarianism include:

1. An analysis of the world in terms of a real or impending catastrophe, which has an immediate effect on the individual's life;
2. A revelation that explains this state of affairs, and which offers some form of salvation or redressing of ills;
3. As part of the revelation, the possession of special knowledge that the disastrous state is the result of the action of malevolent forces (spiritual or secular) which conspire to corrupt and subvert the normal organs of society or the State. Through the possession of special knowledge, the holder has a unique and powerful capacity to fight the malevolent and corrupting forces;
4. A sense of timeliness for action, in that the forces of corruption are nearing completion of their tasks;
5. A conviction that these forces can be defeated because of the special insights, and that the defeat of the forces of evil will result in the ushering in of a new and better world (see **Messianism** and **Utopianism**).

Phenomenology. The study of an individual's subjective experience as a unique perception of the world. Events are understood from the individual's own point of view, rather than focusing on an individual's **behaviour** (see **Behaviour**).

Public Space. A term used by Hannah Arendt to characterise the availability of any sort of mental or physical forum within which free debate can exist without fear of sanction. A particular quality to Arendt's use of the term refers to the process whereby an individual both gains and maintains a sense of reality. The absence of Public Space is a critical element in the development of political violence.

Reinforcer, Reinforcement. An event which increases the future probability of occurrence of a **response** that it follows. Negative **reinforcement** refers to the attainment of this by *taking away* an **aversive** event; positive **reinforcement** achieves this through *adding* or *presenting* a positive event.

Response. The activity of an individual that can be seen, described and measured in some way, either through observation or the use of appropriate instruments (see **behaviour**).

Shari'a. The Islamic laws derived from the Qur'an, Hadith and other holy sources of Islam. More generally, **Shari'a** can refer not just to a narrow sense of codes of law, but to the all-embracing way of life laid down by Allah for Muslims. In this sense, it embraces the values, customs and **social norms** which shape and influence all of human life when seen from a Muslim perspective.

Shi'a, Shi'ite. Refers to one of the two major branches of Islam (the other being Sunni). A characteristic of Shi'a thinking is an emphasis on divine legitimacy, gained through the descent of Shi'a leaders from the family of the Prophet Mohammed (Fatima the daughter of Mohammed and Ali her husband). Three branches of Shi'aism can be identified, related to which of the early Immans they follow. The Shi'a version of Islam differs in a number of significant ways from Sunni versions, and considerable antagonism exists between them. In the Islamic world as a whole, the Shi'a are in a minority.

Social Norms. A group or community's unwritten rules that govern its members' behaviour, attitudes and beliefs.

Utopian, Utopianism. A place, or proposed state, where there is an attainable perfect social and political system. In some respects, a secular equivalent of the **messianic** and **millenarian** perfect state.

Violence. Any form of directed or indiscriminate behaviour aimed at harming or injuring another human being. Whilst recognising in this work the similarity in meaning between the terms **aggression** and **violence, violence** is the preferred term. It is more readily seen as a description of behaviour, and embraces the situation where no particular victim is intended, but rather any person who happens to be there.

Preface

It is difficult to understand the problem of political violence. It challenges complacent views of the orderliness and reasonableness of behaviour, its contemporary relevance obscures objective analysis, and its multifaceted nature leads to complex analysis. Those concerned with its management don't need to be told how complex it is and quite reasonably look to the specialist for useable and comprehensive explanations. But it may be that these expectations are too great for the present state of our knowledge.

In an earlier book[1] I explored the concept of the terrorist from a psychological and behavioural perspective, and sought to challenge some of the assumptions we make about terrorism. In this book, I have extended that analysis to offer an analysis in behavioural terms of the factors that might influence the development of political violence.

In so complex an area, where empirical investigation is sparse and difficult to conduct, discussions of processes must necessarily be speculative. It is possible to draw on well developed psychological and behavioural theories to develop our appreciation of the problems, but the application of these theories to the understanding of political violence necessarily goes beyond the strict limits of empirical verification. One aim of the book has been to extend behavioural approaches further into the realms of socio-political analysis, but focusing on matters related to the control of individual behaviour, rather than the social context in which that behaviour might occur. This broadly corresponds to what Mills[2] has referred to as a 'troubles' rather than 'issues' approach. However, the book may be read at a variety of levels, ranging from an analysis in behavioural terms of fanatical violence, to a more general account of political violence which may be interpreted from a number of social science or psychological perspectives.

Whilst the approach of behaviour analysis is the seed from which the book has grown, the technical accounts of behavioural processes may be skipped without substantial damage to the arguments presented. The reader may draw some comfort from that! Indeed, it would be a great disappointment if it were seen as a narrow psychology book. The study of political violence requires a unique and challenging interdisciplinary approach. Insights into the causes and origins of political violence are not the preserve of any single discipline, and indeed, critically important insights may well be found not in the Social Sciences at all, but in that obscure interface between literary work and society. It is to that broad and less well defined agenda that I hope this book will eventually contribute.

Is there then a solution to the problem of political violence? I suspect not, in the sense of an easily understood formula that can be applied to reduce its incidence, or prevent its occurrence. For the foreseeable future, I think the best we can hope for is a growing understanding of the processes involved. That understanding can then structure and inform empirical explorations where possible, and we can perhaps look forward not to solutions, but to the development of a clearer empirical base from which to generate systematic initiatives.

Writing this book has drawn upon the experience and advice of many people. Where appropriate, acknowledgements to authors for the use of scholarly material is included in the text and Chapter Notes. However, I owe a particular debt to Dr David Rapoport, who made a number of penetrating comments on a draft of the manuscript, and who through his writings has drawn my attention to a particularly fruitful and important area of interface between Political Science and Psychology. His scholarly contribution in this area is considerable, and I gratefully acknowledge the stimulus he has given my thinking. My thanks are due to Ms Helen Ryan who critically read earlier drafts, and to Bryan Watkins of Brassey's Publishers for his encouragement and helpful editorial comments. Much of the conceptual work on which this book is built was made possible by Contracts Numbered DAJA45-86-M-0458 and DAJA45-88-C-0001 from the US Army Research Institute for the Social and Behavioral Sciences through its European Science Co-ordination Office, London. The opinions expressed are those of the author and do not necessarily represent those of the US Army, or indeed anyone else.

The quotation at the head of Chapter 1 is from *The Bell*, by Iris Murdoch,[3] at the head of Chapter 7 from *Selige Sehnsucht* by JW

Goethe, and at the heads of Chapters 4 and 9 from *The Rebel*, by Albert Camus.[4]

The late Bill Wilson was a source of information, help, encouragement and support in this project as in others. His profound knowledge, intellectual stimulus, moral support and above all his friendship, I will greatly miss.

Whilst not always helped by their presence, I am nevertheless grateful for the distinctive contributions made by Alice and Cathy; as ever, I am grateful for Ethel's.

Max Taylor
Corcaigh, Eire
January 1991

CHAPTER 1

Fanaticism and Extreme Behaviour: an Introduction

This chapter introduces and explores the concepts of fanaticism, violence and political violence. It also introduces the behavioural approach used later as the psychological base from which the discussions develop.

'... whose strength is seen only in the sharpness of cast shadows.'
Iris Murdoch – The Bell

Never a day seems to pass without us being confronted in the media by accounts of atrocities in the form of violent political acts. In the Western World, where perceptions of the dangers of political violence seem to be rising, and personal security increasingly at risk, the threat of political violence stands out as being particularly frightening. Such fear may be merited. The scale of political violence, seen most obviously in the form of terrorism, is now so great that only the more dramatic acts which result in large numbers of deaths or injuries warrant wide media attention. The bombing of the Pan Am jet over Lockerbie in 1988 was widely reported, but the almost routine shooting or bombing of members of the security forces in Northern Ireland, or the incidental deaths of Lebanese civilians, rarely merit more than a passing reference. Political violence is a shadow cast over all of our communal lives with frightening potential for involving innocents.

The people who commit acts of political violence frequently appear unexceptional.[1] This makes it difficult for most people to understand how individuals who are in other respects quite unremarkable can commit brutal acts for political ends, often in the cause of freedom or liberation, sentiments which would command general support from

1

most people. Analysing the paradox of the committed person who, in the name of liberalism, can engage in the most profoundly illiberal acts, is perhaps the greatest challenge faced by anyone who attempts to understand the psychological issues involved in political violence. The difficulties of this are so great that we often seek refuge in explanations of their behaviour which focus on mental illness or evilness rather than examine the behaviour itself. Furthermore, there is a widespread assumption, mirrored by items in the press or on television, that the incidence of politically inspired violence has increased, with the implication that this somehow reflects some profound malaise in contemporary society. In fact, this latter assumption would be very difficult to validate but, when examined closely, it is probably as unsustainable as an explanation as are assumptions about the pathological psychological makeup of the individuals concerned. We have very little idea of why political activity becomes the vehicle for violent behaviour; this book attempts to offer some insights and reflections on one aspect of this problem.

Violence, Politics and Legitimacy

Viewed from a psychological perspective, the relationship between violence and politics is complex. Violence, or its threat, is of course used by states as a means of propagating political objectives. Clausewitz's famous aphorism '. . . war is a mere continuance of policy by other means' illustrates this in a way which remains as relevant and accurate now as it was in the nineteenth century when it was originally written. Generally speaking, we regard violence of this form (i.e. warfare) as a legitimate, if regrettable, State activity, provided it is not too frequent!

Under some circumstances, violence to achieve political ends by *non-State* combatants also seems to have international acceptance. In the United Nations debates 'on measures to prevent terrorism and other forms of violence which endanger or take human lives or jeopardise fundamental freedoms' which were held in 1972 and 1973, the view was expressed that '. . . although recourse to violence must ultimately be eliminated from relations between people . . . certain kinds of violence were bred by oppression, injustice, the denial of basic human rights . . . it would be unjust to expect . . . the same code of ethics . . .', for people suffering such injustices.[2] This seems to confer legitimacy on non-State combatants provided they are involved in wars of 'liberation', or equivalents in some sense. The attributes of legitimacy in this context, of course, are complex in the extreme and often seem to be related to political perspectives rather than absolute standards.

These issues make it very difficult to achieve a broadly acceptable consensus about definitions, and identification of problem areas in this field. In this book we will, in the main, confine ourselves to analyses of the nature of political violence in circumstances where there is no such legitimacy, recognising and accepting the difficulties and inconsistencies that might follow from this. Legitimacy is essentially a political concept. By introducing it into our discussion, this is not to suggest that the psychological basis of 'non-legitimate' violent behaviour differs from 'legitimate' as a result of the arbitrary application of notions of legitimacy. But in order to progress our discussion, it has to be recognised that legitimacy is a relevant but contentious issue, where agreement is difficult.

Violence

It is a regrettable fact that the possibility of violence in some form is an inescapable feature of both public and private lives. What we mean by violence can encompass a variety of different activities, and what we might regard as violent behaviour can take many forms, ranging from verbal abuse and threats to physical assault and injury. Public displays of violence, such as a fight at a football game, or private displays, such as might occur in a domestic dispute between husband and wife, are not particularly infrequent in Western Society. Whilst they may not be condoned, they are a recognisable feature of contemporary social living. Added to this, particular culture and social differences may play a role in facilitating or inhibiting the expression of violent behaviour. Perhaps a 'Latin temperament' might lend itself more readily to emotional outbursts as violence, for example, than that of the more restrained 'Anglo-Saxon' temperament.

Sometimes we use violence against ourselves, as in self-injurious behaviour or suicide, but mainly it is done to other people. In certain circumstances, we may even use extreme violence, not simply to injure someone, but seriously to damage or even kill them. Violence of this kind, however, is tolerated only in very limited circumstances. Self-defence may be one legitimisation of extreme violence, as might provocation in some circumstances. In general we can confidently say that in most Western societies, extreme violence is rare at an individual level, but that lesser forms of violence are relatively common.

Contrary to popular belief, if we look at the settings in which most of the violence we see in society occurs (extreme or otherwise) we will note that it is frequently associated with our interpersonal relationships. The foci of violence are usually those situations familiar and accessible to use, and are often those in which our social lives take place – for example the family and the workplace. If we exclude drug related violence and violence associated with crime, an argument or a real or imagined slight provides the familiar background in which violence might develop, and our domestic environment provides the likely location.[3]

One of the most obvious consequences of violent behaviour is the change that it inflicts on the individual it is directed towards. It necessarily changes someone else's personal environment in some way. In this sense, the consequences of violence are external to ourselves; someone is hurt or injured, or an article is smashed or taken away. But we must not forget that the very expression of violence, regardless of the reasons for it, may well *also* have consequences for the person committing the violent act. Furthermore we might sometimes describe such personal effects as positive; we feel better for hitting out at someone, we are no longer uncomfortably angry. When we try to explain or look for the reasons for other people's violent behaviour (as opposed to our own), we often exclusively focus on these personal consequences, as the explanation as to what 'motivates' a person to behave in such a way.

We can describe at least two senses in which this personal quality to violence might occur. The first sense involves what might be termed the positive emotional consequences of expressing violent behaviour to the violent person. Positive consequences can happen when our anger or emotions are dispelled – in simple terms, we feel better for being violent, regardless of what it does to other people. Furthermore, being violent, or being involved in violent events, may also be very exciting. The pleasures for the football hooligan associated with violent confrontations with opposing supporters should not be underestimated, and we do not need to seek meaning for such behaviour outside the positive consequences for the individual involved. Social attenuation of these consequences, experienced perhaps as guilt, does not necessarily diminish its power, nor seemingly does apprehension, appearance in court or conviction. Related to this, being violent *itself* may be positive when it is in association with other emotional states – where sexual pleasure or arousal is experienced at the same time as the violent act, we might describe this as sadism.

There is a second personal sense of the consequences of violence, which again might be described as positive. If we allow ourselves to become violent, our immediate environment changes, altering it and perhaps improving it in some sense for us – an offending member of our family is suitably chastised (and perhaps cowed), our will or view prevails, or someone runs away. Furthermore, by being violent, we might demonstrate our power over people in ways not possible when using non-violent means. In this second sense of positive consequence, therefore, violence results in some sort of structural change in our immediate social and personal world. The effects of violence in this sense might be characterised as having external instrumentality, in contrast to the personal instrumentality which might distinguish our first sense. Related to this, the consequences of violent acts can also be explosively immediate as opposed to the slower changes we see from the more controlled expression of feelings.

In summary, therefore, the personal consequences of violence may be seen to be instrumental in two senses, affecting both the environment in which the violence occurs (someone is hurt, the environment is changed through someone running away, or being killed) and the individual who committed the violent act (who feels better, powerful or more in control). These two aspects of the personal effects of violence are not of course separate from each other. Furthermore, this duality in personal effects can have reciprocal qualities, resulting in each sustaining and enhancing the effects of the other.[4]

Much of the violence of everyday life is domestic in character and related to those situations accessible to us. It may be repetitive and occur often, and it may also result in extreme damage to someone (and even death) in circumstances where the extent of such violence seems out of proportion to the originating conditions (as in most cases of non-accidental injury to children, for example). However, we can generally understand such violence, if not explain it, in terms of some personal and essentially local and probably domestic issue or circumstance. When such violence is repetitive, and appears to be 'out of control' or in some sense disproportionate, this might encourage us to describe the violent person as 'mad', 'fanatical', 'psychopathic', or 'wicked'. We tend to use terms like this indiscriminately when faced with disturbing behaviour we do not understand and cannot relate to our own lives.

There is a further special sense that we might add to the above in which we can identify violence as being instrumental. Again, excluding drug related or criminal acts, violence can of course also be expressed outside of a domestic context, and be personally instrumental, not simply in the senses discussed so far but addressing some more external forum associated with social power. Furthermore, there are sometimes circumstances in which, whilst the personal qualities and consequences of violence may be important, the primary focus can be in some sense *political*. It is this form of violence, as it affects the political process, that concerns this book. Of course, the distinction between personal and political so easily pronounced here may in practice be much more difficult to make, and the distinction, as we will see, will prove to be less than watertight. It would be wrong to move conceptualisations of political violence away from more general analyses of personal violence. Nevertheless, we can identify examples of extreme violence where the *primary* consequence is best expressed in political terms, and where the instrumental qualities of the violence are most evident in the political process. In this sense, violence takes place within a political and ideological context which provides meaning and support in its political dimension. The personal consequences of such violence remain important in understanding its psychological determinants, but the behaviour nevertheless remains in its external focus an essentially political act.

The approach adopted here contrasts with more traditional accounts of the reasons for political violence. These typically emphasise the political context in which violence takes place, relegating the psychological and behavioural forces to which the individual is exposed to a subsidiary mediating role. The image often presented by these accounts is of a relatively passive individual acting as a mediator for the working out of dynamic large scale economic and political forces. Thus, these analyses stress broad social and political features, such as the importance of economic deprivation and unemployment.[5] If a psychological element is necessary in these explanations, they usually draw upon concepts such as frustration[6] to mediate between the economic state and the assumed political violence. Accounts of this kind, whilst fitting well into some political analyses of society, generally lack empirical verification, and the utility of such approaches is seen increasingly to be limited. We can illustrate this lack of utility in a number of ways. Whilst the incidence of unemployment is generally regarded in political commentary as a critical social variable, changes in unemployment levels in societies suffering from major political violence, like Northern Ireland for example, seem to have little or no relationship with the incidence of violence.[7] Likewise, the notion that frustration and similar emotional states have a role in the development of political violence in the form of terrorism has been criticised[8] for distracting attention away from the essential instrumentality of terrorism and introducing an unwarranted implication of psychopathology.

More sophisticated models of the causes of political violence have emphasised the inter-relationship between psychological and social forces on the one hand, and the political context on the other. The inescapable fact that many people experience social and political disadvantage, whilst very few people become involved in political violence, inevitably draws attention to the processes involved in those individuals who do become violent. Generally speaking, political analyses have taken as their primary focus a macro-level of analysis,[9] concentrating in political terms on the dynamic political process as it effects individuals in general in a society. More recently, political analysts have addressed more micro-levels of analysis, focusing on the political processes impinging on the individual.[10] This book offers a similar kind of perspective, but approaches the problem of violent behaviour from a behavioural rather than a political context.

Thus, this book is concerned with the expression of violent behaviour, often of an extreme nature, which is intended in some way to influence the political process. Both personal and political instrumentality, therefore, lies at the heart of the relationship between the violent act and some politically determined end. From a political perspective, the concept of ideology will clearly pay a critical role in this. Our particular focus, however, will not be on the political belief systems that we might label as violent, but on the expression of *behaviour* that merits that attribute. When it is excessive or repetitive, we sometimes call such behaviour 'psychopathic', 'pathogenic' or 'fanatical'. We will use here the term *fanatical* to characterise it, because as we will see later, the connotations of that term readily encompass the notions intended in this analysis.

What is Violent Behaviour?

We have consistently used the term 'violent' and 'violence' in the above, rather than 'aggressive' and 'aggression', to refer to the kind of behaviour we are concerned with. The meanings of the two terms are of course closely linked. In general, the term violence, in the sense used here, refers to the process and character of an act of aggression, and its meaning is broadly synonymous with aggression, although, as we will see, there are grounds for distinguishing between them.[11]

We can develop our discussion further by first considering what we mean by *aggression*, a term which is more commonly used in the psychological literature than violence. A generally accepted definition of aggression is '. . . any form of behaviour directed towards the goal of harming or injuring another living being . . .'.[12] There are features of this definition to which it is worth drawing attention. The first, and perhaps the most important point to note, is that aggression refers to a behaviour, not a state of the individual who is being aggressive. A persistent, but probably erroneous, view has tended to relate aggression to inner causes, such as instinct, emotions, or 'man's nature'. In the sense in which it is used throughout this book, aggression refers not to presumed inner causal states, but to behaviour. Furthermore, by defining aggression in behavioural terms, we are also implicitly defining it as a response to something, rather than a state having no specific origin. Thus, the primary level of causal analysis lies in the context in which aggression occurs, rather than an inner condition. *Violence*, as employed in this book, uses the same behavioural referants. It is used in preference to aggression in this sense only because it further emphasises *descriptive* aspects of behavioural qualities.

This definition also introduces the idea that aggression is directed and purposeful, in the sense that it is intended to cause harm of some form. Harm, of course, can take a variety of forms. In general, we will be concerned with actual physical harm, but of course aggression can be a verbal response just as much as an act of physical violence. However, at this point we can distinguish in one sense between violent acts and aggressive acts. We would presumably not want to regard an accidental injury as an aggressive act, but of course an accidental injury can be described as the result of violence, even if not intended. Violence, as the use of force, therefore, is a broader concept than aggression, in that it embraces intended and unintended use of force. This is a point worth making, for some of the situations which we will consider will refer to the use of force, often of an extreme kind, where there is no *particular* victim intended, but rather a general class of victims, which may be as broad as anyone who happens to be in a particular location. Or perhaps the violent act itself is all that is intended, and any victims that might result are both unintended *and*, in a sense, unnecessary.

Many terrorist bombings fall into both these categories. For example, on Monday, 25 June 1990, the Provisional IRA left a bag or parcel containing a bomb in the porchway of the Carlton Club, an exclusive Conservative Party social club in the centre of London. The

Carlton Club lies between Trafalgar Square and Buckingham Palace and is located in a busy tourist area. At the time the bomb went off, there were many tourists passing by. The explosion did considerable damage to the Club and firemen rescued 24 people from within the building. Nine people were injured in the blast, most of them American tourists, who received injuries from flying glass. Two people were detained in hospital with more serious injuries, a 76 year old porter at the Club, and an 82 year old Club member. The bombing was presumably intended as a symbolic attack, rather than an actual attack. In its statement admitting responsibility, the Provisional IRA said '. . . the IRA has brought the war directly to those who keep the British Army on the streets and in the fields of Ireland. While such occupation continues, and the nationalist people face daily oppression, the policy makers and their military arm will not be safe.' Despite the rhetoric, it is clear that there could be no *particular* victim intended in this bombing attack. The meaning of intention in this situation, therefore, is clearly rather different to that assumed in the above definition of aggression. This further makes the use of the term 'violence', and 'violent', preferable to aggression in the contexts used here.

Conventional definitions of aggression also often add, to the one we have used above, something to the effect that the recipient of aggression '. . . is motivated to avoid such treatment'.[13] In the situations we will refer to, this may not always be the case, in the sense that an important category of violent acts which we will discuss will be that of violence against the individual committing the violence himself to achieve some political end. Political suicide, as self-inflicted violence, is an extreme example of this which we will in fact encounter. Again, the term violence seems preferable in this context to aggression.

This discussion has enabled us to identify our focus as behaviour which is violent, often in an extreme way. Another issue, however, which we need to resolve is what we mean by extreme. We can think of violent behaviour as extending along a continuum describing the extent and severity of violence (reflected in the actual or potential damage produced). At some point along that continuum, a violent act becomes socially and morally unacceptable. Earlier we have noted briefly the ambiguity surrounding the notions of acceptability and appropriateness in the use of violence. These ambiguities are undoubtedly magnified as the extent of violence increases, yet we nevertheless do make qualitative judgements of this kind about violent behaviour. In most circumstances, the judgement of acceptability or appropriateness inevitably involves reference to some standard, very often some form of social quality. Yet to complicate the issue further, the involvement of social referants leads to a further inevitable ambiguity in the attributes upon which we will focus. This is evident in the way that our views on extremeness of violent behaviour often assume that 'by definition' it is contrary to accepted 'norms'. Social norms imply judgements made from some particular perspective; a major difficulty, however, is that there are a variety of social perspectives that might lead to different and often conflicting judgements. We can contrast a social approach, of course, with the much more certain judgements of appropriateness we might make from a moral or religious standpoint. In adopting a social approach, one difficulty that has to be dealt with is the inevitable, if frustrating, lack of universal certainty in the social attributes we might focus on, and the fact that they are situationally and sometimes culturally dependent.

We can clearly see this lack of certainty when we come to examine the circumstances in which violent behaviour occurs. The expression of violent behaviour alone is not generally thought *in itself* to be either abnormal or extreme, and any judgement about this needs to examine the context of that behaviour. Most States, for example, maintain some form of army which is routinely trained in the exercise of violent behaviour, and indeed, in techniques for effectively killing people. Perhaps less obviously, an essential and defining attribute of a civilian police force has been argued to be its capacity to 'exercise non-negotiable force'[14] to effect compliance. The expression of violent behaviour in these contexts (a disciplined army, to effect compliance with the law), given certain constraints, are generally regarded as acceptable and appropriate, and whilst we might be concerned about the *limits* of such violence (hence the constraints), given those limits it is generally condoned. Strangely enough, if I seek to 'take the law into my own hands', and attempt to produce compliance in someone through the use of force in circumstances where, for example, police use of force would be appropriate, I would probably be guilty of an offence. If I did it regularly, and always to a particular purpose, or associated with a persistent theme, I might be called 'antisocial', a delinquent, or some other term. An important issue in condoning violence of this kind is both its predictability (related to legal prescription) and its controlled use (by a disciplined force such as the police).

Many of the issues raised here, of course, reflect upon how we might regard the nature of the State and its relationship with social structures. Consideration of this is beyond the scope of this book except that we should note that the State as an organised political community which exercises control over its population through laws, is not necessarily a neutral context in which society, and the behaviour society condones, develops. Nor, of course, is the State the same as Society, although States often claim to be representative of particular social environments. The State, or at least the executive organs which reflect the political leadership of the State, can of course actively influence the social environment in which we live. It is often asserted that 'the State' can claim a monopoly of violence and States certainly seek in general to limit the expression of non-sanctioned violence by its citizens, often paradoxically through the deployment of violence through its police force, judicial processes and army. The State, through the ideological and social framework it creates, can also play an important role in facilitating and directing non-State violence.

Quite clearly, therefore, a critical issue is the extent to which our thinking about violent behaviour in the political context is related to the role and nature of the State. The State legitimises in some sense violent behaviour, and in doing so may create the conditions in which extreme violence (or the more particular notion of fanaticism) of the kind we are concerned with here can develop; this is one of the central issues we will consider. States create and mould our personal and social environments. The causes of our behaviour, as they relate to our social environment, reflect the conditions (either deliberate or accidental) which as much as anything particular State ideologies have created through the political systems under which we live. Nazi Germany, for example, was a State which facilitated and indeed perhaps made inevitable an extreme expression of violence against particular sections of that State. In that case State policy, informed by Nazi ideology, created a context that not only legitimised the expression of violence, but developed it as a matter of State policy. In considering issues of this kind in this book, our principal concern will not be so much with an analysis of the nature of that ideology as a part of the *political* processes of the State, nor with how it might become expressed in political terms. Rather, we will be principally concerned here with how ideology impinges on the individual in such a way that the psychological and behavioural consequences of particular qualities of ideology gain full expression as violent acts.

In this context, a rather obvious, but nevertheless important point to note is that it is not the State that commits a violent act – it is some of the individual citizens of the State who actually behave in violent ways, either collectively or individually. Whilst the potential framework within a State can facilitate or mitigate against the expression of violent ideology, the psychological and behavioural features of ideology are the essential basis on which individual or group political behaviour develops, dependent for its expression on the immediate behavioural environment of the individual, although of course that environment will in some measure be influenced by the State. At the level of analysis that we are concerned with, a concept like the State is just too big a unit to have any sensible direct *behavioural* meaning. Thus, whilst the expression of ideology in behaviour may be facilitated by the State, it is not necessarily dependent on the State. Nevertheless, we may be able to equate qualitative differences in the influence of the State over behaviour to features of the way a given State is organised. This applies particularly to the quality of State organisation we term totalitarian.

The broad social and political context is of course important in understanding the framework in which any behaviour might occur. Nevertheless, we can identify other more psychological approaches to understanding behaviour, which without diminishing the broader analysis implied by a social approach, nevertheless may help us understand more specifically why particular acts occur. Indeed, a principal weakness of the broader social approach lies in its lack of specificity, making it difficult to understand the *particular* circumstances that influence and control behaviour. As an attempt to develop a more specific analysis in this book, we will adopt an essentially behavioural approach to understanding instrumental violence influenced by, and addressing, political agendas. We will focus on the behaviours themselves, and seek to develop some understanding of the circumstances in which these extreme acts might occur. The analysis presented here will not therefore substitute for social or political analyses; rather the intention is that it will complement these, offering perhaps different or parallel insights into the same processes. Indeed, we can confidently assert that the complex situations which we will encounter will not satisfactorily be dealt with from any single discipline perspective.

Fanaticism

One term that appropriately captures more than any other the kind of behaviour we are concerned with here is *Fanaticism*. In the discussion above, we have introduced a number of terms and concepts that indicate the qualities that interest us; these might be summarised as '*violent political fanaticism*'. Whilst the term *fanatic* captures the psychological qualities of extreme behaviour as it concerns us, it is itself a difficult concept to understand. There are inconsistencies in the way it is generally used, and as we will see, there are uncertainties as to its attributes. On the other hand, the term '*fanatical*' has wide currency, and even if inconsistent, does give a focus to many of the psychological qualities of the behaviour. Associating it with the term 'political' suitably qualifies the general concept of fanatical to reflect our focus here.

We will consider the concept of fanaticism in some detail in Chapter 2. However, a brief introduction here will enable us to set the scene for further discussion and serve to introduce some of the issues involved. The term fanatic seems to have entered the English language in the seventeenth century, when it was used to refer to excessive enthusiasm in religious belief. This usage can be seen in the origin of the word, its roots being in the Latin *fanum*, which means temple or sacred place. Indeed, the term *fanaticus* occurs in Latin literature, where it means 'to be put into a raging enthusiasm by a deity',[15] and Seneca uses the verb *fanari*, to rage. References are found in eighteenth century German literature to fanatics as 'raging fighters for religious principles'. Examples of medieval fanaticism can be seen in the activities of the many Christian millenarian movements, and indeed, more contemporary millenarian movements equally reflect qualities of fanaticism (as we will see later). A word with similar contemporary meaning is zealot, which also has an ancient origin in religious activity, referring here, however, to the first century Jewish religious sect who promoted rebellion against Roman rule. Quite clearly, the 'zeal' or 'fanaticism' that can surround religious devotions has long merited notice as something out of the ordinary, and this has been reflected in our language.

Early usage of fanatic, therefore, is associated with both religion and violence. Contemporary usage of the term, however, has extended its meaning to embrace foci other than religious, and less clearly associates it with violence. This can be seen in the Oxford English Dictionary definition of the word as '... (person) filled with excessive and mistaken enthusiasm ...'. In this definition, both the religious and violent origins of the term seem to have been lost.

However, a critical point to draw attention to in the Oxford definition is the inclusion of *mistaken* along with excessive. A quality of contemporary usage of the term fanatic (but not necessarily its ancient origins) is that it carries with it implied criticism, or negative judgements of some form. As Milgram[16] notes '... fanaticism ... is applied to the state of mind of those who are wholeheartedly committed to a set of beliefs and are condemned for it'.

Milgram's description of fanaticism implies the holding of extreme beliefs, but it also suggests expressing those beliefs with enthusiasm or vigour in some way. This quality may distinguish most people who might simply hold extreme views or beliefs, and even sometimes express them, from the fanatic who *consistently expresses* those beliefs, often in a vigorous and insensitive way. It is of course this expression, which is behaviour in some form, that we are aware of and notice; it is also of course the behaviour that worries us, because that is *all* we have access to. *Expression*, therefore, and *vigour* seem to be the important qualities of the fanatic, and these are evident for our purposes not in the fanatic's systems of belief, but his behaviour. A further critical and important quality which we can identify is the insensitivity of the behaviour of the fanatic to the circumstances in which it occurs. Such insensitivity suggests that concern for the immediate consequences of action may be less important for the fanatic than the expression of the behaviour itself.

As in the case of violent behaviour, one way of thinking about how we use the term fanatic is that we are essentially categorising and describing an individual's behaviour and locating it along some kind of continuum. This is an important point to make in a number of ways, and one which needs to be stressed. Fanatical behaviour may differ in terms of vigour of expression, rather than in terms of qualitative differences from behaviour we might regard as normal. When we realise that fanaticism refers to the expression of behaviour, it becomes possible to observe it, examine its attributes and perhaps identify the circumstances that control it. We need not seek meaning therefore in the inaccessible realms of the human mind or belief systems, but in the events around us. This does not diminish the role of concepts like ideology, attitude or prejudice; but it does enable us to place our analysis within a broader accessible framework. Furthermore, recognising that fanatical behaviour contains elements of what might be termed normal behaviour, from which it differs in degree, allows us to see how those factors that influence normal behaviour might equally operate for the fanatic. We need not necessarily, therefore, create special accounts to understand fanatical behaviour.

Features of violent behaviour like vigour and insensitivity to immediate circumstance, which we will discuss at greater length in Chapter 2, are not the single principal qualities with which we will concern ourselves. Our interest here is not just with qualities of excess, nor simply the expression of violence, but with political instrumentality which such behaviours might show. It has long been recognised that there are circumstances in which politics and violence may be intimately linked: Clausewitz's famous aphorisms '. . . war . . . is an act of violence intended to compel our opponent to fulfill our will . . .', and '. . . war is a mere continuance of policy by other means . . .'[17] readily illustrate the context in which extreme violence, in the form of warfare, can be a part of the political process and the development of politics. In one sense, the violent political fanatic simply illustrates and acts upon Clausewitz's more general point at a personal level.

Warfare as the pursuit of political ends is, of course, not necessarily solely (or even) conducted by Fanatics, nor is fanatical behaviour either necessarily related to or the same as warfare. Nevertheless, warfare may provide one of the arenas for fanaticism. Warfare refers to activities undertaken on a broad social scale in some sense, whereas to label someone as fanatical is to describe a quality of behaviour or action. Clausewitz's assertion quoted above is expressed in terms not of individual acts of violence, but warfare, something conventionally associated with states rather than individuals or small groups; it was certainly Clausewitz's understanding that he was referring to warfare between states in his discussion.

A distinction can be made about the qualities of warfare which for our purposes may be useful; this is related to ideas about restraint and appropriateness of force in warfare, and to the role of warfare in the interactions between states. Where the debate about violent political fanaticism in this book touches on warfare and armies, our concern will not be with the analysis of warfare as such, even though it may represent a form of extreme violence, and may indeed sometimes merit the term fanatical. We will rather be more concerned with what might be termed the 'deviant' excessive qualities of warfare expressed by individuals. As we have already noted, there are rules or norms that we use to make judgements about violent behaviour, whether in warfare, normal political intercourse or social interaction, which even if they are inconsistent, and sometimes even contradictory, nevertheless tend to limit activity. Our concern in this book is where those limits are exceeded, either in the normal political process, or in the rather different, but still essentially political, process of war. This is the broad framework in which we will examine the concept of *Violent Political Fanaticism.*

It is worth noting that any complacency about the notion of the appropriateness of the use of force in warfare should be restrained. There are many inconsistencies surrounding the notion of 'rules' which legitimise the use of violence in warfare, and for that matter in society in general as we have noted earlier. Constraints in warfare have gained international agreement, the most important being the 4th Geneva Convention of 1949. But warfare, both before 1949 and after 1949, has been if anything characterised by a *disregard* for those rules. For example, a generally accepted aspiration in warfare has been that non-combatants should not be involved in the conduct of the war as deliberate strategic targets. Actions in World War II such as the bombing of Dresden and Coventry, and the nuclear bombing of Nagasaki and Hiroshima, were quite clearly intended to inflict extensive damage upon non-combatants. More recent conflicts, such as the Vietnam War, have accelerated the tendency to victimise non-combatants. This is further complicated by the development of Terrorism and State Terrorism as forms of surrogate warfare. Whilst violent actions may gain legitimacy by being part of a war between states (and of course gain further legitimacy by victory), their inconsistency with the comfortable assumptions we sometimes make about warfare is clearly apparent. The moral to draw from this is that extreme and extranormal violence (in the sense of breaking accepted rules) is not confined to relations betweeen individuals.

Returning to the concept of fanaticism, when we use a term like fanaticism to characterise behaviour, we are of course doing something more than simply describing behaviour. Milgram, in the quotation referred to earlier, made reference to the condemnation that seems to be a part of the contemporary usage of the term fanatical. Rather like our use of the term 'terrorism', there is often an implicit moral judgement being made when we refer to someone as a fanatic. In this book we will attempt to exclude implicit judgements of this kind from our discussion, and we will use fanatic and fanatical in a descriptive sense, referring to particular sets of behaviour having certain attributes. But we should note that this is not quite the same as everyday usage. Often, the term fanatic is, as Milgram points out,[18] used to refer to someone who is condemned for holding (but more probably expressing) certain beliefs.

In this respect therefore the term fanaticism is similar to the term terrorism, and as in the case of terrorism, its use often seems to imply a wish both to create a distance from the activity involved, and to indicate that it is in some sense undesirable. This, however, usually depends on the perspective and context from which the action is seen, a point which brings us back to our uncertainty about the grounds we use in making social judgements. It might also, however, be related to the outcome of the activity in question. A single minded and what might be described as fanatical pursuit of something, if successful, may well temper our judgement of fanatical – such a person, if successful, is then perhaps showing perseverance, a much more desirable feature; we might only describe him as a fanatic if he fails. In any event, we should note that there is a measure of relativity in our use of fanaticism which complicates analysis.

The relativity of judgements about fanaticism can be readily seen in the religious contexts from which the term grew. Religious prescriptions, like Jewish dietary prohibitions for example, look strange to the non-Jew and, given the lengths to which it might be necessary to go to obtain kosher food, may well appear to the non-Jew (or even to the non-religious Jew) to be extreme, if not fanatical. But to the religious Jew, such dietary prohibitions are part and parcel of the practice of his religion, where *failures* would attract approbation. This, of course, is not an example of fanaticism nor does it involve violence; but presumably the forces that sustain those dietary prohibitions also sustain the stoning by Orthodox Jews in Jerusalem of offenders breaking other Jewish prohibitions against working on the Sabbath. In this we can see the sense in which our use of the term fanatic, and its association with violence, may simply be an aspect, almost in some senses incidental, to the principal focus of the fanatic's concerns.

An example, related to the above, of what to many people would be a case of fanaticism can be seen in the persistent refusal of members of the Jehovah's Witness religious sect to allow themselves or their children to have blood transfusions. An example of this occurred in June 1990, when the parents of a 2 year old Greek Cypriot child suffering from leukaemia were ordered by a London court to allow their child to receive a blood transfusion. Despite the court order, the child was snatched by the parents from the Great Ormond Street Hospital, and taken from Britain to Cyprus, where the parents went into hiding. The Cypriot authorities also issued a court order to the same effect and the child eventually received a blood transfusion in a hospital in Nicosia. The child's father told reporters that '... Nobody can love my child as much as I do. Of course, we'll do everything possible and sell our belongings if necessary, with the full support of the rest of the family, to save Stephanie's life. But we cannot agree to a blood transfusion.' There are no grounds for doubting the sentiments the father expressed, and every reason to suppose that the parents thought they were acting in the child's best interests. To non-adherents of the sect, this appears extraordinarily insensitive to 'normal' feelings of parental concern when faced with the illness of a loved one. Yet from their own religious perspective, such refusal is neither extreme nor extraordinary, but merely conforming with their particular logic of biblical interpretation. Presumably, in their terms, the maintenance of religious rules is more important than the life of their child, incomprehensible as this may seem to non-initiates.

Our use of the term fanatical, therefore, seems to reflect complex processes involving implied judgements. We can avoid this difficulty, however, by resisting the temptation to describe as fanatical those things which we neither understand nor favour, and using the term instead in a descriptive sense. The attributes on which we might focus are described at length in Chapter 2. We might anticipate one conclusion of that discussion to note that a descriptive definition does not necessarily eliminate uncertainty, but does at least serve to reduce it, for as we will see, the attributes of 'the fanatic' are complex and multidimensional.

What then is the relationship between what we will term fanatical behaviour and political behaviour? As in the case of violence, the issue is one of degree of expression, rather than all or no expression. Thus, we are all from time to time violent, and we all from time to time express political views. Generally, any link between the two is constrained and circumscribed. Where violence and political views might conjoin may, for example, be seen in the form of screwing up and throwing away a paper describing some political event – which could be described as a very mild and essentially inoffensive violent political act. We might even feel led to take part in some protest, for example, about something we think important. These are normal and acceptable behaviours in democracies; they are also, of course, behaviours which might be engaged in by a fanatic, although the fanatic is unlikely to limit his involvement to these acceptable forms of democratic political dissent. The distinguishing quality of the fanatic, as we will see in Chapter 2, may be that he or she differs in two major dimensions – in terms of the intensity of behaviour and the degree of violence expressed. As we will see, these fanatical behaviours gain their political focus and strength through ideology.

The Behavioural Approach

The analysis developed in this book differs from others in the general area of psychological thinking about political activity in that it has a behavioural focus. This leads to an emphasis on environmental qualities, rather than personal attributes, as foci for explanation. Discussion and evaluation of the extensive psychological analyses of the Nazi war criminal from the perspective of their particular childhood pathology, for example, which tend to appear in conventional psychological analyses of political violence, are largely absent from this work. Rather, the environmental contexts, both personal and social, that facilitate the behaviours in question are examined.

We have already noted that the approach adopted here focuses on behaviour, rather than mental events, belief systems, or other essentially inaccessible qualities of people. In focusing on behaviour, particular attention is paid to its environmental determinants. Behaviour does not occur in a vacuum; it occurs in a complex, often reciprocal, system of circumstances and events. These impinge on us through the process we call learning. The idiosyncratic and individual processes of learning account not only for *how* events come to have significance for us, but also *why* we differentially respond to circumstances.

The distinctive feature of a behavioural approach is the recognition that the environment shapes and controls our behaviour through the actions of various events which are technically called *reinforcers*. Reinforcers are events that increase the likelihood of a behaviour which they follow occurring again. Thus, if some action is followed by a reinforcer, it will tend to occur more often. Whilst there may be some universal reinforcers (like water to a thirsty person), many reinforcers are personal and sometimes even appear idiosyncratic, acquiring their properties through learning processes which may well be unique to the person concerned. Such processes may even be accidental, or at least unrecognised by the person. The kind of family we belong to, the sort of friendship circles we create or join, the career or profession we take up (or don't), all influence and create our behavioural world, and determine the significance of environmental events. Furthermore, we are not simply the passive recipients of environmental influences; our actions themselves change the world in which we live, creating a reciprocal and dynamic complex of environmental events. The choices in our lives, the effect we have on our immediate environment, all contribute to the *particular* set of circumstances which at any time impinge on us, and *control* our behaviour.[19]

There is therefore a reciprocal relationship between our actions (behaviours) and the environment which facilitates their expression. The particular mix of circumstances which might result in and control any given behaviour will undoubtedly be very complex. Nevertheless, we can describe in behavioural terms the general processes that might lead to the expression of particular behaviour. A detailed analysis of an individual action may simply not be possible (through lack of knowledge as a result of the passage of time, for example) but in any event may not be necessary.

In developing behavioural accounts, it is useful to bear in mind a fundamental distinction between those circumstances that result in an individual *becoming* involved in a particular role (like becoming a member of the SS, or becoming a terrorist), and those circumstances that *exist* at the time of a particular event. Taylor[20] has discussed this in the context of the development of the terrorist, and Cornish and Clark[21] within a more general framework for the analysis of criminal behaviour. In considering the first element of that distinction, we can note that becoming a terrorist, an SS member, or a political activist is usually something that takes place over a relatively long period of time. Like most life choices, such decisions are the result of a complex series of circumstances, not necessarily unique in themselves, but probably unique, or at least distinctive, in the way in which they are evident and impinge on the individual concerned. These forces no doubt continue to exert effects after the point of formal commitment, initiation, or whatever, and it may well be the case that those circumstances continue to exert some influence on that person's subsequent behaviour. Equally the consequences of becoming involved in a particular role, like membership of an organisation such as the SS for example, would in itself be a source of continuing influence and direction in the circumstances of an individual's life.

Membership of a group often implies joining people with similar interests, frequently at some physical location where meetings take place and where others are excluded (we can here perhaps see the underlying basis for the symbolic importance of 'club houses', for example, in this respect in the development of organisational coherence). Indeed, a physical location can serve to further enhance the development of the attributes of membership of a social group, creating a circle from within which friendships and other forms of social contacts can develop, and serving to focus social contact within a narrowing circle. Political groupings of the kind we will be most interested in may also enhance their 'belonging' by secrecy, confirming and developing the special qualities of membership. A particular quality of the political group may also be shared ideological perspectives. As we will see later, ideology is an important element in the binding together of political groups, and there is a sense in which the discipline of ideology may both sustain group membership and deter questioning and rejection of the group. Membership of a political group implies acceptance of its ideology and this in turn sets the boundaries for independent action. In this sense ideology may serve to augment and exaggerate existing forces towards 'belonging'. These and other associated behavioural consequences might be expressed in terms of group processes and forces. Clearly, these historical and social circumstances can reciprocally interact with the immediate environment and the conditions of the moment that might 'explain' any particular behaviour.

On the other hand, as we noted above, we can distinguish from these general contextual pressures, the events that might lead to the expression of a *particular* behaviour or the choice of a *particular* direction that an individual might take in some situation. In these circumstances, whilst the historical circumstances affecting a person may interact with particular contemporary circumstances, those historical circumstances are not in themselves a sufficient explanation of that particular behaviour. They may set the scene for action, they may account for why an individual is involved in the way he is, but they do not explain the detailed control over particular actions. We can illustrate this with reference to burglary. There are many reasons why a burglar adopts a criminal lifestyle, and places himself in a position to commit a burglary. But these reasons have little relationship to the reasons why a particular house is chosen to burgle. Indeed, it may well be the case that the events determining particular actions such as the choice of a house to burgle by a residential burglar, or perhaps the site of a terrorist ambush, has little to do with any broader historical and contextual contingencies that led the individual to become involved in burglary or terrorism. The reasons for a particular action are the result of particular environmental contingencies and circumstance acting on the individual at that time. In the case of the burglar, for example, factors such as location of the house and the amount and nature of cover are far more important determining factors controlling the behaviour of burglary than the life histories and historical contingencies which affect the burglar.[22] The same may be said for terrorist ambushes.

In spite of the inevitable reciprocal relationship between contextual and immediate causes of behaviour, the above distinction remains a useful one to make, allowing us systematically to structure our analysis of particular events, and thereby avoiding confusion of that analysis with analyses emphasising general social directions. It reminds us that there are different levels to the analysis of behaviour, which whilst they may well share common assumptions, need not necessarily involve assumptions of common forces.

The historical and contextual forces that impinge on behaviour, if they are structured and organised around a particular theme or themes, might be termed an individual's belief system. If that theme is concerned with the way a society organises itself, the distribution of social power, or in terms of the propagation of particular kinds of public policy, again structured and organised around distinct themes, we might refer to this as *ideology*. We can therefore understand the sense in which ideology might influence behaviour through the reciprocal processes described above, in terms of the particular historical contingencies an individual has been exposed to, and the particular consequential value for him which this places on immediate environmental events. All of us are subject to these forces in some measure, of course, and we all behave in ways appropriate to our particular context. It is when these forces gain expression through vigorous action in some sense, that we come close, perhaps, to identifying the qualities that lead us to describe someone as a fanatic. These issues are discussed at length in Chapter 4.

We have already noted that there are many inconsistencies in using terms like fanatic or fanaticism to describe individuals, which can result in difficulties of analysis. One illustration of such difficulties may well lie in our inconsistent and ambivalent approach to violence. This, in its turn, may well be related to the complex effects violence has upon us and upon the environment in which violence is expressed. In the sense in which we will use it here, the political fanatic is concerned with influencing or fulfilling political ideology through violence. An issue of fundamental concern to us in this, therefore, is the way in which the fanatic might employ political violence to effect change in other people's behaviour. Violent behaviour can be very effective in producing immediate consequences, both for the person who is violent, and in terms of the immediacy of effects on the subject of that violence. We termed this instrumental violence earlier in this chapter. As such, in this sense the consequences of violence are reinforcing, and this represents a force of considerable power in influencing behaviour.

We can distinguish between two aspects of the violence we will be concerned with which may help us to understand this issue a little better. We can discriminate between violence designed to induce individuals *not* to behave in particular ways, and violence designed to induce individuals to behave in *different* ways. Technically, the former we refer to as punishment, the latter as aversive learning. Both illustrate what is termed aversive control over behaviour, and the consequences of both kinds of aversive control may well be similar, in the sense that the incidence of a particular behaviour is reduced; but the effects on the recipient of such control may well be very different. At the simplest level, in aversive learning the individual through his actions can avoid aversive effects; in punishment learning he cannot. Furthermore, their long-term effects may well differ. In the case of punishment, when the punishing circumstances have been removed, the punished behaviour may well recur; whereas in the case of aversive learning, the individual learns a new response instead of the punished response, which may well result in a more permanent change in behaviour.

That we can distinguish between these two aspects of aversive control, and furthermore, that we can indicate one kind of aversive control as more successful than the other in changing behaviour in the long term, may seem inconsistent with the ubiquity of punishment as a technique of behavioural control. Examples of punishment used to control behaviour in society in general, for example, are far more common than the use of aversive learning. The critical issue here may be the effects of punishment on the punisher. We earlier noted the effects of violence on the person inflicting the violence, and a similar analysis might be made here. Expression of punishing behaviour may well be highly reinforcing to the individual, *regardless* of the long-term effects on the person punished. We feel better when we hit out at someone, even though a more rational analysis may lead us to adopt other ways of controlling behaviour. The critical issue is the immediacy of effect which results from the use of punishment. To the person inflicting the violence, this immediate effect is highly reinforcing – thus we see another source of the control violence can exert over individual behaviour.

Level of Analysis and Perspective

A discussion in behavioural terms drawing on the concepts outlined above may seem unsatisfactory to some readers if there is an expectation of the analysis of the interplay of complex emotional forces as explanations of behaviour. Descriptions in scientific terms of the stark circumstances and environmental context with which particular *behaviours* might be associated, like a hunger strike for example, may well lack the richness of a description of the agonies of the inner life of a particular hunger striker. Similarly, bald accounts of the pressures of group forces may do little justice to the *experience* of the forces which were felt as 'love' and comradeship for each other that characterised, for example, the feelings of World War I soldiers who 'went over the top' in the near certain knowledge of death. Descriptions of group forces, the constraints of the environment, and so on may not adequately capture the experiences of those circumstances *as they were lived through by the individuals involved.*

An evocative recreation of the experiences of men in the trenches at the time of World War I, in ways which are very relevant to some of the topics discussed in this book, can be found in Frank McGuiness's play *Observe the Sons of Ulster Marching Towards the Somme.* It is an exploration of both the politics of sectarianism and the effects of combat, which illustrates the sheer power of the context in which the soldiers found themselves, and the ways in which they came to terms with that context. As a literary work, it is a revealing psychological and social analysis, and undoubtedly for many readers will contrast favourably with the more scientific accounts attempted here.

But behaviour can be understood at a variety of levels, and the effects of circumstances can be expressed in a variety of ways. It is the case that empirically orientated psychologists have largely ignored the insights of the novelist or playwright as accounts of experience. But the events the novelist describe are also behaviours, and the point remains that hunger strikers *do* from time to time die as the result of a set of events which can be interpreted in behavioural terms. Similarly, World War I soldiers *did* show particular behaviours, which we refer to as 'going over the top', and in consequence were killed in their tens of thousands. Furthermore, when we look at these activities in behavioural terms, there are consistencies, histories, and features of the events in which these things took place that can be identified and described.

We can try to understand events from a variety of perspectives. This book offers one, a scientific behavioural perspective, which might perhaps complement other more literary or social analyses. It may lack the evocative richness of a literary analysis, or indeed a more conventional psychological analysis expressed in terms of mental events. But it enables the development of an empirical account of these complex processes, directing attention to the controlling conditions to which an individual is exposed. Its focus are the factors that influence and direct, and because of this it offers more in terms of future understanding, and perhaps prevention and control, than other kinds of accounts. The account presented here is somewhat speculative. It offers, however, a framework for bringing together a series of relevant concepts within a single consistent and powerful conceptual approach. It develops, therefore, a structure and a means of analysis which enables the reader to better understand the complex phenomena we are dealing with.

Our concern here is primarily with the forces of what we will identify as fanaticism as they impinge on the individual. Violent political behaviour can, of course, occur within contexts such as crowds, as well as within an individual context. Crowd situations, and the social and political forces they imply, cannot in one sense be separated from the individual and his actions. Especially within a violent political context, circumstances where we might look for evidence of fanaticism are frequently those where violence is related to crowd behaviour. The Nazi mob protesting against Jewish businesses, the crowd protesting against a social injustice, the protest march in favour of the abandonment of nuclear weapons are all examples of situations where crowd dynamics may come to affect the individual.

The study of the dynamics of crowd behaviour is an important area of social psychology in its own right. Crowd situations appear to embody forces different from those which control individual behaviour. Many authors, for example, have referred to the sense in which crowd activity loses the constraints that might typify an individual acting on his own.[23] The crowd has been described by Moscovici[24] as '... characterised by unreason ...'. The problem of relating such unreason to the ostensibly rational political process is one of the major problems facing social psychologists concerned with political psychology, and is probably in itself responsible for many of the difficulties in understanding the process of political activity.

Political fanatics may well make use of crowd violence as a means of propagating their own ends. We can see this especially in the context of leadership, where the fanatical leader (like Hitler, for example) might explicitly use and direct the irrationality of the crowd to propagate and develop his own ideological priorities. In this sense, therefore, crowd behaviour may be a tool of the political fanatic. But it is precisely in the area of rationality that we can distinguish between the fanatic in the sense we will use it in this book, and the member of a crowd. As we will assert in our discussions later, the political fanatic is neither irrational nor uncontrolled. His behaviour has a remorseless logic to it, from his own perspective. That perspective, and an understanding of the role that ideology might play in providing the political structure of that perspective, is the critical point of distinction between the fanatic and the crowd member, despite the apparent involvement of both in violent political activity.

One final issue needs to be addressed in our discussion of perspectives and levels of analysis. In developing a behavioural perspective, this account takes as its subject matter concepts which, in the main, are not derived from a behaviour analysis. Rather, the issues addressed take their agenda principally from the political sciences and political analysis. We will seek to maintain a balance between description in the scientific terms of a behaviour analysis, and more general terms, referring to political activity with which we are all familiar. There are, however, problems in doing this, principally in terms of maintaining the balance between the needs of the specialist and lay reader. In particular, the level of technical analysis presented has often been limited to avoid unnecessary confusion for the lay reader. But in doing this, there remains an inevitable danger that it will fail to satisfy either lay or scientific readership. However, if the book tempts the specialist reader to delve more deeply into the issues raised, and tempts the non-specialist to think more behaviourally about the problem, then it will have achieved one major objective.

Looking Ahead

The topic addressed by this book is both complex and obscure. The literature available is enormous, and the wealth of experience of many of the circumstances discussed is vast. As we develop our analysis, we will see that it challenges some of the fundamental assumptions we make about human behaviour. Even though some of the examples discussed are essentially historical, the forces we will identify change and influence contemporary political processes. The Violent Political Fanatic remains with us as a part of our social framework, and continues to influence the course of political development.

Within the psychological approach to this problem, a broadly behavioural emphasis has been adopted throughout this book. This emphasis offers the broad conceptual framework from which we will describe and seek to understand the issues of concern to us. A behavioural approach takes as its subject matter that which we do, namely our behaviour. It does not necessarily speculate or attempt to relate behaviour to presumed mental processes *as explanations*. It addresses qualities of an individual's behaviour that we can see and observe, and seeks to relate those behaviours to the environmental events that change and modify their form and incidence. We sometimes refer to this process as learning. In these terms, therefore, an 'explanation' of behaviour lies in an account of the environmental forces that influence, control and direct a particular behaviour. One important force in learning is the set of historical contingencies the individual has been exposed to. Equally, another and related important force in this context may be the determining ideology an individual subscribes to, as it impinges, shapes and moulds both behaviour and the environment in which he or she lives. These later forces will be very important elements in the processes we will consider in this book.

This account therefore takes as its principal focus those forces that impinge on the individual, and this approach might distinguish this book as a psychological analysis from, say, a political science or sociological analysis addressing the same topic. This is not, however, primarily a technical psychology book. It is intended for the general reader, who has a concern with understanding the problems of fanatical political behaviour. Whilst psychological concepts and evidence are used extensively in the book, no particular background in psychology for the reader is assumed.

The particular examples chosen to illustrate the issues raised in the chapters ahead are somewhat partial. Certainly, they are not intended to be representative of all possible circumstances. They are either primarily West European or broadly Western in focus, and reflect the preoccupations and assumptions of these areas. Even when they go beyond the West in geographical terms (the Shi'ite suicide bombers, for example), the events and circumstances are largely discussed from a Western perspective. The treatment given to each example is relatively limited; quite clearly, the topics covered might well be the subjects of extensive works in their own right, rather than chapters in a book as presented here. This inevitably means that the discussions that follow are selective, focusing principally on supporting the analyses offered in the book.

One final comment is necessary on the conceptual bases of the discussion presented, and on the relationship between that conceptual approach chosen, and broader issues in psychology. This book is primarily aimed at providing a useful way of looking at the problem of political violence; its value to the reader will lie in whether or not the explanations offered help our understanding of the problem. Whilst the discussions are grounded in well-developed psychological theories, the application of those theories to the complex problems of political violence extend them beyond their present empirical bases. Some of the issues raised are probably never likely to be explored in any rigorous experimental fashion – they are too complex, and expressed at too high a level of generality. Others may one day benefit from empirical exploration. This should not, however, limit the value of the discussions presented. This book is an attempt to extend an important psychological debate to an area of considerable immediate social concern.

Summary

The work falls broadly into three broad parts. The first part (Chapters 2 and 3) discusses the concept of fanaticism, and considers some of the related psychological issues. In Chapter 2, the concept of fanaticism is explored, and the historical origins of the concept are considered. Ten features of fanaticism are then identified, which revolve around the fanatic's highly personalised and focused view of the world. These features are developed further in Chapter 3, and areas of psychological analysis that are relevant to them are identified and discussed. Three broad themes are explored: fanaticism and abnormality; fanaticism, prejudice and authoritarianism; and fanaticism and the dynamics of group behaviour.

The second part of the book (Chapters 4, 5 and 6) introduces the relationship between political action and psychological processes, and develops a discussion of the forces that might lead to and facilitate political fanaticism. These chapters are the most technical chapters in the book and explore ways of analysing, from a behavioural perspective, those features of the fanatic identified earlier. The prinicipal focus is on the role of ideology as the vehicle for structuring and organising the behaviour of the political fanatic. A threefold equation relating political ideology to fanatical violence is proposed in terms of militant potential, the totality of ideological control over behaviour and the notion of imminence in millenarian achievement. Chapter 4 examines the concept of Ideology. Starting from a discussion of psychological approaches to Ideology, it develops an alternative behavioural analysis emphasising the relationship between ideology and rule following behaviour. Within this behavioural approach, the notion of militant potential is explored. From the perspective of developing a behavioural analysis, this is probably the most critical chapter in the book, and it is from this chapter that much of the later conceptual discussion develops. Chapter 5 examines the notion of millenarianism, and relates this essentially non-behavioural concept to the processes of ideological control over behaviour discussed in Chapter 4. In particular, behavioural processes that related to the concept of imminence in millenarian attainment are considered. In Chapter 6, Hannah Arendt's concept of Public Space is considered from a behavioural perspective, and is related to the processes of millenarianism and militant ideology. The main purpose of this section of the book is to relate from a behavioural perspective the broader political concept of ideology to aspects of the processes of ideological control that can result in fanaticism.

The final section of the book (Chapters 7, 8 and 9) discusses examples of fanaticism that might illustrate these forces. Chapter 7 discusses examples of suicide related to the attainment of political objectives, drawing on Islamic fundamentalist and Irish Hunger Strike examples. Chapter 8 discusses examples from the Third Reich, focusing on the nature of the forces that resulted in the excesses of the SS. In Chapter 9, the ordinariness of explanations of fanatical violence are considered, and examples of the operation of the forces discussed earlier in less obviously aberrant situations are explored. The examples given relate to an overall theme of obedience. Finally, the broader notion of understanding political violence from a behavioural perspective is considered, and some indications for further analysis are given. The discussion in these final chapters is not in any way intended to be exhaustive surveys of the area, but rather offers illustrative material developing the analysis presented in the first part of the book. The final section of the book is probably the least technical, and can be read without the more detailed analyses of the second section (Chapters 4, 5 and 6). A summary of the technical areas of the book is presented at the end of Chapter 6.

CHAPTER 2

The Concept of
Political Fanaticism

The concept of fanaticism is complex and confusing. This chapter examines the concept, and goes on to identify ten of its features that help to illustrate its meaning. These features extend the discussion to examples of political violence.

Our concern with political fanaticism revolves round two broad themes – the particular behaviour of the fanatic, which is evident to us in some sense, and the political instrumentality of such behaviour. In the following chapter, we will focus on issues related to the first of these themes, by considering some of the conceptual issues related to our use of the term fanatic, and the identification and description of the behaviour of the fanatic within political and non-political contexts. Later chapters will consider the forces which might affect the nature and instrumentality of fanatical behaviour as it relates to violence within a political context.

As we use the term 'fanatic' in everyday language, it seems to refer not so much to behaviour, but rather to some kind of inner state which in a diffuse and general way is said to *cause* behaviour. The fanatic is said to show qualities of 'fanaticism', a state assumed to give rise to particular attributes. Rather than focus on behaviour, we seem to assume that fanaticism is a quality of the individual, which simply finds expression in what he does. Therefore whilst we may recognise it by the extreme quality of behaviour, the term tends more often to be used as reference to an inner condition, rather than a description of behaviour. It follows from this, therefore, that if fanaticism is a quality of an individual, we may describe fanaticism as a hidden or latent quality.

The above is not just a semantic issue, but a specific example of a more general tendency to describe the causes of behaviour in mentalistic, rather than behavioural terms. As such, it represents in a specific situation a major problem of psychological analysis. We might for example describe aggressive behaviour as the *result* of anger, as we might similarly describe tears as *caused* by sadness. There are alternative ways of depicting these situations, and there is some controversy as to the relationship between the states we feel (such as sadness and anger) and the expression of behaviour. But at least both sadness and anger are discernible emotional states as far as the individual is concerned, for which there is a considerable measure of common understanding about what is being experienced. Controversy exists not so much as to whether they are experienced, but as to their causal relationships with behaviour. We can, however, distinguish the notion of fanaticism from states of this kind like anger or sadness. It makes little sense for example to say 'I feel fanatical' in the sense in which you might say 'I feel sad' or 'I feel angry' as a label describing a broadly agreed set of experiences. We can distinguish therefore between terms which refer to and label emotional states like sadness and anger, and terms like fanatical and fanaticism, which have no clear emotional correlates in the same sense.

Emotions, of course, might be in some sense involved in examples of fanaticism, but fanaticism does not seem to be properly described as an emotional state. When we use the term fanaticism in the psychological sense, it is at best a loosely defined descriptor referring to a higher and more general level of expression, and whilst we might implicitly make assumptions about causal states related to fanaticism, if they exist at all, they clearly are different in character from the kinds of causal explanations of other psychological phenomena like emotions. General and unspecific terms like fanaticism which have a loose reference to behaviour (criminal might be another example) are often used not just to describe acts, but also, by implication, to indicate presumed causal states. What is worrying is that we don't even necessarily recognise the assumed causal implications of these terms.

Implicit assumptions of this sort can present problems for analysis. By using them as qualities of an individual (even if we don't recognise this usage), we make their investigation, and eventual control, much more difficult. Reference points move from the external, observable and essentially controllable environment, to a secluded and essentially unobservable mental world of traits and predispositions. It does not necessarily follow that we should dismiss accounts of behaviour in terms of emotional states such as sadness or anger. But because fanaticism is not a term that obviously refers to emotional states, it does allow us to question the value of similar usage in its case.

We can therefore question the value of accounts of behaviour expressed in such mentalistic terms in the case of fanatic and fanaticism. Nevertheless, there are many circumstances when we do predict someone's future behaviour not simply from observation of past occurrences of that behaviour, but from what we know of the individual concerned, and from what we loosely term their attitudes and beliefs. Behaviour is on the whole organised, and people do show consistency in what they do. This consistency in part provides the basis of our anticipation of other people's future actions. We often explain that consistency by reference to 'belief systems' or similar concepts. With reference to our broad political focus, another notion we might draw on to help explain such organisation of behaviour might be ideology.

Belief system and ideology seem part of the process by which past experiences and events come to be expressed in and influence present behaviour. Both are higher level concepts, relying on inference rather than direct observation for evidence of their existence. They might be said to refer not so much to causes of behaviour, but to descriptions of the processes underlying the organisation of behaviour in time, and in this sense can therefore be distinguished both from emotional states and the concept of fanaticism. We will develop in Chapter 4 the concept that ideology is the expressions of the 'rules' that determine and regulate our behaviour.[1] The position presented here takes the view that the processes involved reflect the particular history of the individual concerned, and are essentially the aggregation and expression of learned relationships between the settings in which a particular individual lives (his environment) and his behaviour.

In general, everyday experience suggests that it would be wrong to infer a direct relationship between belief systems and particular behaviour. In so far as we can assume attitudes reflect belief systems, the lack of success which has bedevilled efforts in health education to limit smoking illustrates this. Despite high levels of knowledge of the dangers from smoking, and negative attitudes to smoking, for example, smokers are extraordinarily resistant to any change in their smoking habits (more appropriately termed smoking behaviour). In most cases it might be better to see belief system as characterising behavioural frameworks, rather than predicting particular relationships between behaviour and its consequences.

We might at this point note one quality of the fanatic which is relevant to this, and which may help us to distinguish the concept of the fanatic from other related ones. For the fanatic, his belief systems or ideology are often clearly apparent and explicit. In the case of the political fanatic, this may simply be that he necessarily makes them apparent, given the essentially public qualities of the political process. But to attract the term fanatic, he must show that his belief systems are consistently and remorselessly controlling his behaviour, unlike the 'normal' political activist, whose actions might be characterised more by duplicity than consistency! In any event, as we examine this in more detail, we will see that the qualities we recognise as explicit are quite complex and overlapping.

Whatever the relationship may be between ideology or belief system on the one hand, and behaviour on the other, we can generally use the term fanatic consistently, using distinctive qualities of an individual's behaviour on which to base our judgement. Whatever controversy might exist about causal states, this consistency of usage suggests that there are certain features associated with the behaviour of the fanatic that we can recognise. We must stress, however, the difficulties that can arise when we forget we are describing behaviour, and imagine we are describing 'qualities' of the person concerned. When we do this, we lose the precision a behavioural analysis allows, and we introduce unwarranted assumptions about motivation and cause. What, then, are the qualities that distinguish the behaviour of the fanatic from others? Below we will examine further the concept of the fanatic, explore some of its attributes and qualities, and discuss ways in which we use this term.

The Concept

In this book we will use the term fanatic to refer to behaviour which is excessive and inappropriately enthusiastic and/or inappropriately concerned with significant life purpose, implying a focused and highly personalised interpretation of the world. In the political sense of primary concern to us, we will use it to refer to behaviour which is strongly influenced and controlled by ideology, where the influence of ideology is such that it excludes or attenuates other social, political or personal forces that might be expected to control and influence behaviour.

We have noted earlier in Chapter 1 that the term fanatic appears to have made its appearance in the English language in the seventeenth century, and was used originally to refer to 'excessive enthusiasm in religious belief'.[2] The important element of this definition is the term 'excessive'. Enthusiasm (perhaps expressed as commitment to a view) is not an unusual feature of most people's lives, and indeed we may feel that a lack of enthusiasm *for anything* may be indicative of a diminished life. It is not, therefore, the display of enthusiasm, which in the religious sense we might term devotion, which warrants the term fanatic. It is when this enthusiasm exceeds some boundary and becomes excessive that we begin to use the term. In this sense, therefore, fanaticism seems not to be a quality of particular behaviour, but one of degree or vigour in expression. The difficulty is, of course, what do we mean by excessive, and how do we recognise the boundaries?

The way that we have used the term excessive is rather like the way that we use the term abnormal – that is to say, it is a comparative term, making reference to some often implicit standard (the boundaries referred to above). The standards we use might be derived from a variety of sources, and because it is often an implicit judgement, we are unclear and even inconsistent in our use of them.

One standard we might identify is derived from what is essentially a statistical approach. For example, we could in many situations envisage a continuum of vigour of expression of behaviour – religious devotion expressed as church attendance is quite a good example even though it is not directly linked to political violence. There is some level of church attendance, for example, that many members of a particular religion might maintain, and most members broadly conform to that level of attendance. This may be an attribute of church membership, and represents an average level of attendance, which serves to summarise the population of church goers. A continuum describing church attendance of a particular religious congregation could be constructed, ranging from no attendance to frequent, multiple daily attendances. All members could be located somewhere on that continuum, probably clustered around some point (perhaps the average or the modal level). If the critical dimension along which behaviour might vary is agreed to be incidence of church attendance, then differences in an individual's attendance from the average might be termed deviant, and perhaps in unusual and extreme circumstances even attract the term fanatical (attending mass two or three times a day might merit such a term if it persisted over long periods). However, whilst we can identify two senses of deviation in this particular example, it is that involving *more* attendance that would probably most readily attract the term fanatic. If *everyone* attends at some time, for example in a society where religious observance is a necessary part of the social structure, then total *non*-attendance would attract opprobrium, and might as readily qualify for the term fanatic. This might be the case in some fundamentalist religious sects, for example, or perhaps in a future radical fundamentalist Islamic State.

Statistical views in these terms are powerful influences on our judgements. But they do not imply any prescription in our judgements. Were we to use this approach alone, it would be essentially a value-free judgement. A contrasting alternative approach, emphasising values in judgemental qualities, is that which makes reference to moral, ideological or religious *prescriptions*. This is a more socially defined approach, making reference to accepted wisdom, and perhaps proscriptions, as the arbiters against which standards of behaviour might be based. The ways in which we make judgements about violence often reflects this kind of approach. As a general statement, a controlled measure of personal violence is socially acceptable but, in general, violence that results in tissue damage is not acceptable. But at different times, the *degree* of violence that is acceptable varies. Corporal punishment in school, for example, was in the past far more acceptable than it is now. Parental chastisement of children, including beatings, is less condoned now than it was, although chastisement of other people's children has never been condoned, at least in the recent past.

By this view, therefore, standards that apply will vary, depending upon such factors as moral climate and cultural influences. In the heterogeneous societies of today, it is very difficult to identify acceptable broad cultural norms, and there may even be little uniformity within a diverse multicultural society. When we try to judge 'excessive' by reference to conflicting and inconsistent cultural values, therefore, we must expect inconsistency and confusion over attributes. This is an inevitable and perhaps insoluble problem, which we see expressed in broad social terms when particular standards derived from one culture or tradition are imposed upon a different culture. Both may be sincerely held, and both may have internal logical consistency, yet may conflict so profoundly that massive social disruption and violence results. The attempted introduction of Moslem Shari'a law in the predominantly Christian areas of Southern Sudan illustrates this. The threat of imposition of Shari'a law has served, amongst other things, as a catalyst to precipitate a vicious civil war which has seriously distorted the economic and social fabric of Sudan, made worse by profound physical catastrophes of desertification and flood. Yet the religious priorities which underlie this conflict remain unyielding on both sides, in the face of terrible starvation, migration on a largely unrecognised scale and profound misery.

Whilst the historical expression of fanaticism was associated with religion, religious fanaticism is not, of course, a historical phenomenon, and in the contemporary world adherents of religions (or religious-like movements) display fanatical behaviour from time to time. Because most religions make absolute moral and social claims, issues related to 'standards' (in the sense discussed above) become very relevant. Indeed, it might be suggested that there may be particular qualities of some kinds of religious belief that tend towards the excessive qualities of expression we term fanatical and, indeed, may be related to the occurrence of violence. We will encounter some of these qualities later when we consider the processes related to ideology (for in this sense, religious belief shares much in common with political ideology).

Whilst we can identify uncertainties about the conceptual bases of our judgements about fanaticism, the discussion only becomes meaningful when some particular behaviour occurs. In the context of religious belief, excessive and fanatically violent expression can take two general forms (which parallel the expression of violent political fanaticism): it can be expressed against others, either non-believers or the less enthusiastic fellow believer; or it can be expressed against the individual himself. The all too frequent victimisation of one Christian Sect by another (for example, Protestant by Catholic, or Catholic by Protestant, depending on historical period and location), or the excessive and often fatal zeal of the Flaggelants[3] illustrate these forms. The later form of self-victimisation, which we shall discuss later (Chapter 8) in the context of political suicide, is particularly disturbing and contrary to normal expectations of appropriate behaviour, but we will find it of particular value in furthering our understanding of the forces underlying fanaticism in general, and political fanaticism in particular.

Contemporary usage of the term fanatic has extended beyond the religious context, to refer to the more general expression of extreme behaviour. Perhaps this shift in emphasis from religion is associated with the declining role of religious ideology in people's lives, and its replacement by political ideology. This shifting of emphasis may also, however, indicate an important developmental quality of fanaticism; that fanaticism is not necessarily associated with religion as such, but with the expression of particular belief systems and ideological qualities (reflecting the degree of control that 'rules' of behaviour have over what we do), which the religious may share with some political activists. Alternatively, perhaps some forms of political ideology have enough in common with religious ideology simply to substitute one for the other. The processes we focus on we will assume to be probably the same in both religious and political contexts, and in what now follows we will tend to use *ideology* to refer to both religious and political contexts.

Ten Features of Fanaticism

Our everyday use of the term 'fanatic' is not confined to behavioural descriptions. If we are to explore this issue further, we must address non-behavioural analyses and constructs. Inevitably, in so doing we will lose the precision of behavioural accounts. Nevertheless, it is worth examining, in some detail, the qualities we use when referring to fanaticism, for even if they may be non-scientific, their identification will help us to better understand and identify the concept. They may well overlap and show interrelationships, and they may be inconsistent at times, but their identification and description reflects the usage we make of the term. The order in which they are presented here does not imply conceptual importance, nor logical priority, although the second quality discussed, personalisation, may in some sense have more global characteristics than the others mentioned. Perhaps the features we will note are in some senses aspects of related processes, seen from different perspectives. Whether or not they have a quality of interrelationship, or whether they are distinctively different, collectively they will help us to identify this complex concept.

Some ten qualities of the fanatic are described below. The overlapping qualities of these features indicate the fuzzy boundaries of the concept. Our use of the term is related to the aggregation of all or some of these qualities which contribute to and determine our use of the term 'fanatic'. Precision of identification of the concept is not absolutely necessary for our purposes. Fanatic or fanaticism is not a diagnostic category, and therefore uncertainties of identification present less difficulties here than in other contexts. We should note, however, that in the main, the display of one or more of these qualities is not in itself sufficient to merit the use of fanatic. Indeed, we all probably possess in some measure some or many of the qualities we will identify. Their vigour and persistent display *in some measure of combination* may be the necessary defining quality of the fanatic. What that combination might be remains a matter of judgement.

(i) Focusing

We all concentrate on, and limit ourselves in some measure, to those activities and aspects of our environment that are important to us. Such limiting, or focusing, can take a variety of forms; we work singlemindedly whilst at university for a degree, we spend our free time enthusiastically practising a musical instrument, or we play golf regularly and with determination. We can distinguish this acceptable level of involvement, however, from one of the striking and immediately apparent features of the fanatic – excessive and all-absorbing focusing on the issue of concern to the fanatic, to the exclusion of almost, or perhaps even all, other things. The fanatic follows the logic of his own behaviour to the total exclusion of all other alternatives, regardless of social approbation, and more general social or broader cultural norms. Furthermore, such focusing seems to result in the fanatic's lack of concern with the broader consequences of his actions. In this respect, the fanatic seems to be unaffected by the logical or moral paradoxes in which his behaviour results. This is not to say that the fanatic is unaware of this; but rather that it does not seem to matter to him. Such focusing is not limited to a narrow range of behaviours, but rather also extends to other aspects of a person's life. Focusing is not simply, therefore, an obsessive preoccupation with certain activities (as might be the case in clinical obsessive states) but a much broader interrelationship between the fanatical focus and everyday life.

Supporters of extreme political ideologies, like religious movements, often show qualities of this focusing aspect of fanaticism. An example can be seen in an extreme political context in the actions of supporters of Sinn Fein, the political wing of the Irish terrorist group, the Provisional IRA, who passed a motion at their annual conference in 1986 supporting the 'right to life', with the exception that it should not apply to what they term the 'armed struggle'. To the committed, the illogicality of supporting 'right to life' movements (in the context of anti-abortion) and the pursuit of a campaign of victimisation and murder in Northern Ireland seems to be resolved by focusing on the narrow ideological framework of that political movement, to the exclusion of the broader political, social and logical context.

The inconsistency of this motion is astonishing only in the context of normal political and social conditions. In the focused world of that particular terrorist group, and its supporters, the assertion more properly typifies the kind of logic which can characterise both the fanatic's and some terrorist's rationales. The overriding concern is with the single issue, or group of issues, around which the individual defines himself; other issues become defined in those terms, and become subservient to them. In the terrorist context, the achievement of ultimate goals overrides all other considerations, and moral consistency, amongst other issues, becomes subservient to the attainment of overall ideological objectives. Bombing campaigns in Northern Ireland and the United Kingdom in general, therefore continue to place infants, children and indeed fetuses at risk, showing scant regard for their 'right for life', presumably because they are incidentally involved in the broader process of the 'armed struggle'. Alignment with 'right to life' movements, especially in the Republic of Ireland, has obvious political and propaganda value for audiences within a predominantly Roman Catholic country, but the cynical and focused logic of the ideology as it impinges on Sinn Fein members excludes the paradox it implies.

The remorseless following through of the fanatic's logic, regardless of the broader implications, was graphically illustrated in an interview with Gerry Adams, the leader of Sinn Fein, the political wing of the Irish terrorist group, the Provisional IRA.[4] In the course of the interview, he acknowledges that he is '. . . involved in an organisation that supports an armed struggle that is responsible for the death of non-combatants'. But when asked how he '. . . feels about the enormity of taking a human life and about the terrible grief and torment this causes close relatives and friends, even of combatants', his answer is not to respond to the human anguish caused by the deaths, but to simply draw on ideological assertions stressing the moral correctness of the Provisional IRA's activities. 'I have had to think this through for myself and I sometimes envy those who can take a straightforward line on this one way or another. I don't want to give the impression that I am wracked with scruples or that I am some kind of confused bleeding heart but I have resolved for myself the issue of taking the lives of combatants. I support the right of the IRA to do this and while I don't take any pleasure in anybody's life being taken and am often momentarily taken aback by it, I believe the IRA is morally justified in doing this and I am morally justified in supporting their right to do it.' It is difficult to envisage a more compelling example of focusing, where an assertion of moral correctness dismisses the routine horror of deaths caused by the Provisional IRA.

(ii) Personalised view of the world

The feature of fanaticism described as focusing might in one sense be a specific aspect of a more general process of the personalisation of the world which seems to characterise the fanatic. Personalisation refers to the fanatic's exclusive concern with his own ideological construction of the world, to the exclusion of alternatives. It can be thought of in two ways:

  a.   personalisation in the sense of personal preoccupations dominating how the world is interpreted and seen;
  b.   personalisation in terms of how events unrelated to the individual in any direct sense are taken as having a personal reference and involvement. Focusing may describe a process which exacerbates the effects of personalisation, or it may, from another perspective, be seen as an element of personalisation.

In the first sense used above, processes like personalisation are not unique to the fanatic. Some parallels with this usage of personalisation, for example, can be seen in the feature of the psychological development of children, known as egocentricism. This is an element of normal development associated with children from around two to about seven years of age. It refers to the young child's inability to understand that someone else may see the world in a different way from him. For example, the child describes things from its own visual perspective, and in early life seems unable to give an account of the same scene from someone else's view. Some more general qualities of this may persist into adolescence, as in the adolescent's inability to see that others may not be preoccupied with *his* problems in the same way he is. Of course, we all tend to view the world from our own perspective (both literally and figuratively), so in a sense we all suffer from this quality. It is when it is present in excess that we might associate it with fanaticism.

However, if this aspect of fanaticism parallels the developmental processes noted above, then unlike in the adolescent, the fanatic's preoccupation, at least in the political context, is not particularly with personal problems, but with the personal view of the world derived from his own particular ideological position. Ideology in this sense, therefore, perhaps substitutes for personal preoccupations. But although we can distinguish between the focus of the personalised preoccupation of the fanatic and the adolescent, the processes whereby such preoccupations come about may well have similarities; in any event, the result is very similar. The fanatic's view of the world, his particular interpretation of events, or the significance of particular acts which characterise his approach seem only to exist from his particular standpoint, and other perspectives are either ignored, judged irrelevant, or incorporated into the personalised view.

An example of personalisation might be seen in the animal rights activists who become involved in the militant expression of their views through attacking laboratories using animals, or shops and stores selling animal products (such as fur coats). The basis of the animal rights activists' views is their objection to the exploitation of animals for human benefit. Objections are raised, for example, to experiments on animals which might inflict pain or distress. This is a controversial area, where arguments against causing distress to animals are countered by the potential benefits from research with animals, in terms of, for example, the development of new drugs or improved understanding of the working of the brain.

The general principle that unnecessary distress to animals should not be caused would probably command wide support. The problems revolve of course around the notion of 'unnecessary'. The Animal Liberation movements have extended a concern with animal welfare, however, to the exclusion of concern with the welfare of others who may become involved in their actions. The militant expression of animal liberation supporters, and their particular personalised view of the world, seems to exclude the risk to others, animal and human, in which their activities might result. An illustration of this occurred in June 1988, when two animal liberation supporters were gaoled in London for arson attacks against stores selling animal fur products. The fires they set caused over £4,500,000 damage to the stores, and resulted in a loss of trading to the stores of a similar amount. Reports at the time stress the potential for loss or damage to human life from these fires, that was fortunately avoided. These considerations appear to have played little role in the decision to cause the fires.

These arson attacks were just one of a series of incidents designed to intimidate people involved in what the animal liberation movement supporters regard as cruel activities. Laboratories involved in scientific work using animals were prime targets for such intimidatory action. A typical incident involved the animal laboratories of the Institute of Psychiatry in London which was broken into in February 1988, when between 70 and 100 white rats were removed. The Physiology Laboratories at Oxford University have also been the target for several such attacks, and these have extended to threats and direct intimidation against the head of those laboratories, Professor Colin Blakemore. He has received anonymous telephone calls threatening to kill him, and his wife whilst pregnant, received telephone calls hoping '. . . her baby is born deformed'. Another animal researcher in London University, Professor Ian Steele-Russell, has received similar threats against himself and his family, which he takes sufficiently seriously to not allow his children to leave his home unaccompanied. The capacity of groups of this kind to inflict serious life threatening damage should not be underestimated, as events in the United Kingdom in May and June 1990 have shown, when an infant was seriously injured in a car bomb blast in Bristol.

Animal liberation supporters seem to be so absorbed in their own set of concerns with animal welfare, that they exclude consideration of the welfare of others; this well illustrates this sense in which personalisation can characterise the fanatic. It also shows that, in this case, the excessive and absorbing preoccupation with cruelty and oppression of animals, when expressed in a militant fashion, results in the oppression of people. A preoccupation with the personal can also be seen in the interview with Gerry Adams, the leader of Provisional Sinn Fein, referred to above. He was asked if he thought '. . . he should not be a party to the infliction of . . . appalling grief and injury on so many people, through his support for the "armed struggle" . . .'. His response reveals a striking concern with the personal effects of such grief and injury on himself, rather than on the relatives and friends of those killed and injured. '. . . But yes, I have regrets. It is a drain emotionally and physically and in other ways. There are moments of great sorrow or great tragedy. . . . You reflect, you contemplate, tragedies happen that shouldn't have happened. But as I have said before, I can defend to myself and to my conscience my support for the right of the IRA to wage an armed struggle.'

The generality that the concept of personalisation in this sense might have is illustrated further by the comments of Hannah Arendt in her account of the trial in Jerusalem of the Nazi war criminal,

Adolph Eichmann.[5] Eichmann was heavily involved in organising the murder of Jews (and others) in the Concentration Camps, and is widely described as a fanatic. In a discussion of the quality of his evidence in the trial, she notes that '. . . The longer one listened to him, the more obvious it became that his inability to speak was closely connected with an inability to *think*, namely, to think from the standpoint of somebody else. . . .'

As we have noted above, the processes we have identified here as personalisation may be seen from another perspective, related to the fanatic perceiving events in which he is not involved as having some direct *personal* meaning. Sometimes the fanatic can give the impression that events related to the particular *external* focus of his beliefs are felt as something happening to him, rather than a third party actually involved. Ideological preoccupations with injustice, for example, often seem to result in the individual *feeling* the injustice as if it had happened to him. The process whereby an individual shares another's experiences and feelings is termed empathy, and in this sense, the personalisation of the fanatic might also be related in some sense to empathetic processes.

In behavioural terms, empathy can be seen as a process of imitation, and perhaps what we see in this quality of fanaticism is the ability of an individual to imitate, or empathise, with the feelings of others in the absence of the actual circumstances which give rise to those feelings. They are evoked instead by reading, hearing or perhaps seeing on television, or as a spectator, examples of injustice and oppression. A particular issue we should note here, however, is that in the case of the fanatic, such empathy is focused in the sense previously noted; it seems to be related not to the 'human condition', or some general theme of (say) oppression, but to a particular and often highly defined group which has some real or symbolic significance in terms of a particular ideological perspective. Perhaps the animal rights activists also show this focused quality with respect to the subject of animal experiments, in contrast to their views of the consequences of their actions on other people.

An example of such empathetic personalisation can be seen in the account which Michael Baumann, the founder of the West German terrorist group, the 2nd of June Movement, gives of his own development into terrorist life. An attempt on the life of a student activist, Rudi Dutschke, appeared to have a profound effect on Baumann. As he describes '. . . The bullet might just have well have been for me. . . .

I now felt I had been shot at for the first time. So it became clear to me
... we must now fight without mercy....'[6] In this situation, Baumann was not shot and does not appear to have been involved in the
events around the attempt of Dutschke's life, but he describes the
effects almost as if he had been. The effects on him were clearly
profound, and he gives great weight to this example as a critical
feature in his development as a terrorist.

(iii) Insensitivity

Another feature of the fanatic which we can identify is his insensitivity
both to other people, and to normal social pressures. The fanatic
becomes insensitive to the expected limits to behaviour; the standards
which others might apply appear to leave him untouched. This
quality may well be related to those described above, and indeed is
implicit in the examples given. As in the case of focusing, we might in
one sense see it as another facet of personalisation, again viewed from
a slightly different perspective.

A reciprocal relationship can be identified between behaviour and
the environment in which that behaviour occurs. Thus, in normal
circumstances, our behaviour exerts an influence on others, but
equally the behaviour of others influences us; we act and react
together, in relation with our physical, social and personal environment. We are concerned with what others might think of us, we seek
approval or praise for what we do, and we give praise for things done
to us. This reciprocity in relationships seems either to be lacking in
the fanatic, or to be severely attenuated in a political sense in critical
areas related to the fanatic's particular perspective. In other respects,
however, the behaviour of the fanatic may be quite normal and
appropriate and show qualities of reciprocity.

Members of the 'Moonie' sect, adherents of the Reverend Sun
Myong Moon, show what can only be described as fanatical devotion
to their leader, and to the sect. Often the act of joining and becoming
a 'Moonie' is a source of great distress and concern for family and
friends. It not only results in the 'Moonie' leaving home, but an
abandonment of all the values of their former life, especially with
respect to their family relationships; they effectively acquire a new
family, disclaiming and repudiating their earlier one. Yet the distress
this causes leaves the adherent untouched. If a problem is acknowledged, it lies not with the devotee, but with the rest of the world and
the rejected family and friends. The devotee becomes insensitive to

those aspects of his environment (family, friends) that affect the rest of us in some measure.

(iv) Loss of critical judgement

We often assume implicitly that people's behaviour when dealing with choices in some sense reflects a process of optimisation. That is to say, we act in ways that will ultimately be to our benefit. What benefit might mean, of course, will be dependent on the particular individual and his circumstances, but given the possible variety of individual circumstance, there is a surprising degree of consistency in what is recognised as being desirable. Given a variety of contexts and situations, one person's benefit may, of course, be another's disadvantage – claims of universality may well be suspect. Benefit in this sense need not necessarily mean change in something, of course, but maintenance of present conditions of relative comfort, or lack of discomfort. Maintenance of equilibrium, or balance, may be a feature of optimisation, where benefit is interpreted in terms of balance. When we successfully 'optimise' in this sense, we might be said to be exercising our critical judgement. Similarly, when we make what seem to be situationally appropriate choices, or avoid behavioural choices that might disadvantage us, again we might be said to be exercising our critical judgement. The notion of judgement, therefore, refers to personal benefit, but is probably expressed in terms of some broader social contexts.

The universality of these assumptions in practice may be questionable, of course, but in general we certainly assume that the operation of processing something like this are important in the regulation of behaviour. In contrast, however, the fanatic does not seem to show evidence of optimisation in the sense discussed above. He often seems to act in ways which expose him to public approbation in settings where he seems to have a choice of possible options and in particular where options to avoid approbation exist. Such failure to optimise behaviour in the fanatic may be described as a lack of critical judgement. This becomes evident therefore where the fanatic appears to embark on courses of action that seem contrary to that individual's interests, when interpreted from more normative perspectives.

The lack of critical judgement shown by the fanatic is evident in his failure to be sensitive to expected 'benefits' from situations. The issue here, of course, is again how do we judge 'benefit'? What standards apply to this? By the standards of the society in which the fanatic lives, his actions may well be contrary to the interest the *broader* society might identify. The issue here is similar to the problem of 'excess' discussed above, and the problem lies in the contrast between the fanatic's particular ideological priorities and broader social norms. In so far as the fanatic is concerned, of course, his actions are presumably consistent with his interests as expressed from his particular ideological perspective. The benefits to himself seem to outweigh or replace those normally expected by society. In a sense we can see this as yet a further aspect of personalisation, where the fanatic's particular set of values overrides those of society in general.

A failure to optimise decisions in the way we have discussed does not necessarily imply social criticism. Many people may resist the temptation to steal or cheat, and thereby improve their material conditions, because they feel other values are more important, like honesty or honour. Indeed, there is a long tradition of embracing poverty and abandoning material possessions amongst religious adherents. In a material sense, the vows of poverty of the monk represent a failure to optimise; in another sense, of course, because it may result in benefit in the hereafter, the abandonment of present material wealth may be a positive step 'optimising' future benefits. This may be an example of fanatical behaviour; it may also be an example of lack of critical judgement, but it does not necessarily follow of course that such choices are either illogical or socially inappropriate.

Indeed, we can develop this theme further. What we have termed here in one context as loss of critical judgement may lead, from time to time, to what we sometimes call 'selfless', rather than fanatical, behaviour. If someone experiences disadvantage for adherence to his principles (ideology) *with which we agree*, for example, we might prefer to call it selfless sacrifice, rather than fanaticism. Indeed, moral and religious prescriptions exist for behaviour of this kind. 'Greater love hath no man than this, that a man lay down his life for a friend'[7] illustrates an extreme example which nevertheless in principle would attract broad admiration. This illustrates the inconsistency of usage which we have noted earlier, but does not necessarily invalidate an analysis of such behaviour in terms of benefit. The 'selfless' may well be influenced and controlled by that benefit (if only in the personal consequences of adherence to principles – a powerful enough reinforcer of behaviour) in the same way as we might suggest for the fanatic. The way in which we might make judgements about this is also revealing. Skinner notes[8] that 'We give credit generously when there are no obvious reasons for . . . behaviour. . . . We give maximum credit when there are quite visible reasons for behaving differently.'

In our discussions in Chapter 1 of the features of a behavioural approach, we noted the idiosyncratic qualities of reinforcement. By this, we mean that the events that may serve to reinforce and control the behaviour of one person may well be different from those that reinforce another person's behaviour. What we have discussed above may be a reflection of this general process, expressed in the context of particular ideological frameworks. The critical issue may be the extent to which a particular ideological framework may serve to reorder or establish reinforcing qualities. One important role of ideology, therefore, may be defining the reinforcers that control our behaviour.

(v) Inconsistency and tolerance of incompatibility

A further quality of our use of fanaticism seems to be an absence of the necessary logical consistency which we might feel should characterise normal belief systems and behaviour. Furthermore, and perhaps critically, this lack of consistency appears to leave the fanatic untouched. We can see this very clearly in the case of the religious fanatic for example, who might well espouse a doctrine of love, but, as with the adherents of the Reverend Sun Myung Moon noted earlier, abandon family and kin, much to the family's very evident distress.

However, as with the qualities already discussed, this inconsistency lies in the contrast between the fanatic's values and actions with those actions expected by the broader community in which the fanatic lives. It is inconsistent to us, because we expect something different. To the fanatic, there appears to be no difficulty in accommodating to his choice of action, because it is consistent with his ideological position from his perspective. Again, in a sense we may see this as another aspect of the processes we have described above, resulting from the fanatic's focused and personalised view of the world.

Heinrich Himmler, Reichsführer SS in Nazi Germany, illustrates the inconsistency and tolerance of incompatibility that can characterise the fanatic. He was leader and organiser of the SS, the principal organ of oppression against the Jews in Nazi Germany. As we will discuss later, the SS were directly responsible for the deaths of millions of people in appalling conditions; yet Himmler, in the knowledge of these deaths which he both initiated and to a large extent controlled, had scruples at eating meat from slaughtered animals, and had what has been described as a hysterical opposition to hunting animals. He said to his doctor '. . . How can you find pleasure, Herr Kersten, in shooting from behind cover at poor creatures browsing on the edge of a wood, innocent, defenceless, and unsuspecting? It's really pure murder. Nature is so marvellously beautiful and every animal has a right to live. . . . You will find this respect for animals in all Indo-Germanic peoples. . . .'[9] In Himmler's case, respect for 'animals' did not, it would seem, extend to the Jews, or other inmates of the concentration camps, whose very existence ran counter to Nazi ideology. We might see parallels here with the views of the anti-vivisectionists and animal rights activists, who seem able to inflict damage to humans in the defence of animal rights. We can see even more striking parallels with anti-abortion activists who bomb abortion clinics (with the potential for serious injury or death to anyone caught in the blast) in the name of 'right to life'. It requires no great stretch of imagination to see further similarities with the terrorist's stated concern with 'justice' and 'human rights' in the context of bombings and ambushes of civilians.

The inconsistency evident in Himmler's views was not unusual amongst Nazi activists in general. Contrary to post-war stereotypes, members of the Nazi movement were not necessarily twisted psychopaths. Some perhaps were, but that did not characterise the SS member, let alone the ordinary Nazi Party member. Yet both the SS, and the broader party membership, condoned, if not supported, unrivalled atrocities. As Fest notes,[10] this was made possible by placing the 'duty' of operationalising Nazi ideology before other societal values. In this situation, where ideology conflicts with other values, the fanatic's resolution to the paradox is to adhere to his ideological imperatives. In the face of this, inconsistency and incompatibility with other social norms ceases to be a problem.

(vi) Certainty

The features discussed so far all cluster around common themes of the fanatic's separation from the normal consequences and constraints of events and circumstances, insensitivity and personal focusing. A further elaboration on those themes that we can identify is the certainty with which the fanatic undertakes his activities. The fanatic has no doubt as to the appropriateness of his actions, and the energy, single-mindedness and insensitivity with which he pursues his ends seems to imply the quality of certainty.

We can see in this notion elements of focusing and insensi\
noted above, but it seems particularly to reflect the vigour .
characterises some aspects of the fanatic's actions in attaining his
ends. The fanatic is not *just* single-minded or focused, but he energetically and vigorously directs his activity and pursues his ends. This
pursuit admits of no deviation or recognition of moral dilemma. All of
the examples given above, including that of Heinrich Himmler, illustrate this feature of fanaticism. Like many senior Nazis, Himmler
expressed no doubts in his anti-semitic views; he pursued them
energetically and vigorously despite inconsistency and contradictions.

An example of the certainty which characterises the fanatic was
shown by the Nazi leadership in a rather unusual way. For a variety of
reasons, active resistance to Hitler's policies among the German
people was limited in the extreme. Of course, one important reason
for this may be that his policies commanded broad popular support.
'... the German resistance movement did not exert the slightest
influence on the course of history...'[11] summarises quite clearly the
results of such limited resistance that existed. However, as the defeat
of Germany seemed more likely as the war progressed, there were
efforts made by the Nazi political and military leadership to remove
Hitler, by assassination, and to begin negotiations with the Allies.
These efforts culminated in the famous von Stauffenberg plot of 20
July 1944, generally regarded as the only significant act of resistance
in the whole of the period of the Third Reich. Many of the conspirators such as Karl Fredrich Goerdeler and Wilhelm Leuscher (and von
Stauffenberg) were well aware of the significance for negotiations of
the slaughter of the Jews, and seemed to have been motivated as much
by moral outrage as by concern for German national survival. Yet the
preparations for negotiations with the Allies that were made if the plot
had been successful revealed, according to Hannah Arendt,[12] a star-
tling perception of the issues that might arise in any negotiations. The
conspirators appeared to believe that the basis for negotiations included matters such as '... the re-establishment of the national
borders of 1914, with the addition of Austria and the Sudetenland ...
a leading position for Germany on the Continent ...'. Indeed, some of
the lesser conspirators appeared to have played an active part in the
extermination programme, and the conclusion that the conspirators
viewed that programme as a difficulty in negotiation which could be
surmounted rather than a source of moral deadlock is a tenable
hypothesis. If this is the case, then the ultimate irrelevance of the fate
of the millions of Eastern European Jews seems to have been regarded

as common ground by the conspirators between themselves and the Allies, illustrating not only the absolute certainty with which they held their anti-semitic views, but many of the other qualities described here. Even in the face of defeat, a fanatical ideology continued to influence and determine actions.

(vii) Simplification

In the political fanatic's description of his world, an overwhelming impression is the simplicity of the structures he uses to describe political processes, in contrast, of course, to the everyday experience of the reality of political life. The world of the political fanatic often seems black and white – imperialists or non-imperialists populate the world, or communist conspiracies colour and influence all actions. The religious fanatic has a similar view, perhaps seeing the devil (or God) always present and responsible for events. Furthermore, the attributes of those whose views do not correspond to the fanatics are also often characterised in simple terms. In Nazi Germany, Jews were the root of all evil, notwithstanding empirical evidence to the contrary, or even personal experience of 'good' Jews. A simplified caricature of the Jew served as a focus for legitimising the atrocities committed against them.

Caricatures of this kind are, at one level, a form of propaganda; the cartoons of George Gröss, for example, illustrate the simplification in description and illustration of negative qualities. They at least have the virtue of some artistic merit; most of this material is offensive and obscene. But what for the rest of society remains propaganda (however effective), for the fanatic it seems properly to characterise his views. The naive but vitriolic anti-semitic propaganda of Nazi Germany looks today to be excessive and bizarre; but the assertions of the 'Master Race' and its strange notions of hereditary superiority, and the image of the grasping and malevolent Jew seeking to subvert the 'Herrenvolk', properly characterised the Nazi view of the world . . . and the chilling truth remains that most Germans of that time subscribed to those views.

Propaganda of this form is not confined to the Nazi period. Contemporary use of similar simplified racial propaganda can be seen in the material disseminated by the Ku Klux Klan, an American racist organisation '. . . committed to the interests, ideas and cultural values of the White Majority'. The Ku Klux Klan does not confine itself to black racism, and embraces Jews and other racial groups in its propaganda material. Mock boat tickets are available, for example, for the 'Coon-ard Lines' offering one-way boat trips to Africa. The ticket is illustrated with crude racial drawings, and offers the traveller 'All the bananas and choice cuts of missionary desired. ... Barrels of axle grease for hair. ... Plenty of wine, marijuana, heroin and other refreshments.' On the ticket stub is a drawing of a stereotypical Jew, inviting travellers to take part in a draw. 'If the pumps stop working and boat sinks, the nigger whose number is drawn gets a free life-jacket from big-hearted Izzy Pilebaum. Otherwise $500 each, cash.' The racial stereotypes in material of this kind are obvious, and are grossly offensive. Yet whilst propaganda of this kind is unlikely to gain new adherents, the potential power of this material amongst the already committed should not be underestimated.

The process of simplification also seems to extend to treating the individual drawn into the particular ideological framework as illustrative of group members, rather than individuals. What we have identified here may well be closely related to the process of stereotyping. This is discussed later in Chapter 3, in the context of prejudice, but we might note here that a stereotype refers to a group of persistent preconceptions and expectations about a particular group – 'they all look alike to me' captures this notion, in the sense that it refers to a mythical aggregation of 'they' (as members of a racial, political, or class based group), rather than the individuals that make up that group. This example also captures the negative qualities of stereotyping, in that by saying 'they all look alike', it implies they are not worth identifying individually.

(viii) Resistance to change

The apparent isolation of the fanatic from the circumstances that affect other people's behaviour is further evident in the fanatic's resistance to change. The insensitivity and personalisation discussed above is, of course, an aspect of this. It may be a matter of debate whether the reluctance of the fanatic to change his views is because he is unaware of the problem (resulting from his insensitivity), or whether he simply does not wish to change his views because he knows he is right (certainty). In any event, resistance to change may be a higher order attribute, drawing on the qualities already discussed to become evident.

Another sense in which we might conceptualise the fanatic's resistance to change is in terms of the vigour and perseverance which seems to characterise him. We have already made reference to the vigour of the fanatic's activities reflected in many of the features discussed before. Vigour is, of course, related to perseverance and tenacity in the face of adverse circumstances, and may in fact be a further perspective of the insensitivity of the fanatic.

(ix) Disdain/dismissal

The net result of all these facets of fanaticism discussed above, as far as the recipients of the fanatic's behaviour is concerned, may appear to be disdain for, if not dismissal of, his perspective, beliefs and actions. After all, all the features so far considered result in what for a recipient of a fanatic's actions may well be negative consequences. This disdain may even extend to lack of regard for the lives of others, so focused and intense is the concern with ideological priorities.

The persistent victimisation of members of the security forces in Northern Ireland, for example, is undertaken with no apparent regard for the families of those bombed or shot. The disdain this seems to imply on the part of the paramilitary groups involved may extend to a failure to apologise, show remorse, or admit to a mistake when someone wholly unconnected with the security services is killed or injured. Where apologies are given, there is often a sense of appeal to their own supporters, with a stress on the rightness of the cause *despite* some unfortunate mistake, rather than a genuine expression of sympathy with the bereaved. The quality of personalisation referred to above also seems to play a role in this. A concern with the effects of a mistake on themselves, rather than on the family (as illustrated in the interview with Gerry Adams quoted above) illustrates a disdain for other parties, as well as personalisation.

What the Press Association described as a 'bungled IRA bombing' illustrates the lack of concern with the lives of others that can characterise violent political fanatics. On a November evening in 1988, a bomb was concealed in a van and left outside an unmanned police station in the village of Benburb in Northern Ireland. A short warning was given to the security authorities, and the bomb exploded at about 10.50 pm. Responsibility for the attack was claimed by the Provisional IRA. The police station was unmanned at that time, as it was known to be every evening. As the bomb exploded, a resident of the village, 67 year old Barney Lavery and his 13 year old granddaughter, Emma Donnelly, were passing the police station in their car. The car was hurled into a field, and they were killed immediately.

A further eight civilians were injured. No members of the security services were hurt or involved, and none were in the vicinity of the explosion. The irony of this incident is that the two people killed were Roman Catholics, a part of the community the Provisional IRA would claim to represent.

It seems unlikely that this incident, in itself minor and relatively commonplace except for the deaths, was in fact bungled. It was common knowledge that there were no security force personnel in the police station at that time of night, and the night itself was foggy, limiting the capacity of the security services to respond to the short warning given. No doubt the *particular* deaths of Mr Lavery and his granddaughter were not deliberate or intended, but some measure of civilian casualties was an almost inevitable outcome. After all, the attack was carried out in the knowledge of civilian movements around the village, no security force presence and with what can only be described as a lack of concern for its consequences. That this was not a particularly unusual incident can be seen by the fact that in the same week, two other attacks were reported, both with enormous potential for injury and death to civilians. In the first, two grenades were thrown at workers repairing a damaged police station in Dungannon. In the second, a rocket-propelled grenade was fired at two police vehicles, which missed, and demolished a butcher's shop. Fortunately, there were no injuries in either case.

The processes underlying these behaviours are not, of course, confined to terrorists. Regrettably, we may be looking at general processes resulting from exposure to ideologies that become evident in certain circumstances. Lapses in the behaviour of members of the security forces in Northern Ireland, for example, which do from time to time occur, may be amenable to similar kinds of explanations. To serve in such a hostile environment may well result in conditions like those we might characterise later in this book as ideological control. The discussion in Chapter 9 of the events at My Lai in Vietnam may relate to this.

Herman Göring, in an address to SS members in 1933[13] described general principles that capture the essential qualities of terrorist incidents like those described above: 'You can't make omelettes without breaking eggs. Don't shout for justice so much. ... Even if we make a lot of mistakes, we shall at least act and keep our nerve. I'd rather shoot a few times too short or too wide, but at least I shoot.' Göring's chilling phrase might be used by any contemporary terrorist group to dismiss any objection that might be raised to bombing and killing civilians, let alone anyone else. His comments certainly apply to the examples given above. For people not involved or caught up in the ideology, it is difficult to understand the kind of processes this comment illustrates, but it may be that this disdain for others is the inevitable consequences of the processes of fanaticism. Göring's comments also illustrate the importance of action for the fanatic; the fanatic seems impelled to act on his ideological priorities.

We can see the process of disdain in operation in other ways, reflected in the names given to those who might oppose the fanatic's perspective. Pigs, infidels, papists, heretics, unbelievers are all terms which illustrate this. Bandura[14] suggests that at least for the terrorist, this renaming of victims (and thereby diminishing them) plays a role in making the terrorists' actions acceptable to themselves. Lest this should give the impression that this process is confined to dissident terrorist groups, we should also note that states (or their leaders) are just as capable of illustrating this process as an individual. As far as challenges to state power is concerned, an attempted coup is never conducted by 'freedom fighters', or groups seeking democracy. For example, the serious riots in July 1990 in Kenya were described by the Kenyan President, Daniel arap Moi, as the result of a 'power-hungry' and 'bent on subversion' Cabinet Minister, Kenneth Matiba. Because the riots have challenged the one-party system in Kenya, they are described as a matter of 'state security'.

We might refer in passing here to links that might be identified with prejudice behaviour, and the self-confirming qualities of prejudice. We might note here that negative beliefs and actions result in responses to behaviour that sustain and justify further negative action. Self-sustaining qualities of this kind may be important in helping to explain the persistence of fanaticism despite objective evidence which seems to contradict the fanatic's views.

(x) Contextual facilitation

Whilst the fanatic might be insensitive to the reciprocal social and moral qualities of behaviour as the rest of the world might experience them (as argued in the discussion of insensitivity for example), nevertheless, some qualities of reciprocal forces do seem to influence the fanatic. One example of such reciprocity is the self-sustaining quality of fanatical behaviour discussed briefly under Disdain/Dismissal; but this can be considered in a broader framework, where the particular environmental and social context which the fanatic creates for himself further sustains and develops fanatical behaviour.

There is every reason to suppose that the fanatic, like most people, exercises some measure of choice over his social contacts. He chooses his friends and his social circle. He also selectively exposes himself to current events and entertainment through the newspaper he purchases or the television programmes he watches. As we all do, he creates for himself a distinctive world, which is part of the broader social world, but limited in some sense through his own choices. This, of course, applies to us all, and the fanatic is not unique in this. We all in some measure create our own world which reflects our own interests and experiences. In the case of the fanatic, this leads to the construction of what might be termed a fanatical world, where, in so far as is possible, the social contacts and exposure to news confirm and sustain the fanatic's preoccupations. Thus, in this sense, given the ideological control which fanaticism implies, the environment he creates further feeds and develops existing excessive qualities.

When ideology becomes so important an element of life, perhaps this is an inevitable outcome. The interaction and effects of all the kinds of processes we have discussed above may well lead to the creation of a self-sustaining and facilitating context, almost a parallel, separate but distinctive sub-culture that directs and sustains the fanatic, through selectively reinforcing the incidence of ideologically appropriate behaviour. The selective use of information that characterises the prejudiced (and discussed in Chapter 3) may be relevant to this.

The Status of 'Fanatic' and 'Fanaticism'

We have seen above that we can identify a number of elements of meanings to the concept of 'fanatic'. Given such an array of qualities, the precise attributes we use when describing someone as a fanatic of necessity becomes somewhat blurred. On the other hand, the above discussion has served to identify qualities that however conceptually complex they might be (in terms, for example, of their social attributes and referrents), can be expressed in behavioural terms. Most, if not all, of the ten features described above can be reduced to aspects of behaviour. The precision this can give the analyst should not be overemphasised; the inherent linguistic and social confusion of the concept is not resolved by a behaviour analysis. Yet we will see that the various features of fanaticism we have identified recur as signifi-

cant elements in our later discussion. Those features may be interpreted as evidence of a process (or series of processes) in their own
right, or they may be seen as attributes of other more complex
underlying processes. However we see them, they are the behavioural
referrents which we will keep returning to.

The descriptions of fanaticism detailed above broadly conform with
those of other authors who have discussed this issue. In particular,
Rudin,[15] in his extensive phenomenological account of fanaticism,
notes the importance of the intensity of expression of fanatical behaviour, and also the problem of values in describing fanaticism. He
adopts a very different conceptual approach to that of the analysis
presented here, however. Even so, a particular point he underlines,
which is not inconsistent with the approach adopted here, is what he
terms the *multilayeredness* of the problem. In his view, fanaticism does
not reduce to a single feature, but rather extends across a broad
spectrum of activities, sometimes as a peripheral and sometimes as a
central factor. In many ways, the ten features of fanaticism described
above are more specific elaborations on that theme, within a behavioural context.

In the light of this discussion, we can see that the use we will make
of the concept of fanaticism in this book is somewhat restrictive when
compared to everyday usage of the term. As we have noted, our
principal concerns here are with the political expression of fanatical
behaviour. Yet the concept of fanaticism is not something confined to
the political arena. In the contemporary world, it may well be the case
that our encounters with and experience of fanaticism comes most
obviously from within a political context. But on the basis of the
discussion in this chapter, we might expect to see examples of what we
term fanaticism in a variety of contexts. Although not central to our
concerns, we will cast some light on these more general processes
through our discussion of the particular problem of political fanaticism.

Throughout our discussion, a recurrent theme has been the importance of political ideology in structuring and shaping the behaviour we
are primarily concerned with. Indeed, it is the involvement of ideology that enables us to distinguish political fanaticism from other
forms of fanaticism. However, qualities of ideology are also, as we will
see, something which in themselves shape and develop violence. In
the next two chapters, we continue our conceptual analysis by considering the psychological context to fanaticism (Chapter 3), and
what we mean by ideology (Chapter 4).

CHAPTER 3

The Psychological Context

After discussing the complex relationship between fanaticism and abnormality, the chapter goes on to explore how fanaticism relates to prejudice and authoritarianism. The links between group behaviour and fanaticism are then discussed.

In Chapter 2 we have identified and described some of the principal features that are associated with our use of the concept of the fanatic and fanaticism. Can we now develop some psychological meaning from these features? Fanatic is not a technical word in any psychological sense and is not a concept enjoying psychological currency. Hence, perhaps not surprisingly, the concept of the fanatic has received relatively little comment in psychological terms. If considered at all, it might be subsumed under general analyses of violence and prejudice, or alternatively, within the context of mental health. On the other hand, in the light of our earlier discussion, analyses of processes underlying states such as prejudice might be thought to be relevant to the ways in which we use concepts like fanatic and fanaticism. Indeed, despite a relative lack of analysis and lack of technical meaning, our earlier discussion does suggest that there are distinctive, if complex, attributes of fanaticism, and that those attributes might serve to distinguish fanatical behaviour from other behaviour.

One of the few authors to address the concept of fanaticism is Rudin.[1] He takes a broadly phenomenological approach to its analysis, and because of this, his approach largely lacks reference to empirical constructs. In consequence, he makes little reference to contemporary insights into psychological processes. Empirically orientated approaches, such as a behavioural analysis, are in contrast wholly lacking in reference to fanaticism. Yet, as we have seen, the term fanatic does refer to identifiable and reasonably systematic qualities of behaviour. Can we therefore identify from the broader psychological and behavioural literature concepts and processes that might help us better understand the qualities of the fanatic, and later to develop the more behavioural accounts outlined in Chapter 1? We will test the utility of this in three broad illustrative contexts: fanaticism and abnormality; fanaticism, prejudice and authoritarianism; and fanaticism related to the dynamics of group behaviour.

Fanaticism and Abnormality

One starting point for exploring the psychological dimensions of fanaticism is to consider its relationship to concepts of abnormality, and its links with mental illness. When using the terms fanatic and fanaticism, we often use 'fanatic' to refer to the individual and what he does, whereas we seem to use 'fanaticism' to refer to the process which produces, or is responsible for, the activities we label as fanatical. In using the words in this way we seem implicitly to assume that there is a state of the individual (fanaticism) that gives rise to the fanatical behaviour we observe. Because fanatical behaviour is somewhat out of the ordinary, we sometimes refer confusingly to this state as abnormal, or perhaps more accurately we refer to the behaviour we see as abnormal. The latter is more accurate because, of course, all we see is the behaviour on which we make a judgement, rather than the presumed process of fanaticism that may underlie it.

We have shown earlier, in Chapter 2, that we can clearly distinguish some qualities of fanatical behaviour from other more 'normal' behaviour. If we emphasise this line of argument, we may well also be assuming implicitly that because we can distinguish fanatical behaviour from other behaviour (i.e. in some sense it is deviant), it therefore falls within the realm either of abnormality or of mental health. If we take abnormal to mean infrequently occurring behaviour, then of course fanaticism is by definition abnormal, simply because it is different from and generally occurs less often than other more 'normal' behaviour. But when we use fanatic and fanaticism in these ways, we can readily assume that we are looking not only at an unusual or unlikely activity, but also at activity that is the result of a state (called fanaticism) that is also abnormal. We can see here a way in which fanaticism becomes related to mental illness, because our views about mental illness are intimately bound up with our notions of unusual and unlikely states.

We should note from the outset, however, that fanaticism is not recognised as a diagnostic category in mental illness. It does not appear, for example, in the Diagnostic and Statistical Manual (DSM-III) of the American Psychiatric Association,[2] a widely used and authoritative classification system for the description of psychological disorders. On the other hand, many of the qualities of behaviour that we have identified in Chapter 2 can, in some circumstances, be regarded as qualities of recognised abnormal behaviour states. The perseverative qualities of fanatical behaviour, for example, which was a common thread running through many of the features of fanaticism we described, such as focusing, the personalised view of the fanatic, and insensitivity to change, may well be thought to have qualities in common with obsessive compulsive states, for example.

Elements of Abnormality

To develop this issue further, we need to consider both what we mean by abnormal, and how abnormality relates to mental illness. A dictionary definition of abnormal may well make reference to 'deviating from type or normal', where normal refers to 'freedom from emotional or mental disorder, typical or usual'. A useful definition of abnormal in these terms might be 'Conduct which does not fit into the normal pattern of human behaviour; or an inability to use the powers of logic and thought processes regarded as normal by society resulting in a failure to comprehend normal social discourse or to express views which other people would regard as normal.'

When we examine this in more detail, however, it becomes clear that there are a number of issues which complicate our discussion. To the lay reader, reference to difficulties in deciding what we mean by abnormal behaviour probably seems to be an example of academic pedantry, rather than a practical problem. However, surprising as it may seem, the first point we must make is that there are no clear-cut technical definitions of abnormality which command general authoritative acceptance on which we can draw, nor are there any accepted practical ways to infallibly recognise abnormality. The concept of abnormality is complex, but rather like fanatic, because we use a single word to refer to it, we can be beguiled into thinking that the word refers to a single unitary concept. However, once we recognise its complexity, we will begin to see the relative qualities to which it refers.

There are a number of ways in which we can approach the problem of defining abnormality. These might take a social, legal or medical framework as their starting point. In the following, we will broadly follow the essentially psychological framework developed by Rosenhan and Seligman,[3] who refer to seven elements of abnormality. A discussion of these will help us both to explore and structure the concept in our particular context. Some of the elements Rosenhan and Seligman refer to are qualities of which only the individual concerned can be aware. Some of them refer to behaviour in a social context. A crucial point to note, however, is that whilst not all of these elements need to be present to refer to behaviour as abnormal, at least one (and probably more) must be present for us to use that term.

The first element of abnormality to which Rosenhan and Seligman refer is *suffering*. If someone feels inconsolably depressed or miserable, and such feelings become unbearable, then we might refer to that state as abnormal because, of course, such a state of suffering does not characterise most of our lives. On the other hand, there are clearly circumstances when being depressed is an entirely appropriate state. If a loved one has died, or your life circumstances have suddenly and massively deteriorated, as a result of redundancy for example, depression, and the state of suffering that might imply, may well be an appropriate response. If that depression and consequent suffering continues or seems out of proportion to events, then we might well refer to the state as abnormal. The important issue here is, of course, context. The settings in which suffering as depression, anxiety and so forth occur influence the way in which we regard it. But, of course, we must always remember that suffering, in this sense, is also a common quality of life. We would probably be unlikely to refer to it as abnormal on its own, in the absence of other qualities of abnormality.

The second element of abnormality to which Rosenhan and Seligman refer is *maladaptiveness*. Behaviour that contributes to individual or social well-being is regarded as adaptive. Conversely, behaviour that diminishes well-being is termed maladaptive. Individual well-being is generally taken to mean the capacity to work and the capacity to enjoy appropriate relationships with others. Social well-being refers to adequate functioning within the particular social context in which the individual lives. Excessive violence, for example, might be thought to diminish both individual and social well-being by interfering with the capacity to enjoy relationships with others, and by probably breaking the social norms (perhaps expressed as laws) of the society in which the individual lives. Profound depression may have relatively little impact on the individual's social well-being, but might well seriously diminish his individual well-being. The residential burglar, in contrast, may function perfectly adequately in an individual sense, but by breaking the law, he diminishes his capacity to live within accepted social norms (again expressed as laws). Not all of these would be termed abnormal in a psychological sense, and we would probably place greater emphasis on disturbances in individual well-being rather than social well-being in Western societies. Would we make the same judgement with respect to more collectivist societies (such as Japan)? Again we see the importance of context.

Rosenhan and Seligman's third element is *irrationality and incomprehensibility*. Where an individual's actions seem lacking in logic, or where an individual shows evidence of forms of incomprehensibility such as thought disorder, then we may well refer to that person as abnormal. Persistent perseveration and obsession with dieting, such that the individual loses massive amounts of weight that puts life at risk, as occurs in anorexia nervosa for example, would clearly attract the term abnormal. Persistent refusal of food is incomprehensible, in that it is beyond the understanding of most of us. It is also irrational, because it will result eventually in profound tissue damage and even death, and we assume that individuals are motivated to avoid such outcomes. We would therefore describe such behaviour on these grounds as abnormal. In the case of anorexia nervosa, we would of course have other additional grounds on which to make our judgement, such as its maladaptive qualities.

The fourth element Rosenhan and Seligman refer to is *unpredictability and loss of control*. Our world is broadly speaking highly predictable, and predictability certainly characterises our social relationships. When we develop a relationship with a partner, for example, we expect the attributes we find attractive in that person to persist, or at least to change very gradually. Likewise, the relationships we establish at work are premised on a degree of predictability. Indeed, we complain, and perhaps go on strike, when circumstances in our work are changed in arbitrary ways. Another way of looking at the same issue is to refer to behaviour as being controlled, rather than constantly changing in unpredictable ways, for unpredictability might be seen as an attribute of loss of control. Such predictability on the part of others contributes to our ability to anticipate and control our own environment, of course. Lack of predictability of behaviour in these

terms is certainly an attribute we might use when referring to abnormality. Again, however, context may be important. Excessive anger
and aggression, if we do not know the reasons for it, may appear to be
behaviour out of control and unpredictably. When we know why it
has occurred, we might temper our judgement.

Vividness and unconventionality are the fifth element of abnormality
described by Rosenhan and Seligman. On the whole, those things
which most individuals would do are accepted as being conventionally normal, and conversely those which most people would not do
tend to be regarded as abnormal. This of course draws our attention
to the origins of our behaviour, especially its social origins, in that
what people conventionally do varies from place to place and from
time to time. Again, we see an element of relativity in our judgement
when we draw on concepts of unconventionality. Vividness similarly
relates to unconventionality and frequency. Infrequent vivid behaviours, that are also unconventional, are likely to be regarded as
abnormal.

Another and sixth element of abnormality, described by Rosenhan
and Seligman, is *observer discomfort*. Activities that disturb or frighten
us are often regarded as abnormal, perhaps because they disturb our
well-being. Sometimes this might occur when behaviour breaks implicit rules that govern our relationships with others. Nudity, for
example, under some circumstances might be said to break implicit
rules about modesty, and might in some circumstances cause offence;
similarly, a person with a speech defect who breaks implicit rules
about verbal fluency might perhaps frighten us. We might, on occasions, be tempted to regard both circumstances as abnormal.

The seventh and final element of abnormality which Rosenhan and
Seligman describe is *violation of moral and ideal standards*. We often have
both implicit and explicit notions about the appropriateness of behaviour, derived from a variety of religious, moral and ethical prescriptions. We also have notions, sometimes difficult to articulate systematically, about ideals against which we measure the appropriateness
of behaviour. We expect people to have regular and appropriate jobs,
and we expect people to support their family financially. Tramps and
drop-outs, for example, violate these expectations of ideal behaviour
and we may well, in consequence, describe such people as abnormal.
Offenders against religious codes are probably less likely these days to
be described as abnormal, but in the past this was not an unusual
attribute to be used as a quality of sufficient abnormality to merit
institutionalisation. For example, it is not unknown, nor that unusual,

for present day elderly residents of mental hospitals who were committed there in their childhoods to have been committed for offences against morality, such as giving birth to an illegitimate child.

Given these various elements of abnormality, what then do we mean when we refer to a behaviour as abnormal? In most of these elements, a measure of social relativity and judgement is apparent. The use of moral attributes illustrate this in a most obvious sense, but so do those elements described as vividness and unconventionality and observer discomfort. Similarly, expectations of appropriateness (which are related to, but not equivalent to, moral judgements) likewise illustrate a measure of social relativity. We can conclude, therefore, that in these terms alone, there is a lack of absoluteness in the concept of abnormality.

This lack of absoluteness is also evident, however, in the lack of a single attribute of abnormality that we can identify. The elements described above in combination may refer to an appropriate judgement of abnormal, but singly, or collectively in some circumstances, they may not. The judgement we make is more complicated than simply referring to a list of qualities; it *is* a judgement, with all the uncertainties that implies. The problem of relativity is perhaps an inevitable quality of judgements of this kind, and is not solved by changing the focus of our debate from the attributes of abnormal to the attributes of normal. Rosenhan and Seligman define normal as '... simply the absence of abnormality', which further emphasises the point that the complex of issues we view from these perspectives all have qualities of uncertainty and relativity inherent in their usage.

Yet despite all the above, the concept of abnormal remains a critical element in judgements and diagnoses of mental illness. The notion of mental illness generally presupposes the identification of a state of abnormality having elements in common across a variety of behaviours, and the diagnostic label used serves both to categorise and to indicate techniques for addressing the abnormal state. Categorisation is often used as a means of relating abnormal behaviours through some common presumed underlying state. Thus a diagnosis of anxiety state can serve to link very disparate behaviours, such as phobic states, trauma and panic attacks to an underlying theme of anxiety. Having labelled something an anxiety state, those techniques appropriate to the management of anxiety states then become available for use with this particular problem.

Describing behaviour as the result of mental illness can also imply judgements about the broad causes of particular kinds of behaviour, which also in turn might well have implication for the treatment of the abnormal state. Generally speaking, three broad categories of underlying explanations are used in making judgements about mental illness. These are sometimes referred to as *models of mental illness*. The *biological model* assumes mental illness to be the result of a physiological or biochemical deficit or state. The behaviour we see as symptomatic of mental illness is therefore the manifestation of this underlying physical state. The *psychodynamic or existential model* assumes mental illness to be the result of disturbances or unresolved qualities of psychological development, expressed in terms of the dynamic elements of psychosexual development identified by Freud, or as elaborated by his various followers. Again, the behaviour we see is symptomatic of an underlying state. The *environmentalist model* in contrast to both the above seeks the explanation of mental illness in terms of the situation and environment in which the individual lives and works. This might be expressed in behavioural terms, or in cognitive terms, but contrasts with the other models by making reference to the interactive qualities of behaviour with the explanation of abnormality essentially lying outside of the individual, rather than as a symptomatic feature of an internal quality.

When we link abnormality to mental illness, we also tend to imply that something should be done to *change* the abnormal state. By analogy with physical illnesses, we often assume that mental illness represents a state of dysfunction, which must be remedied. If abnormal behaviour is linked with mental illness, we might then assume that describing something as abnormal brings that individual within the ambit of therapeutic intervention. This would of course be an erroneous assumption, however, and one that would present us with considerable difficulties in the context in which we are discussing fanaticism.

Fanaticism and Normality

In many ways our discussion in Chapter 2 parallels the discussion above. In the case of both abnormality and fanaticism it is possible to describe a series of qualities to help us to make our judgement, but in both cases, those qualities may be *necessary* conditions, but not in themselves *sufficient* conditions for making our judgement. Furthermore, in the discussion here and in Chapter 2, we have made reference to the importance of social context, which inevitably introduces a further measure of arbitrariness and relativity into the judgement.

Is, then, the fanatic abnormal? By the standards of the above discussion the simple answer to this is that under some circumstances he is and in other circumstances he isn't! When we are offended or frightened by the fanatic's behaviour, when some activity is maladaptive or irrational, when it violates moral or ethical standards, when it appears unpredictable, then we might well describe fanatical behaviour as abnormal. When we agree with the objectives of the political fanatic, even if we disapprove of his methods, when we place 'blame' for some action not on the individual but in the social context in which he lives, then we may well not regard such behaviour as abnormal, and describe it as contextually appropriate and normal, even if it meets the *necessary* conditions of abnormality described above. Or, of course, to make matters even more complex, we might decide that even though an individual meets both the necessary and sufficient conditions for abnormality, we will condone what he has done, because we agree with his broad intentions, if not his methods.

These conclusions are not unique to discussions of fanaticism. Taylor[4] concluded that it was inappropriate to term the terrorist abnormal for similar kinds of reason.[5] The terrorist, of course, commits horrific crimes (for most if not all terrorist activity that we notice is by definition illegal), but committing a crime is not a necessary quality of abnormality. Many people commit crimes, relatively few are caught, and even fewer are regarded as abnormal in the psychological sense we are using here. Even committing an horrific crime, involving gruesome violence for example, is not necessarily indicative of abnormality in either a psychological or legal sense. The mass murderer Denis Nilsen[6] was not regarded as abnormal (in the legal sense of diminished responsibility) despite the fact he probably killed in excess of 15 men in the period from 1978 to 1983. In one sense, of course, the very fact that he murdered anyone places him in the category of abnormal from a statistical point of view, in that very few people kill anyone, let alone more than fifteen people. Equally, from most moral perspectives, his behaviour would be seen to be abnormal. But in the technical legal sense, and probably in the psychological sense, he was not abnormal.

Paradoxically, notwithstanding our discussion of the features of abnormality above, perhaps the most striking quality of those features is their 'statistical' normality, in the sense that we all show from time to time some of these attributes in some measure. If we consider this with the qualities of the fanatic which we discussed in Chapter 2, we can conclude that systematic analysis of our use of the concepts may lie not in qualitative contrasts with normal behaviour, but rather in quantitative terms as matters of degree. The problem is that differences of this kind do not readily fall into the context of abnormality, nor indeed should they.

Given all this, it seems inappropriate to describe the fanatic as abnormal. We can certainly conclude, therefore, that fanaticism does not necessarily have the qualities of a diagnostic category in mental illness. Nevertheless, there remains a persistent tendency to place the fanatic within the context of mental health, if not mental illness. There are some grounds for this. We can, for example, identify parallels with fanaticism in a number of relatively common psychiatric states. The obsessive-compulsive clinical state, for example, seems to have elements in common with fanaticism. The fanatic shares with the obsessive-compulsive a pervasive obsession with a theme, and both may well energetically and compulsively pursue that theme in spite of social disapproval. The persistent theme of perfectionism which authors such as Watzlawick[7] have emphasised as a quality of fanaticism certainly seems to illustrate obsessive-compulsive qualities. Similarly, the utopian themes which may well be important elements in the development of violence in fanaticism discussed in Chapter 5, just as millenarian motifs clearly relate to notions of perfection and persistent striving for a 'better' state.

However, the fanatic does not appear to perceive his obsessions as irrational or aversive to himself. Such a perception may be an important feature of obsessive-compulsive states, and if so, would in itself serve to distinguish the fanatic from them. On the other hand, there remains a sense in which the fanatic might be said to be 'driven' to do the things he does, which is a feature of compulsive states. Perhaps conclusively, however, unlike the compulsive, the behaviour of the fanatic does not seem to have the stereotyped and ritualistic qualities which characterise compulsive behaviour. The fanatic in his actions, as we saw in Chapter 2, is undoubtedly flexible in the means by which he pursues his ends.

Other kinds of clinical parallels with fanaticism can be developed which make reference to the delusional qualities of the fanatic, and perhaps the fanatic's propensity to paranoia. Paranoia refers to the holding of chronic, highly systematised and apparently incurable delusions which are held without general personality disorganisation. The delusions often make reference in some way to persecution or some kind of grandiose reinterpretation of the world, and seem to involve interpreting common or chance events from a personal and highly organised viewpoint.

The fanatic and the paranoid may well share common elements, and in practice, it may prove difficult to distinguish between them, especially where the paranoid individual expresses his paranoia in some form of extreme behaviour, perhaps even in a political context. The selectivity in perception of the fanatic certainly seems close to that of the paranoid, and the abrasiveness and argumentativeness associated with paranoia readily fits the image of the fanatic where the paranoia addresses a public issue.

Another clinical parallel with violent political fanaticism is what is variously termed the antisocial personality, the sociopath or the psychopath. The anti-social personality (in contemporary clinical usage, this is the preferred term) refers to a state, the hallmark of which is '... a rapacious attitude towards others, a chronic insensitivity and indifference to the rights of other people that is marked by lying, stealing, cheating and worse ... contact with anti-social personalities may be downright dangerous, for many of them are outright criminals ...'.[8] The idea of a sociopathic state has attracted attention for a considerable time, and it has at various times in the past attracted terms such as moral insanity, or disorder of the will. More recently, it has been regarded not in the context of moral offences, but rather as a psychiatric state, appropriate for treatment, rather than correction. However, given that the principal attributes of the anti-social personality are usually criminal acts of some kind, such individuals frequently find themselves within the criminal justice system, rather than the psychiatric system.

The clinical diagnosis of anti-social personality in DSM-III requires not only that the individual shows anti-social behaviour, but also that such behaviour has been longstanding, and that it shows at least four examples of particular anti-social behaviour such as irresponsible parenting, inability to sustain sexual relations with a partner, recklessness that endangers others, repeated lying, failure to honour financial commitments and unlawful behaviour such as pimping, theft, drug dealing and prostitution. Other authors, however, have emphasised psychopathy, rather than anti-social personality, as the appropriate descriptive label, and have focused on slightly different attributes. Cleckley,[9] for example, lists unreliability, insincerity, pathological lying and deception, egocentricity, poor judgement, impulsivity and lack of guilt or remorse.

Such stringent diagnostic criteria may well exclude many individuals who would be termed fanatical from its diagnosis, yet it is quite clear that the attributes of the anti-social personality and the psychopath in some measure overlap with those of the fanatic. In particular, in the context of political violence which is of principal concern to us, the violent qualities of the psychopath or anti-social personality seem relevant. Hare[10] noted that '... some serial murderers, contract killers, mercenaries, armed robbers and kidnappers are psychopaths in the classic sense ...'. In the sense in which we are concerned with violence as part of the political process, it cannot be regarded as mindless or unstructured, as might be thought to be the case with the psychopath or the anti-social personality. On the other hand, the lack of remorse, the insensitivity to the plight of the victim, are all part of the qualities which we have described as being elements of fanaticism.

Perhaps, therefore, the fanatic is psychopathic, anti-social, or paranoid in some senses. Or perhaps he shows some qualities of the obsessive-compulsive. Or perhaps he does meet some of the attributes of abnormality identified by Rosenhan and Seligman.[11] But does this, or any of the concepts of abnormality considered above, progress our understanding of the fanatic? The simple answer to this seems to be 'no'. The fanatic is clearly unusual, and his attributes clearly in some measure overlap with many of the qualities of abnormality we have identified above. But using the term abnormal in a technical sense, with all its implications of illness and treatment, does not help us develop our understanding. In particular, it seems to divert attention from the striking *rational* and organised qualities of the political fanatic. The terrorist, for example, may well commit horrific acts, with seemingly little or no regard for the victim. Yet the act is to some purpose – it may be violent, the victim may have no relation to the ultimate political objective, the act may disregard and violate normal standards – but it has some purpose in a broader political and often media-related framework. This is not to imply that the act therefore becomes acceptable. We are quite entitled to make condemnatory judgements about such behaviour. But we cannot dismiss it as abnormal in any technical sense, and we have to respond to it in different ways.

Fanaticism, Prejudice and Authoritarianism

Abnormality in a clinical sense, therefore, may not properly characterise the fanatic. Nevertheless we may be able to identify features of some related psychological phenomena, which do not necessarily assume abnormality in any clinical sense, that may reflect upon fanaticism. One area we might profitably explore is the links between fanaticism and psychological processes such as those evident in prejudice. Prejudice refers to '. . . an attitude towards the members of some specific group, leading the person who holds it to evaluate others in a characteristic fashion (usually negative), solely on the basis of their membership of that group'.[12] Prejudice is usually expressed towards members of a group as a class, irrespective of the attributes of particular members of that group. These aspects of prejudice may well be qualities which might be thought to share common elements with fanatical behaviour.

There are a number of qualities of prejudice that seem most obviously to relate to fanaticism. For example, a tendency to rigidly held views which seem resistant to any change through rational argument is one obvious area in common; insensitivity and focusing seem to be other qualities. Prejudice and fanaticism might therefore be thought to refer to similar qualities of individuals, although fanaticism might in one sense be seen as a higher order term – it is perfectly possible to refer to someone who is fanatically prejudiced, for example.

In psychological terms, an important quality of prejudice is that it refers to a means of organising, interpreting and recalling information about the particular group prejudiced against. It makes reference, therefore, to a particular way in which a belief system (or, in more general terms, an ideology) impinges on how an individual interacts with the world. We can speculate here how a quality of the politically committed might interact with these processes. One feature of political ideology is that it provides a coherent world view, which in some senses might be thought to substitute for a belief system derived from the more normal mix of sources. This may enhance the development of qualities of prejudice. Related to this, the prejudiced person tends to notice and remember only certain kinds of information about the prejudiced group. The actions of the group subject to prejudice seem to have no effect on the prejudiced person, other than to confirm the prejudice.

The cognitive components of prejudice are organised around what are termed stereotypes. Stereotypes refer to the expectations and beliefs we hold about members of particular groups. Once formed, stereotyping results in very persistent preconceived notions about the prejudiced group. In the prejudiced, such stereotypes are associated with negative emotions or feelings about the group concerned, and this is often related to action of some form. The result of this is that the prejudiced individual has a way of looking at the world which is highly selective and resistant to change, regardless of actual event. In this respect, we can of course see many similarities here with fanaticism. The fanatic may not necessarily be prejudiced against groups defined in terms of personal attributes like race in the sense in which we tend to identify racial prejudice; and indeed, the negative qualities of prejudice need not necessarily characterise the fanatic. But the rigidity of cognitive structures, and the *process* of assimilation and use of information which characterises the fanatic, clearly illustrates common elements between the fanatic and the prejudiced.

An important and relevant aspect of prejudice which may have a bearing on understanding the processes of fanaticism is the self-confirming nature of prejudice. The fanatic and the prejudiced share an insensitivity to these circumstances that might be expected to change their views. At least some of the basis for this may be the way in which holding extreme views exerts an impact on behaviour. The prejudiced may treat those who they dislike in particular ways, which in turn may well result in those subject to prejudice responding in particular ways, each of which may well sustain and fulfil each participant's expectations. This is one example of the reciprocal qualities of behaviour–environment interaction which we have noted earlier. There is soundly based experimental evidence to confirm that this process does in fact occur, and furthermore, the negative features seem particularly susceptible to this 'spiral' of self-confirmation.

The above indicates some of the psychological qualities of prejudice that seem to have elements in common with fanaticism. However, our discussion of prejudice can go beyond the attitudinal area and extend to considerations of personality. There is some evidence to suggest that persons who are prejudiced share certain common personality characteristics, notably authoritarianism. Adorno and her colleagues[13] have made a considerable contribution to this debate in their identification of the 'authoritarian personality'. Personality refers to traits or characteristics that predispose individuals to behave in particular ways. In this case, highly authoritarian individuals show patterns of submissive obedience to authority, which is paradoxically associated with punitive rejection of groups other than their own.

Allied to this is a tendency for the authoritarian to see the world in rigid black-and-white terms. The authoritarian has, for example, been repeatedly shown to be more likely to use punishment in dealing with other people. (In this context, it is of significance to note that the initial work on authoritarianism was undertaken to try to understand the psychological correlates of the rise and development of the Nazi movement in Germany in the 1930s and 1940s.)

Parallels with some of the features of our discussion in Chapter 2 are again clearly apparent. Rigidity and insensitivity are all features of authoritarianism *as well as* fanaticism. It might also be argued that conformity is a feature of the fanatic as well as the authoritarian, and it is tempting to speculate that in both fanaticism and authoritarianism (and no doubt other states as well) we are looking at the manifestation of a particular set of fundamental personality characteristics, interacting perhaps with particular historical and situational forces to result in particular consistent behaviour patterns.

Prejudice and authoritarianism do certainly seem to have elements in common with our concept of fanaticism, although which concept is primary in a causal sense would be difficult to establish. Presumably, some prejudiced individuals might also be referred to as fanatical, as might authoritarians. Whether prejudice, or the processes that lead to it, represents the underlying basis on which fanaticism *also* builds is not clear. However, we can see that there are many attributes in common, both in terms of processes and particular features. Perhaps the clearest link between them, however, is the sense of extremeness both imply. Prejudice, along with fanaticism, are generally viewed as negative states by those not subjected to them. In the context of ideal social relationships, both seem extreme.

Whether both are reflections of underlying fundamental qualities of personality also remains unclear. We often seek explanations of behaviour in terms of constitutional differences between people when we do not know the reasons for particular behaviours. Yet everything we have discussed about fanaticism (and we could equally follow the same themes in prejudice) emphasises the role of social context in providing the attributes on which we make our judgements. Given that the qualities of this social context that we focus on are both arbitrary and relative (as they will inevitably be), it seems unlikely that we will identify constitutional differences between people that will adequately explain either fanaticism or prejudice in this sense.

On the other hand, it does seem from the above that we can identify some constitutional psychological processes that relate to the psychological basis of fanaticism, and these processes may well have links with the origins of prejudice. They may not adequately 'explain' issues, but they do enable us to locate the problem of fanaticism within a broader framework. There are differences between fanaticism and prejudice in some respects, however, especially in the apparent capacity of the fanatic to make evident his extreme views through action. It may be that in this respect the fanatic demonstrates an extreme position on a continuum describing the processes underlying prejudice, where extremity is related to expressing, rather than simply holding, extreme views. The differences between the fanatic and the prejudiced or authoritarian may be considerable in terms of the focus of their behaviour, but the processes whereby they are acquired and occur may well be similar. Our knowledge in this area is limited, but the above seems to help us to understand at least some of the factors involved.

One word of caution is appropriate, however. In the above accounts of the relationships between fanaticism, prejudice and auth-oritarianism, and the discussion of abnormality, we have made refer-ence to dispositional qualities of people, in terms of constructs such as personality (as in the case of authoritarianism) or related implied abnormal psychological processes. We should note, however, that when we attempt to account for other people's actions, it has been shown that we tend to show distinctive biases in the kinds of expla-nations we choose that are not wholly based on objective evidence. In particular, we have a strong tendency to overemphasise dispositional features of people at the expense of situational and environmental causes. 'He is that kind of person' (with its implied reference to personality-like qualities) is an example of the dispositional assump-tion we tend to make in explaining another's behaviour, a tendency which is apparent even if we know an individual's behaviour is not entirely under his own control. The more extreme a person's behav-iour is, the more likely we assume dispositional causes.

This process is termed by social psychologists as the *fundamental attribution error*. Conversely, we tend more readily to attribute the causes of our own behaviour to situational causes. We can illustrate this by considering examples of clumsiness. If we stumble and fall, we might blame an uneven pavement; if someone else stumbles and bumps into us, he is careless. It may well be the case that we are more aware of the situational factors affecting our own behaviour than those affecting others. These, and other related social psychological processes, clearly influence the way in which we make judgements about the causes of behaviour, and should serve as a warning against uncritical acceptance of explanations expressed in dispositional terms. This cautions us even further that we must be very careful in evaluating the attractiveness of dispositional explanations of fanaticism in terms of abnormality, prejudice and authoritarianism.

Fanaticism and Developmental and Group Processes

Our attempt to seek for parallels of fanaticism with other psychological processes has so far yielded, at best, provocative relationships, rather than straightforward explanations. Furthermore, we have some grounds for being sceptical about the validity of some kinds of explanation. However, a more satisfactory form of psychological explanation of fanaticism than hitherto encountered may be possible, in terms of its development and relationship to group processes. At several points in the discussion above and in Chapter 2, we have suggested that we might regard the fanatic as expressing behaviour which is at some extreme point on a continuum of potentially normal behaviour. Rather than seeking special kinds of explanations of fanaticism, in terms of abnormality or personality for example, the ideas of process and continuum might be useful qualities to focus on. It would clearly be naive in the extreme to imagine that a single explanation of the kinds of complex behaviour which might characterise the fanatic is possible anyway, and in any event, in particular cases, it would probably prove difficult to gain sufficient information to assess the utility of such explanations. Nevertheless, whilst particular explanations of fanatical behaviour may be inappropriate, we may be able to reflect upon the processes that might contribute to the development of fanaticism.

A useful starting point in the analysis of developmental processes is to make a fundamental distinction between the forces that might give rise to *involvement* of the fanatic in some cause or other (ideological or religious) and the circumstances which might surround the expression of a particular *act*. 'Involvement' circumstances may well be quite different (although possibly but not necessarily related) to more specific 'act' circumstances. If we focus on the 'involvement' forces in a political or religious movement (which seems to provide the necessary context for the expression of the fanatical in the sense we have discussed here) we can describe a general framework of increased involvement and development of fanatical behaviour, in terms of processes of incremental progress. These will vary from person to person and circumstance to circumstance, but can be seen as resulting from situational causes (being born into a religious or terrorist family, for example), personal causes (joining a political party or membership of a circle of friends), or the occurrence of a particularly significant or traumatic event (the death of a friend or a perceived or actual insult). Given this framework, we might relate these initiatory events to other psychological variables such as particular types of personality, for example (bearing in mind the caution expressed above), social variables such as poverty or situational qualities of an individual's life such as loneliness perhaps. In any event, the outcome of these forces may result in the membership of a particular group, defined around an ideological focus.

The reasons for contact with the particular group will of course be many and diverse. For some people, presumably ideology (political or religious) gives the individual certain 'rules' that he might follow that help in making sense of the world. It also offers in both a general sense, and probably a specific sense, a means of social support, defining both a conceptual group and probably a physical group to belong to. In this sense, the effects of ideology might be like that of belonging to an interest group (like a club for model aircraft enthusiasts), but because an ideological framework is broader in aspiration than an interest group, so it embraces more aspects of life. (Although we might note that a striking feature of magazines for interest groups is that they convey a focused enthusiasm, an all-embracing quality verging on the extreme.)

Once a member, it is not difficult to see how the attractions of, and forces confirming, group membership might explain the incremental process of involvement and absorption with a theme, and the increased focusing which might characterise the development of the fanatic. We can draw on explanations in terms of well established social psychological processes to help our understanding of this. For example, relative uniformity of views within a group serve to reinforce conformity of individuals within the group, which allied with concepts of group behaviour and decision making like 'Psychological Traps'[14] may offer a potential mechanism to explain increased polarisation and movement towards extreme behaviour.

Psychological traps refer to circumstances where an individual, having decided upon some course of action which will yield a desired goal, finds that the process of goal attainment requires a continuing and repeated investment in some form over time. Embarking on a process of involvement with an ideological goal, for example (through joining a political movement), is likely to be a lengthy process. If political aspirations are expressed in terms of a radical change in social organisation, for example, this is likely to be a very long term goal. Repeated investment (in a psychological sense) will probably be required of that individual to sustain involvement, yet the eventual goal may continue to remain very distant. Somewhere in this process, Brockner and Rubin note that it is not uncommon for people to find themselves in '. . . a decisional no man's land, where they have made a substantial investment but have not yet achieved their goal'.

At this point, the individual experiences a decisional crisis. The investment (of time, energy and hope) may seem too large, given other circumstances, to continue in the absence of a readily attainable goal. On the other hand, withdrawal means the abandonment of what has gone before, and the individual may feel a commitment, if only to justify the investment already made. '. . . To the extent that they do continue investing in order to justify prior commitments, they are said to be entrapped. When taken to an extreme, the choice to escalate commitment to a chosen course of action can produce irrational behaviour with disastrous consequences.'[15] Brockner and Rubin describe at length empirical evidence which supports this notion, in a variety of contexts.

At a rather simple level, they describe what they term dependency traps. We make use of the services of a wide range of health professionals. Continuing interaction with them develops a sense of dependency, deepening on an incremental basis as we make use of their skills. If something goes wrong with that relationship, however, whilst we have the capacity to change, very often the dependent patient finds difficulty in doing so. It may be difficult to terminate a long standing psychotherapeutic relationship, for example, even if it no longer serves any purpose. So much time, energy (and perhaps money) has been invested into the pursuit of therapeutic goals, that the client may find himself resolving the decisional trap by tenaciously clinging to the relationship with the therapist even though it no longer is appropriate or productive.

On a larger scale, Government decision making can show evidence of entrapment. For example, there have been a number of analyses of the decision-making processes employed by the United States Government to escalate its commitment to the war in Vietnam in these terms. The process of incremental escalation of entrapment as experienced by a decision maker are well illustrated by the comments of Bill Moyers, a contributor to the decision-making process of President Johnson's Administration. 'With but rare exceptions, we always seemed to be calculating the short term consequences of each alternative at every step of the policy making process, but not the long term consequences. And with each succeeding short-range consequence we became more deeply a prisoner of the process.'

The notion of psychological traps has great appeal in the analysis of fanaticism. We have noted that there are few qualities of the fanatic that would lead us to propose explanations in terms of abnormality in the sense of mental illness. The principal quality of the fanatic's behaviour is its extremeness, rather than anything else. Psychological traps offer us a means of understanding how the extreme qualities of fanatical behaviour might develop from relatively mundane origins, in terms of a development process of incremental decision making. Furthermore, it has the virtue of explaining the development of extreme behaviour not in terms of inherent qualities of that individual (in terms of constructs like personality, for example), but in terms of a general and dynamic process applicable to a wide variety of situations and behaviours not limited by individual qualities.

Concepts like psychological traps also help us to understand some of the reasons why extreme political movements continue to command support despite the atrocities so often associated with them. Hewitt,[16] in a comparison of public attitudes to terrorism in Uruguay, Spain, Italy, Germany and Northern Ireland, has noted that the views of supporters of terrorist movements are largely unaffected by events in the terrorist campaign. There are, of course, profound methodological problems associated with the measurement of public opinion in environments subject to terrorist action. Yet such evidence that exists does suggest that support at a variety of levels for terrorist groups like the Provisional IRA is largely resistant to particular events. The more gross examples of violence that attract international attention, such as the bombing of the Remembrance Day Service in Enniskillen in 1988, appear to produce limited short term and negligible long term effects on public support for the terrorists and their political wing, Sinn Fein. We can understand some of the processes that lead to this by considering the sense of entrapment experienced by the supporter. Extreme nationalism of the kind which presumably characterises the Sinn Fein supporter makes enormous psychological demands. The supporter has a great deal invested (in a psychological sense) in support for the terrorist group and is, in the sense we have used above, trapped into that support. The more atrocities that occur, the more psychologically entrapped the individual becomes. Indeed, we might hypothesise that atrocities might even lead to enhanced commitment, rather than diminished. The naive expectations on the part of policy makers that atrocities will in some sense diminish terrorist support is clearly erroneous.

In addition to processes such as psychological traps, we can also identify other developmental features that might contribute to the fanatic's extremeness, especially in the political or ideological context of concern to us. Political activity most commonly gains expression in groups of some kinds, as of course does most religious activity. There are features of group membership and more general social interaction that can enhance the pressures towards extremity we have identified above. One such force is what has been termed 'group polarisation'.[17] This refers to a common feature of group decision making which leads to increased polarisation. Group discussion leads people to become more extreme in their judgements and opinions about particular courses of action. For example, if someone mildly held views in opposition to some particular action, group discussion can result in the development of that person holding more firmly opposing views.

There are two general explanations that have been proposed for why this process of polarisation takes place, both of which have received empirical support. The first of these explanations makes reference to *social comparisons*. This approach makes two fundamental assumptions: it assumes people wish to maintain positive self-images of themselves, and that an effective way of achieving this is to compare oneself favourably with others. Most people assume that when compared with other people they have some favourable qualities in some sense. In the context of group discussions, it is reasonable to assume that group members believe their views to be more extreme (or perhaps just different) than others in a valued and appropriate direction. Put at its crudest, we generally assume our own views to be superior (more enlightened, more correct, and more approximating to an ideal state) than those of others. Yet in a diverse group, it is impossible for this to be the case for all members, and as discussion or exchange of views develop, it becomes clear that an individual's views may not be as extreme (or as 'right', or as orthodox, or as committed) in the desired direction as he at first thought. Recognition of this puts pressure on group members to shift to more extreme positions. In summary, the process of movement to extreme views results from the recognition that an individual's views are no better than some notional average.

The second explanation of group polarisation makes reference to the *persuasive arguments* theory. It is a reasonable assumption that in the course of discussion people will present arguments that support their own point of view. Furthermore, it is also reasonable to assume that some of the arguments presented will not be ones previously considered by other group members. Combining these two assumptions, we might predict that the group will shift its view to correspond to the view supported by the largest number of arguments. The greater the number and quality of arguments, the greater the probability that some group members will be influenced by them.

Another relevant social psychological process to draw attention to is what has been termed 'Groupthink'.[18] Cohesive groups tend to engage in a number of faulty decision-making processes. These involve rigidity in the appraisal of situations, simplified and stereotyped views about the outcomes of decisions, and belief in the morality of their decision and its invulnerability to failure. In a sense, there is an overwhelming quality of wishful thinking in such groups. Victims of groupthink fail to examine information that indicates errors in their plans, or fallacies in their supporting arguments. Perhaps because of all this, such groups fail to develop contingency plans to deal with things going wrong.

There is extensive evidence to support the existence of processes such as those discussed above which result in more extreme decision making in groups. Such processes should not be seen as independent, but rather interrelated, resulting in reciprocal and interactive effects. Most of the work refers to formal decision-making groups, such as those that might exist in higher government policy making bodies, where the practical implications of this are considerable. For example, there is evidence that processes like group polarisation and groupthink may well have contributed to the decision by the Argentinian President Galtieri, in association with his advisers, to invade the Falkland Islands, thereby precipitating the Falklands war, and the eventual defeat of the Argentinian armed forces. But the processes also operate at a much lower level, and do not require the formal structure and heightened circumstances of a war cabinet to find expression. Meetings between friends or colleagues are as much groups in this sense as are formally constituted groups, and we would equally expect to see the power of such group forces at the level of even casual interaction.

We can see from the above, therefore, processes that might lead the individual into increasingly extreme positions. A quite reasonable starting point of a concern with social injustice might, therefore, incrementally drift to an escalating involvement, joining with others, and eventually resulting in behaviours which at the outset might well have been abhorred by the individual, but given the processes involved, now seem quite reasonable to that person. This is, of course, a critical issue. To the outsider, who only sees the end result of the dynamic forces that produce our behaviour, a particular activity may appear extreme. To the individual concerned, however, who has experienced these processes, behaviour may well have a clear and obvious logic and consistency (albeit personal). We see here the contrast between the public logic we bring to bear in making judgements about the behaviour of others (with implied social and ideal referrents) and the essentially personal logic as evident to someone who has experienced the dynamic forces that result in behaviour. This is, of course, exactly how we might characterise the insensitivity and focusing of the fanatic we referred to in Chapter 2. We can particularly see here the inappropriateness of drawing on concepts such as abnormality to explain fanatical behaviour. Our judgement about abnormal is usually based *only* on evidence available now, rather than an account of the processes of development of that behaviour. Apparent irrationality, for example, may well evaporate when the developmental logic becomes apparent.

The reasons for the expression of *particular* fanatical behaviour, as distinct from envisaging *the process* whereby fanatical behaviour might develop, might on the other hand be appropriately sought in the situational features of the immediate environment in which the fanatic finds himself. *The process* of involvement may well itself specify particular expression of fanatical behaviour; the accident of circumstance or utility in some sense, may all guide and determine the particular acts concerned. The analysis proposed here is similar to that proposed by Cornish and Clark[19] in their analysis of criminal behaviour, and we can gain some further insights into this by looking at that analysis.

Cornish and Clark propose, in their analysis of crime, that a fundamental distinction be made between criminal involvement and criminal events. The circumstances that lead a residential burglar to embark on a career of crime, for example, may include a wide variety of factors, including psychological, social and development factors, as well as what they term a 'readiness' to commit burglary. This is related to, and tempered by, his previous history and learning, the family and cultural context he comes from, and is also related to the burglar's financial and social need and expectations. Once made, the decision to commit a burglary itself then specifies a further series of options and decisions the burglar must take. These are in terms of choice of area from which a house is chosen, the general type of house to burgle, and the choice of a *particular* house from those in the chosen area.

They term this the 'Rational Choice' perspective on offending, and it emphasises the personal (as opposed to public) logic and consistency underlying what we might describe as deviant and illegal behaviour. Useful parallels can be drawn between this two-stage analysis of offending and how we might analyse fanaticism. Of course, the kinds of activities we focus on in looking at the fanatic may well be more extreme than those characterised by residential burglary (although if we apply this analysis to other crimes, this may not be so). But the distinction between process and event may well prove of great value.

The brief account presented above may help to locate the concept of the fanatic within a psychological framework emphasising development and social processes. Inevitably, because it is a general account, it is expressed at a general level and may lack the incisiveness and appeal of the case history. In particular, by emphasising developmental and situational forces effective in both 'involvement' and 'act' features, it may appear to underestimate the importance of dispositional personal factors we considered in the early part of this chapter (but note the warning about the fundamental attribution error). From the perspective of analyses of particular states that might be termed fanatical, such as terrorism, the above seems to be a plausible account.[20] Furthermore, we can see how various group and social forces (such as psychological traps) can augment and enhance the factors that fuel the dynamic pressures towards the development of extreme behaviour.

The Context

In this chapter we have discussed briefly three broad areas where psychological insights may provide a context to further our understanding of fanaticism – the concept of abnormality, the processes of prejudice and the social and developmental forces of group membership. The importance of these areas lies not only in the particular insights they offer, but also in drawing our attention to the discrepancy that can exist between public perceptions and private experience of the forces that control our behaviour. This discrepancy seems to lie at the heart of any psychological analysis of fanatical behaviour, and reflects directly on the various features of fanaticism we identified in Chapter 2.

This chapter has served to set a broad context for the analysis of extreme behaviour. Its relevance lies in reflections on concepts and processes that might help our understanding, rather than a discussion of the detail of any particular act or individual. Such detailed discussions are probably inappropriate anyway, given the multitude of different circumstances when we encounter extreme behaviour. Whilst our discussion so far has yielded interesting insights, only in the discussion of developmental and group forces have we come close to an analysis of the fanatic at an individual level. Notions of prejudice, authoritarianism and abnormality are suggestive in offering comparative frameworks, but seem limited when applied at the individual level.

We have not so far, however, addressed the issues that might contribute to the *political* qualities of the kinds of fanaticism which are of principal concern to this book. In the following chapters we will address these issues within the broad context of the kind of developmental processes we have identified here, by developing an analysis of *particular* settings and circumstances that may contribute to the distinctive qualities of political fanaticism. The starting point for this is an analysis in psychological and behavioural terms of the ideological context in which political fanaticism might develop.

CHAPTER 4

Political Behaviour and
its Ideological Context

The psychological bases of ideology are initially discussed, leading to the conclusion that present accounts are inadequate. An alternative interpretation in behavioural terms of the concept of ideology as rule-following behaviour is then presented. Following from this, militancy as an element in ideology is then discussed as an example of rule-following behaviour which has a critical role in political violence.

'But ideology, a contemporary phenomenon, limits itself to repudiating other people: they alone are the cheats. This leads to murder. Every dawn masked assassins slip into some cell; murder is the question today.'

Albert Camus – The Rebel

A distinctive quality of the behaviour of the politically committed, whether we term it fanatical or otherwise, is that it is highly organised and directed towards particular ends. There is a simple way of illustrating this. The political activist can usually describe specific objectives towards which he is aiming, and furthermore, can relate current behaviours to those objectives. For him, those objectives might be characterised as ideology. The extent to which an individual's behaviour closely follows ideological prescriptions may be one element of what we mean by political fanaticism. Ideology, as we will see, provides the situation, as well as content, of political behaviour. It is worth noting that we might also characterise the religious enthusiast in the same way.

Generally speaking, in contrast to the ideologically committed, the non-activist lacks in any personal sense the explicit capacity to describe the all-embracing aims of the behaviour that characterise his political views. Even in those limited circumstances where we can express overall objectives that matter to us, they are often disorganised and may well be mutually contradictory. The individual who has a distinct and compelling enthusiasm (we might even refer to fanatical enthusiasm) for soccer or music, for example, is an example of this 'partial' ability to describe objectives. But such people lack the all-embracing directive qualities we associate with committed political or religious behaviour.

The characteristic organisation of political behaviour of the politically committed may be apparent in two ways, one focusing on the context in which politics takes place, and the other on psychological qualities. Firstly, viewing political behaviour in terms of its context, we see that it invariably takes place within some kind of structured and organised arena; a parliament or legislature of some kind, a smoke filled room of a party caucus, or the discussions of a terrorist group identifying the choice of a target. This context both refines and supports political behaviour by facilitating the emergence of analyses of current circumstances and providing immediate subsidiary objectives for the activist to achieve.

In this sense, because the structured context creates a forum of some form for meeting others, political behaviour seems also to be essentially a form of group behaviour, the groups varying in size and function depending on the nature of the political activity involved. These groups (like all groups) command loyalty, give structure to the participants, and provide support and direction. As a result of this, individual actions of those involved are influenced by a complex sequence of reciprocal social influences, mutually selecting and reinforcing appropriate behaviour. It is these influences that we call group processes. These processes may well be important elements in the determination of political behaviour (we encountered some of them in Chapter 3), but we must also note that these processes are in themselves insufficient to account for the complex qualities of political behaviour. This is especially so where it impinges on fanatical behaviour. Group forces may well contribute to the processes that shape and direct fanatical political behaviour, but do not seem to be a sufficient account of the direction of the behaviour, and more particularly, of its overall organisation and coherence over extended periods of time.

A critical feature of our experience of political behaviour is the degree of generality we see in its expression. Politically active individuals seem to share common political activities, or perhaps more appropriately, they behave in similar ways, which seem appropriate to and consistent with generalisations we can make about overall political frameworks.

The ubiquity of membership of political parties, for example, illustrates the extent to which commonality in political behaviour can be found. The degree of intensity of expression of behaviour, or the particular choices that an individual might make within a framework such as a political party, may well vary. In recognising such relative contextual conformity, we generally describe the bases of such behaviour by reference to the notion of ideology.

We noted earlier that the structural qualities of political activity seem insufficient to explain the temporal organisation of political behaviour. On the other hand, the second quality of the organisation of political behaviour, the psychological qualities of ideology, do seem to fulfil that role. We will discuss this at length below. Our concern in this chapter, therefore, will be with developing an understanding of the organisation of political behaviour through the psychological qualities of the concept of ideology. In doing this, we will retain and eventually return to our ultimate concern with extreme political violence and fanaticism. The argument will assume that what we refer to as ideology provides the basis on which the structure and direction of political behaviour develops, and from which in turn violent political behaviour may grow. Ideology is the means by which political behaviour acquires both meaning and also legitimacy. In this chapter, we will initially discuss the concept of ideology in general, developing the behavioural perspective introduced in Chapter 1. We will extend the discussion to our specific concern with violent political behaviour towards the end of this chapter, and in Chapters 5 and 6. To anticipate later discussions, we will consider issues related to both the content of ideology (in terms of militancy and messianism) and the process of ideology (in terms of imminence and lack of public space).

The discussion presented here will necessarily gloss over many points which a more detailed analysis would consider. Furthermore, by adopting a behavioural perspective, issues of concern from other perspectives will not necessarily be given due weight, at least in their own terms. As a review of psychological approaches to ideology (or as a related account of the influence of ideology on psychology) it will therefore appear to be lacking. The area generally referred to as political psychology, with its emphasis on phenomenology and psychodynamic explanation, will certainly not receive the due weight its

proponents might consider appropriate. On the other hand, the behavioural emphasis developed here complements that adopted in
other chapters, providing a basis on which later discussion of the
relationship between ideology and fanatical political behaviour can be
developed. We should also note that our focus is essentially on the
influence of political commitment on an individual which results in
fanatical political violence. Our analysis may also prove to be an
element in understanding less extreme political behaviour, but our
intention here is not to present an overall account of the influence of
political thought on behaviour. Billig *et al.*[1] offer interesting reflections
on this more general issue, which are not entirely inconsistent with
those developed here, although they draw on different conceptual
perspectives.

Perspectives on Ideology

Ideology is a difficult concept to examine in behavioural terms. The
Greek origin of the term relates it to 'ideas', not behaviour, and a
contemporary dictionary definition[2] gives an archaic meaning to the
term 'ideology' as the Science of Ideas. Current usage of the term
'ideology' seems to have its origins in the nineteenth century post-
revolutionary French political movement, the Ideologues. Early, if not
initial, use of the term itself has been attributed to Antoine Destutt de
Tracy.[3] In original use, it described the particular qualities of the
study of ideas developed by the Ideologues. Their principal concern
was with how the individual combined sense impressions into beliefs,
an undertaking which in its time was challenging to orthodox (and
largely religious) views about the nature of belief. In many ways, the
Ideologues anticipated many aspects of contemporary psychology,
although they are rarely credited with such influence in accounts of
the historical development of psychology.[4]

Conventional psychological definitions of ideology reflect these origins, but generally do not make reference to ideas as such but to more
specific, but related, inner states such as beliefs and attitudes. Rokeach[5] illustrates this in his definition of ideology, which is also typical
of how other authors have approached this issue. '. . . an ideology is an
organisation of beliefs and attitudes – religious, political or philosophical in nature – that is more or less institutionalised or shared
with others, deriving from external authority . . .'.[6] Whilst this definition may not particularly offer a behavioural perspective, and indeed offers no views on the relationship between beliefs and attitudes

and political behaviour, it nevertheless does include a number of features which are worth drawing attention to, and which will progress our discussion.

The first point to note is that ideology in the sense used by Rokeach refers not just to politics, but to other forms of activity as well. In Rokeach's definition, ideology refers to the framework in which various kinds of behaviour take place, and from which we can understand that behaviour, rather than any particular kind of behaviour as such. In this sense, ideology describes a process or context, expressed perhaps as a particular set of concepts or rules from which our actions are developed. In these terms, we can therefore reasonably talk about religious ideology as much as we can refer to political ideology. Both refer to the framework that provides overall structure and direction to behaviour, and which sets in motion particular kinds of choices of activity. For the religious, of course, this may seem to be a strange use of words, for they are probably more accustomed to talk about 'faith' or dogma, rather than ideology. Nevertheless, whilst we typically find ideology used only within a political context, it seems reasonable in these terms to extend its usage beyond politics to other areas.

The second point we might note from Rokeach's definition is that the concept of ideology has a quality of sharing associated with it. Other people also 'subscribe' to an ideology, and ideology takes its meaning from some form of public statement of its principles. This, in turn, implies that ideologies have a structure that can be articulated, and because of this, can be judged in terms of internal consistency. This may be what Rokeach means by referring to 'institutionalised'. The reference to '... derived from external authority...' further emphasises the formality of expression we associate with ideology, as well as indicating one potential source of legitimacy for ideological views. That formality derives in the main from the communicative and essentially written nature of ideology. Because ideology is public (at least to initiates) and articulated in some way, it can therefore also be subject to logical analysis. Indeed, its public and articulated nature may well serve to emphasise the importance of consistency, refining and developing its expression.

This raises an interesting issue. Whilst, in Rokeach's view, ideology is expressed in psychological terms as beliefs and attitudes, the origins of the particular qualities of ideology lie not in the internal processes of the individual, but in the external expression of precepts by some authority *from* which the individual might derive attitudes. Attitudes and beliefs, therefore, are only hypothesised mediating structures, rather than determinants of ideology as such. This effectively *inverts* the relationship we might assume. We will note in our later discussion the extent to which many authors, whilst accepting Rokeach's general definition of ideology, fail to recognise its implications in this respect. They persist in seeking *inner* causes to ideology as expressions of psychological qualities, rather than recognising the essential external quality of the content of ideology as it might control or influence behaviour. The importance of the written nature of ideology cannot be understated, and this of course gives us some appreciation of how the written word can wield such power.

However, our concern with ideology is not because it offers a way of organising beliefs and attitudes, in the terms used by Rokeach. Our principal concern here is with behaviour, and our interest in ideology arises from a concern with political behaviour rather than attitudes. We might, therefore, both anticipate our later discussion and summarise our concerns with ideology by developing Rokeach's definition referred to above and extending it in a behavioural framework. In this sense, we might view ideology as a common, public and broadly agreed set of externally derived *rules* which influences an individual and which help to regulate and determine behaviour, giving it consistency with past action, and helping to generate appropriate behaviour in novel environments. We should note that we may be using 'rules' in a slightly unusual sense here, and we will return to this issue later. Ideology in the sense we use it here is also related to the concept of 'values' used by Camus[7]. In his terms, values mark a transition from facts to rights, and the articulation of values in some form represents the sense of ideology as used here. In the sense used by Camus, values relate to action; however, as Camus notes, values not only precede action, but are pre-existent to action, a view not inconsistent with that expressed here.

Further exploration of the concept of ideology will help us refine the extent to which we can make use of it in the explanation of political behaviour. It will also enable us to place into broader perspective issues which relate to the concept of political behaviour. At the outset, we should note that when we look at ideology, and try to identify the attributes of a particular ideological position, we are not, of course, undertaking a psychological or behavioural analysis. Rokeach's emphasis on the external origins of ideology emphasises this. Analyses of ideology are literary and essentially political undertakings, looking at people's actions in political forums of some kind from a political perspective, and trying to place order on their activities from that perspective. Ideological analysis is therefore not so much concerned with the individual, and his political actions in this sense, but the activity of groups of people doing political things. Thus, concepts like 'left wing' or 'right wing' may be used to summarise particular clusters of attributes – political views based on Marxist writings, for example perhaps attracting the term left wing. Other kinds of concepts may be used in particular settings – imperialists and freedom fighters seem to be examples of terms that describe particular clusters of attributes related to the nature of government in particular areas. The important point to note is that these essentially *political* terms do not necessarily imply parallel *psychological* explanations.

Because ideology is something which is expressed, and seems to generally have an origin with a particular authority, it can be assessed in terms of its logic and internal consistency. Ideological principles can be identified, for example from Marxist views, that might guide the adherent in broadly consistent ways, specifying his actions in logical and predictable terms. Ideology, therefore, sets out a series of broad propositions (referred to above as rules), and offers an analysis that an individual can subscribe to. In subscribing to an ideology, the individual has a means of working out consistent responses to circumstances, either by application of the particular principles, or by reference to the authority. A 'scientific analysis' from a Marxist perspective of a social problem would indicate the former; reference to the Bible or *Mein Kampf* for guidance on some problem might illustrate the latter. In behavioural terms, we would refer to the influence ideology has over an individual as being 'controlled by an ideology'. We can see in the above, therefore, that ideology can serve either to create the behavioural 'rules' referred to in our earlier development of Rokeach's definition of ideology, or to contribute to the conditions that enable those 'rules' to be expressed.

Ideology serves to link people together along a common dimension. It is presumably perfectly possible to have a single subscriber to an ideological position, but generally we restrain our usage to the collective expression of particular views. Perhaps because of this, ideological statements appear general and address broad issues. Particular ideological statements might from time to time arise, an example of which might be 'Do not eat South African fruit.' But ideology in the sense used here does not particularly concern itself with the agricultural practices in South Africa. Rather the purchase of South African fruit is an element of some broader strategy both to demonstrate opposition to the South African regime, and perhaps to inflict on the country some kind of economic disadvantage. The ideological logic is expressed at a much more general level than the particular behaviour that might from time to time be derived from it.

Ideology is also something that may serve as a framework to link together particular kinds of people. Geographically or racially based ideology might be termed nationalism and uses, as its principal attribute of both membership and concern, reference to that geographical or racial grouping. Ideology might also link together, however, more conceptually defined groups; religious ideology, for example, addresses a very broad spectrum of people – the believers in a particular religion. In a further and more constrained example, we can see that members of a particular socio-economic group might be the focus of class-based ideology. Sometimes ideology can focus on several such groupings, linking together otherwise diverse groups – class-based religious ideology would be one example of this. In this sense, therefore, ideology defines a group to which the member can belong. It might be an ill defined conceptual group, like the member of a class, or it might be a very particular physical group, like membership of a church or club, that meets regularly and provides a focus for social activity.

Another quality of ideology that we can identify is that it offers guidance about how to respond to things of which the individual has no experience, and perhaps no control over. The public finances of a State are something over which an individual citizen, in the main, has relatively little control. For most wage earners, the redistribution of wealth, for example, is something which that individual can do little about at a personal level. Most wage earners are unlikely to be in positions to generate new wealth, and in any event they can do little to effect direct change. A particular ideology (like Marxism) offers the individual a means of coming to terms with and understanding differences in the distribution of wealth, and gives direction to action, perhaps in concert with others, to effect change. In this sense, ideology provides the individual with a 'ready made' set of responses to particular novel situations, which will be both generally consistent with things he might have done in the past, or will do in the future, and with others who share these concerns, however they have arisen. In the terms we have used earlier, this is another example of ideology as the development of behavioural rules, and it illustrates the sense in which behaviour is controlled by ideology. By acting in concert with others, the individual can, of course, often exert influence in a way that is not possible when acting on his own. This is perhaps a further important factor in understanding the attractions of political ideology and the influence it might have over the individual's behaviour.

A number of authors have noted the importance of ideology for the individual when faced with lack of certainty. Religions illustrate perhaps best of all the extent to which such uncertainty can influence the extent to which ideology can determine behaviour. Religious doctrine is invariably based upon assertions of truth related to authority. A religion may be based on God's word, but God in general is not available to help deal with the numerous small issues on which the devotee may need guidance. His Word, therefore, needs to be mediated in some way, and furthermore, such mediation needs to be available to consult and refer to. This is often achieved by a prophet, or prophets, who mediate between God and the devout, and produce written statements of ideology to guide the faithful. The Torah, the Bible and the Qur'an are obvious examples.

God is, however, not directly available to the faithful, and the adequacy and nature of His ideological guidance must inevitably attract some measure of uncertainty, especially if that guidance (expressed in holy writings) was written a long time ago, as is the case with most contemporary religious authorities of this kind. There is some evidence that the strength with which an individual subscribes to an ideology, at least within a religious context, is in some circumstances paradoxically inversely related to the degree of certainty he might have in the authoritative bases of that ideology. In an interesting and important study of the effects of failure of religious prophecy, Festinger *et al.*[8] described a religious sect which gathered around a particular prophet who foresaw the end of the world. After predicting the final day and time, the sect prepared itself; but at the final hour, nothing happened, and the prediction failed. The challenge to the ideological credibility of the prophet and the sect resulted for some members in disillutionment and withdrawal from the group. But for the majority, after a brief period, they became even more ardent members of the sect. They moved from being essentially inward looking (they saw themselves as the possessors of special and divine knowledge not available to others, a chosen few), to actively proselytising their faith amongst others, seeking expansion of the sect through conversions. We might speculate about the influence of psychological traps, and other social psychological processes, in the development of this.

There is, therefore, a complex relationship between ideology and certainty, which presumably also has a bearing on the relationship between ideology and behaviour. Ideology seems to provide us with ready-made solutions to problems; it specifies choices for us, and offers a structure to enable us to understand the events in our environment over which we have no experience or control. In the terms introduced earlier, we can, therefore, describe ideology as behavioural 'rules'. We can also describe behaviour as 'controlled' by ideology. Our adherence to a particular ideological position, however, does not necessarily seem directly related to utility, at least in the sense of ideology successfully predicting outcomes (as in the case of Festinger's religious group described above for example). Of course, there is one sense in which ideology by definition has utility. Whether or not the framework offered by an ideology is 'correct' in any objective sense, simply by virtue of providing a framework to guide behaviour it is successful. In this sense it reduces uncertainty, and perhaps enables the individual to evaluate the relative merits of environmental events as they impinge on him.

Reduction in uncertainty may be a very powerful force motivating the acceptance and adherence to an ideology. From time to time, we all experience social anxiety, or doubt the direction our lives are taking. Because ideologies of the kind we are discussing offer a sense of certainty, as well as a clear structure within which individuals can order their lives, it is not surprising that adherence to an ideology offers the insecure individual many attractions. This is not to suggest that adherents to an ideology are insecure or anxious. Rather, it is simply to note that the sense of certainty and security that an ideology can offer, as well as the broader supportive context in which ideologically controlled behaviour might develop, has many attractions.

We are more accustomed to look at the development of security as a childhood phenomenon, as a feature of child rearing practices. But the features of early learning that determine childhood insecurity are equally apparent and operative in adult life. In this sense, the social *and* cognitive structure that an ideology can give an individual may be an important determinant not only of the extent of ideological control over behaviour, but also of the forces attracting an individual to the ideology in the first place. The sense of 'conversion' which might characterise acceptance of an ideology may well be related to this.

Psychological Approaches to Political Ideology

There are always difficulties in using concepts from one discipline to set the agenda for analyses in other disciplines employing different conceptual systems. No more than in other areas, this has proved to be a problem in psychological approaches to understanding political ideology. Psychological studies addressing this problem, as distinct from the behavioural approach adopted here, can be described under two broad headings: those that have primarily taken ideological and political concepts as a starting point, and tried to identify psychological correlates of those concepts; and those that have started from primarily a psychological position, and tried to relate psychological concepts to political ideological activity. The former we will characterise as the Political Starting Point, the latter as the Psychological Starting Point. As we review these approaches below, we should note that the two starting points do not necessarily define mutually exclusive areas.

The political starting point

One striking feature of political activity is the difference in political positions that can be characterised by the left and right, or liberal and conservative. Indeed, it is sometimes claimed that this is a universal feature of political organisation, reflecting underlying fundamental social and political processes. Certainly, experience in the Western democracies suggests that political activity is broadly ordered along a continuum describing a conservative-liberal dimension. What might be termed left wing or liberal views have a consistency and overall logic to them, as do what might be termed right wing or conservative views. Contemporary left wing views generally relate to things like replacement of national spending on armaments with spending on social services, public provision of health care and education, and social and racial integration. Contemporary right wing views generally relate to polar opposites of these; reductions in State spending, and reduction in taxes, provision of a military potential, and greater encouragement of individual provision for welfare rather than public provision. We should note, however, that these views may well be related to particular historical and social conditions, and therefore what particular issues might be viewed as characterising the left wing, for example, may be a relative judgement which changes over time.

Yet even though left and right may be dependent on, and related to, social and historical conditions, the degree of consistency which both clusters of views show has led some authors to explore the extent to which such a left-right dichotomy reflects important personal and psychological qualities of people. The consistency of left-right is of course most obviously evident where political parties are organised in terms of left-right views. But it can also be discerned in political systems where political groupings are not ordered along that dimension. In the United States, for example, the major political parties are relatively loose coalitions of a variety of political positions. Yet within these coalitions, left and right wing elements can be identified *of both* Democratic and Republican parties.

One notable exploration of this approach can be found in the work of Hans Eysenck.[9] He devised a psychometric scale to measure liberal and conservative attitudes, which in his view broadly corresponded to the left-right dichotomy. The scale uses statements with which the respondent either agrees or disagrees – the nature of the answers given are then used to construct a score which locates an individual on a radical-conservative dimension. The kinds of issues addressed by Eysenck's scale can be seen in the type of questions asked. '*Our treatment of criminals is too harsh; we should try to cure them, not punish them*' and '*Ultimately, private property should be abolished and complete socialism introduced*' are examples of questions where agreement indicates a radical position. '*Production and trade should be free from government interference*' and '*"My country right or wrong" is a saying which expresses a fundamentally desirable attitude*' are questions where agreement indicates a conservative or right wing perspective. Eysenck assumes that attitudes, as expressed by agreement or disagreement with the kind of questions above, cluster around particular positions. These positions we describe as radical or conservative. '. . . to say that a person is a Socialist or a Conservative immediately suggests that he holds not just one particular opinion on one particular issue, but rather that his views and opinions on a large number of different issues will form a definite pattern . . .'.[10]

To be useful in understanding political or ideological behaviour, Eysenck's approach must assume a correspondence in some sense between attitude and behaviour, something which is by no means certain or established. A more fundamental difficulty for this approach, however, is the extent to which an *individual's* views may be inconsistent, and not cluster in the way that Eysenck assumes. Consistency in a political sense may not necessarily equate with consistency in the psychological context. It seems perfectly possible, for example, for someone to hold *both* left and right wing views as defined by Eysenck, about different issues. An individual may, for example, be all in favour of socialised medicine, and a strong supporter of State intervention in industry and commerce. He may also be an ardent racist, desiring segregation and discrimination of people on the basis of colour. The views are only inconsistent if the political bases of fundamental assumptions about the psychological radical/ conservative dimension are accurate.

These difficulties can in some measure be overcome if other attributes of the radical/conservative dimension are identified. One approach has been to look for more fundamental psychological qualities that perhaps underpin this dimension, such as, for example, receptivity to change in social and political organisation. Bird[11] proposed this for example, and in terms of the contemporary political scene such an approach seems to have some relevance. Difficulties again emerge, however, over people's capacities to hold inconsistent views, and the fact that changes have occurred to both left and right wing ideologies over time. Agreement with general principles about women's suffrage, for example, would hardly generate the passions they once did, and would probably now be encompassed within most contemporary right wing ideologies. Yet during the 1920s, at the height of the suffragette movement, views on women's suffrage would probably have been one of the attributes used to distinguish radicals from conservatives.

An alternative approach to this problem has been developed by Silvan Tomkins,[12] who has characterised political activity of the right and left in terms of the ways in which people use information, and the ways in which they solve problems. He relates these to people values, and uses the terms humanistic ideologies to characterise broadly left wing ideology and normative to characterise broadly right wing ideology. The use of normative and humanistic as opposites along a psychological dimension of some form, which also characterises Eysenck's approach, is retained by Tomkins. The humanistic/ normative dimension can be illustrated by reference to a number of issues which discriminate between them. '*Man is an end in himself*' (left wing and humanistic) contrasts with '*. . . the valuable exists independent of man*' (right wing and normative); '*values are what man wishes*' (left wing and humanistic) in contrast to '*values exist independent of man*' (right wing and normative); '*man should satisfy and maximise his drives and affects*' (left wing and humanistic) in contrast to '*man should be governed by norms which in turn modulate his drives and affects*' (right wing and normative).

Tomkins, therefore, distinguishes between the right and left in terms of their underlying values. He suggests that humanistic (and left wing) dimensions emphasise a person's wants and experiences;

normative (right wing) dimensions emphasise norms, rules and modes of action. Using these assumptions, more general efforts have been made to relate these dimensions to personal qualities of individuals, expressed in terms of personality.[13]

Tomkins offers a more complex and sophisticated set of attributes on which judgements and categorising of ideology might be made than other authors, but it is difficult to see how it escapes from the same sort of criticisms levelled at the earlier approaches. The persistent series of sex scandals, for example, that seem to emerge from time to time around politicians of both the left and right suggest that normative pressures are not always sufficient to temper what Tomkins would call other humanistic pressures! More seriously, it offers few insights into the ways in which left wing groups (reflecting humanistic ideologies) can, in the context of extreme radical views, demand of their adherents an extreme degree of obedience and conformity to rules, a characteristic of right wing (and normative) attributes. The high degree of conformity demanded by extreme left wing terrorist groups has been termed 'the paradox of conforming anti-authoritarians' by Post.[14] It is a very evident feature of radical terrorist groups such as the Provisional IRA, which demands obedience of members and followers, and inflicts on recalcitrants gross punishments which in other contexts would be termed the barbaric attributes of right wing repression. There is an echo in this of Camus'[15] comment that the revolutionaries' claim to freedom leads to servitude.

A further problem of all these approaches is that they often seem to represent a 'leakage' of the author's own political values into the presumed 'objective' psychological categories used. Perhaps this is inevitable if the starting points are political, rather than psychological, categories. Tomkins's views on normative and humanistic values, for example, seem to be almost caricatures of the liberal-conservative dichotomies that characterised social movements in the 1960s. They may be argued to encapsulate fundamental qualities, but those qualities look decidedly dated and very much based on social context when viewed with hindsight. Adorno's work on authoritarianism[16] referred to in Chapter 3 and noted below similarly seems to draw on a caricature of the archetypal Nazi, and may well reflect more on post-war sentiment rather than on psychological reality.

In general, we can conclude that attempts to develop relevant psychological dimensions from a political and ideological starting point seems to have limited utility. Perhaps the difficulty lies in assuming that what makes sense from the perspective of establishing conceptual clarity and uniformity for political and ideological concepts also makes sense in psychological terms. A major weakness seems to be the extent to which people's behaviour, and indeed attitudes as well, do not consistently conform to assumed generalised ideological and political prescriptions.

The psychological starting point

In contrast to those discussed above, psychological starting points to the analysis of ideology have generally attempted to relate psychological qualities as states in some sense more fundamental than socially determined ephemera, to features of ideology. Typically, they have tended to focus on the relationship between political activity and personality, assuming personality to be a fundamental psychological quality of people. Personality has been defined as '. . . the combination of relatively enduring characteristics of an individual that are expressed in a variety of situations'.[17] This approach to ideology therefore focuses on the role of relatively stable internal qualities of individuals, expressed as personality, and relates these to forms of political expression.

As a matter of common observation, we might note that, on the whole, an individual's behaviour is relatively predictable and organised. Personality theorists assume that such stability and organisation is the result of particular qualities of the individual, often termed personality traits. The qualities may be related to and modified by situational and environmental factors, but in the main are assumed to be invariant and in some way constitute attributes of that person. Such attributes may be inherited, or they may have their origins in the interaction of inherent properties with significant events, usually (but not necessarily) in early childhood.

Most approaches to ideology from this perspective have emphasised psychodynamic approaches to personality derived from the work of Freud, and have especially emphasised the role of the unconscious. Typical of these approaches is Davies.[18] He asserts that in his view '. . . the most fundamental contribution to political psychology was made by Freud . . .' and he goes on to discuss the origins of political behaviour, including the role of ideology, in psychodynamic terms. Consistent with Freudian theories, these approaches tend to interpret fundamental qualities of political activity as a form of disguised, unconscious and unfulfilled psychosexual aspiration and adjustment.

Davies's account of political development[19] is expressed in these terms, and he develops themes which have been introduced by other authors, such as Lasswell.[20] Lasswell in fact related his theory more directly to political activists, and developed the notion of three political 'types': the Agitator, the Administrator and the Theorist. Lasswell related these types to Freudian psychodynamic theory, in terms of sexual repression and its relationship with power. However, Lasswell (and most other theorists in this mould) failed to relate these rather general assertions and interpretations to the specifics of ideology as we know them, and in particular, the left-right dimension that, however elusive it may be, seems to be so prominent a feature of actual political behaviour.

Psychodynamic explanations certainly accord well with literary analyses and pretensions, and psychodynamic accounts in consequence frequently inform fictional and biographic accounts of political events or political figures. The main theme they emphasise in analyses of ideology is the role of sexual repression, and its relationship with power. Thus, the political activist in some sense resolves his particular developmental psychosexual problems by becoming involved in political activity. That political behaviour and the ideologies that inform it are concerned with the regulation of power, and control over others in some sense, cannot be disputed. Whether psychodynamic explanations represent a useful contribution to understanding political behaviour, however, is a much more difficult judgement to make. Looking at psychology as a whole, it is rather surprising that this area should be so dependent on Freudian speculation, given the limited role that Freudian accounts play in other areas of psychological analysis. Perhaps this is related to the very evident lack of conceptual development in the area of political psychology, and the paucity of empirical research.

An approach which has elements in common with the psychodynamic theories noted above can be seen in the attempts that have been made to relate presumed fundamental personality attributes like authoritarianism to particular ideological positions. Concepts like authoritarianism have a more coherent empirical base than most psychodynamic constructs, and to some extent lie outside the Freudian framework. They are also, however, amenable to psychodynamic interpretation. As we have noted earlier, the origins of work on authoritarianism lay in attempts by a number of workers to try to understand some of the psychological bases of the events which characterised political life in Nazi Germany. A group of workers, led

by Adorno,[21] described what they termed the authoritarian personality, which they associated with right wing fascist political views. In
their view, the authoritarian tended to see the world in rigid black and
white terms; for example, either you were a member of a particular
group, or you were not. Authoritarians showed patterns of submissive
obedience to authority figures, but showed punitive rejection of
groups other than their own. In many ways a typical authoritarian
was the embodiment of the stereotyped Nazi, including the implied
negative criticism of such a comparison. Links between authoritarianism and the psychodynamic approaches outlined above lie in the
assumed developmental features of the authoritarian. These are
thought to be the result of early childhood experiences and parenting
practices, and draw on conceptual assumptions similar to psychodynamic accounts.

We can see that the concept of authoritarianism seeks directly to
link personality with one aspect of political behaviour. Its influence on
both psychological thinking and more general approaches to understanding political extremism, especially of the right, has been considerable. Unfortunately, when more detailed analyses of the relationship between authoritarianism (as measured on the scale developed
by Adorno *et al.*) and actual behaviour, as distinct from attitudes, are
undertaken, the assumed causal qualities of authoritarianism are far
from clear. Ray,[22] for example, reviews this area, and coherently
analyses and discusses many of the empirical weaknesses in studies
addressing the concept of authoritarianism. As with the more explicit
psychodynamic accounts, and for broadly similar reasons, the concept
of authoritarianism as a fundamental basis for ideology seems want-
ing.

An approach from a different psychological tradition which
attempts to relate ideology to personality can be seen in Eysenck's two
factor theory of ideology. Eysenck assumes that the left-right dimension is also a psychological dimension, as well as political, as we have
noted above in our discussion of his radicalism-conservatism scale. He
introduced, however, a second and more fundamental dimension
along which personality attributes of ideology might be located –
tough mindedness and tender mindedness.[23] The tough minded person is a materialist and pessimist; he is irreligious, fatalistic and
sceptical. The tender minded person is idealistic, intellectual, concerned with free-will, and is religious and dogmatic. The tough
minded person deals with the environment either with force (as a

soldier might) or by manipulation (as a scientist might). The tender minded person '... deals with problems either by thinking (philosopher) or by believing (priest). The best way of describing this factor is by stressing the practical-theoretical dichotomy ...'.[24]

Tough minded and tender minded are not themselves primary personality factors in Eysenck's terms, but are linked to personality by their relationship with Eysenck's concept of extraversion-intraversion. This is, in Eysenck's view,[25] a fundamental personality dimension, in contrast to the radicalism-conservatism dimension, which he regards as an attitudinal dimension. The tough minded are related to extraversion, and the tender minded are related to introversion.

Eysenck's analysis is both stimulating and controversial. It has the virtue of having an empirical basis, in contrast to the Freudian speculations which characterise so much of this area, and this has important implications for the theory's predictive power. Analyses of scores of politically active individuals on Eysenck's various scales have revealed provocative results, the most striking of which is the extent to which extreme left and right wing individuals (as identified by extremes of scores on the radicalism/conservatism scales) show similarities on the tough minded/tender minded scales. Both extreme right and left wingers show similar attributes of tough mindedness, favouring 'authoritarian' approaches to social organisation. This would certainly help us to make some sense of Post's observation[26] of the 'paradox of the conforming anti-authoritarian', the tendency of extreme left wing groups to be overtly and brutally conformist in the application of their radical ideology. It has to be noted, however, that other authors have disagreed with Eysenck's analysis, and called into question the relationships he describes.[27]

Whether Eysenck's views can be supported or not, his approach does seem to represent a substantial development on the rather less specific and conceptually and empirically limited analyses based on psychodynamic theory. It moves the explanation away from the hidden inner world of unconscious motives, and its fundamental theoretical assumptions are much more accessible to empirical analysis and assessment. As a theory, it results in a demythologising of political activity, and enables us to move closer to analyses of political behaviour. It also enables us to move away from the assumptions or implications of inadequacy in development which so often seem to be features of psychodynamic explanations of the supporters of extreme ideologies. On the other hand, its proposed relationship of political activity to inherent (and in Eysenck's terms) genetically determined qualities of the individual, such as extraversion and intraversion, seems to leave little room for situational influences. Yet an inescapable and fundamental feature of political activity, especially as we have noted it in the context of political violence, is the importance of situational and environmental factors.

Ideology as Rule Following Behaviour

We now move away from the analysis of ideology from a broad psychological perspective, to a more specific behavioural analysis. The discussion that follows in the next two sections is somewhat technical, drawing on concepts from a specialised area of psychology. The basic approach is not that complex, however, and the reader who wishes to avoid the technicalities can skip the next two sections of this chapter, moving to the summary at the end of the section on *Fanatical and Violent Political Behaviour as Rule Governed Behaviour.*

The fundamental problem with the approaches to ideology we have encountered so far is their reliance on essentially mentalistic concepts to explain behaviour. They seek to explain behaviour by reference to internal predisposing states, a point of view which seems both lacking in empirical support and unnecessarily limiting in conceptual terms. This criticism applies as much to Eysenck as to other authors. Furthermore, perhaps because such explanations 'push' accounts of behaviour inside the individual (in terms of thoughts, attitudes and traits) such authors also begin to consider ideology as something separate from, and outside of, the broader framework in which politics, as an aspect of social living, take place.

In particular, they fail to make a fundamental distinction between ideology as a *process* structuring and influencing behaviour, and the content of *particular* ideologies. The extent to which ideology controls and influences our behaviour can be seen as something apart from particular ideological prescriptions, the content of ideology. This distinction is an important one to make, and relates to the distinction made in Chapter 1 between becoming involved in some activity and the circumstances surrounding and controlling a particular action. It enables us to look at ideology as a multifaceted force influencing behaviour. At one level, we can see the role of ideology in providing the direction and coherence of behaviour in terms of particular ideological prescriptions. But perhaps more importantly, we can see at another level why certain kinds of ideologies become strong controllers of behaviour. We will look for understanding of these forces in those processes we know to control other behaviour – the environmental and contextual forces we have referred to in Chapter 1 as contingencies of reinforcement.

A behavioural account undoubtedly has some prospect of remedying the deficiencies noted above. Yet at first sight, behavioural approaches of the kind we have discussed in Chapter 1 also seem lacking in some respects. Accounts of the direction and control of behaviour in terms of environmental consequences (such as reinforcement) are unquestionably powerful when applied to circumstances where we can identify a direct relationship between behaviour and reinforcing (or aversive) consequence. If we do something, and immediately we receive a reward of some kind, the controlling effect of the reward on subsequent behaviour will be readily apparent. Accounts of this kind seem lacking, however, when they are applied to behaviour determined and controlled by more distant ends. Yet it is of course the importance of such distant ends that characterises both religious and secular ideological behaviour. The political activist may immerse himself in meetings, protests, etc., on a day to day level, and we can readily enough identify immediate reinforcers in the nature of the friendships formed, social contact and group approval. But of course the political activist's behaviour is *also* directed towards the attainment of some more distant and general objective, such as changing the political party in power, effecting some change in the law or change in more general social conditions, or even the overthrow of society and its replacement by a new and better order. How can the day to day behaviour we observe to be the stuff of politics be related in any direct sense to outcomes of this kind, when such outcomes are so far removed and distant from the particular behaviour we are concerned with?

One useful way of explaining the effectiveness of control of delayed outcomes on present behaviour is to propose some form of chaining, whereby particular relationships of behaviour and consequence are *directly* linked, one to the other, to the more distant end. Thus, we can envisage a complex sequence of events, each related to the next, that might explain an individual joining a political group, becoming more and more involved in it, and finally moving towards violent political activity of some form. Such a chain would envisage an incremental movement towards the distant behaviour state through a complex series of interrelated activities. Models reflecting this approach can be identified in the literature on terrorism, and we will use this area in the following as a specific example of the more general issue of fanaticism. The increasing involvement of the West German terrorist Michael Baumann (founder of the 2nd of June Movement) described by Kellen[28] illustrates this. Like many terrorists, Baumann did not suddenly embark upon a terrorist career. Rather, he seems to have gradually moved towards it as he became increasingly marginalised from society, drifting into political radicalism, and eventually terrorism. As his increased involvement developed, so other associated events helped to sustain him. It is worth noting that the attractions of his life style increased as he became more marginalised, for as he notes, '. . . if you had long hair, there were always an incredible number of chicks hanging on to you . . .'.[29] The interrelationships of the various factors associated with his development as a terrorist are inevitably highly idiosyncratic, and difficult to anticipate, yet on looking back, a chain of interrelated events can be discerned. A process of this kind is inevitably peculiar to the individual involved, although nevertheless lawful to the observer given hindsight. An explanation in these terms has already been anticipated somewhat in Chapter 3, in the discussion of developmental and 'involvement' processes in the development of fanaticism.

Even if idiosyncratic, the processes whereby a person becomes a member of a terrorist group, and the incremental approach to violence that might imply, may well be forceably explained in these terms. Expressed generally, the starting point for an individual, a sense of injustice, a particular precipitating event, or even more remotely a friendship, may appear very far removed from a terminal point, placing a bomb or shooting a policeman. But we could readily envisage a process whereby they would be linked through a complex sequence of interlocking but idiosyncratic circumstances. We would be developing in such an explanation an account of the 'internal' logic of that behaviour, which of course would contrast with its apparent illogicality when viewed from the perspective of broader social norms and expectations. Social psychological processes of the kind described in Chapter 3, such as entrapment, would readily fit within this framework, interacting with and shaping the chained and incrementally progressing behavioural sequences.

Yet even when viewed from a terminal point and with the benefit of hindsight, the process of 'becoming' a terrorist in these terms may seem obscure and difficult to understand. In the particular case of terrorism, the behaviour involved grossly departs from normal rules of conduct and expectations. In these circumstances, rather than look for lawful behavioural relationships as explanations as we have above, we may feel we should have recourse to explanations in terms of mental illness or deviance in some sense to help us to understand what seems to be inexplicable behaviour. If we could clearly see the sequence of events that led to that point of placing a bomb, and if we could recognise the complex series of reciprocal relationships between particular behaviour and outcomes, the logic of development may well become clearer, and appear less mysterious. The difficulty is, of course, that such clarity of hindsight is not generally possible. Detailed reconstruction of the events which might determine a particular behaviour, however simple, is something that in complex social settings can only ever be imperfectly guessed at. All is not negative, however. Explanations of these kinds have utility in some circumstances, by at least offering a framework for further analysis, removing the behaviour in question from the realms of inaccessibility. Taylor and Ryan,[30] for example, have used this kind of explanation to attempt to describe the development of fanatical behaviour in the context of terrorist violence, by drawing on the idea of incremental development in terms of chains of behaviour.

But there are further difficulties with such explanations. The most important one is that they appear to be both unnecessarily mechanistic and deterministic, and dependent on *post hoc* analysis. Indeed, this is of course the same kind of criticisms that can be levelled at Freudian and psychoanalytic explanations. The length of chain that would need to be postulated to explain any particular behaviour in these terms may well be of enormous length, stretching (literally and metaphorically) the credibility of the analysis. Equally, whilst behaviour may well be determined by the contemporary and historical environment in which it occurs, analyses of this form over-emphasise the *inevitability* of particular circumstances, giving a false sense of predictability and inevitability. One certain feature of the development of the terrorist, for example, is that whilst many people experience circumstances that may be correlated with induction into a terrorist life style, relatively few people actually become violent terrorists.[31]

Another and perhaps fundamentally problematic aspect of such explanations is the implicit assumption that behaviour has a beginning and, more particularly, an end from which we can look back in analysis. This seems to ignore the reciprocity and dynamism of behaviour, devaluing the flexibility which seems to characterise it, and assuming a linear relationship between environmental events and behaviour. Such criticism should not necessarily result in a rejection of this kind of explanation, however; but the limitations it implies should be recognised.

An alternative analysis from a behavioural perspective is to develop explanations in terms of what has been called rule following.[32] The control exercised by distant outcomes which is so much a feature of all behaviour, not just political behaviour, may well be better characterised as being mediated by a rule which relates those distant outcomes to particular behaviours, rather than by an inevitable chain of responses and consequences. A rule is a verbal description of relationships between behaviours and consequences, especially aversive events and reinforcement. 'If you touch that stove when it's hot, you'll burn yourself' or 'Tell that joke to Jim, he'll like it' are very simple examples of behavioural rules. They describe what is technically referred to as a *behavioural contingency*, or relationship between an event and behaviour. A behavioural contingency consists of a description of a response, a description of an outcome, and the identification of circumstances of some form in the presence of which the response will produce that outcome. Those circumstances in which a response will produce the outcome are technically referred to as *discriminative stimuli*. In the example above, in the presence of a hot stove (. . . a discriminative stimulus . . .), touching that stove (. . . a response . . .) will present an aversive burn (. . . an outcome . . .). Another simple example might be the events that confront a comedian, where in the presence of a receptive audience (a discriminative stimulus), telling a joke (a response) will produce a rewarding laugh (an outcome).[33]

A rule, therefore, is a generalisation about the circumstances that control behaviour (both positive and negative) that have applied in the past, or *will* apply in the future. Another way of expressing this relationship is to refer to *contingency rules*. The examples given above illustrate simple contingency rules that might exist. The first, for example, is of the form that might be taught to a child, the second is perhaps a more complex example. In the former, the particular environmental event that will produce the aversive outcome (the discriminative stimulus) is the stove; in the latter it is a receptive audience. Outcomes, of course, can be positive or negative, again as illustrated above.

In terms of understanding complex behaviour, the utility of an analysis in terms of contingency rules can be contrasted with the chain analysis of ideological behaviour detailed above. The chain analysis emphasises the importance of immediate acting circumstances in the control of behaviour. Such behaviour might be termed contingency controlled, as opposed to rule-governed. The distant outcomes in themselves have no necessary relationship with the immediate controlling contingencies. The individual might 'drift' towards something (like involvement with terrorism), but that eventual state has little or no relationship with the particular circumstances that affect the individual at any given time. An analysis in terms of contingency rules, on the other hand, emphasises the relationship between present behaviour and some deferred consequences. The rule effectively mediates between present behaviour and that deferred or distant consequence. By drawing on the same explanatory and conceptual framework, therefore, we can identify two very powerful but different kinds of explanation. In any given complex situation, we will presumably not be concerned with them individually, but in some kind of reciprocal combination.

The postulation of such contingency rules does not imply mentalistic explanations of the kind referred to earlier in our description of psychological approaches to ideology. The importance of introducing the concept of rules lies not in substituting one obscure kind of explanation with another.[34] Rather, by looking at rules as verbal descriptions (for both the speaker *and* the listener[35]) mediating distant outcomes to immediate behaviour, we are indicating a process whereby such rules might develop which is both consistent with and complementary to other kinds of behavioural explanations. It recognises and draws upon the powerful situational forces which we know to control behaviour, and places them in a context which enables us to explain the complex organised qualities of behaviour over time.

Rules can be abstractions from inevitable immediate environmental contingencies, or they can be abstractions or analyses of contingencies that have occurred, or will occur. One very powerful form of rule noted by Skinner,[36] which is based on the latter, is an ethical, religious or government law. These are almost invariably injunctions (for example, the sixth commandment instructs 'Thou shall not commit adultery'), although in application, the injunctive quality may be softened, resulting in a description of immediate contingencies ('If you do, I will leave you'). That very softening reflects the combination of a contingency rule (the commandment) with an immediate circumstance (or contingency) affecting present behaviour referred to above. Indeed, the notion of ideology as we have discussed in this chapter fits into this particular framework for rules, in that ideology frequently is a series of injunctive prescriptions of behaviour, which on analysis soften to more explicit descriptions of immediate contingencies. We might even describe this contingency based softening of ideology as the pragmatic *process* of politics.[37] In summary, for the purposes of our discussion here, it is sufficient to note that rule following behaviour offers a means of relating distant objectives and outcomes to immediate activity.

In elaborating on Rokeach's definition of ideology at the beginning of this chapter, we referred to ideological as '... a common and broadly agreed set of rules to which an individual subscribes which help to regulate and determine behaviour'. The utility of this definition is now apparent. Ideology gives the individual a set of rules that help to determine behaviour. The circumstances in which behaviour occurs gains its 'meaning', or perhaps we should say its apparent purposiveness, by reference to some distant end. This end is expressed in terms of a rule, rather than by reference to the immediate circumstances prevailing at the time. The distant end therefore shapes and conditions behaviour. In analysing the process of this, we can begin to see interrelationships between what might otherwise seem very disparate and unrelated activities. By reference to rules in this sense, for example, we can readily see the way in which rules can substitute for, and 'short-circuit', experience of particular behavioural contingencies.

Thus the political activist takes part in a variety of activities, all of which are structured around and controlled by broad ideological rules which control his behaviour. The source of the rules are authority of some kind, and they are expressed in some transmittable verbal medium (like writing, for example). The importance of transmission of verbal rules through some medium is of considerable conceptual importance in this analysis,[38] and of course this is a particularly appropriate quality for analyses of political ideology. Thus, the rules that structure our behaviour come from the Bible, the writings of Marx, Hitler's *Mein Kampf* and so on. Usually, the rules expressed in works of this kind are very general, and do not offer particular detailed prescriptions for behaviour. We therefore see the development of additional rules elaborating and expanding on the original rules, through commentaries and Papal encyclicals. These ancillary developments may well more closely relate to immediate contingencies. It is not without significance that a feature of the ideologically committed (both secular and religious) is their regular attendance at study groups, discussion forums and services at which the general rules are worked out into a more particular form. Thus the general ideological rules become expressed in more particular ways such that the individual can both more readily learn them and the behavioural contingencies implied by the rules more readily and effectively exert their influence.

In passing, we might also note the important immediate circumstances which will also apply in this process, and may serve to interact with and supplement the more distant rule related contingencies. Meetings and discussions of the kind noted above may serve to refine ideological prescriptions, but they also exercise considerable control over behaviour themselves, through social reinforcement and the forces of group behaviour we have already discussed. Thus, when looking at the long term focus of rules, we cannot ignore more immediate contingencies that might act as subsidiary supports.

Rules do not exercise perfect control over behaviour. Even the most enthusiastic devotee to a religion may from time to time lapse and sin (the strength of the rule governed contingency, however, might be indicated by the extent to which he is aware of sinning and the nature of that awareness). We can say in general that the degree of control the environment exercises over behaviour is related to the kind of reinforcing contingencies that might operate on an individual. The most important element of this is the adequacy or otherwise of the reinforcing consequences in such contingencies. Where the relationship between behaviour and its consequences are unclear, or where the consequences are not particularly distinctive or are perhaps multiple, so the particular control of any one contingency over behaviour will be less than absolute.

Likewise, we need not assume that all rules when expressed are necessarily effective. Malott[39] distinguishes between 'hard-to-follow' rules and 'easy-to-follow' rules. The 'easy-to-follow' rules describe relationships where behaviour will produce an outcome which is probable and sizeable, even if delayed; they may also involve other probable and sizeable subsidiary contingencies (for example, aided perhaps by study groups, social contact, and other qualities of the environment in which the individual lives as we have noted above). We might embark on an arduous programme of study, not because we are reinforced by reading course books, but because at the end of the programme we receive a degree or diploma that makes it more likely that we might earn a higher income. A considerable aid to this process (as any evening student will know) is the informal contact a student has with others in his position. In a more technical discussion, Cerutti[40] has referred to subsidiary contingencies of this kind as 'collateral consequences'.

'Hard-to-follow' rules, in contrast, describe contingencies that are either improbable or have outcomes that are small (in terms of either aversive or reinforcing consequences), and are perhaps lacking in subsidiary 'easy-to-follow' rules. We might also envisage circumstances where rules might conflict – for example, some of the health related activities we *should* perform to ensure a healthy future may conflict with other rule-determined behaviours related to earning a living, or making professional or occupational progress. Thus, we might work in unhealthy or dangerous environments, placing health at risk where the balance of rules related to occupational advancement is more powerful in terms of outcome.

Developing this theme, therefore, we might describe someone who is ideologically committed as being under the control of particular rules, derived from whatever ideological source. The origins of such control lie in the normal learning processes with which we are familar, and relate to the situational consequences of behaviour. It is important to stress that whilst this may appear to be a relatively simple and straightforward explanation of how ideology might come to occupy an important role for an individual, the processes that will occur for the individual will of necessity be complex, reciprocal and interactive. An explanation of the behaviour may be made by reference to relatively simple processes, but the operation of the processes we have identified may well be extraordinarily complex.

We should note that whilst we have drawn attention to the role that rule following might have in explanations of ideological activity, this is not to say this explanation *only* serves this form of behaviour. Rather, it would seem likely that *all* forms of behaviour are subject to the control of rules of some form. The difference between the ideologically committed and others is that perhaps for the ideological the rules can be expressed in a relatively clear way. Ideology is necessarily transmittable through a verbal or analogous medium. Furthermore, such rules may be 'easy-to-follow', and as we noted earlier, have a measure of cohesion and strength because they are expressed. Indeed, by virtue of being expressed, they may gain further cohesion and power through specifying clearer relationships. Thus the behaviour of the ideologically committed may appear more organised and directed because the rules are more clearly articulated and interrelate in clearer, logical and powerful ways. The relationships between immediate *and* distant outcomes become, therefore, more explicit, and able to exercise closer control over behaviour. In summary, therefore, our behaviour, whether ideologically based or otherwise, remains both controlled by rules relating distant outcomes to immediate events and by immediate contingencies. For the ideological, the rules may be more explicit and logical, and additionally supported by powerful subsidiary contingencies.

This analysis is somewhat speculative, in that empirical verification of these concepts in terms of the large scale activities implied by political behaviour are lacking. On the other hand, the analysis offers considerable conceptual advantages over other psychological speculations in this area. By relating ideology to rule following behaviour, we are describing a process whereby particular ideologies, expressed in rules, gain control and influence over behaviour. Furthermore, an important point to stress is the significance of the rhetoric and content of ideology. It is the content of ideology that defines the rules. In the main, analyses of the effects of ideology on behaviour tend to distance themselves from the content of ideology, by offering alternative explanations of its influence through various presumed psychological mechanisms. Viewing ideology in the way proposed here leads us to examine what constitutes the expressed principles available to followers on which behaviour is based. In this respect, this analysis is consistent with Rhodes's[41] very practical discussion of the influence and importance of Nazi ideology in Germany. It also offers us a perspective from which to analyse particular ideologies, for given such a process, we can now look at the functional relationships of particular political activity. In general terms, the position advanced here is not a unique development in analyses of political behaviour. It bears some similarities with other perspectives emphasising functional relationships, such as that developed by Dietrich[42] of the rise to power of the Nazi party. However, in contrast to the position developed here, Dietrich's analysis is based on the related area of social behaviourist principles.[43] Skinner's notion of rules seems to be an important conceptual advance over Social Learning Theory in the area we are concerned with, however, offering a specificity in analysis which is consistent with the power to apply it to more general situations.

Fanatical and Violent Political Behaviour as Rule Governed Behaviour

From this short analysis, we can see how ideology, seen as the expression of explicit and internally cohesive and logical contingency rules, helps to relate distant events to immediate behaviour. Our analysis does not need to draw on special explanations, but rather uses existing powerful explanatory frameworks. By referring to rule-governed behaviour, we can see how ideology relates to authority (as the source of rules), and how ideology provides rules that determine our behaviour. The focused way in which the political fanatic, for example, seems bounded by his ideological assumptions to the exclusion of all else (as discussed at length in Chapter 2) illustrates in a simple way the rigid and insensitive nature of rule governance.

This approach also sets the scene for an analysis of the relationship between political violence and ideology, in terms of a framework in which particular ideological priorities might be expressed. An important implication of this discussion is that in the conceptual terms discussed here, political violence is not necessarily a primary, and therefore distinctive, quality of either ideology or the politically active, although it may be that violence is more likely in some ideologies than others. Nor need we look for particular individual qualities that allows for the expression of that violence. Rather, violence can be seen as an instrumental quality of ideology, its incidence being determined by the interaction of ideology as contingency rules, the particular content of ideology, local and immediate behavioural contingencies and situational factors. Indeed, under some circumstances, violence may simply be a rather minor element linked with, and subsidiary to, other more powerful controlling contingencies. The effects of such violence may, of course, be profound on the recipient, or the society in which such violence takes place, but as far as the violent person is concerned, it may well be an incidental element in the broader contingencies controlling behaviour.

In attempting to understand the determinants of ideological behaviour from this perspective, we can assume that both immediate contingency relationships and more distant rule-governed contingencies interact and control our behaviour. As far as rule governed contingencies are concerned, they may exercise effective or ineffective control. For most people, we can see examples of both kinds of rule following, and the contradictions and uncertainties we observe in people's behaviour may be related to the balance of effective and ineffective rules, or the conflict between rules. It is reasonable to assume such a balance is related, at least in part, to the degree to which rules are articulated. The case of the fanatic seems to represent a situation where a form of ideological rule exercises extensive and powerful control over behaviour.

Such effectiveness of control may indicate the main reason for the distinctive rigidity of the fanatic's behaviour. A feature of the fanatic we have noted earlier in Chapter 2 is his remorseless and unshakeable adherence to a particular position, *and to the logical following through of that position* regardless of whether such behaviour conflicts with moral prescriptions. Perhaps what we see in the fanatic is an individual showing in fact two distinctive qualities of behavioural control. The first is that the fanatic's behaviour is under close control of ideological rules (in the sense of effective rules used above) which by virtue of their origins are for that individual easy-to-follow rules, or have similar strength through subsidiary consequences and supports. The second quality is that circumstances or contingencies in his immediate environment exercise reduced control over behaviour, with limited or no supportive contingencies. It has been recognised that close control by rule following contingencies results in insensitivity of behaviour to immediate circumstances.[44] Such insensitivity in the particular circumstances we are concerned with may be a very significant element in the development of this particular quality of fanaticism. Indeed, Skinner[45] describes many of the features of behaviour which we have identified as fanatical in Chapter 2 in terms of the qualities which he sees as typical of rule-governed behaviour – lack of variety in response and reasons, an emphasis on truth, and so on.

We noted in Chapter 2 that the fanatic's behaviour can be thought of as having qualities similar to those of normal people, differing along a continuum of some kind, rather than differing in absolute terms. Perhaps one way of characterising that continuum is in terms of the extent to which the fanatic's behaviour is closely controlled by a limited set of rules which are relatively constrained in extent and closely interrelated. This contrasts with the relative multiplicity of rules that might control normal behaviour, and the extent of control exercised by immediate circumstances.

If we express this difference in such a way, this is not simply a tautology, nor is it an elaborate version of the kinds of mentalistic accounts noted above. An individual can be 'fanatical' about a variety of things – he might follow a sport fanatically or become wholly absorbed and involved in an aspect of work. All are examples of the control exercised by behavioural rules. The nature of the particular rule following behaviour will clearly determine the focus. The distinctive quality of fanatical political behaviour is the extent of control which is itself a reflection of the all-embracing qualities of political ideology, in contrast to the limited scope of sport related rules, for example. In describing ideologically controlled behaviour in this way, and in particular by relating it to the behaviour of the fanatic, we are not therefore only describing the nature of behavioural control, but also describing the processes whereby such control develops. This seems to be an advance on other ways of conceptualising the problem.

We can also now distinguish between the processes that might allow the expression of ideology, and the qualities of a particular ideology. Rules refer to the set of contingencies relating distant outcomes to behaviour (the process of ideology). On the other hand, the particular content of rules (or in technical terms, the contingencies they imply) refer to their ideological content and prescriptions. The content qualities of ideology, whilst relating to more general rules, are likely to involve more immediate circumstances, relating to events on a day to day level. This distinction is probably most apparent in religious ideologies, where there is often a very direct link established between behaviour and ideology. Particular activities relate to ideological prescriptions, through subsidiary activities such as prayer, retreats and abstention from particular foods.

This approach, therefore, seems to free the analysis from the constraints imposed by *political* conceptual consistency, and the assumption that political consistency also characterises behavioural consistency. Left-right might be a useful category for political analysis, as a means of describing ideological content, but we do not now need to seek some inherent psychological or behavioural meaning in that description, nor look for meaning in terms of particular personal attributes. We are also now able to look at ideology in terms of function and utility for the individual, rather than seeing ideological content as something that exists in its own right without reference to the behavioural contingencies it might create.

Summary: Ideology and Rule Following

This summary reviews the principal areas of discussion of the last two sections.

> ▷ A fundamental distinction is made between ideology as a *process* structuring and influencing behaviour and the *content* of a particular ideology.
> ▷ A characteristic of ideological behaviour is its concern with distant, and probably ultimate, ends, perhaps related to social change, or religious fulfilment. This can be distinguished from the more immediate circumstances that constitute subsidiary elements of that larger process which might be characterised as political behaviour.

▷ Traditional behaviour analyses relate immediate circumstances to distant ends through some kind of chain of circumstances, resulting in perhaps incremental development of someone towards the distant end. The weakness of this approach when applied to political behaviour is that it is heavily dependent on hindsight. The end either seems accidental rather than deliberate, or it implies an inappropriately mechanistic and deterministic view of human behaviour, which is not borne out by everyday experience. This fails to capture the essential quality of political behaviour, which is that it does have a coherence and direction over time.

▷ An alternative way of relating distant ends to immediate behaviour is through the concept of rule following. A behavioural rule relates a distant outcome to particular behaviour. A rule is generalisation about the circumstances that control behaviour.

▷ The process of ideology can be characterised in behavioural terms as '. . . a common and broadly agreed set of rules to which an individual subscribes which help to regulate and determine behaviour'.

▷ The actual control over behaviour at any given time is the result of the interrelationship between immediate circumstances and rule related distant outcomes.

▷ Fanatical behaviour can be characterised as behaviour under powerful and effective rule control, with reduced control of immediate circumstances. This helps to explain the rigidity, insensitivity and focusing of fanatical behaviour.

▷ The difference between fanatical behaviour and normal behaviour can be thought of in terms of a continuum reflecting degree of control by behavioural rules. The fanatic's behaviour is closely controlled by a limited set of rules which are relatively constrained in extent and are closely related. This contrasts with the relative multiplicity of rules that might control normal behaviour, and the extent of control exercised by immediate circumstances.

The Context of Ideology: Militancy

We can now turn to our principal concern: how ideology becomes associated with violence. In the remaining discussion of this chapter, and in the next two chapters, we will be concerned with this issue. We have noted that the process of ideology can be conceptualised in terms of rules, but such rules have particular qualities by virtue of their content and nature, that relate to the expression of violent behaviour. Two principal qualities of the *process* of ideology will be discussed in the next two chapters in relation to their capacity to facilitate violence – millenarianism as particular qualities of ideological content, and lack of public space as a quality of the process of ideological control over behaviour. A particular quality of ideological *content* – militancy – that clearly relates to violence will be disposed of relatively briefly in this chapter.

We can see violence in ideology as an aspect not simply of the process of ideology (as may be the case with millenarianism and public space as we will see later), but also the expression and articulation of the qualities of particular ideological content, expressed as rules (in this behavioural sense), which characterise that ideology. This is an important point to make, for in the context of a militant ideology, it emphasises the relationship between ideological rules (perhaps expressed in a general way as rhetoric) and behaviour. This, in turn, enables us to separate out kinds of ideology related to violence by relating its rhetorical expression to particular behaviour. We might even envisage a continuum of ideological expression that relates to violence, and we might see that expression in the articulation of that ideology, in whatever form it takes.

The extent of violent and combative rhetoric in any particular ideology can be described as its degree of militancy. Militancy is clearly the most obvious content quality of potentially fanatical ideologies that has a bearing on the expression of violent behaviour. We can distinguish between ideologies that *directly* relate militancy to behaviour, and ideologies that have militant, combative *potential* which in some circumstances can lead to violence. Ideologies that explicitly encourage violence as a means of attaining a desired goal may be relatively rare, but perhaps can be seen in some anarchist movements, such as Nihilism. An example of Nihilist ideology can be found in the writings of Sergei Nechayev, who aspired to the destruction of society to prepare for a better, utopian, order to replace it. As far as Nechayev was concerned, the revolutionary who would achieve this desirable utopian end state '... knows only a single science: the science of destruction'. Sometimes, the term 'propaganda of the deed' was used to describe Nechayev's views, which of course emphasises the direct behavioural references to his ideology. If we could express Nihilist ideology in terms of behavioural rules, they would, of course, directly relate destructive violence to positive distant outcomes in terms of a changed social order.

Nihilism is not typical of ideologies involving violence, however. It is unusual to find explicit violence expressed as an essential and necessary element of an ideology. More usual is a less direct relationship with violence, where militancy rather than violence better expresses its focus. Revolutionary ideologies in themselves, because they look forward to some better state, do not necessarily prescribe violent behaviour. The anticipated change might be achieved through gradual change, or political activity through democratic institutions. But in circumstances where the ideology indicates means to achieve the desirable end state, interference with such means may well have the *potential* for expression in violence. In circumstances where ideology is expressed in terms of inevitable outcomes (the fulfilment of the class war, for example, or the attainment of the thousand year Reich) *and* where personal action may play a part in attaining or hastening the attainment of the political objective, so there may be a particular potential for violence. This is discussed at some length in the next chapter in the context of millenarianism.

Where ideological rhetoric makes reference to 'cleansing the world' of some racial group, such as the Jews, we can see at its clearest the origins of rule governed contingencies relating behaviour to violence. More subtly, but equally clearly, we can see how Qur'anic injunctions and consequences to apostasy in Islam can result in attempted violence against the author Salman Rushdie after the publication of his book *The Satanic Verses*. These examples illustrate how explicitly militant expression of ideology can in turn gain expression through violent behaviour.

In pursuing the discussion developed in this chapter, we can also speculate about a further way in which once violence is introduced into ideologically determined behaviour it may increase in occurrence. The immediacy of consequence to violent behaviour has already been noted in Chapter 2 as a powerful reason for its persistence, despite frequent social disapproval. Such immediacy of effect may be important in enhancing the relative importance of a narrowly defined and limited array of contingency or controlling relationships. Thus, those behaviours that result in violence may be reinforced by fulfilling ideological priorities, establishing powerful contingency relationships within the overall context of broader ideologically specified rule-governed contingencies. We can see examples of this in the way in which Allen[46] describes the way in which the Nazis came to power in the German town of Northeim. The selective victimisation of townspeople, the sporadic upsurges in violence related to electioneering, all indicate the action of local and essentially immediate factors, which whilst they were consistent with the broader Nazi ideological framework, also seemed to enhance the commitment of the committed by creating a sense of progress and change.

Attempts have been made to relate notions of the kind described above to the development of more macro-social units, such as cultures. This is not the same as ideology, of course, and perhaps addresses a level of analyses even more general than that addressed here. Malott[47] and Glenn[48] introduce and develop these ideas in the context of cultural anthropology, drawing on the work of Harris[49] and the approach to anthropology known as Cultural Materialism. This is an empirical analysis of culture entities drawing on similar assumptions to those developed here, especially the primacy of behavioural approaches. The details of this analysis need not particularly concern us, however, other than to note the broader generality of explanations of macro-social processes in terms of rule following behaviour.

The distinctions we have made in this chapter help us, therefore, to analyse ideologically determined behaviour. One further issue remains – how do the contingency relationships we have described as ideology come to affect an individual? Why does an ideology with one set of attributes come to be chosen (or exercise influence) rather than another? In practice, the answer to this question may prove very complex. Some ideologies seem to be expressed in terms of 'easy-to-follow' contingency rules, and this in itself may account for their spread. It is often asserted, for example, that Islam has continued to grow and gain adherents amongst tribal peoples because it is so attractive, offering a relatively simple and direct route to salvation expressed in terms meaningful to native peoples.

The importance of the certainty which an ideology offers should not be underestimated as an attracting force. Nor should the role of ideology in meeting an individual's sense of belonging be underestimated. In both circumstances, adopting an ideology (at a cognitive *and* social level) may serve as a powerful mechanism for reducing social anxiety. Indeed, there are well established relationships between fear and anxiety and an increased desire to be with others[50] (referred to as affiliation). The basis of this seems to be a reduction in anxiety produced by the presence of others. It is important to stress, however, that whilst the pathologically anxious may well find strength, support and relief from adherence to an ideology, this is not to suggest that ideologically committed people necessarily suffer chronic anxiety, or are insecure or in need of social affiliation. Some perhaps are, but many are not. It would be wrong and misleading to assume that there are special reasons that can be identified for adherence to an ideology, any more than similar special reasons are necessary to explain any of life's choices.

This last point needs to be stressed. Despite the inevitable uncertainties of analyses of this kind, we can say with some confidence that we do not need to produce special accounts of ideological behaviour which are different from accounts we might make of other kinds of behaviour. Understanding the processes of why a particular ideology comes to control behaviour makes reference to no less (and probably no more) complex events than those involved in understanding any of the choices associated with major life events, such as career choices. Our analysis of ideology here (and similarly terrorism in Taylor[51]) draws on, therefore, the kinds of structures and concepts that we might use to describe other complex behaviours, and will presumably be expressed in terms which will include amongst other things early experiences, the learning and development of particular contingency rules and the reciprocal influences of social reinforcement through group membership. The list will be long, sometimes idiosyncratic and undoubtedly complex, reflecting situational, familial and social influences. We should also note that in some cases (or perhaps even many), there might even be no other explanation than the fortuitous combination of circumstance.

Overview

We have in this chapter discussed the nature of ideology, and attempted to develop a notion of ideology in a behavioural context, as distinct from a psychological or political context. We have identified ideology as 'a common and broadly agreed set of rules which regulate and determine behaviour' where a rule is a verbal description of a behavioural contingency, relating distant outcomes to immediate behaviour. Ideological rules, therefore, relate both to the nature of behavioural control and to the process of expression of ideological content. We must look to the particular content of any ideology to determine its potential for success in gaining adherents, and its potential for expression in violence, but we need also to look to the processes that allow ideological expression if we want to understand violent political behaviour.

Ideology, therefore, is little more than the collection of rules, more or less clearly articulated, but which gain coherence through expression, which relate distant consequences to immediate activity. To merit the term ideology, the rules must have some measure of coherence and internal consistency. Furthermore, the rules must have some measure of utility in some sense – at their simplest, the rules must help the individual attain the expressed ideological end state. In religions, this is difficult to judge, because in the main, the end state is something which occurs at death – you go to heaven (or hell). But of course other subscribers to a religion can't know if this is true. Utility in religions in this sense, therefore, has to be judged in other ways, perhaps by reference to subsidiary states. Political ideology can, however, be more readily judged in these terms. The subscriber to a political ideology can ultimately know, at least in principle, if the objectives are attained.

Analysing ideology in terms of rule-following contingencies controlling behaviour offers attractive advantages. One of its principal benefits is that it offers a potential mechanism whereby broader social and political forces might influence behaviour. In the way in which we have used the concept, rule following may both complement and mediate the effects of social psychological processes on behaviour. The level of analysis presented here of course lacks specificity, and all that can be developed in this chapter is a broad outline of a general approach. For the purposes of this book, and its objectives, this is sufficient, although the professional reader will undoubtedly feel the need to examine the notions developed in greater detail. More detailed discussion of particular circumstances occurs to some extent in later chapters, when we look at ideological behaviour related to the Nazi movement, political suicides, terrorism and situations involving authority. What is clearly lacking in the analysis presented above is empirical verification of the concepts in appropriate situations. In this respect, this chapter might perhaps be regarded as setting an agenda for further research to elaborate on the behavioural concepts proposed.

If we turn our attention to the processes of ideology, we can identify qualities of ideology which, in the context of the militant ideology of particular interest to us, make expression in terms of violence more likely. Two of these processes are discussed below in the next two chapters – 'Millenarianism' as a further content element of ideology, and 'Public Space' as a process variable. Neither of these terms are derived from behaviour analysis, and they do not make particular reference in their normal usage to behavioural concepts. Nevertheless, as we will see, they do complement and extend our behavioural analysis of ideology.

We will anticipate the discussion somewhat, to place the next two chapters in context. It is proposed that there are factors related to particular kinds of ideology that make the expression of violence more likely. One of these we have noted already is in terms of the rhetoric of any given ideology, and the extent to which it prescribes violent behaviour, or has within it a considerable militant potential, either directly or as a result of other events. The two other factors which we will discuss in some detail in the next two chapters are Millenarianism and Public Space. The position developed here which relates Militancy, Millenarianism and Public Space is that, in combination, they facilitate the expression of ideology as violent behaviour. The precise nature of such combination and their relative weighting may be unclear. But their presence, it is argued, is necessary to facilitate the expression of any ideology as violence.

CHAPTER 5

Millenarian Motifs

Factors associated with political and religious millenarianism are related to political violence and fanaticism as examples of rule-following behaviour. It is argued that millenarianism is one important factor related to the development of political violence. The importance of the concept of imminence of messianic attainment as a behavioural variable in the development of violence is emphasised.

What has emerged from our discussion of ideology in Chapter 4 has been a conceptual mechanism to relate distant ideological objectives to immediate behaviour, through behavioural rules. In addition we have briefly seen how given this process, one obvious particular quality of ideological content that is relevant to political fanaticism – militancy – can influence behaviour through specifying particular kinds of rules. These rules either give rise to violent behaviour directly, or create circumstances where violence is likely. Given this, we can now examine how other aspects of ideology might influence behaviour. In particular, we will examine how qualities of particular types of ideologies might relate to violent behaviour. An emphasis on the qualities of ideology follows from the recognition of the role of the content of ideology as the source of behavioural rules. We are also now in a position to look at how some of the features of fanaticism described in Chapter 2 might become associated with political ideologies which result in violence, and we will see how the behavioural qualities of those features become evident.

We will develop this issue by focusing on one of the features of fanaticism that we noted in Chapter 2 – utopianism or millenarianism – as the basis for our discussion in this chapter. The particular expression of an ideology in millenarian terms may be quite complex, but we can identify a number of 'symptoms'[1] or fundamental qualities which relate to the millenarian experience:

1. An analysis of the world in terms of a real or impending catastrophe, which has an immediate effect on the individual's life;
2. A revelation that explains this state of affairs, and which offers some form of salvation or redressing of ills;
3. As part of the revelation, the possession of special knowledge that the disastrous state is the result of the action of malevolent forces (spiritual or secular) which conspire to corrupt and subvert the normal organs of society or the State. Through the possession of special knowledge, the holder has a unique and powerful capacity to fight the malevolent and corrupting forces;
4. A sense of timeliness for action, in that the forces of corruption are nearing completion of their tasks;
5. A conviction that these forces can be defeated because of the special insights, and that the defeat of the forces of evil will result in the ushering in of a new and better world.

If we refer to the distinction made in Chapter 4, millenarian aspirations are in one sense an element of ideological content expressed in some way. But these aspirations also create a set of circumstances that seem to specify qualities related to processes of behavioural control, as well as ideological zealotry. A millenarian ideology specifies particular kinds of both distant and immediate objectives, and therefore particular kinds of rules, but the way in which these rules interact with behaviour describes the process of millenarian attainment. The *particular* content, like the influence of explicit militancy, may also produce distinctive effects in the way in which ideology is expressed. In this way, we will argue, ideological content plays a role when associated with millenarianism in the development of violence. It will be argued, therefore, that millenarianism along with other qualities of ideology, provides an important setting condition for the development of violence. It does this through both the distinctive millenarian content, and the process of attempting to attain particular millenarian ideological objectives.

We will begin our discussion by considering what is meant by the concept of millenarianism. In doing this, we will touch on issues related to the religious origins of the concept. Indeed, we will see that our discussion frequently revolves around religion related concepts, if not religion as such. This reflects the literature in this area. Because much of this literature makes little reference to psychological states, let alone behavioural variables, we will from time to time move away from our behavioural analysis to consider basic issues related to millenarianism. Our central theme will, however, recur.

Millenarian, Messianic and Utopian: the Terms

Looking forward towards a promised better, utopian or perfect future is a quality of many, if not most, religions. Millenarianism implies something rather more than this, however, related to a particular analysis of the state of the world at the moment, special knowledge, and a role for personal action to attain the future state. Given the religious origins of the term fanatic we noted in Chapter 2, it is not really surprising to find parallels between those religious origins of fanaticism and features of utopian movements, although the nature of those parallels may not be clear. One area for exploration may be the links between them in terms of the common qualities of religious and utopian ideologies.

Religious utopian movements are often referred to as millenarian or messianic movements. Millenarian literally refers to a thousand years, and has its origins in Christ's prophesied reign in person on earth, biblically foretold in Revelations 20: 1–5. Messianism refers to the belief in a Messiah, variously regarded as the promised deliverer of the Jews, Christ, or in a more general sense, a liberator or leader from oppression, or a leader to the righteous way. Given in this sense their common Judaic and Christian origins, both millenarian and messianic aspirations are closely related, the Messiah by some views leading his people into the biblical utopian thousand years. Millenarian and messianic aspirations are not, of course, confined to Judeo-Christian cultures, but we do not seem to use different religious terms to describe utopian views from other religious or secular traditions.

Usage of the terms utopianism, millenarianism and messianism has changed and developed somewhat over time. If we are to be linguistically accurate, utopianism properly refers to some form of secular aspiration, in contrast to millenarianism and messianism, which both have a religious context.[2] The critical distinction might be thought to be that a utopian society is the product of human action, whereas a millenarian or messianic society is either the product of, or awaits, divine intervention. This distinction can, of course, become blurred, when religious millenarian aspirations also require some form of human intervention to be effected, or when secular utopian ideology draws on notions like the 'inevitability' of class warfare, for example.

In contemporary usage, however, millenarian tends also to be used in a secular context, without *necessarily* assuming messianic leadership, or indeed any particular Christian or other religious context. In contrast, messianism does tend to assume a more specific religious context. All, however, refer to closely related concepts, and in practice are frequently used interchangeably. The looseness in usage may hide, however, a complicated relationship between the terms, and this can be illustrated by reference to the issue of leadership. Messianism emphasises the prophetic, and perhaps divine role of the leader, but the nature of leadership cannot be ignored in a millenarian or utopian context. The purely political leader may well claim prophetic messianic qualities, both for himself and for his followers; Hitler and the Nazi movement, for example, illustrate this.[3]

For our purposes in this chapter, utopian, millenarian and messianic will be used in a broadly interchangeable way, and consistent with the literature in this area, will be treated as largely synonymous. We will do this despite the distinctions that can be made between them. For the sake of consistency, we will tend to use millenarian as the generic term in both secular and religious contexts, without making any assumptions about divine or secular origins. This usage largely reflects that of the anthropological literature, whence much of the systematic work in this area originates.

Millenarian themes are important elements of the Western political and cultural heritage. Plato's 'Republic', for example, is an early description of an idealised utopian society that continues to exercise enormous contemporary influence over political and philosophical thinking, despite its ancient origins. Drawing on more explicitly Judaic and Christian bases, millenarianism in a religious sense, and also in the secular sense of utopian, has played an important part in both literary and philosophical exploration of society, reflecting social and religious aspirations almost from the very origins of our culture. Davis[4] categorises and discusses this extensive historical literature, and Morrison[5] explores some of the uses which literary and philosophical explorations of these themes, especially utopian, may have served. Their importance as what he describes as literary 'thought-experiments'[6] for example, offering a way of exploring potentially innovative social arrangements without actually creating the utopian society, was arguably an important element in progressing cultural and social experiment. A good example of this is the way in which the form of Plato's utopian society remains an implicit aspiration underlying the thinking of many contemporary political theorists.

Sometimes, millenarian theory has been translated into practice as a way of progressing a social development. Nineteenth-century social visionaries, such as Robert Owens, actively developed millenarian (or in his terms utopian) communities at New Lanark in Scotland, and at New Harmony in the United States. Contemporary communities such as Twin Oaks,[7] which have explored Skinner's utopian ideas expressed in his book *Walden Two*,[8] similarly enable the practical exploration of utopian social organisation. Secular social explorations of this kind can be distinguished from religious millenarian communities, which often function solely to prepare believers for the millennial event. In these latter religious circumstances, the community structure is often merely a means towards an end, as distinct from an end in itself in secular communities.

Interesting and important as such issues may be, our concerns here are not with exploring the broader social role of millenarianism. Our concern is primarily with the effects of the ideological qualities of millenarianism (in terms of both process and content) on the individual that may become embroiled in these movements, and we will see that millenarianism may have a role to play in the development of the extreme political behaviour we have referred to as fanaticism. This is not to say that political fanaticism need necessarily involve utopianism, messianism or millenarianism; but rather that the *processes* which result in millenarian movements, and influences and determines the adherent's behaviour, will enable us to further develop our concept of the political fanatic. Indeed, even at this early point in our discussion, we might assert that the revolutionary political movement that might result in fanatical violence might well always have millenarian elements in its ideology. Furthermore, it will be argued that qualities of millenarian ideology may well play an important role in the development of violence in the pursuit of fanatical objectives.

The relationship between extreme political views and millenarianism referred to above may be contentious, but can be illustrated in two ways. Marxism may be thought to represent a generic form of an extreme left-wing political ideology, and in so far as it does, it and related ideologies show intimate, if complex, millenarian (or more properly utopian) aspirations. Lukes,[9] for example, describes this complex relationship. Marxists have, in fact, ambiguous and ambivalent views on utopianism. On the one hand, as Lenin[10] said, utopianism represents '... idle guesswork about what cannot be known ... '. On the other hand, whilst the precise Marxist utopian dream may be unclear, the expectation and achievement of it as an inevitable historical process, is not. A much clearer right wing example can be seen in fascist, and more particularly, Nazi ideology. The 'thousand year Reich' so often referred to in Nazi writings and propaganda is of course both literally and figuratively millenarian.[11]

Imminence, Millenarianism and Behaviour

Many religious and secular social movements sustain themselves by not only offering a means of making sense of the world, but also a prospect of the future. Such movements are not necessarily millenarian simply because they have future changes in view, however. Millenarianism involves not simply a view, or indeed a certainty, about the future, but also a series of quite distinctive additional qualities associated with the nature and process of the expected changes. It is these qualities which will be discussed later that may contribute to the frequent association of millenarianism with violence and terror, rather than millenarian ideology as such. This has been admirably discussed at length by Rapoport.[12]

The revelation of response to impending disaster, and as a consequence of that, looking forward to an *imminent* utopia, as distinct from some general diffuse aspiration to change for the better, is probably one of the most important qualities that is critical in millenarian aspirations.[13] Imminence refers not simply to the eventual attainment, even if inevitably, of some desirable future state, but rather that such a revelatory state is brought nearer by the disastrous present and is 'soon to happen'. Its attainment may indeed be the result of inevitable forces, or it may have become achievable through human action. In any event, the foretold desired state is on the threshold of coming, and *will* come. The special knowledge revealed to the initiate relates not only to an analysis of the present, but to millenarian attainment itself.

The religious fervour that surrounded the return of the Ayatollah Khomeini to Iran in 1979 seems to capture this sense of imminence. Khomeini's arrival was not simply the fulfilment of revolutionary social and religious aspirations associated with the defeat of the Shah's regime. It was taken by many to reflect a much more profound and fundamental change in the nature of the Shi'ite world (and indeed the world in general), heralding the beginning of the foretold new and prophetic Shi'a Islamic State. Indeed, many Iranian Shi'ites believed that the Ayatollah Khomeini was the long awaited al-Mahdi, the re-embodiment of the infant son of the Eleventh Iman, Mohammad el Muntazar, the Twelfth Iman of the line of Ali, who went into occulation in 873. (An interesting contemporary related Shi'a messianic theme seems to be associated with the Iman Musa al-Sabr, a Lebanese Shi'ite leader who disappeared on a visit to Libya in 1978.)

From a different Islamic perspective, contemporary fundamentalist Sunni analyses suggest the development of millenarian qualities associated with imminent attainment. In the writings of Qutb,[14] an important influence on Sunni fundamentalist thinking, there is a striking analysis on the disastrous state of the world, followed by the assertion of the necessity to rediscover the 'true' Islamic way. In the book *Milestones*, one of his most influential works, the opening lines assert[15] 'Mankind today is on the brink of a precipice, not because of the danger of complete annihilation which is hanging over his head – this being just a symptom and not the real disease – but because humanity is devoid of all those vital values which are necessary. . . .' He goes on to claim that 'It is essential for mankind to have a new leadership!',[16] and after discussing the failure of the West to offer appropriate values to guide man, he asserts that 'Islam is the only system which possesses these values and this way of life.'[17] Sivan[18] notes the urgency of Qutb's tone, and the need to move quickly to redress problems before it is too late. The solution offered by Qutb is unquestioned acceptance of God's law expressed in the Shari'a,[19] and Jihad against enemies and unbelievers both within and without Islam.[20]

Qutb's influence can be seen in the writings and action of Muhammad Abd al-Salam Faraj, a participant in the successful plot to kill Anwar Sadat, the Egyptian President, in October 1981.[21] The theocratic demands of these interpretations of Islam are millenarian in character, and the believer is required uncritically to accept God's word as expressed through the Qur'an and other Holy writings. In Faraj's writings, the assassination of Sadat is expressed within a millenarian context, and the sense of imminence is evident in the belief that the death of Sadat, as both the symbol of evil and a corrupter of Islam, would itself result in the intervention of God on earth to aid the founding of the prophesied Islamic State. Consistent with this belief, as far as can be judged, the plotters made no preparations for the assumption of power, since once the call to Jihad was obeyed, human preparation was unnecessary and God would intervene. It would be erroneous to dismiss the significance of this background to Sadat's assassination, even though the promised millenarian fulfilment did not appear to occur in this instance.

Millenarian hope can be distinguished from some general hope of change that might characterise most religious movements. In issues that concern us, it seems to be the strength of adherence to the millenarian ideology (or perhaps more properly expressed as the control the millenarian ideology exercises over the individual's behaviour), *and* this quality of *imminence of attainment* of the desired state that may serve to facilitate the expression of millenarian ideology through violence. Thus the critical variable in psychological terms that enables us to distinguish potentially violent millenarian movements from other non-violent millenarian movements may be the factors related to the concept of imminence of attainment. Imminence of the millenarian ideal is also the quality that makes possible action to prepare for or speed the advent of it. The threshold of a definite temporal or spiritual end becomes visible. Given other ideological supports relating either access to the new world, or the time or nature of arrival of the prophesied end to particular kinds of human activity, it may also make possible individual action.

In a *religious* context, the benefits that imminent millenarian fulfilment might bring about need not necessarily be evident in this life, of course, and they may well refer to some non-material state of benefit. However, such change as might occur usually *also* includes a change in earthly conditions. Burridge[22] captures this admirably in the title of his book on millenarianism – *New Heaven New Earth*, which is itself an allusion to Revelations 21: 'And I saw a new heaven and a new earth: for the first heaven and the first earth were passed away.'[23]

In the context of *secular* political millenarian movements, however, the future offers certainty of imminent change on this earth, usually in both social and material terms. Furthermore, its attainment relates to human action in some sense. In this measure, therefore, it might be thought that all revolutionary political movements have qualities of millenarianism – the adherent gains admittance not simply to a body of special knowledge, but also to a route which will lead to some improved future which is attainable through social and political activity. The issue of its imminent attainment, however, again seems to be the critical quality linking political aspiration to action. The sense of urgency, allied with an assumed disastrous present, which can be seen to be evident in much terrorist propaganda,[24] may be a reflection of this quality of millenarian imminence expressed in contemporary political terms. We can see here, therefore, how this aspect of the broad qualities of millenarianism is closely related to the

expression of millennial aspiration through action. Indeed, imminence in both secular and religious contexts may serve as a bridge
linking relatively non-specific ideological prescription and consequences to behaviour.

In behavioural terms, the achievement of the millenarianism state
relates to the prospect of immensely powerful reinforcers. That millenarianism refers to the attainment of reinforcing states is perhaps
obvious enough, but the ideologically fundamental issues these reinforcers relate to means they are of enormous power. Rules that specify
relationships between these very powerful reinforcers and behaviour
would be expected to have great potency and potential to control
behaviour. However, in any millenarian ideology, these reinforcers,
even if powerful, are distant. It is with respect to this issue that the
notion of imminence again becomes of great importance. In terms of
rule-governed behaviour discussed in Chapter 4, the notion of imminence may be a critical variable in the relationship between distant
rule-mediated reinforcement and immediate contingency control.
One way of thinking about imminence may be to see it as a shift in the
control of behaviour from distant rule-related contingencies to more
immediate contingency control, as the cataclysmic event approaches.

Another way in which we might conceptualise the behavioural
factors associated with imminence may be in terms of the nature and
quality of rule control over behaviour. Hayes *et al.*[25] describe three
different kinds of rule-governed behaviour, which relate to the contingencies that motivate what an individual does with respect to the
rule. The most fundamental example of rule-governed behaviour is
what they term *pliance*[26] (derived from *compliance*). Put simply, this is
rule-governed behaviour characterised by following a command.
Many religious precepts can be characterised as examples of pliance
(such as the injunction on Moslems to pray in particular ways at
particular times). A second kind of rule following is termed *tracking*[27]
(suggesting following a path, perhaps related in some sense to the way
the world is organised in physical or social terms). This implies a
greater degree of control by immediate factors over the behaviour
specified by the rule than is the case with pliance. The third less well
understood form of rule following is termed *augmenting*.[28] This relates
to the extent to which other rules can enhance the capacity of a given
rule to control behaviour. Augmental rules rarely occur on their own,
but are rather associated with other forms of rule governance.

To describe ideological control as a single dimensional example of
rule following would of course be extraordinarily naive. In such a

complex area, a variety of kinds of rules and contingencies presumably affect an individual's behaviour. In the case of imminence, what we may be seeing is a move away from primary control over behaviour being exercised by pliance rules, to the more immediate sensitivity implied by tracking rules. Additionally, the conditions which give rise to the sense of imminence may also be another way of describing the role of augmental rules in enhancing tracking control. In any event, we can see clearly that the relationship between behaviour and millenarian development is emphasised by imminence.

Imminence, therefore, is an important element of ideology of this kind in both the religious and secular context. In conditions where a millenarian ideology lacks the dimension of imminence, we might expect to see powerful control by ideological rules primarily of a prescriptive kind (pliance) derived from the ideological source. In rigorous religious communities, for example, the extent of ideological control might be evident as an excessive conservatism, reconciling the individual to the social context defined by the ideology. For our purposes, we should note that such rigorous rule following rarely gives rise to violence, and is characterised more by withdrawal from the wider world than engagement in it to effect change. Indeed, such rule governance may give rise to an acceptance of conditions, rather than challenge. In contrast, the development of a sense of imminence (which we can characterise as a move towards control by tracking and augmental rules) appears to result in an engagement with society, which given the essential qualities of millenarianism ideology necessarily leads to efforts to effect change and fulfilment of the millenarian ideal.

Of course, where the achievement of the millenarian end is subject only to the whim of the Deity, action as such by believers will have presumably no effect on the nature of the imminent, or even distant, end. But even in these circumstances, the faithful might well prepare for the end, even if they cannot influence its coming. For the religious, action in the form of observance (ritual devotions or following 'the law', for example) may be sufficient. The contribution the individual might make may well be in terms of more strict observance of religious rules, indicating stronger faith. We can see this in the development of some religious utopian communities which were established to await the end of the world (the discussion later in this chapter of the Rappite community illustrates this). Religious observance served to prepare the initiates, and perhaps determined their selection as the chosen group to be saved. However, when the millenarian state appears to be imminent in ideologies that allow personal action to influence events, so the pressures to act become that much greater. This may be because of the reinforcing value of the now approaching end (resulting as far as the person is concerned in increased motivation), and the increased degree of control exercised by the negative features of the disastrous present, resulting in a shift in control between different kinds of rules and between immediate and distant contingencies.

In the political context, there seems to be no real equivalent to the essentially individual inward preparation of the religious. Where political aspirations address broad social conditions, so the adherent's actions required by ideological rules (enhanced by imminence) must, of necessity, directly address social structures. Given that attempts to change or influence social structure can in some circumstances meet strong resistance, we can immediately see here one simple route whereby the political millenarian might become involved in violence as a reaction to resistance to change. Where a millenarian ideology is explicitly violent, or has militant potential, we can see a further pressure towards violence. Furthermore, on the basis of the above discussion, we might speculate that imminence may be a factor in realising militant potential in ideology, although empirical evidence to support this view may be difficult to identify. The increased militancy of Iranian Shi'ites since the abdication of the Shah can perhaps be explained in these terms. Indeed, from an historical perspective, there certainly seems to be evidence of increased militancy associated with the rise of imminent millenarian aspirations in other religious communities.[29]

Not all political or secular millenarian movements address broad social change, of course, and the extent of aspirations to this may well be an important factor in the development of violence. On the other hand, where millenarian religious doctrine *also* has a strong social and societal focus (as in Islam in general, and Shi'ites in particular), both religious and social aspirations may combine, resulting in a force of great strength. For both the religious and the secular, imminence-related actions hasten, or even bring about, the desired millenarian objective.

It may also be possible to envisage transient states of imminence developing, related to local situational pressures. In the context of the group forces we have already identified, the possibility of the attainment of some important local goal may, in extreme circumstances, give rise to conditions like those already discussed within a broad ideological framework. The bases of such an effect may, for example, lie in the particular extreme reinforcing value of the particular objective. For soldiers in combat, meeting expectations of courage, regimental tradition, and the like in extreme life-threatening circumstances, when allied to simple survival, may temporarily give rise to conditions not unlike imminence in the sense in which we have used it here. Another factor in the military situation may well be the totality of behavioural control that the soldier is exposed to. We will encounter this again in our discussion of obedience in Chapter 9, in the context of the atrocities at My Lai.

We might summarise this discussion by noting that imminence may affect the control of distant consequences over behaviour (serving to increase ideological control by mediating between consequence and behaviour, or by making the consequences appear less distant). In the secular context, it may also in some measure shape and specify the nature of particular ideologically specified behaviour. The notion of imminence also draws our attention to the important quality of 'time' in millenarianism as one of the factors which contribute to the development of violence.[30] The impending achievement of the millenarian end also has a parallel in the urgency of action expressed in much of the terrorist communication noted earlier. We can conclude that from a psychological perspective, the temporal distance of significant events seems to be an important factor in how we evaluate events, and such temporal factors merit much greater exploration in the factors that precipitate political violence. We can readily accommodate these notions within a behavioural context, in terms of strength and effectiveness of reinforcing events, and the qualities of rule-governed behaviour contrasted with immediate contingency control.

Millenarium Movements

From our perspective, imminence is an important quality in the development of violence in millenarianism. There are, however, other attributes of millenarianism relevant to our concerns upon which authors in this area have focused. Both Burridge[31] and Cohn[32] discuss these attributes at some length. They may also, in some measure, contribute to the processes we have identified above. In the discussions of these attributes, the concepts and terms used make little reference to psychological or behavioural concepts. In pursuing this discussion, therefore, we will examine them in their own terms, placing them where appropriate in a psychological and behavioural context.

A critical concept which both Burridge and Cohn agree to be fundamental, and which we need to examine at the outset, is the relationship between millenarian activity and the concepts of 'salvation' or 'redemption'. Given the broadly secular context of the kind of political action which we are concerned with in this book, these essentially religious terms may seem unusual concepts to introduce. Furthermore, given the behavioural framework we have adopted, these terms may appear somewhat incongruous. However, both Cohn and Burridge use the religious term 'salvation', or something close to it, to describe the consequence of *secular* millenarian activity in terms that are in fact consistent with a behavioural analysis. By pursuing our discussion of these concepts, we will also reveal interesting behavioural parallels between the process of religious and secular millenarian aspirations, reflecting on the common roots of both.

We are familiar with the term salvation when used in a religious sense, as deliverance in some sense from sin. Particular religious interpretations may elaborate on this notion, or relate it to other elements of religious doctrine which need not concern us here. There is, however, another equivalent sense in which we can use the term to mean avoidance of disaster. These two usages of salvation are, of course, very closely related in the sense that sin, in most religious contexts, is perhaps a most fundamental disaster. Religious ideology usually relates the conditions in which sin can be avoided and salvation attained to religious devotion or observances. Indeed, it might be argued that religious ideology is, in essence, a series of prescriptions (or rules) to achieve salvation. Furthermore, a common theme in religions where individual action can contribute to salvation is that a failure to attain, or strive for, it may well result either in personal or social apocalyptic consequences. The devotee has a great deal to gain, therefore, by religious observance to avoid fundamentally damaging consequences.

Related themes to these can be discerned in secular millenarian political movements with political ideology occupying a similar role to revealed religious doctrine. Political ideologies in these circumstances also often emphasise negative outcomes for not following ideological prescriptions. Ideological positions predicting the disastrous outcomes of present social or economic conditions, for example, are a feature of many political movements (revolutionary and otherwise) as well as being an essential quality of millenarian movements. Contemporary concerns over the destruction of the environment, with its potential apocalyptic consequences, and the rise of environmentalism as a political force seem to illustrate this. There is clearly a sense in which adherents of these ideologies might see *their* membership of *their* particular movement as offering special insight into the problems of the world, *and* the means of avoiding and solving those problems. In this way, therefore, we might speak of salvation in a political as well as religious context. We can also make some sense of the notion of salvation from a behavioural perspective. In a behavioural sense, salvation may be seen as a form of avoidance learning. Membership and participation in political millenarian activities may offer political salvation (in creating a new world) as avoidance of the apocalyptic consequence of the present political system, just as salvation in a religious sense may offer salvation or *redemption* from the essential sin of present life at the point of apocalyptic judgement.

Millenarian movements expect the attainment of a new order as the consequence of their activities. The resultant new order, however, is not simply a transformation and improvement on present conditions, but the achievement of something which is radically different. In the terms we have introduced above, the millenarian aspiration (religious or secular) is nothing less than salvation. As Cohn notes, the millenarian pictures salvation as '... total, in the sense that it is utterly to transform life on earth, so that the new dispensation will be no mere improvement on the present but perfection itself ...'. It is worth noting that we can see here a distinction between the gradual incremental change more usually associated with utopianism,[33] and the more dramatic *and total* change in attaining the millennium. The role of imminence in this context is of obvious importance, and we can see how changes in factors such as imminence that might influence the realisation of millenarian aspirations might have enormous control over behaviour.

Burridge[34] particularly relates the concept of salvation in millenarian movements to a quality of perfection, but emphasises the attainment of this through the notion of *redemption*. As with salvation, this is a word having most obviously religious connotations but which, like the concept of salvation, can equally have meaning in the political and secular contexts of concern to us. Redemption, in the sense used by Burridge, refers to the fulfilment of debts or obligations. He assumes, perhaps not unreasonably, that a quality of social living is the development of a network of obligations and debts. For example, the child is in a sense obligated to its parents for its nurture or to 'society' in some general sense for its education and cultural heritage. In the aphorism 'paying our debt to society', Burridge illustrates one sense in which this notion of obligation might be interpreted. Social networks in this sense involve complex interactive and reciprocal systems of obligations which constrain and limit our capacity to behave. This analysis can probably be extended to all societies, although the quality of obligation is probably more explicit in some than others. Traditional Japanese society, for example, seems to illustrate a very explicit recognition of the role of obligation and mutual obligation creating the rules for social interaction.[35] Burridge suggests that the 'perfectionalism' of millenarian aspiration involves a state of 'unobligedness', a state of total freedom achieved through fulfilment of obligation and debt through salvation in the sense used above.

This is most readily understood in a religious context of course, and it offers one approach to understanding the sense in which 'peace' is often used in a Christian context as a metaphor for the utopian achievement of the second coming. In terms of the above discussion, it represents the attainment of perfection as freedom from all obligations. Indeed, the idea of 'freedom' is also sometimes used to metaphorically describe the millenarian end.

There are interesting parallels to be drawn between Burridge's notions and the reflections on freedom from the behavioural perspective of Skinner.[36] Skinner discusses at some length the notion of freedom and the ways in which we use it. He concludes, somewhat controversially perhaps, that freedom is reduction in, or abolition of, aversive control (that is to say, control exercised over behaviour by either punishment or avoidance conditions). In behavioural terms, if the mutual obligations that constrain our activity are aversive in some sense (as the use of terms such as 'obligation' suggests), then the conditions resulting from the removal of these aversive conditions may well also constitute the attainment of freedom in the sense used by Skinner, as well as in Burridge's view. We can also see, following on from our discussion of salvation, how in the sense used here, salvation (as avoidance of aversive consequences) might also equate with or contribute to freedom. The state of 'unobligedness' Burridge refers to therefore may well be a state where the individual's behaviour is not subject to aversive control. We should note, to round off Skinner's argument, that such a state of freedom is not in Skinner's terms absence of *all* control; some degree of positive control remains. In a practical sense, we can see the exploration of Skinner's ideas in his fictional account of a utopian community, *Walden Two*.[37]

Burridge develops his notions in a slightly different direction from Skinner, however. From an anthropological perspective, Burridge draws our attention to the fact that in his view '. . . all religions are basically concerned with power . . .'. Leaving aside the qualities of any particular religion and religious practice, Burridge argues that they all involve '. . . the discovery, identification, moral relevance and ordering of different kinds of power, whether they manifest themselves as thunder, or lightning, atomic fission, untrammelled desire, arrogance, impulse, apparitions, visions or persuasive words. Within these terms a spiritual being, whether thought of as a deity or ghost or human being or angel or goblin or fairy, becomes a named and identified source or principle of power. . . .'[38] Accepting this, if we assume that political aspiration is also concerned with the exercise and control of power, then we can see that there may be a further common process relating religious and political millenarianism through the search for and control of power. In behavioural terms, such religious and political processes may become evident in the same way, and have parallel behavioural effects. There are obvious links here with Skinner's emphasis on the social uses of aversive control.[39] Religion is, of course, not solely concerned with power, and Burridge's assertion may seem controversial, at least to religious adherents. But through the common link of power, we can see how religious and secular political millenarianist aspirations might have elements in common.

In summary, therefore, millenarianism in these terms might be thought to be concerned with the ultimate redistribution of power. The millenarian outcome in both secular and religious terms is one where power is redistributed in such a way as to result in freedom (in Skinner's terms), redemption or unobligedness (in Burridge's terms). We might note that where action of any form is required to hasten the millenarian ideal (as the notion of imminence so often implies), it follows that some distinction between believers (and hasteners through their actions of the millenarian event) and non-believers will emerge in terms of access to the millenarian final state. The non-believer is damned to hell, or fails to participate in the millennial ideal. We can see, therefore, a further element in the bases of the apocalyptic themes that characterise millenarian movements.

A further important quality of millenarian outcome, however, is that the change it looks forward to, perhaps because it is total, will also be sudden. Millenarianists generally envisage a cataclysmic change of some form, rather than a gradual development, change or improvement of conditions. In Christian terms (for of course Christianity is a millenarian religion) the world will end and God will, in some sense, reassert His control of the world through His direct presence and intervention in human affairs. The righteous will be saved, but the sinner will be damned. The state of salvation, whilst ill defined, is often metaphorically referred to in terms of peace or quietness. The end, when it comes, will be sudden, violent, and irreversible. The images of the Book of Revelations, which has had a profound effect on many millenarian movements, illustrates both the process and outcomes of cataclysmic change. The change envisaged in millenarian aspiration is not only total and sudden; it can be, as we have noted earlier, *imminent.* Imminence in the context of totality of change is a very important quality associated with millenarian aspirations, and quite clearly may serve to distinguish some millenarian movements from others. Furthermore, and more importantly, we can now see how that quality of imminence has important psychological consequences which materially change the behaviour of millenarian adherents.

An Example: George Rapp and the Rappites

Christianity is in a general sense a millenarian (or messianic) religion, but the expectation of ultimate salvation it offers is for most adherents ill defined. The world will at some point end, and in the terms of the Nicene Creed ... And he shall come in glory to judge both the quick and the dead ... The believer looks ... for the Resurrection of the dead, And the Life of the world to come, 'but at least, in orthodox belief, is given no particular time at which to expect this dramatic change. In general, therefore, whilst Christianity may claim millenarian qualities, because it lacks the quality of imminence it would be inappropriate to describe it as a millenarian movement in the sense we have used it. We might controversially speculate that this may be one reason why contemporary Christian behaviour rarely extends beyond limited ideological prescriptions, expressed as observance of ritual.

On the other hand, within Christianity from time to time clearly defined and explicit millenarian sects develop. They acquire meaning and form through Christian belief, but are not typical of orthodox Christian worship in that they do have a striking sense of the imminence of prophetic fulfilment. Whilst such sects are on the whole marginal to orthodox Christian religions, they are not necessarily insubstantial. The contrast between these millenarian sects and the orthodox Christian believers often lies in the extent to which religious ideology exercises control over behaviour. In terms of the discussion in Chapter 4, we might express this in terms of the strength of rule following, and is perhaps related to the nature of the behavioural rules, which are themselves related to the *relative* distance between immediate behaviour and its distant end. Again, we see a critical role for the concept of imminence as a variable mediating distant consequence of rule-governed behaviour (in the sense used in Chapter 4) to immediate behaviour.

An historical example of a very successful and numerous Christian millenarian sect can be seen in the community established at Harmonie in the United States by George Rapp.[40] We will consider this community at some length, for the features of this sect offer a good illustration of the development of a successful non-violent millenarian movement. Their non-violent qualities may more readily help us to focus on the processes involved. Its religious context sets the scene for much of their activity, but the features of the Rappite community also offer useful parallels for understanding contemporary political millenarian groups.

George Rapp was born in Iptingen, a village bordering the Rhine, in 1757. His early life was characterised by growing dissent from the official church, which culminated in the development of his own sect. This sect attracted a considerable following. It was frankly millenarian in outlook, and an essential element of belief was a confident expectation of the imminence of the millennium. The members of the sect actively sought to prepare themselves for the millennial event, and the influence of millenarian ideology on their behaviour was profound. As in similar sects, Rapp's most ardent followers, for example, abstained from sexual relations unnecessary because of the imminence of the millennium which would render sexual reproduction irrelevant.

Much of Rapp's preaching was based on his interpretations of the Book of Revelations. His followers were expected to show complete obedience to Rapp (as God's representative), perfect love to each other, and order in their affairs, however trivial. They aspired through religious devotion and observance to attain a state of perfect Harmony (hence the choice of name for the community they eventually founded) as preparation for the millennium. Their religious observance extended to pacifism, for sect members were forbidden to bear arms. Their beliefs gave rise to inevitable disputes with the civil authorities, and eventually led Rapp to move his community from southern Germany to the United States. He initiated this move in 1804, and his intention was to establish a perfect community in which the devout could await and prepare for the second coming.

In 1805, the Harmony Society was founded, which was to be the vehicle for the development of the Rappite communities in the United States. The first community, Harmonie, was established at that time on the Connoquenessing Creek in Western Pennsylvania. It survived with difficulty at first, but eventually prospered. By 1814, it had established itself as a reasonably affluent self-sufficient community, with the capacity to 'export' its agricultural and manufactured surpluses to the surrounding area. In 1814, however, Rapp decided to abandon the Pennsylvania site, and moved the community to the banks of the Wabash River in what was then largely unexplored territory, now in the State of Indiana. Probably both economic and religious reasons played a part in this decision, but undoubtedly the latter were the most important. Isolation from the rest of the world seems to have been a critical element in this. The second community, again called Harmonie, was established in virgin territory. As before, after a difficult beginning, it flourished, quickly becoming self sufficient, and again selling its surplus production and productive capacity (milling, for example) to the surrounding community.

Both Harmonie communities lived under strict religious observance. Property was communally owned, and work and trade was undertaken as communal activity, rather than based on individual initiative. George Rapp maintained close and total control over the life of the community which maintained strict order, with a curfew at 9 pm. Taylor[41] describes the way of life as follows:

'Each morning a cart went round collecting milk; it carried a placard with special instructions about jobs to be done. Then, summoned by French horns, men, women, and children marched together to the fields, or to the various manufactories. They were dressed alike; the men in jackets and pantaloons recalled the Rhineland *tracht*, the women in grey dresses, their hair scraped up and under a cap.... Later, the Harmonists' movements were controlled by a bell in the steeple of the church, a thing of great wonder on the frontier.'

The Harmonie community was orderly, controlled and devout in its ideological and religious observances. It maintained economic ties with the outside community, but there was little social interaction between inhabitants and its neighbours. Because it was relatively isolated from the world at large, the dynamic structure of the community is very clear, and because of this, we can see the control which ideology can exercise over behaviour. Furthermore, it illustrates how that control is evidenced as rule following. The ideology derived from Rapp was transmitted to his followers in terms of the structure and content of their social living. This structure was very clearly expressed as behavioural rules, which served to both control the day-to-day activities of the community and to relate those activities to the attainment of the ultimate millenarian objectives. The virtue for our purposes of the Rappite community is that it serves as an example of the small, explicitly religious millenarian sects that have developed. More recent and much more extensive millenarian social systems, such as in contemporary Iran, are less isolated and more complex, but still illustrate the same features of social control through ideological rule following.

Harmonie was also a very successful economic enterprise, no doubt the result of the efficiency and effectiveness of the communal ideology developed by Rapp. Despite this success (or perhaps because of it), Rapp initiated a third further move of the community in 1824, to the banks of the Ohio some 18 miles from Pittsburgh. The site and buildings of Harmonie were sold to Robert Owen, the British utopian theorist and early socialist, who established a secular utopian community on it, now called New Harmony. The Rappites, for their part, moved to Economy, the name chosen for their new settlement on the Ohio.

The changes in the community sites ordered by George Rapp do not simply seem to have been the whim of a despot. They were each separated by 10 years (arrival in the USA in 1804 and the foundation of Old Harmonie, the movement to the Wabash in 1814, and the move to Economy in 1824), and seem to have been related to Rapp's interpretations of the second coming. The community as it developed was transitional, focused only on preparing for the second coming. Perhaps Rapp saw the moves as helping that focusing, by emphasising the temporary nature of the physical development of the community. Contemporary surprise at the change of sites, and apparent uprooting and disruption of the economic potential of the communities, stems from using the wrong frame of reference in judging the effectiveness of the communities. Their economic success, which other millenarian communities of this kind tend not to achieve (and of course on which we tend now to focus), was largely incidental to the Rappites' overall purpose.

Leadership

There are two broad senses in which we can consider the effects of leadership on fanaticism in general, and millenarianism in particular. The first relates to what might be termed qualities of leadership, and the capacity of the leader to exercise influence over others.[42] Psychological analyses of the nature of leadership, and the personal qualities associated with effective leadership, have proved complex and somewhat incomplete. There are grounds for suggesting, however, that qualities such as self-confidence, need for achievement and dominance are associated with the successful leader, and that qualities such as expression of inferiority, tendency to elicit sympathy and deference are absent. Psychological studies therefore tend to confirm the commonly held stereotype of the leader as a dominant and confident person (both for men and women). A need for power is also sometimes included as an attribute of the leader (presumably related to the theme of dominance). However, studies also suggest that the situation in which the aspirant leader finds himself are also important elements in whether any leadership potential is fulfilled. Thus, whilst there may be distinctive qualities of leaders, which *particular* leader might emerge will be dependent on the situation at the time.

Once a leader has emerged, however, the very fact of leadership and control places within the hands of the leader great potential to sustain his position. The forces of mass influence and crowd behaviour[43] become available, and were used to great effect, for example, by Adolf Hitler. We should note, however, that whilst the leader may be in a position to exercise control over forces of mass influence, there is a considerable body of work which emphasises two further features. Leaders are susceptible to influence by those who follow. Leadership appears to be a reciprocal relationship, rather than one embodying a single relationship of leader *to* follower. Furthermore, there are 'audience' characteristics that are relevant, for example in the sense that there are occasions when people want to be led. Some of the qualities of fanaticism which we have identified earlier are relevant to both of these. For example, some features of fanaticism may well lend themselves to use by a leader, and indeed because of reciprocal relationships might draw both leader and follower towards more extreme positions. Features such as the tendency towards focusing, insensitivity, etc., all may allow the leader powerful means of exercising additional influence and control, and himself being controlled.

We can, however, identify a second sense of leadership. This might be characterised as the situation where the leader is the source of refinement for ideological prescriptions, shaping, clarifying and directing ideological priorities. It refers in a sense to the content and bases of ideological direction. This aspect of leadership is intimately related to that described above, of course, and the way in which the leader exerts his influence is clearly related to the direction the leader wants to take. The direction he takes is also related to the needs of his followers. The reciprocal relationship described above will, of course, operate in this respect as in others. The direction the leader might take, and its relationship to *ideology*, can be identified as the separate feature of particular relevance to us. It is this second sense which we are primarily concerned with here, and in the following we will not discuss at any great length the effects of other qualities of leadership (although the issue does become relevant in Chapter 9). Indeed, this important issue might well be the topic of a substantial work in itself, and is in the main beyond the scope of our present discussion.

Within any political group, we might encounter leadership at various levels (depending on its size). The principal leader (in the role occupied by, for example, Hitler) occupies a different relationship to his followers than the leader of a small subsidiary unit. Both these relationships will be different from that occupied by the leader of a small revolutionary organisation. Within a substantial terrorist organisation, the differentiation of function (perhaps expressed in terms of cells) gives a variety of leadership roles. At lower levels, we may be dealing with a process familiar through the study of small group dynamics. At higher levels where strategic decisions are made *and* where public as well as private leadership is involved, we might expect to find more complex features.

In the second and more limited sense identified above, in both religious and secular millenarian movements a leader of some form is almost invariably involved who either creates the ideology, or interprets ideology derived from an authority. Furthermore, we might usefully distinguish between original leaders (who create an ideology) and subsequent leaders of that ideology who elaborate and develop the original theme. In a religious movement, such a leader is often regarded as a prophet, someone who interprets or reveals God's will, and perhaps in some sense precedes the millennial event. George Rapp, in the example described above, is quite clearly an example of such a prophetic leader, who saw his task as preparation of his followers for the millennium. There is little evidence to suggest, however, that Rapp saw himself as having a divine role in the millennium itself. The term which refers to the promised deliverer of the Jews, the Messiah (the anointed one), does imply this more extensive role, but this term has also come to mean a more general religious liberator of a country or people – hence the use of the alternative term messianism for millenarianism.

More rarely, the millenarian leader (or perhaps more properly the messianic leader) will himself claim to be the deity, wielding supernatural or magical powers to achieve the millennium, and creating his own ideology to achieve it. The Reverend Jim Jones, the founder and leader of the People's Temple, who eventually initiated the suicide of more than 900 adult and child followers of his sect in 1978, illustrates the development of claims to messianic leadership, initially as a prophet, but later as a divine figure. At the sect's foundation, Jones occupied the role of a prophetic leader, interpreting scripture and counselling his followers (demonstrating very effective qualities of leadership). Later however, as his sect developed, his actions became more extreme and he began to claim divine powers and attributes for himself. He seems to have staged miraculous healings, and on one occasion he threw his Bible to the floor whilst addressing his followers, because 'too many were looking to it', rather than to him.

In political millenarianism, the role of a leader seems to be equally important, although it is quite possible to envisage a millenarian movement lacking a leader in this sense. The Nazi movement in Germany in the 1920s and 30s was a good example of a political millenarian movement,[44] and of course Adolph Hitler occupied the role of leader (Führer), and arguably prophet (in the sense used above). Through his personal appearances, and the highly effective State propaganda apparatus developed by Joseph Goebbels, he both reinterpreted the history of past German defeats, and guided what might be termed the country's resurrection and salvation (in the sense used earlier) towards the inevitable 'Thousand Year Reich' through Nazi ideology. It is worth noting that both Goebbels and Hitler were well aware of the techniques of mass influence, and showed a detailed knowledge of the work of Le Bon.[45]

The relationship between the action implied by the process of imminence and the role of the leader in millenarian movements is of critical importance. The leader directs and focuses existing millenarian aspirations already implicit in the ideology of a movement. Actual or claimed ancient origins of an ideology may well also serve to add credibility to the leader's guidance. Thus in the case of Christianity, whilst orthodox Christianity as we have noted is little more than nominally millenarian, the potential for explicit millenarianism lies within its ideology. From time to time a leader or prophet may therefore capture this latent quality, making it explicit (as George Rapp did). In the case of political millenarianism, the leader may well play a more explicit developmental role, in that the ideological support for imminent millenarian achievement is often contingent directly on him (as was the case in Nazi Germany, and the dependence of Nazi ideology on Hitler's personal role). The forces that control and direct the behaviour of the messianic leader may, of course, be very complex. The lure of power (or the reality of exercising it), for example, is a factor that cannot be ignored. Indeed, the power of prophetic interpretation from the ideological authority may itself be an important element in sustaining and directing the leader's actions, quite aside from the attractions of exercising power in any other sense.

The political millenarian cannot look towards divine inspiration or authority in the sense that the religious can, although he can make reference to concepts like historical necessity or tradition in ways similar to the use of authority in religious ideology. But perhaps the development of the quality of imminence necessarily requires reference to an authority analogous to divine authority, or at least the postulation of absolute values or circumstance. The use made of the Jews by Hitler in the development of Nazi ideology may in fact illustrate this. The Jews were presented as the cause of Germany's ills *as they always had been*. The truth, or otherwise, of such an assertion is, of course, irrelevant in this context.

In this respect, the influence of the leader may be critical in releasing the militant potential of an ideology. The extent to which a later leader can build upon, and perhaps distort to his own ends, an existing ideology is clearly an important feature of political violence. We have noted that, in origin, ideologies are often expressed in general ways, requiring interpretation to make them relevant to the needs of the moment; this is particularly the case with the major contemporary religious movements. Thus, from a common Christian base, ideologies as diverse as pacifism and the racism of the Ku Klux Klan can be derived. The realisation of the detail of ideologies of this kind depends greatly on the qualities of the leader of the moment, who of course in turn derives added authority by association with the original ideology.

The Social Context to Millenarianism and Imminence: the Cargo Cult

There is another element we can identify, however, which may have a critical role in the development of imminence in millenarian ideology. Christianity has the potential for millenarianism, which frequently results in the development of millenarian *movements*. Explicit sects that set themselves apart from society, making the commitment to reject materialism in the way that the Rappites did, for example, are more infrequent. There are, however, recurrent geographical and temporal pockets of Christian millenarianism which can be identified and which are associated with distinctive socio-economic circumstances. Social and economic context, therefore, seems to contribute to the development of this quality of millenarianism.

In Medieval Europe, Cohn[46] notes that 'in the valley of the Rhine ... one can detect an unbroken tradition of revolutionary millenarianism down to the sixteenth century. In some areas of what are now Belgium and Northern France, such a tradition can be traced from the end of the eleventh to the middle of the fourteenth century, in some areas of Southern and Central Germany from the middle of the thirteenth century down to the Reformation; after which the beginnings of a tradition can be observed in Holland and Westphalia.' The Rappites referred to above are, of course, a later example of this same tradition, originating from one of those areas. The feature that Cohn identifies and relates to these developments is the social upheaval of the times having exaggerated effects in these places, involving in the main changes in agricultural practices, and related profound social and economic changes. Harrison[47] similarly relates the development of millenarian sects in eighteenth and nineteenth century Britain to the social changes resulting from the Industrial Revolution. Furthermore, a similar kind of interpretation emphasising social change has been offered for the selective development of non-Christian millenarian movements in various parts of Polynesia and Oceania.[48]

It is worth elaborating on an example of Pacific experience of millenarianism, for until now, our discussion has been largely Christian and European in focus. In contrast to this, anthropological investigations of millenarianism, on which much of our conceptual knowledge of millenarian processes are based, has been largely conducted in the Pacific area, and the most systematic analyses available tend to use these examples. For our purposes, they have the virtue of illustrating processes emphasizing social change with examples outside of the familiar West European context of most of the examples in this book.

The advent of Europeans to Polynesia during the nineteenth century dramatically and materially altered traditional ways of life, and brought about profound social disruption. Whilst, as Burridge points out, explanations of millenarian movements *purely* in terms of socioeconomic change are insufficient to explain their selective rise, nevertheless, such changes undoubtedly provided the setting conditions in which millenarian groups could develop.[49] The fact that in the Pacific region their focus was often on the products of European culture most evident to the native islanders, i.e. material possessions, clearly emphasises this. The best known examples of this are the so-called cargo cults.

'Cargo' is a pidgin English word which refers to all the manufactured goods possessed by Europeans. The word suggests something brought in, rather than made in the locality, and a feature of cargo cults is that they refer to the possession not of the skills to produce and make goods, but to the manufactured products themselves. In the cults, the 'cargo' is not to be purchased or acquired in any conventional (to the West) sense; rather proper ritual will produce the cargo (the ritual in pidgin is termed the 'Road Belong Cargo' – Rot bilon Kago[50]). The fulfilment of this is that the 'cargo' is brought to the islanders as cargo in something – generally a mythical boat or aircraft.

Cargo cults, therefore, appear to be related to the impact of European civilisation in general, but especially material possessions, on an existing less materially endowed social system. They are relatively common in parts of Polynesia and Melanesia in locations where there has been extensive contact with Europeans (e.g. coastal areas of Papua/New Guinea, for example), but are very rare in areas where contact with Europeans has been limited. Missionary activity seems to be related to the development of the cults, and rudimentary elements of Christian ritual often provides the bases for the development of the cargo cult ritual.

Probably the most extensive and comprehensive description of the circumstances and development of several cults is presented by Burridge.[51] As he notes, a common theme discernible in cargo cults is that white men and their possessions provide the background against which myths and religious practices develop as attempts to assure a re-distribution of the white man's goods to the native communities. An underlying theme seems to be that by the possession of goods, native communities could attract some measure of the power usurped by the Europeans. Burridge argues that the cults do not develop spontaneously, but seem to occur within particular social and historical frameworks, where the cult enables the native peoples to make some sense out of the profound changes affecting their communities as a result of European contact. The cults, therefore, have an instrumental quality, aiming to redress real or perceived economic and social disadvantage.

One typical example given by Burridge[52] of the development of a cargo cult is on the Melanesian island of Tangu. The first direct contact between the natives of Tangu and Europeans is thought to have occurred before World War I. Quite early in these encounters, myths began to develop amongst the Tangu which seem to have been an attempt to enable them to understand the very evident material discrepancies between the native community and the white men. These myths involved two brothers, ancestors respectively of white and black men. Because of some mythical act, the white ancestor was endowed with ability and inventiveness, the black ancestor with dull attributes. Explanations and fulfilment of the myths, in terms of brothers sharing their wealth, or alternatively the 'white' brother being forced to do so, provide the background in which the cargo cults on Tangu developed. Myths of this type are not uncommon in other parts of Melanesia and seem to readily fit into indigenous religious views.

The role of myth and ritual in Polynesian and Melanesian native society is complex, but some understanding of it is essential in understanding the features of cargo cults. In general, it can be said that native religious observance is based on a principle of reciprocity, where the performance of ritual results in reciprocal action on the part of the spirit world. The ghosts of ancestors play an important role in Melanesian society, actively intervening in the physical world in support of their living relatives. Ancestral activity of this kind is an important element in enabling the native community to make sense of how material things are produced and obtained. The native recognises his impotence in making things grow successfully, for example, but his ancestor can and does intervene in the growing process to his benefit. This is based on reciprocity of obligation, where performance of ritual places obligations on the ancestral spirits. Whilst the ancestors are the object of religious devotions, therefore, they are not treated as deities in the Western sense of religious worship. The two brothers' myth needs to be seen in this context.

Early missionary activities seem to have been interpreted as the fulfilment of the first interpretation of the myth (i.e. in terms of sharing), and Lidz *et al.*[53] suggest that the adoption and participation in Christian ritual by the native communities should be understood in this light. Of course, despite native compliance with Christian ritual, the white men's goods inevitably remained largely confined to the white community. In terms of native cultural expectations, Christian ritual failed to create the reciprocal production of material goods. In terms of myths described above, Burridge suggests that this led to an increased acceptance of the second interpretation (i.e. the white men being forced to share their goods with the black men). Lidz *et al.* suggest that the cargo cult is a response to this by the development of alternative rituals designed to produce the ritual obligations on the spirits to produce cargo.

In Tangu, all that seems to have been lacking for this interpretation of the myth to develop fully was a leader to organise and develop this theme. Inevitably, a native leader emerged who achieved this in 1937. He was called Mambu, and took the title of 'Black King'. His particular ideology claimed that the deities who manufactured the white men's goods had already despatched the goods to the black men. The perfidious whites, however, had intercepted the packages, changed the labels, and redirected them to themselves. Mambu claimed that if the natives did as he bid them, a ship laden with goods ('cargo') for all would duly arrive. Those who ignored his advice would be destroyed. This later element reflects in a rather different context the common apocalyptic theme of most millenarian ideologies noted earlier.

Aping elements of Christian missionary practice, the followers of Mambu erected sacred buildings on which they placed a red flag and cruciform. '... in or by it recruits to the movement were "baptised" by having their genitals sprinkled with water, breechclouts and skirts having been stripped off beforehand and buried'.[54] After the 'baptism', the faithful wore European clothes. This inevitably attracted the attention of the colonial administration, and the activities of Mambu and his followers were suppressed. But the memory of Mambu persisted, and in time became absorbed within the original two brothers' myth.

The elements of this particular cargo cult reasserted itself after World War II. During that war, Tangu was occupied by the Japanese, and subsequently liberated by American and Australian forces. The island then came under Australian administration, and the native communities enjoyed a period of relative affluence, based largely on war damage compensation. As this short period of prosperity waned, so the attractions of the cargo cult seem to have increased, and further prophets in the Mambu tradition emerged, drawing on the already well-known myths. These prophets essentially replicated the millenarian aspirations of Mambu; adherence to ritual and obedience to the prophetic leader would result in the imminent attainment of cargo, and perhaps also (and probably rather more significant in the post-colonial ethos of those times) the elimination of whites.

The focus of a cargo cult, as indicated of course by the term cargo, is on material conditions. The context in which the cults occur seems to be the material disparity between white colonial or missionary cultures and black native cultures. The circumstances of the Tangu cults are broadly replicated in the numerous examples of Polynesian and Melanesian cults, and it illustrates the general features of their development. Its millenarian quality is the attainment of cargo through divine or spiritual intervention. It seems reasonable to conclude, as Burridge does, that particular social conditions, involving upheaval and change, facilitate the development of millenarian conditions as illustrated by the cargo cult. One issue remains, however. An element of the cargo cult that is important in its evolution for the participants, but at first sight seems problematic for the behavioural analysis proposed here, is the role of myth in the development of the cult, and more generally in the societal context in which the cults develop. This has been discussed in a related context by Malott,[55] who considers this general issue in the context of the development of the 'sacred cow' as a critical element of Hindu culture. He makes a convincing case for seeing the role of myths of the kind discussed above as elements of rule-governed behaviour. The myths serve as a means of mediating between distant contingency relationships which *are not direct acting* and immediate behaviour, where the myths have their ultimate origins in the reinforcing contingencies described by contingency rules. In this sense, therefore, myth is a socially appropriate form of verbal expression of the contingency rules operative.

In contrast to the above account, we should note that some authors have offered explanations of the cargo cults in terms similar to some of the psychological accounts of ideology discussed in Chapter 4. We have already noted in that chapter that explanations of ideology have often been framed in terms of psychoanalytic constructs, and explanations in similar theoretical terms have been used to account for cargo cults. Lidz *et al.*,[56] for example, attempt to relate the development of cargo cults to features of psychological development in childhood. Using Piaget's developmental framework, they draw analogies between the way children understand the world and features of cargo cults. Lidz *et al.* assume that cultural changes mirror individual changes, and that concept development in childhood as the child grows can be thought to parallel cultural development as that culture responds to change. In turn, they relate these speculations to features of psychoanalytic thinking. Whilst such explanations have a literary attraction, perhaps the principal problem for them is that the assumptions required strain to breaking point the bounds of credibility.

Contemporary examples of social conditions affecting the development of a millenarian movement in a secular and non-Christian context can be seen in the effects of the social upheavals that preceded the development of the Nazi movement in post World War I Germany. The social upheavals of that time seem to set the scene for the development of its millenarian potential[57]; the defeat and abdication of an 'invincible' sovereign in the Kaiser, followed by profound social deprivation, appear to have materially contributed to a desire for social change, culminating in the development of a particularly repulsive millenarian movement led by Adolph Hitler. Whether a leader (Hitler simply being one of many who might have risen) was the inevitable consequence of this, or whether Hitler was able to make use of these conditions which without him might not have taken a millenarian direction, is of course a moot point.

The examples described above are important not only in developing our notions of millenarianism, but also in developing our concept of ideology. Millenarian ideology can clearly be influenced by situational variables such as socio-economic change. This lends further support to the application of our earlier analysis of ideological activity as rule-following behaviour to millenarianism. In particular, it illustrates that particular situational conditions can attenuate and modify the contingencies which relate distant outcomes to immediate behaviour. It is, perhaps, in this respect that we can see both the role of socio-economic influences and imminence as behavioural variables.

Action

The literature on millenarianism emphasises the collective nature of millenarian movements, and accounts frequently make reference to groups who become caught up in a millenarian expectation. It is not clear, however, whether the experience of millenarianism is necessarily a collective phenomena. Hermits, or others who retreat from the world, may well do so in expectation of a millenarian outcome for which they alone are preparing; we may not be aware of them, however, because of their solitary state. On the other hand, those millenarianists which we notice (or historians, or the media notice for us) are generally collective, involving sometimes groups of considerable size. This may well of course distort our view of the importance of collectivity.

Where millenarianism takes the form of retreat from the world as preparation for the millennium, communities often further isolate themselves by becoming self sufficient. The community created by George Rapp at Harmonie on the banks of the Wabash, for example, illustrates this. Indeed, its members were not only self sufficient, but proved to be a highly successful economic unit, both supporting themselves and selling their surpluses to the wider community. In this respect, it is now without significance that the third community site chosen by Rapp on the banks of the Ohio river was called Economy. Much of the community's success must be attributed to Rapp himself, and the particular millenarian ideology he created. The failure of the New Harmony community founded by Robert Owen, which took over the Harmonie site in 1824, demonstrates that the inherent economic potential of the site was not sufficient to sustain a community in the absence of an appropriate community structure and ideology.

A quality of religious millenarian movements is their anticipation of and dependence on the supernatural. Christ will come, for example, and His coming will change the world. Human intervention may temper or amend that change in some way, but essentially, human activity ceases to be meaningful in the sense in which we know it when God's will rules. Human action may change how that coming impinges on us as individuals (through salvation, for example), but the nature, extent and form of divine intervention usually remains beyond human control and influence. If we are sympathetic to the millenarian religious ideology, we might refer to the changes as supernatural; if we are less sympathetic, we might refer to them as magic. In any event, the change when it comes has an automatic quality in which humans as a category are largely either incidental or acted upon.

Secular millenarian notions do not, of course, anticipate supernatural change in the same way; change when it does come is through human action. Nevertheless, there are elements in common between secular and religious millenarianism in this respect. In both, the final outcome is often seen as inevitable, cataclysmic and total, arising out of the impending disastrous state of the world; in this respect, the quality of inevitability is important. Despite the fact that the secular millenarian does not have recourse to divine agency to effect change, nevertheless it is often asserted that it will come, and concepts like historical necessity are often drawn on to substitute in the secular world for the capacity of the divine to force change. The French revolutionary group, *Action Directe*, claim as justification for their acts the fact that '. . . they can regard the present with the insights of tomorrow . . . and recognise that the historical task of the communists – both as a faction and as an organised *avant garde* of the proletariat – is to understand the movement of capital in its entirety . . . to understand . . . the development of the revolutionary consciousness of the proletariat . . .'.[58] The special 'insight' of the processes of social change which the terrorist has implies a determinism that seems almost divine in character, a paradox that does not seem to affect the most atheist adherent. Marxist doctrine on historical progress can often seem to have this quality, and when absorbed into revolutionary ideology, it makes it possible for many of the qualities of religious millenarianism to occur within a secular context. A more obvious example of inevitability in this sense can be seen in some contemporary environmental movements. Our profligate use of natural resources, destroying 'the balance of nature', can acquire inevitable and apocalyptic qualities quite close to those often anticipated in explicitly religious movements.

These forces become even more potent when the millenarian leader begins to claim supernatural, if not divine, properties. Nazi Germany was largely a secular state, and Nazi ideology certainly did not propagate a Christian view of the world in any orthodox sense. Nevertheless, it did contain many deeply mystical elements (often expressed through the use of symbols in the rituals of membership in Nazi organisations) and made constant reference to the inevitability of the Nazi régime as a means of expressing the aspirations of the German people. In many ways, it substituted a form of nationalism for Christianity, where nature and the inevitability of eugenics substituted for Christ's intervention.

We can see how the inevitability of millenarian achievement relates to the concept of imminence. It can be expressed in terms of how the ideological contingencies relating behaviour to distant outcome are expressed. In the terms used by Malott,[59] and as noted earlier and discussed at length in Chapter 4, these forces may become evident as variables affecting the nature and degree of behavioural control which rules might exercise.

Fanaticism and Millenarianism

The attributes discussed above give some indication of the kinds of qualities we might expect to find when identifying a social movement as millenarian. Any given movement will not necessarily display all these qualities of course, nor are they all equally important. Their relative relevance may well change as a movement develops, and particular circumstance may well be more important in determining any balances that might emerge, rather than any particular formula. Our particular concern is not so much with the social forces they imply, however, but rather with how those forces might impinge on the individual, particularly in the context of political aspirations, and the development of violence.

We can identify a number of themes that might be relevant to our purpose, developing further the notion of the fanatic and how ideology affects fanatical behaviour. The totality of the millenarian view, and its undoubted profound significance for the adherent, can in part help to explain why we might be tempted to use the term fanatic to describe millenarian followers. If the world, as we know it, is about to come to an end in some cataclysmic way – if that change is inevitable, but through some action personal salvation is possible – if in the political and religious context it becomes possible to achieve power – if a leader focuses and helps us to realise this unique and profound potential – these are profound and all-embracing qualities. Is it surprising that when all these are expressed in a coherent ideology, the faithful follower may become so totally absorbed and involved that he shows those qualities such as focusing, a personalised view of the world and insensitivity, which we have described earlier in Chapter 2 as the attributes of a fanatic?

We can also see how the original religious meaning of fanatical takes form and substance in the context of millenarianism. But we can equally see that similar forces may become evident in a political and secular context. Burridge's view about the role of power as the principal quality of religion is one way of looking at this in the political context, resulting, of course, in the inevitable social conflict this may give rise to. But we can also see that secular millenarian aspirations draw on very similar attributes as religious millenarianism in so far as they might affect the individual. Both secular and divine aspirations seem to result in similar behavioural features.

In the context of the discussion of ideology in Chapter 4, and the proposition that ideology in behavioural terms can be characterised as rule-following behaviour, we can see how features of millenarianism can alter behavioural contingencies as examples of kinds and qualities of rules. Apocalyptic consequences clearly relate to strength or potency of outcomes in the behaviour-distant contingency relationships. Imminence similarity may relate to potency of outcome, as well as contributing to subsidiary contingencies. Empirical verification for these interpretations may well be difficult to achieve, but we can see directions for further development and exploration, drawing on a framework for understanding derived from a well established perspective. What otherwise may appear to be an inaccessible social process can now be seen as an element in the broader contingencies that control our behaviour.

Millenarianism, Fanaticism and Violence

In the above discussion, we have from time to time noted qualities of millenarianism that might relate to violent behaviour. Quite clearly the relationship between millenarianism and violence is complex. Millenarianism does not necessarily lead to violence, and there are numerous examples of millenarian movements which are peaceful and indeed avowedly non-violent. The Rappites are a good example of an historical movement showing these attributes. On the other hand, it seems that millenarianism can, under some conditions, at least become associated with violence. Interpretations of recent Shi'ite violence, for example, emphasise this.[60] We will argue below that there are in fact inevitable attributes of millenarian ideology, albeit in the context of other facilitating states, that actively contribute to violence.

We can see that millenarianism, when expressed at the individual level, may have qualities of the fanatical, as we have defined it earlier. What we term fanatical may well, of course, be the proper (in its context and in its own terms) expression of religious belief for that believer and others who share those beliefs. We must remember the issue of relativity in the nature of judgements about fanaticism here; the quality of excess that may appear to the non-initiate, for example, may simply be devotion to the initiate.

Whether millenarianism 'releases' those individual qualities we have identified as the attributes of fanaticism, or whether millenarianism complements and interacts with other determinants, is not clear. On the whole, the position favoured here is that millenarianism constitutes one of the complex of forces which contributes to what we term fanatical behaviour, as a critical element of the qualities of ideological, or 'rule-following' behaviour that characterises the fanatic. We may see this becoming evident in the way it might play a role in modifying the contingencies relating distant events to immediate behaviour, in the sense described in Chapter 4. In any event, we can see that millenarianism offers at the very least a vehicle for the expression and direction of fanatical behaviour, contributing to its intensity of expression, as well as its focus and character. What remains, is to consider the relationship between millenarianism and violence.

In our discussion of violence in Chapter 1, we noted that whilst violence is a ubiquitous feature of social life, its expression is on the whole bounded by constraints. There are generally accepted limits which restrain our actions, expressed both as moral limits and legal constraints. The frequent failure to keep within these limits in no way invalidates the general point that there are limits *to which we aspire*, the boundaries of which we can recognise when we have exceeded those limits. In behavioural terms, those limits clearly constitute examples of pliance rule-following behaviour as discussed earlier,[61] a behavioural contingency relating distant outcome to particular behaviour, the broader consequences of which can be seen in terms of facilitating, or even making possible, social living.

Millenarian ideologies are of course varied and there is no evidence of any universal qualities of violence that necessarily characterise millenarianism. Of course, where features of a particular millenarian ideology directly address constraints against violence, we would then expect there to be some effect on violent behaviour. Experience suggests that on the whole, where millenarian movements drawing on Christian ideology have any impact on these restraints, they take the form of a *strengthening* rather than a reduction in constraints. The Rappites, for example, illustrate how a Christian millenarian movement developed a *non-violent* ideology, resulting in the creation of a pacifist community.

However, this may disguise a very important issue. We have noted that millenarianism as it interests us involves belief in an *imminent* and *total* change in present conditions. Whatever particular ideological or religious perspective may develop to predict that end state, the notions of imminence and totality are fundamental qualities of millenarian movements. These notions must, however, of necessity impinge on the nature of the constraints that bind society (in behavioural terms, the rules we follow), if for no other reason that the constraints will shortly be replaced by other kinds of rules (those derived from the fulfilment of the particular millenarian ideology). We have noted already that amongst the Rappites, the more ardent believers abstained from sexual relations (a deviation from generally accepted behaviour appropriate in its context), not, it would appear, because of any special wish for purity, but because given the imminent end as they saw it, there was no need for sexual reproduction. Similarly, the pacificism that might characterise millenarian movements is itself, as Rapoport noted,[62] a breaking away from social constraints that allow the use of violence. '... whether one chooses pacifism or terror, one is still rejecting the existing conventions governing coercion ...'.[63]

This latter point is important when trying to understand the behavioural conditions that might occur in millenarian movements. Groups like the Rappites may well have led very orderly and ordered pacifist lives. But both the orderliness and the pacifism are not qualities that we normally find in human organisations, and they were not consistent with, nor related to, the social conditions in which they originally lived in the Upper Rhine. We can recognise this when we examine the conditions in which George Rapp led his followers to the New World.[64] Their move was no doubt the result of a complex of forces, one important one being the demands of the Elector of Württemberg for military service in support of the Emperor Napoleon Bonaparte. The pacifism of the Rappite sect came into conflict with the secular authorities in Württemberg, and steps were being taken to enforce military service on the Rappites at the time that they left for America. Had Rapp not led his followers away from the problem, would that community have remained pacifist and acquiesced to demands for military service, or would it have resisted enforced military service? It seems likely that the Rappites would not have acquiesced, and had they not avoided the problem by moving to America, perhaps we might remember the Rappites in terms of resistance and violence, rather than pacifism.

Of course any speculation about the potential for violence in the Rappite community is hypothetical, and cannot be answered from this distance. But in identifying the conditions in which we might pose that question, we can see one of the important elements that might lead the millenarian into violence. Popper,[65] in his discussion of utopia and violence, notes that a quality of utopianism (which in our terms we will refer to as millenarianism) is its certainty, and its imperviousness to what he terms 'rational' or 'reasonable' argument. In the behavioural terms we have used here, the contingency rules which control millenarian behaviour are both powerful and 'easy-to-follow' (in the terms used by Malott[66]), and supported by probable and sizeable subsidiary contingencies. If you know you are right, then the give and take associated with argument cannot exist, because from the millenarian perspective, there is nothing to argue about – all is certainty!

Behavioural Processes

We have expressed above the links between fanaticism, millenarianism and violence in behavioural terms. In any millenarian ideology, ideological precepts are explicit and firm. They are also necessarily rigid, in that they specify *the* route to attain the millenarian ideal. In behavioural terms, we can express this as fixed and rigid powerful rules. They are also probably 'easy-to-follow' rules, and therefore exert very powerful control over behaviour. Changing circumstances, changing environmental constraints, all of which might. reflect changes in the contingencies which might normally be expected to influence these rules, now no longer produce the subtle changes of accommodation that characterise everyday life. Imminent attainment of the millenarian end further exacerbates the nature and extent of behavioural control by ideologically determined rules. Thus we see an increasing spiral of control, resulting in the focusing, etc., which we associate with fanaticism.

Secular millenarian groups concerned with political change share these forces with religious millenarianism. However, the inevitable social focus of a political millenarian movement (of the right or left) gives rise to further issues which may exaggerate the control exercised by rule-governed contingencies. When faced with the pressure to implement the social change that millenarian political aspirations might demand, we know that if that pressure persists, society may begin to adopt more and more coercive measures in response. But by causing social and political unrest, or failing to comply with government injunctions in some way, we see a further pressure towards violence. Most states reserve the right to enforce compliance when faced with what, to the executive, is intransigent opposition. Indeed, the police, as one of the major organs for enforcing social order, specifically have the right to *enforce* compliance when compliance is not forthcoming.[67] Experience suggests that, eventually, social groups that resist social or political pressures are either coerced into compliance or more rarely, the groups move away from social confrontation.

But, of course, the normal limits to behaviour, expressed in immediate contingency control, no longer apply, *because* of the nature of millenarian behavioural rules. One result of this is that the limits on possible responses to violence too may no longer be effective. Given these conditions, all that is left for a political millenarian group is forceful rejection of compromise and, when conditions facilitate it, violence. We can look on this as an example of punishment learning. We know that when faced with aversive consequences, an organism seeks to avoid those aversive consequences, either by escape (which is effectively what Rapp did), learning a new response (denied by millenarian ideology through the control it exerts over present behaviour), or through aggression. Where no escape is possible, aversive events lead to violence, in this case untempered by the normal contingencies limiting the expression of violent behaviour.

This brief argument also enables us to understand why, as Rapoport notes, many millenarian movements which begin life as pacifist communities later turn to violence. Where pacifism is the behavioural response to a millenarian ideology (as distinct from, say, a moral or social ideology), interaction with a society that places demands upon the millenarian community will, in time, result in resistance to those demands, if they impinge on, and conflict with, some critical element of millenarian ideology. At this point, we might expect the community either to withdraw physically (and perhaps relocate), removing the pressure from itself, or become militant.

Not all millenarian ideologies are the same, of course, and within any given community the relationship between ideology as expressed in contingency rules and behaviour may well change over time. Similarly, militancy does not necessarily imply violence against others; it might result in non-violent passive resistance or, as we will consider at some length later, it might mean violence against the person themselves, culminating in martyrdom. The quality of imminence may again be important here, and the extent and expression of violence may be related to measures of imminence. This in its turn, however, will be related to the relationship between the achievement

of millenarian aspirations and human action. In religious millenarianism, the possibility of divine intervention regardless of human action
is always there. Millenarian groups are often vague and uncertain
about the relationship between divine and human intervention, and
this might well attenuate the extent and nature of action through
imminence. In contrast, in political millenarianism, there is a sense in
which human agency and action can necessarily directly influence the
advent of millenarian conditions (outside of notions like historical
necessity, inevitable crises of capitalism, or catastrophic environmental change).

The political millenarian, therefore, may well be ideologically more
susceptible to violence as an agent for hastening change, because in
the secular world of affairs it is possible to hasten the political
millenarian event in a way not always available to the religious. The
political millenarian is also likely to be concerned with social structure, and thereby impinge on areas of political and executive power
(which the religious millenarian is not so likely to do). He is, therefore, much more likely to encounter agencies for social control (like
the police) who may well respond to his activities with violence. We
can see, therefore, the development, if only in outline, of a series of
reciprocal relationships that will drive and create violent conditions
for the political millenarian, and sometimes, but more rarely, for the
religious millenarian also.

The critical issues that are relevant to our considerations, therefore,
are the totality of millenarian ideology, and the notion of imminence
in millenarian achievement. We might even represent this as the basic
equation relating violence to ideology. In themselves, both conditions
do not necessarily give rise to violence in the form with which we are
concerned. But when combined with themselves, and perhaps aug-
mented by other qualities, they become the necessary, but not sufficient, reasons for the expression of violence. The particular qualities
of ideology that are relevant to this equation have already been
considered in Chapter 4. We now move on in the next chapter to
consider and extend our discussion of the other variable in the
equation, the notion of totality in ideology.

CHAPTER 6

The Totality of Ideology: Public Space

Public space is introduced as a factor in the development of political violence. Public space refers to the circumstances whereby people gain and maintain their sense of reality. Lack of public space is related to the development of political violence through behavioural mechanisms of rule following. The chapter ends with an overview of the preceding three chapters.

In Chapter 4 we indicated behavioural mechanisms to describe the control that ideology can exercise over behaviour. In some circumstances, we noted that the controlling forces (expressed technically as contingency rules) can exercise very powerful, even total, control over behaviour. Thus we see behaviour becoming very ideologically focused, to the extent that we might say that it shows attributes of political fanaticism. The extent to which fanatical behaviour is narrowly directed towards highly specific objectives, we have suggested to be the result of control exercised by powerful rule-governed contingencies that serve to relate behaviour to distant ideologically defined behavioural goals. In the particular context of a militant ideology, this can clearly result in the expression of violence *as part of* the behaviour controlled by ideological rules. In that sense, therefore, ideology itself, and particular content attributes of ideology, can lead to violence.

There is an additional sense in which we can relate ideology to enhanced probability of occurrence of violence. This is not because of ideological prescription as such (in the sense of militancy of millenarianism as ideological content), but because of the way in which the particular rules expressing ideological qualities exercise control. Imminence as an element of millenarianism has been discussed in

Chapter 5 in this context as a quality of how a particular kind of ideology affects behaviour, as well as having relevant elements of content that might facilitate violence. We can extend this part of our discussion further by considering another rule-related quality, referring on this occasion to the extent and nature of the control ideology might exercise over behaviour. The degree to which a particular ideology influences not just specific political or religious behaviour, but extends to all forms of behaviour, whether directly related to ideology or not, can be termed the totality of ideological control. This can be identified as a process variable of a kind similar to millenarianism in describing the influence of ideology over behaviour in general and violence in particular. As such, it is the second element of the equation (along with millenarianism) relating violence to ideology referred to in Chapter 5. In this chapter we will explore this sense of totality of rule control.

Public Space

We will use the discussions by Hannah Arendt of her concept of *'public space'* as our starting point for this exploration of totality of ideological control as a process variable. Arendt uses the term public space to refer to the nature and extent of social and political interaction and communication available to a person. Public space is '. . . the space within the world which men need in order to appear . . .'.[1] In a more general sense, public space might be defined as 'the availability of any sort of mental or physical forum within which free debate can exist without fear of sanction'. This concept is introduced and developed at some length in a number of her works, notably in *The Human Condition*.[2] She uses the concept of public space to refer to a conceptual space rather than a real physical space (although the conceptual space and an actual physical arena in which political activity might take place might from time to time coincide). It refers to what Parekh describes as 'a space of appearance',[3] in which men act, 'see and be seen, acknowledge and be acknowledged by others'. Importantly, it is a way of conceptualising the capacity of people to discuss and compare their interpretations of the world. Arendt regards this capacity to interact with others as a critical factor in the development of our sense of reality. In the absence of public space, an individual *loses* all sense of reality and becomes disorientated. This essentially philosophical observation has profound implications for our understanding of the behavioural processes which underlie the origins of political violence, as we will see later in this discussion. We might note that the emphasis on interactive qualities presumably also reflects her overriding concern with political life as a form of interaction between people. Interestingly, her emphasis on 'public' seems to imply an essentially behavioural framework – public space as the world of appearances is also the world of behaviour, as opposed to other less accessible inner and mentalistic psychological states.

Arendt's views are closely related to her interpretation of the events that resulted in the Nazi atrocities, and the influence of her early work in this area is apparent, especially her paper *The Concentration Camps*[4] and the book *Origins of Totalitarianism.*[5] She expresses and develops these ideas further in her account of the trial of Adolph Eichmann, the discussion of which is particularly relevant to our concern with fanaticism.[6]

Arendt uses the idea of public space to illustrate the political and psychological effects of totalitarian political organisation on individuals. As a political theorist, her particular concern is with the nature of political life, and the expression of that life in social organisation. However, her work has a bearing on psychological interpretations of how political ideology influences what we can (and cannot) do. In her view, for example, the atrocities of the Nazi era can only be understood in terms of the influence of ideology on behaviour, and she uses the concepts of public space to illustrate how ideological processes resulting in totalitarian regimes like the Third Reich might function. She similarly, although probably rather less successfully, extends her analysis to the conditions prevalent in the Soviet Union at the time of Stalin, drawing parallels between Stalinist Soviet Union and Nazi Germany in terms of both general social conditions and the particular extreme conditions of the concentration camps of Nazi Germany and the labour camps of the Stalinist Soviet Union.

As she develops the concept of public space, it does not particularly make reference to psychological concepts, although it is certainly expressed within a broad psychologically orientated framework. Her starting point, however, remains an analysis not of psychology, but of politics based upon psychological qualities. This means that her work is not constrained by any particular systematic psychological position (although she certainly makes psychological assumptions). It also means, however, that her work does not readily fall into or correspond with psychological structures as explanations, and this may present something of a problem for our purposes.

Notwithstanding the above, implicit psychological assumptions can be discerned in Arendt's work, and she seems to have been predominantly influenced by both humanistic psychology and the European psychodynamic traditions. Contemporary thinking about her work tends to emphasise these approaches[7] and she is frequently referred to as belonging to the phenomenological tradition. Such perspectives might be thought to conflict with those adopted in this work, and indeed it seems likely that she would have rejected the scientific empirical and behavioural framework developed in this book. In her paper on the concentration camps,[8] she seems to be asserting that both the concentration camp guards and inmates (as people who have experienced what she terms 'unimaginable' violence) are '... men who can no longer be psychologically understood ...', by what she refers to as 'commonsense' methods. Her dismissal of 'commonsense' seems to imply a dismissal of scientific psychology in understanding the horrors of that time, because of the sheer magnitude of the affront to human existence exemplified by the concentration camps.

We can, of course, distinguish between the assumptions Arendt might have made in developing her concepts, and the utility of the concepts themselves. Whether or not her analytical assumptions correspond to those of this work, her concept of public space does have considerable value in the behavioural context adopted here. Therefore, despite any reservations implied by her position about the approach adopted here, we will draw on her concepts, but attempt to place them within a more scientific and behavioural framework.

She suggests that public space has three essential attributes; in their absence, it cannot occur. These attributes she identifies as human *plurality*, *speech*, and what she terms *public objects*. By *plurality*, she means the extent to which men are free to act independently of others. In Arendt's terms, freedom for the individual is characterised by the capacity of that individual to do different things from other individuals, or to express and act upon different views. This does not mean that free actions are necessarily independent of others, or unrelated to the actions of other people. But it does seem to imply that there is the capacity (or perhaps potential) for such to become independent of others. This seems to be most obviously expressed in political debate. In this sense, therefore, the 'space of appearance' which seems to be so critical an element of Arendt's views on public space is essentially a forum for reciprocal debate, rather than doctrinal assertion. Parekh illustrates plurality[9] by using an example of a slave. The slave lacks the element of plurality, for he is the master's property, and is unable to do things independently of his master. In a sense, the slave's views are simply an extension of his master's (or are treated as such by others). Furthermore, the slave has no capacity or prospect of changing these conditions. The very nature of slavery denies the plurality essential to the creation of public space.

An analogy with a slave appears in Arendt's paper on the concentration camps.[10] In it, she compared the position of the concentration camp victim to the slave, and noted that the inmate of the concentration camp was in fact in a worse position than the slave, in that the camp inmate not only lacked freedom, but was also withdrawn from sight, and therefore withdrawn from the protection and knowledge of men. The capacity to interact publicly with others (not simply people outside of the camp, but between inmates as well) was literally and figuratively removed from the concentration camp inmate to an extreme degree. 'The concentration camp inmate has no price, because he can always be replaced and he belongs to no one ... he is absolutely superfluous.'[11] The inmate quite literally lacked value, and a symptom of this is amongst other things the lack of the attribute of plurality, the capacity to act independently of others.

Plurality seems to be used in this sense in ways related to the use made by both Skinner[12] and Burridge[13] of the concept of freedom, noted in Chapter 5. Arendt's concept of plurality seems quite closely related to Burridge's notion of 'lack of obligation', and to Skinner's notions of 'lack of aversive control'. Indeed, in some senses Skinner's interpretations seem to be particularly close to Arendt's. Although as we have noted, Arendt did not express her concepts in behavioural terms, there is frequently an implicit acceptance of the importance of behavioural referrents for many of her concepts, and she acknowledges what appears to be the importance of the environmental context in which behaviour takes place. Nowhere is this more so than in her discussion of the concept of public space, with its emphasis on essentially interactive behavioural qualities.

Plurality in the way in which she uses it implies a capacity to communicate, and Arendt suggests that this is a second element of public space. She uses the term *speech* to refer to this, but communication seems in fact to be a better way of expressing this attribute, for she does not appear to intend to limit it to speech alone, but includes other forms of communication, such as writing. She suggests that speech in a sense *creates* a conceptual space between people, by using language in some form which makes communication possible. Presumably this also includes all the additional social and cultural assumptions implied by language structures, etc.[14] Furthermore, she notes that the more formal speech is, evidenced for example by the use of ritual, the more it in fact creates and enhances distance between speakers. Paradoxically, however, speech also serves to *bridge* the conceptual space by *allowing* communication as interaction and argument.

The analogy of the bridge is important to the way Arendt links the concepts of public space and speech. As in real situations, a bridge can separate people, but it is also the means of bringing people together. In Arendt's terms, argument and reasoned opposition (in the political context she is primarily referring to, but perhaps we could also extend it in a more social context), serves the very important function of creating public space. But the language in which argument is expressed, and in which replies, interaction, as reciprocity might take place, also serve to 'bridge' the gaps between people. To this extent, it diminishes the extent of conceptual public space and reduces plurality. Arendt seems to imply that agreement between people reduces the extent of human plurality, presumably by reducing the extent to which an individual can act independently of others. This seems to suggest that her ideal image of political society seems, therefore, to be one in which people argue rather than necessarily agree. Paradoxically, democratic decision making, as we are used to it in social democracies of the West, followed by defined and agreed action acted upon by an executive, seems by definition in these terms to reduce public space.

The third attribute for the creation of public space which Arendt identifies as necessary are *public objects*. She uses the term public in this sense to refer to common objects, that is to say, things which are in principle available to all. They are external to the individual, and exist independently of the individuals involved. As objects, they might be physical (as in public parks and items of household furniture) or they can be conceptual (as in laws and institutions). Public objects enable public space to be created. Using the analogy of the bridge again, public objects both create differences and reduce differences through allowing shared access by virtue of being public. Public objects thus always provide the focus, and perhaps the stimulus, for the development of public space. The three essential features of public space are therefore brought together in the sense that it is '. . . when independent men come together to talk about public objects . . .' that creates public space.[15]

The relevance of public space for our concern with the role of ideology in behavioural control lies with the occasions when circumstances conspire to produce, in Arendt's terms, an *absence* of public space. When deprived of public space, '. . . an individual's life acquires an eerie sense of unreality, as happens in a mass society and under tyranny when isolated individuals, thrown back on themselves, live a "shadowy" existence and search for reality in intense private sensations or acts of violence'.[16] It has long been recognised that the crowd, for example, significantly alters the nature of the controls over an individual's behaviour. Within a crowd, behaviour which would be inappropriate for the individual seems to be facilitated, and crowd membership appears to reduce or alter the limits to the expression of socially extreme or otherwise inappropriate behaviour. Le Bon[17] recognised this, and a recent resurgence of interest has emphasised the relevance of Le Bon's earlier observations.[18] In her discussion of the absence of public space, Arendt seems to be referring to processes analogous to those that operate in the crowd.

Authors such as Le Bon have used concepts like hypnosis to explain the attributes of lack of public space. In her discussion of these issues, Arendt does not use these same conceptual and psychological structures. Rather she suggests that it is the sense of unreality resulting from lack of public space which limits, or abolishes, what Arendt terms the capacity to *think*. By thinking, interestingly, she seems to adopt almost a naive behavioural notion of 'silent dialogue', a form of internal speech which parallels external speech as communication. Thinking in this sense, however, is not always used by Arendt in the same way in which it might be in a psychological sense. To Arendt, thinking seems to be an important *conceptual* notion, rather than referring to what we might call the psychological process of thinking. Thinking, in her sense, is more a quality of plurality (referred to above) than a necessary psychological phenomenon. It seems in part to refer to the common ground of public objects which, within a given culture, we all in some sense access.

She refers to Adolf Eichmann, for example, as someone deprived of public space both by circumstance and his own actions, and who because of that lost the capacity to think. She does not, however, seem to mean this in any technical or public psychological sense. Whatever cognitive processes Eichmann possessed presumably remained.

Rather, she seems to suggest that Eichmann was, in a sense, unfree to move or act outside of the narrowly defined conceptual boundaries created by himself, his immediate environment and the ideology he was exposed to. Thus, in some way, what she refers to as his loss of 'thinking' might as readily be expressed as a loss of sense of perspective. He was unable to relate his activities to the broader situation. In Eichmann's own accounts, written by himself in Argentina, and the transcriptions of police examinations in Jerusalem, she notes[19] his frequent use of clichés to describe the reasons for his actions. His trial judges referred to this, when they told him that all he said was 'empty talk', the implication being that he was deviously covering up his real thoughts. But Arendt notes that '. . . the longer one listened to him, the more obvious it became that his inability to speak was closely connected with an inability to *think*, namely, to think from the standpoint of someone else'.[20] The qualification of the final part of that quotation is of some significance, and gives some further indication of Arendt's use of thinking. We can see in particular reference to the fundamental role of both communication *and* public objects. This is developed further in the following quotation about Eichmann, drawing together all the three elements of public space which she describes: '. . . no communication was possible with him, not because he lied, but because he was surrounded by the most reliable of all safeguards against the words and presence of others, and hence against reality as such'.

Clichés might be thought of as a form of automatic speech. They are a ready made response to situations where we do not have to reason out a response. They often take their origin from a simplified version of a world view, and allow the user to appear to offer views which are in reality little more than evasions. The typical political interview is replete with clichés of this kind, and illustrates what Arendt means by lack of thinking. As a form of communication, clichés avoid the need to discuss, but allow the participant to take part in the process of discussion. They sustain the façade of communication, shorn of content or genuine affect.

The absence of thinking, as a limitation on both external and internal speech, Arendt relates directly to the occurrence of atrocities in general, but specifically to atrocities resulting from the Nazi régime and Stalin's régime in the Soviet Union. In her view, the absence of public space which resulted from Nazi totalitarianism, for example, meant that the Germans were unable to exchange opinions, and in particular express the dissent and argument necessary for the production of public space as referred to above. The absence of public space also limited the extent to which behaviour was controlled by moral and historical public rules that might limit the expression of violence or the acquisition of socially appropriate behaviour. Arendt seems to argue that through the absence of public space, the independence of action (which we call freedom) becomes limited. In this context, she relates the concept of freedom to the capacity and ability to behave and to express ideas in a social context through communication. This absence results, in her view, in the conditions that enable and facilitate the expression of extremes of violence.

Arendt argues, therefore, that the absence of public space is an important element in political organisation and political theory. Its relevance for our purposes lies in its being a quality of political ideology, for it is in the social expression of ideology that the conditions for enhancing, or limiting, public space occur. We have noted that much of Arendt's work draws on examples from Nazi Germany, where its particular ideology embodied many of the features of lack of public space – severe and coercive limitation on the expression of dissent, and virtually no opportunity for critical analysis of Nazi actions. The almost total lack of resistance to the Nazi State illustrates, in Arendt's terms, its success in limiting public space.

The more obvious and dramatic examples of loss of public space in the political arena inevitably focus on large political units. By becoming the government of the country, for example, the Nazi Party was able to impose its ideology on others, thereby producing the conditions that are symptomatic of loss of public space. But we need not assume public space to be *only* a quality of large numbers or national political processes. Similar effects in much more modest circumstances can be seen in the ways in which some political organisations control their members. Such organisations generally lack opportunity to coerce a large population, but they effectively control and limit the actions of those sympathetic enough to their ideals to become involved. The Irish terrorist group, the Provisional IRA, and its associated political party, Sinn Fein, exercises an intense authoritarian ideological control over its members in ways which lend themselves to interpretations in terms of lack of public space. The mechanisms of control extend from group pressure to physical coercion, and ultimately death.[21] A similar analysis of some extreme religious sects might also be appropriate.

Related Psychological Concepts

Because it is developed within a different theoretical and disciplinary framework (principally political theory), the concept of public space lacks a clear psychological frame of reference. The three critical attributes – plurality, speech and public objects – allude to concepts that may have psychological referrents, but quite clearly embrace political and social assumptions as well. Furthermore, as far as Arendt was concerned, these latter assumptions were probably more important to her overall analysis than any attempts at placing them within psychological theorising. Indeed, as we noted earlier, at a more profound level Arendt's more general writings would also suggest that she would reject the determinism that generally characterises empirical and scientific psychological analyses.

On the other hand, the idea of public space, and the psychological forces it seems to imply, does readily fit into social psychological thinking in a number of ways, in particular in the area of group behaviour. Furthermore, in the context of our analysis of fanaticism, it does seem to supplement and augment the account of developmental processes introduced in Chapter 3. The kinds of forces identified in that chapter may well represent both the manifestation of lack of what Arendt characterises as public space at the psychological level, and furthermore indicate psychological processes that might contribute to the restriction of public space.

One obvious area of psychological relationship with the concept of public space lies in analyses of prejudice which were discussed at some length in Chapter 3. The processes which are related to Arendt's concept of public space readily relate to the prejudiced individual, particularly with respect to the self-confirming nature of prejudice. The notion of plurality, for example, seems to be compromised by the existence of stereotypes, which limit and shape the views an individual has, regardless of how actual events might impinge or relate to those views. Similarly, the selectivity of attributes on which to focus, so critical in the self-confirming cycle of prejudice, also readily relates to Arendt's notions of plurality and communication. Indeed, the process we might identify here clearly serves to link Arendt's concepts with the psychological bases of fanaticism considered earlier.

As a quality of particular ideological parameters, public space seems to be an 'involvement' factor (in the sense described in Chapter 3). In fact, it might be thought of as characterising in a political sense the extent to which the kind of ideological developmental processes identified earlier are exercising control over behaviour. Psychological traps, for example, may well serve to polarise views, but they also might be characterised as diminishing through their action public space. In this sense, psychological traps serve to reduce the sense of plurality, a concept which as we have seen Arendt regards as essential to the maintenance of public space. They might be thought to do this in two ways. First, by increasing the control which *historical* choices have over behaviour, and secondly, by so doing, diminishing the extent to which individual 'choice' in contemporary action becomes possible. Such limitations on possible choices for action must inevitably diminish the extent to which an individual is capable of acting independently of others, at least to the extent that others have shared common experiences. Similarly, the 'trap' qualities of decision making also become apparent in areas like communication, influencing and limiting 'the space of appearance'.[22]

The forces we have described above also have elements in common with what has been termed 'groupthink'[23] (referred to briefly in Chapter 3). Groupthink refers to 'the deterioration of mental efficiency, reality testing and moral judgement resulting from group pressure'. When groupthinking occurs, decision makers seem to lose contact with the circumstances around them, and see themselves as invulnerable, believing that they simply cannot make mistakes. It occurs in highly cohesive groups led by dynamic leaders, where the tendency to hold on to shared views becomes so strong that they totally ignore external information which is inconsistent with their views. This concept has been used to help to explain the disastrous attempt at invasion of Cuba at the Bay of Pigs in 1961 by CIA-trained Cuban exiles, which was followed through in circumstances which seem to indicate a significant degree of separation and unresponsiveness from the realities of the political and military situation involved. In some ways, the concept of groupthink seems to parallel closely the effects of lack of public space.

Indeed, we could go further than the above, and assert that membership of any group, and exposure to the forces operating within groups, inevitably results in some measure of reduction of public space in the sense used by Arendt. Given that almost everything we do is related in some way to group membership, or has a group quality to it, this means that the potential for restriction on our 'conceptual' public space is considerable. This may become apparent at the simplest of levels. Co-operative activity, for example, a ubiquitous quality of social living, necessarily restricts the extent of choice available to an individual. In psychological terms, the processes involved in co-operation have been characterised as 'social exchanges'. What is exchanged may vary from actual goods and services, to less tangible qualities of relationships, such as love, status, and information.[24] The dimensions along which such exchanges take place (co-operation-competition, bargaining and perceived fairness or equity) are familiar features of our normal social interaction. But the very lawfulness of these processes necessarily limits the qualities of plurality in Arendt's terms.

Perhaps the most obvious area in which social psychological forces might be thought to impinge on the development of public space, however, is in the area of conformity and social influence. In these circumstances the social processes we observe explicitly and actively limit plurality, by constraining, influencing or changing the choices we might make in systematic ways. In the sense used above by Parekh,[25] these forces indeed make slaves of us. In a political context, these forces are of considerable importance. It might be argued that politics is necessarily concerned with influence, and similarly that it is necessarily a social phenomenon. Analyses of group forces of this kind, therefore, reflect upon the very essence of political life. Group forces may represent a common ground therefore between political theory and psychology.

The situations in which we find ourselves of course exercise considerable influence on us – in a social sense, perhaps the most powerful focus of all influences are towards conformity, compliance and obedience. Conformity occurs when behaviour changes to adhere to accepted standards or beliefs. In a sense, therefore, conformity can characterise the nature of non-coercive social influence over us. We might characterise the ebb and flow of political life in these terms. In contrast, compliance and obedience imply a more directive and perhaps coercive quality, where behaviour changes as a result of direct requests (in the case of conformity) or commands (in the case of obedience).

Conformity is a pervasive quality of life. It is neither good nor bad in itself, but simply a quality of social interaction observable in all societies. The expression and features of social conformity, however, may well vary from place to place and from time to time. We may not even be aware that the norms of behaviour we follow are in fact examples of conformity to social rules. British and American habits of queuing, for example, reflect such conformity. Following these rules can appear so natural and obvious a feature of social organisation that it can come as a profound shock when visiting countries where different patterns of queuing take place. In that context, pushing to the front in a queue is not necessarily the rude and anti-social behaviour it might be in the United Kingdom or the United States. Queuing behaviour is a rather trivial example, but nevertheless real, of social influence and conformity. But conformity has also been shown to exercise a control over behaviour in much more disturbing ways. Experimental evidence suggests that conformity can materially affect and amend the judgements an individual makes in groups,[26] by influencing judgements in accord with group views rather than personal views, even where these conflict with objective evidence. The concept of groupthink discussed above of course illustrates this. That the extent of conformity is influenced by the nature of the group (attraction of the influencing group, its size, the presence or absence of social support and the sex of that social support) merely confirms the systematic qualities of the power it might exercise over behaviour.

Compliance with a direct request represents probably the most frequent example of social influence. Whilst compliance to a request may seem a rather obvious way of changing behaviour, we should note that in the main, social compliance does not occur in the absence of a preliminary context that both sets the scene for compliance and makes it more likely. Such scene setting may also serve to diminish our awareness of the extent of such compliance. Two factors are conventionally identified which result in enhanced compliance – ingratiation and multiple requests. Ingratiation refers to increasing the extent to which an individual is liked by the decision maker, because we tend to follow the instructions of those who we like. 'Like' is used in this sense in a rather broad way, referring to those qualities of individuals that lead us to rate them favourably, such as shared opinions or excellence in some task performance. Another important related quality to this, which has a double-edged element to it, is what is termed 'other-enhancement' – a rather grand word for flattery or undeserved and exaggerated praise for others. The value of 'being a good listener' in ensuring compliance is probably also related to this. Multiple requests increase compliance in rather different ways, in that an initial request, regardless of outcome, serves to increase the likelihood of subsequent compliance. The 'foot-in-the-door, small request first, large request later' type of high pressure salesmanship is an example of this technique applied to compliance to buy something.

The most obvious sense, however, in which compliance can be

achieved is through issuing a direct order as a *command*. In this respect, context is important, and the most effective command is achieved when authority figures are in some sense involved in issuing orders. The military is one very obvious example of this (where interestingly uniforms in a general way probably contribute to this), as are bosses in a business organisation, and referees in sporting events. Even relatively mild authority situations, however, can induce compliance with commands through obedience, sometimes to quite extraordinary effect. The most famous experiments that have demonstrated this were performed by Milgram[27] and his colleagues where it was demonstrated that volunteer subjects would take commands from an experimenter to inflict apparent pain on innocent experimental subjects. The typical experimental situation used is well known. Milgram instructed volunteers in an experiment on the effects of punishment on learning to administer increasingly severe electric shocks to a learner if he made mistakes. The learner was in fact a confederate of the experimenters, and no actual electric shocks were administered (the learner faked pain). But the volunteers were not aware of this, and a staggering 65 per cent complied with the orders of the experimenter to continue administering shocks which they thought were 450 volts at their highest!

Milgram's experiments have had an important influence on discussions of the nature of authority and the extent to which individuals can be induced to inflict pain and apparent damage on others. The work has been used as evidence to help explain, for example, the apparent compliance of the Nazi guards in the concentration camps, who performed unthinkable atrocities '... because they were ordered to ...'. We will analyse this particular issue further elsewhere, but we might note the following factors appear important in determining compliance in these experiments:

> ▷ the experimenter was of 'high' status (and wore a form of uniform associated with status, a white coat);
> ▷ the experimenter explained that he (not the volunteers) was responsible for what might happen; and
> ▷ the degree of apparent electric shock incrementally increased, representing a form of psychological trap.

These specific factors readily relate to more generally applicable frameworks.

The ideas discussed above have been explored to some extent in terms of analyses of the development of people involved in systematic torture of prisoners. Haritos-Fatouros,[28] for example, describes the training procedures used for military police by the Government in Greece during the time of the military dictatorship from 1967 to 1974. The analysis was based on the official court records of the trial of participants, and interviews with 16 ex-military policemen. Haritos-Fatouros extends the analysis presented by Milgram somewhat, to include their selection procedures, the binding factors to authority which produced group cohesion, and the learning mechanisms involved. However, his analysis is consistent with that offered here, in terms of the importance of learning processes in the production of the deviant behaviour.

Features of social behaviour such as conformity, compliance and command act upon us in systematic ways. They are aspects of normal social intercourse, and in the main cause us relatively little concern. That they influence in Arendt's terms the nature and extent of human plurality cannot be denied. But in practical terms and under normal circumstances in the sense of the political framework she was referring to, their influence is limited. However, the issue we are confronting is not one where circumstances are normal, but rather circumstances where forces towards extremes are already apparent and where a complex of factors related to the psychological effects of ideology interact. In these circumstances, we can see quite clearly how factors related to the concept of public space can quite successfully crystallise and focus these forces.

We can also examine these issues from a slightly different perspective, emphasising not so much the general social context to the forces we are concerned with, but their specific organisational context. We tend not to think of informal social groups as forms of organisational structure, retaining the latter to describe the more formal business or commercial structures that are established to serve a particular purpose. However, the directive and controlling nature of groups (even if informal) clearly lend themselves for consideration within the 'purposive' framework of political fanaticism.

Crenshaw[29] has discussed the importance of organisational pressures within the context of terrorist groups which is of particular relevance to our concerns here. She contrasts analyses of terrorist groups which assume their purposiveness to be related to their overall *external* ideological goals, with analyses that see terrorist groups as being responsive to *internal* organisational pressures, rather than *external* ideological priorities. Both factors may from time to time be identified, and sometimes presumably these both lead to the same actions. Indeed, in practice it may be difficult to distinguish between them. But for our purposes, to be able to make such a distinction may be very important. Crenshaw suggests that the terrorist group functions like any other organisation, which over time acquires as its principal priority its own survival. This analysis is very compelling when contemporary terrorist groups are considered. The Provisional IRA, for example, appears to have steadily diminishing popular support, and consistently and embarrassingly fails to gain significant public representation in either Northern Ireland elections or elections in the Republic of Ireland. It seems to be an organisation that is locked into a struggle not for justice in Northern Ireland, but for its own existence. That sometimes this coincides with broader political aspirations increasingly appears to be accidental, or at least subsidiary to the task of sustaining its own existence. However we express it, we can see here another sense in which the effects of lack of public space become evident in an organisational setting.

Indeed, once this is recognised, other aspects of terrorist behaviour become more readily understood. Cordes,[30] for example, has drawn attention to qualities of terrorist communications about their actions, in terms of such things as press releases and newspaper articles. She notes that whilst they are usually about an action aimed at some broader political objective of some form (a bombing or shooting, for example, of a representative target), paradoxically analysis of the contents of communications suggest that their target audience is frequently not the oppressed group they claim to represent, nor the society victimised in some way by their action, *but their own supporters.* She terms this the 'autopropaganda' aspect of terrorist communications. We can readily see that 'autopropaganda' complements and extends both Crenshaw's analysis briefly discussed above, and the analysis presented in this chapter. In the terms we have used here, it illustrates the inward focusing which characterises lack of public space.

This analysis, therefore, complements that offered above, and allows us to see another perspective on the notion of public space. The increasing and probably inevitable pressure of the organisational forces to begin to exercise their own influence at the expense of ideological priorities merely serves to substitute one form of totality of control over another. It is an interesting speculation to consider whether in such circumstances we effectively see an enhancement of the extent of organisational control, thereby further diminishing what we have termed public space.

Behavioural Interpretations of Public Space

The above offers some reflections on the nature of psychological forces related to the concept of public space. Through analyses of group behaviour, we can begin to see the nature of ideological control in the context of Arendt's analysis of public space as it might be expressed in social psychological terms. We can, however, further extend our analysis by adopting a slightly different perspective, developed from the behavioural accounts already introduced. Chapter 4 offered an account of the effects of ideology on behaviour which described ideologically determined behaviour as a form of complex control-reflecting rule following, as distinct from control of behaviour by immediate contingencies. Strength of ideological control was related to the extent to which behaviour came under the control of such rule-governed behaviour, perhaps to the exclusion of sensitivity to direct-acting contingencies. We can extend our appreciation of Arendt's notion of public space in similar terms. What Arendt describes as public space may be seen as a description in terms of political theory of the conditions that facilitate the development of, and sensitivity to, direct-acting contingencies. Plurality, speech and common objects are all ways of describing from a political perspective aspects of the environment that facilitate immediate sensitivity to circumstances. They all refer in some measure to the reciprocal and generally immediate state of controlling and being controlled that describes social interaction in Arendt's implied ideal political forum.

In contrast, where ideology becomes all important, as in the circumstances Arendt refers to as totalitarianism, perhaps what we see is the overwhelming influence and power of behaviour controlled by ideological rules at the expense of reciprocity and immediate contingency control. We can see this in a number of ways. For example, amongst other things, the distant explicit ends of the Nazi State reduced those features of the environment that might temper the restraints that limit our behaviour in relation to others. Where ideology defines a group of people as inferior (the Jews, for example), those features of the environment which regulate our relations with that group become lessened, changed or eliminated. In those circumstances, the expected immediate reciprocal behavioural consequences of encountering Jews does not occur. Jews who fail to meet the negative stereotypes, for example, and are friendly or helpful or in other respects like other 'more approved' people, have no effect on behaviour, because such local and immediate circumstances exert less control over behaviour than more negative ideologically defined rules. Ideological prescriptions substitute for other controlling forces, and in particular, the reciprocity that determines our social life is either abolished or attenuated. We can see, therefore, the diminution of public space in the political sense as the shift in behavioural control from reciprocal immediate contingency control to rule-governed behavioural control.

Analyses of this at the political level are lacking. Furthermore, whilst it may be possible to illustrate the processes using examples (as indeed we do in later chapters), those examples necessarily lack the strength of empirical exploration. We can, however, also explore by analogy what this might mean by looking at examples outside of the political context of states of lack of reciprocal control, where there is relevant experimental and empirical evidence to help our discussion. By exploring the expression of these forces in analogous situations, we can better understand their parameters.

One way in which we can illustrate the behavioural qualities of public space is by considering the circumstances of an individual who has no interaction with the world. Such a person by definition lacks public space. Arendt in fact uses as an illustration of this state the slave or the concentration camp victim, but we might equally use the example of the individual who for whatever reason (psychiatric or otherwise) is mute. This is a less emotive example than those chosen by Arendt, appears at first sight to be less extreme, and is altogether a more frequent and mundane state of affairs. It shares, however, many of the attributes of her more dramatic examples. Furthermore, because it is more frequent, it is relatively easy to identify, and generally occurs within an accessible clinical context. For these reasons, it has received much more empirical attention.

Mutism is a complex state, but generally refers to an inability to speak appropriately, i.e. in normal conditions of social interaction; we will exclude from our consideration those who are mute by virtue of physical defect or deficiency. If we consider the mute from the perspective of the three attributes of public space Arendt describes (plurality, speech and public objects), we can see that the mute meets those qualities described for *lack of* public space. Such a person lacks speech in the obvious sense, but also in the more extended conceptual sense used by Arendt. If such a person is confined in a psychiatric hospital, he would undoubtedly lack the condition of plurality, and given the present state of such institutions, both literally and figuratively will lack public objects in Arendt's sense. The mute person is bounded and limited by those elements of his environment that impinge on him, and by virtue of these limitations is seriously hindered in his capacity to act upon his environment. The environment he creates for himself, and the one which we arrange for him (i.e. the hospital), interact and conspire to enhance the lack of public space, in Arendt's terms. The reciprocal dynamic of behaviour is lacking in this example, in the same sense that it is lacking for the slave, or the concentration camp victim. In another context, this might also be what we refer to as institutionalisation.

However, in the case of the mute, we can at least take steps to restore that dynamic by teaching the mute to speak. Lovaas and his colleagues, for example,[31] have described systematic procedures for reintroducing speech in mute children and adults in psychiatric contexts, using reinforcement procedures of the kind we have encountered earlier. For our purposes, the important point to note in these studies is that whilst the initial stages of vocabulary learning are difficult, later stages become much easier and are accompanied by improvements in related, but not directly targeted, areas like social interaction. By improving speech performance, therefore, not only does speech behaviour change, but other behaviour, especially related to social interaction, also changes. This is because it becomes possible for the individual to act upon his environment, and in turn be acted upon – the reciprocal dynamic of behaviour and environment again becomes possible.

Restoring speech in the mute may not be the same as restoring public space in the political sense used by Arendt. Public space is, of course, essentially a political concept, and it refers to political circumstances and behaviours related to political ends. The mute, and any changes we might produce in his behaviour, is a much more domestic matter lacking both the gravity and context of political life. But the *processes* we might refer to that explain both the changes and consequences may be rather similar. To pursue the analogy further, as the mute regains speech, he makes possible other changes that allow him to interact with his environment – his demands can be made known, his wishes and his likes and dislikes can be expressed; similarly, the wishes of many others can be made known to him, and he can respond to them. What the treatment procedure effectively does is to replace the control over verbal behaviour of the factors which produced mutism, by restoring immediate contingency control. In a literal sense, we effectively restore speech, we develop plurality and make possible the public objects around which public space can develop.

In a behavioural and psychological sense, the state of the mute before treatment is very much like that of individuals in totalitarian states. What Arendt terms lack of public space is analogous with the pre-treatment mute, who albeit for different reasons also lacks in Arendt's terms public space. Both are not under the control of immediate contingencies, and therefore lack '. . . the space within the world which men need in order to appear . . .'.[32] In behavioural terms, the differences we see between them are quantitative and differences of degree, rather than qualitative and differences of substance.

Public Space and Millenarianism

In behavioural terms, lack of public space appears to be, therefore, an attribute of ideological control, describing degree of control, and/or changes in the relationship between long-term rule-governed behaviour and short-term contingency shaped behaviour. Expressing it in this way enables us to relate the concept of public space to those factors already discussed relating ideology to extremism and fanaticism. From this perspective, we can also see that the behavioural correlates of public space may well interact with other aspects of ideology, especially that described in Chapter 5 as millenarianism. Indeed, the *form* of ideological control by a millenarian ideology may well result in what we have termed here lack of public space. The extent of commitment, and nature of the eventual utopian society, evident in the believers of millenarian religious movements, for example, illustrate elements of lack of public space. This may be an inevitable feature of ideologies involving millenarianism, but it might also be a variable that can be used by the millenarian leader to enhance control over his disciples.

The Rappites referred to in Chapter 5 illustrate this.[33] Not only did they have a total ideological commitment before they left Germany (as illustrated by the extent to which they refused to follow government demands about conscription), but they also served to enhance the expression of that commitment by the development of their utopian communities at Harmonie and eventually Economy. Withdrawal from society, setting themselves apart from the normal demands made on members of a broad community, and the development of very strict inter-community rules, illustrate this. George Rapp, in moving his community every ten years or so, also seems to have had an intuitive grasp of the need to retain the separateness of his community from the outside world. The disruption, and self-inflicted adversity this resulted in, very effectively served to undermine those features of community life that might have led to the creation of conditions like those that characterise public space.

Indeed, the subservience of personal needs to community goals that characterised the Rappites illustrates the substitution of direct-acting immediate contingency control by rule-following distant objectives. The powerful control such distant rules commanded is illustrated by the way in which the community weathered the deliberate changes in location which Rapp required. The social disruption caused by the moves to the various sites must have been traumatic for the community members, as much as anything because it emphasised the temporary nature of their conditions of life. On the other hand, within the millenarian context, this may be quite reasonable, for the Rappites confidently expected the millennial state to arrive within their lifetimes. Viewed from outside that ideological constraint, we can see how ideology, expressed in behavioural terms, both served to direct and control the behaviour of the community members. The organisational focusing which characterises developed terrorist groups[34] seems to be an example of the same process.

Like many active terrorist groups, the Rappites can be characterised as living in a condition of millenarian expectation *and* a lack of public space. Their particular ideology created a social system that both sustained the ideology and retained control over community members. It was a totalitarian community, in that it demanded total subservience of the individual to the community. In demanding that subservience, and in creating the social structures that implied, it also lacked public space. In contrast with the active terrorist group, it is worth noting that it was also probably both benevolent in intent, and probably benevolent as experienced by its members. However great these qualities of benevolence may have been, they do not of course necessarily undermine the analysis.

Fanatical Behaviour – An Overview of Chapters 4, 5 and 6

We can now draw together the various qualities that we have identified which contribute to the control of fanatical political behaviour. This summary provides a rather technical account, which may be of particular interest to the professional reader. It serves, however, to summarise the principal arguments presented in Chapters 4, 5 and 6.

Political behaviour, in a clearer way than other kinds of behaviour, gains its coherence and dynamic from both its ideological context and content. We have described ideology as a common and broadly agreed set of rules which regulate and determine behaviour. A rule is a verbal description of the relationship between behaviour and its consequences (technically referred to as a behavioural contingency), which serves to relate distant outcomes or consequences to immediate behaviour. Behavioural rules are generalisations about contingencies that control behaviour that have applied in the past, or will apply in the future. In a political context, rules, therefore, relate to the process of expression of ideological content. Other non-political behaviour is also directed towards distant ends, of course, and is similarly controlled by rules in this sense. Ideological control can be distinguished, however, from other forms of behavioural control as rule following in a number of ways. One important way is that for ideology to be meaningful it must be explicitly articulated and expressed. It is the control exercised by formally expressed ideology (and the cohesiveness, organisation and consistency this implies) in the form of contingency rules that distinguishes political behaviour under ideological control from other kinds of directed behaviour. The essentially written qualities of ideology enhance this process.

The distant focus of rule-following behavioural control can be contrasted with more immediate forces characterising immediate contingency control. We have suggested that in general our behaviour is controlled by the dynamic interaction of both immediate contingencies and more distant contingencies which are mediated by behavioural rules. In cases of ideological and political control over behaviour, it was suggested in Chapter 4 that the balance between distant control versus immediate control tips towards the distant rule control rather than immediate contingency control. The balance between the two, therefore, becomes distorted. This results, amongst other things, in an incremental focusing and strengthening of control by ideological rules, reflected in insensitivity, focusing, loss of critical judgement, certainty, etc. These are the features of fanaticism described and discussed in Chapter 2.

Generalities about the development of ideology control over behaviour are problematic. The nature of an individual's encounters with political activity, the relationship such encounters have with life style, peer groups and social relationships in general, are necessarily idiosyncratic and unique for that individual. Furthermore, issues like the nature of leadership of political movements also serve to complicate general analysis. Nevertheless, a useful distinction can be drawn between the process of coming under the influence of ideological control and the circumstances that might influence the expression of particular behaviour in a local context. This distinction between 'involvement' and 'act' circumstances was made in Chapter 3, and remains a useful one in this broader context. It emphasises the multifactorial process of development, and directs our attention to the dynamic reciprocity of behavioural control. In the case of fanatical political behaviour, we might characterise the process of development as reflecting increased reciprocal influence of ideological rules paralleled by diminished control by immediate contingencies. Personal and situational factors no doubt enhance and drive that process.

Ideology as a process in itself, therefore, appears to have particular effects on behaviour of the kind we have noted above, but those effects may be exaggerated or amended by the qualities of particular ideologies. This may be especially important when we consider the relationship between violence and ideological control. In Chapters 4, 5 and 6 we have represented the basic equation relating violence to ideology as militant potential, the totality of ideology, and the notion of imminence in millenarian achievement. In themselves, each condition does not necessarily give rise to violence in the form we are concerned with. But when combined with themselves, we have argued that they create conditions for the expression of violence.

Militant potential refers to the extent to which there is an explicit involvement of violence in ideological prescription, and the extent to which violence is condoned by that ideology as a means of achieving its ideological end. Thus, eliminating the problem of Jews in the way it was expressed in Nazi ideology would be an example of militant potential in ideology; hastening the inevitable end of capitalism through provoking and exposing its contradictions would be another example. Such potential might be thought to interact with another quality of ideological content – millenarianism, the looking forward to a perfect or ideal future state achieved by following ideological rules.

Almost by definition, political ideologies either are explicitly millenarian, or have within them the potential to be millenarian. This may be especially the case with militant or revolutionary ideologies. The particular quality that seems to be related to both the extent of ideological control and the expression of violence in millenarian ideologies is experience of the degree of imminence of attainment of millenarian ideological ends. Imminence has been suggested to be the quality that makes possible action to prepare for, or speed the advent of, the millenarian ideal in that some definite temporal end becomes visible. The notion of imminence is a critical factor relating time to ideology. Given other ideological supports relating either access to the new world or its time or nature of arrival to particular kinds of activity, imminence may make possible individual action. Indeed, imminence in both secular and religious contexts may serve as a bridge linking relatively non-specific ideological prescription and consequence to behaviour. In terms of the ideas of rule-governed behaviour discussed in Chapter 4, the notion of imminence is a critical variable in the relationship between distant ends and immediate behaviour. Imminence serves to enhance that relationship, affecting in some sense contingency variables, changing the value of terminal reinforcing states, or influencing the strength of rule following.

The final element in the equation linking violence to ideology is the totality of ideological control. This might be thought of in terms of the extent to which rule-following behaviours predominate over more immediate contingency control. In Chapter 6 we have explored the relationship between Arendt's notion of public space and the nature of rule-following control over behaviour. The notion of public space, whilst derived from political theory rather than psychology or behaviour analysis, nevertheless represents a useful way of characterising the enabling nature of ideological control. Through the concept of lack of public space, we can see how ideological control can in itself limit and attenuate other moral and historical factors that might control behaviour. The quality that Arendt refers to as 'lack of thinking' (in her discussion of the Eichmann trial), the focused and highly structured world of the fanatic, the urgency of millenarian imminence, all reflect on the concept of lack of public space.

If we bring together the qualities of the totality of ideological control over behaviour, with inherent features of ideology and the particular ideological qualities of militancy and millenarian imminence, we are confronted with forces of enormous power and direction. The reciprocal dynamic of behaviour, which we have expressed as the relationship between immediate contingency control and distant rule-following contingencies, is a useful conceptual model in which to bring together these disparate forces. Expression in these terms also enables us to locate our explanation within a behavioural framework of known utility, which might at best offer opportunities of empirical verification. In specific circumstances, it must be stressed that the argument is not that all the forces we have identified must necessarily and uniquely be present as elements in the equation to result in what we have termed fanatical violence. Leadership, specific ideological content, economic circumstances, social context, are all factors that might additionally influence this process. Rather the argument is that sometimes individually, but more especially when they do combine, we see their expression in behavioural terms as fanatical violence.

In the remaining chapters of this book, we now turn our attention to analyses of particular circumstances that illustrate the forces we have discussed above. Two principal areas of illustration have been chosen – the idea of the political suicide as a form of self-victimisation, and the victimisation of Jews and other ethnic groups during World War II. The processes which can be identified in these two example areas are in themselves of great interest, of course. But for our particular purposes, they serve to illustrate the fulfilment of the processes we have discussed above. Our analysis will of course be both partial and selective, focusing on example rather than exhaustive commentary.

Both areas of illustration develop a theme of victimisation and violence, directed against others or against the self. This contrast is quite deliberate, even if it may appear rather surprising. The comparison is chosen because it serves to illustrate the behavioural nature of ideological control, and the importance of situational and rule-governed influences on behaviour. Violence is of course a reciprocal of victimisation, and in the sense in which we will use it, victimisation refers to the result of violent behaviour.

CHAPTER 7

Self-victimisation and Politically Motivated Suicide – a terrible strength

Suicide as an example of political violence is discussed in the context of the hunger striker and Shi'a suicide bombings. Such self-victimisation is related to broader issues of terrorism and political violence. The processes associated with self-victimisation are discussed as extreme examples of behavioural rule following.

> ***Never more you stay encompassed***
> ***In the shadow of the night,***
> ***You are raised to new desire***
> ***To a higher form of union.***
> *J. W. Goethe – Selige Sehnsucht*

Many people find the idea of self-inflicted violence both disturbing and difficult to understand. It seems a particularly paradoxical behaviour contradicting cherished assumptions about the role of rationality and logic in human affairs. Yet examples of self-victimisation, even resulting in the extreme consequence of death, can be identified. Where this might occur outside of the context of clinical depression, or in someone who is deluded, it certainly seems to merit the term fanatical. Where it also occurs in a political context, it falls within our area of interest as an unusual but revealing example of fanatical political violence.

Perhaps one of the reasons why we find self-victimisation disturbing is its challenge to usually unchallenged fundamental assumptions. One such underlying assumption we often make about behaviour is that the individual, through his actions, seeks to optimise and gain benefit from the opportunities of his environment. Furthermore, there is a further pervasive assumption that human beings seek to maintain a state of equilibrium in some sense, giving relative freedom from stress and discomfort. Self-victimisation challenges this simple view of human behaviour. The inevitable operation of a hedonistic homeostatic mechanism, which this view at least in a simple form seems to assume, *must* be inappropriate if an individual's actions lead to harming himself in some way, or even ultimately death.

There are other perspectives which we can bring to bear on this issue, however, which might also serve to illustrate the processes we have identified in earlier chapters. We have already discussed some alternative views of the determinants of human behaviour, and in particular we have noted the extent to which an individual's behaviour is controlled by its consequences, especially reinforcement. Reinforcement, of course, refers not only to some kind of gain (such as improved financial position, lessening of hunger or improved well-being). It can refer to the avoidance of aversive consequences, as well as to other more individual or idiosyncratic circumstances such as social approval. These idiosyncratic and personal reinforcers may well contrast with the more obvious reinforcing states. This is a more sophisticated position to take than the simple homeostatic view outlined above where benefit is related in some sense to physical well-being.

We will argue in this chapter that self-victimisation in the political context illustrates the process of ideological control resulting in violence which has been discussed in earlier chapters. In doing this, we will also address the issue of whether self-victimisation challenges the idea of control over behaviour by reinforcement, the fundamental premise on which the account proposed in this book is based. The answer proposed in this chapter is that it does not necessarily do so. The idea of control of behaviour by its consequences can readily encompass self-victimisation, even to the extent of suicide, where the *consequences* of self-victimisation (presumably other than pain or discomfort) are sufficiently powerful to sustain the pain or discomfort associated with self-injurious behaviour. We will examine this in more detail below, but it is worth noting that there are clinical parallels such as self-injurious behaviour which might support this view.

There is a useful distinction we can make at the outset. We can distinguish between suicide *per se*, and suicide as self-victimisation (an example of which is politically motivated suicide), in terms of the focus of the behaviour. Suicide *per se* in the terms we will use it has an essentially personal focus, whereas suicide as self-victimisation has an external, and in the terms of concern to us, political focus.

Camus[1] in his discussion of 'The Rebel' was aware of the distinction between suicide and suicide related to some other social context. Referring to the individual who commits solitary suicide, he notes that '... he never uses, in order to dominate others, the terrible strength and freedom which he gains from his decision to die...'. The use of that 'terrible strength' in the political context is the primary focus of our concern. It is also worth noting that whilst a successful suicide as self-victimisation is unquestionably an extreme act, some suicides *per se* can also be understood in a more general context of benefit to the individual. These may be a special case, but religious or moral prescriptions aside, suicide can of course be a logical, and to some people, appropriate, response to intense pain or the prospect of a continuing progressive illness. This is not to say, of course, that all suicides are the response to logical and rational evaluation of such things as future pain or physical deterioration; such suicides might indeed be a small minority of the total, and may indeed be special cases. Furthermore, there is very clearly a psycho-pathological dimension to suicide, associated for example with depression.[2] In fact, suicide is not such an infrequent event; somewhere in the region of 1 in 10,000 people are thought to commit suicide, although the actual figure is largely unknown (due to errors or distortions in reporting procedures). However, the essentially personal focus of such behaviour remains its critical quality.

This personal quality also characterises another form of self-destructive behaviour which seems to be relatively common in the contemporary Western World – anorexia nervosa. Anorexia nervosa is widely regarded as a pathological clinical state, although it has no clear physical cause. It can result in serious physical deterioration, and even death. Whilst there are characteristic psychological states associated with it (such as an obsessive concern with body image) not all anorexics show such symptoms. The French philosopher, Simone Weil, died as a result of anorexia nervosa. Whilst the coroner's verdict on her death was that she 'killed herself by refusing to eat whilst the balance of her mind was disturbed', she herself remarked before her death that her hunger was for God, not her waistline. Perverse as it may seem, refusal of food as a form of suicide as self-victimisation may well have a personal logic and justification. Indeed, recent feminist critiques of anorexia nervosa emphasise this point, and furthermore draw our attention to its societal dimension.

What makes suicide as self-victimisation a particularly appropriate behaviour to focus on in our discussion of *political* fanaticism is that its very paradoxical qualities highlight the utility of our earlier discussion of ideology as rule following. The argument may well apply to a variety of circumstances (such as anorexia nervosa) although we will confine ourselves here to the political context. Self-victimisation ceases to be paradoxical when we see it as an example of behavioural control exercised by powerful rule-governed contingencies derived in the case of our interests from articulated, usually written, political ideology. Its paradoxical qualities lie in the contrast between immediate contingency control (reflecting perhaps the hedonistic assumptions we often make about behaviour) and rule-governed control (mediating distant contingencies). Chapters 4, 5 and 6 have identified and discussed the extent, nature and potential for ideological control over behaviour. Self-victimisation may be seen as a dramatic example of the manifestation of that control in particular and distinctive circumstances.

The Public View

Perhaps, we find non-hedonistic motivated behaviour, such as self-victimisation, so difficult to understand that we have developed strategies for coming to terms with it. In describing behaviour in general, Skinner[3] has noted that 'We give credit generously when there are no obvious reasons for the behaviour. . . . We give maximum credit when there are quite visible reasons for behaving differently. . . .' Self-victimisation clearly falls into those situations where there are '. . . visible reasons for behaving differently . . .' and certainly we seem to applaud, and sometimes admire, the person who does things contrary to culturally and socially determined expectations. The pervasive imagery of the glorious sacrificial hero, so prevalent in radical millenarian movements, for example,[4] illustrate this, where the ideological supports relating it to virtue sustain and enhance commitment.

Is it this quality of self-victimisation that we refer to when we describe someone as a martyr? It may well be. If so, we can distinguish between the context that might support the martyr and the particular personal circumstances that lead an individual to become a martyr. Skinner's comments certainly help us to establish the nature of the facilitating context to martyrdom. Perhaps, in a personal sense, the particular features which result in martyrdom lie in the individual's particular history and circumstances *allied* to a condoning culture. In the examples used in this chapter, religion (including both Christian and Muslim) might provide the facilitating circumstances (expressed as ideology) that allow it and value it. Religion as such, however, does not seem to be in itself a necessary basis on which to see the development of martyrdom, and particular cultural factors also seem to have pivotal roles. Toloyan,[5] for example, describes the special role of martyrdom in Armenian culture as a form of legitimisation of Armenian terrorism, related to the particular historical circumstances of Armenia. An analysis in similar terms might well be applied to Ireland, a country from which many of the examples used in this chapter are drawn.

The political effectiveness of the hunger strike, for example (which we will consider later), seems to be at least partly dependent on a process like that outlined by Skinner. Indeed, in the more general political context, we might note the importance and effectiveness of the peculiar qualities of credit in self-victimisation. Not all forms of extreme self-victimisation attract credit, however. Compare the position of the individual suffering from anorexia nervosa (a state of self-induced starvation) with the hunger striker. Notwithstanding some contemporary feminist views, it might be argued that the difference in public regard between the two lies in the extent to which the individual is seen as being in control of his own actions, and the ends to which the actions are directed. We might assume that some underlying history and pathology of the anorexic, for example, *removes* the element of personal control and choice over eating behaviour which is conversely *attributed* to the hunger striker. Furthermore, the anorexic is often assumed to be acting for personal and immediate reasons (relative weight from day to day, appearance), whereas the hunger striker is assumed to be acting for personal reasons related to some more distant end (social change or political advantage). Indeed, we might further distinguish between them in terms of distant rule-governed behaviour (the hunger striker) as opposed to immediate contingency control (the anorexic). These are powerful arguments, and we will consider these issues in detail later. At this point, however, it is sufficient to note the important point that the effects of non-pathological self-victimisation can extend beyond the individual, to become an element in a broader political context.

The Political Dimension

The examples of self-victimisation developed in this chapter all gain their political meaning through some effect, or attempted effect, on the political process. It is this feature, along with the notion of choice noted above, that makes them noteworthy and draws our attention to them as worryingly powerful, if bizarre, acts. There is no doubt that other forms of self-victimisation occur which do not address this context, but we are usually unaware of them if their agenda is wholly personal. Furthermore, and perhaps inconsistently, even if we are aware of them, we tend to locate primarily personally motivated self-victimisation within the context of psychopathology, as we might view the person who slashes his wrist, for example, as a cry for help and attention.

Within the political arena, and particularly within the context of terrorism, the processes of self-victimisation as discussed here may well be related to what Taylor[6] has referred to as 'the paradox of morality'. This paradox refers to the apparent contradiction between the moralistic rhetoric of the terrorist and the all too frequent death or injury of people having no particular connection with the terrorist cause which results from the terrorist's actions. This paradox seems to be resolved by either reinterpreting victim qualities (through denigration), or denial of responsibility, attributing the responsibility for deaths to some other agency. In the case of self-victimisation in the context of terrorism, for example, the victim may well be the terrorist. The circumstances surrounding the dirty protest of Republican prisoners in Northern Ireland immediately before the hunger strikes, which is discussed later in this chapter, are one illustration of this. The processes which help the resolution of the paradox of morality appear to be powerful, and with respect to our concerns, denial of responsibility of the individual inflicting damage on himself seems to be particularly appropriate to consideration of the hunger strike.

A good example of an attempt to move the focus of responsibility in a terrorist incident and thereby resolve the paradox of morality in a more general sense can be seen in Menachim Begin's account[7] of the bombing of the King David Hotel in 1946. The Irgun, of which Begin was a leading member, bombed the hotel as the centre of the British Administration in Jerusalem. More than 200 people were killed or injured. Begin seeks to diminish the blame for the deaths that might attach to the Irgun or himself, by accusing the British authorities of lethargy and inaction in responding to a warning that a bomb had been planted. The responsibility for the inevitable potential for death and injury in placing a bomb in such circumstances seems to be thereby lost, and is shifted to some other agency, in this case the victim. We will see a similar process operating in the examples of self-victimisation discussed below. Responsibility for whatever outcome there may be is moved away from the perpetrator (who is in the case of self-victimisation also the victim) to some other agency. The potential political power of such a process is of course considerable.

Political Suicide as Part of a Terrorist Act

The death of a terrorist in the context of explicit terrorism is relatively rare. Indeed, there are good grounds for supposing that, with one exception, deaths of terrorists during acts of terrorism are the result of error or accident; that exception lies in a form of Islamic terrorism. Unique amongst terrorist acts, some instances of Islamic terrorism have been characterised by the deliberate suicide of the terrorist as part of the act of terrorism. Acts such as these might also especially attract the term 'fanatic', given what to most observers is their bizarre nature, and as we will see, their religious context.

The Middle Eastern suicide bombings during 1983-84, attributed in the main to Islamic Shi'ite groups, has drawn our attention to this unusual form of terrorism. From the perspective of gaining the operational objectives of the terrorist, such bombings are unquestionably successful in reaching their chosen target, causing considerable damage, and exposing weaknesses in a militarily superior opponent. In some ways it might have been predicted that this method of delivering bombs (for that is the effective result of the Shi'ite attacks) would have been more widely adopted, for in a sense, the suicide attack is the ultimate rational way of ensuring the success of a mission, offering a cheap (in financial terms, if not human) form of guided missile. They have, however, been given an exaggerated significance by Western analysts, probably as a result of their bizarre nature. The response of Western security services to them has been greatly out of proportion to the threat they pose.

As they have impinged on the West, the principal targets for contemporary suicide attacks have been United States installations in the Middle East, principally in Lebanon. Extensive attacks of this form have occurred against non-Western targets, however, in other contexts in the Middle East, notably the recent Iran-Iraq war. We can begin to understand these actions, however, when we think about them within the broader context of Islam, and especially the Shi'ite sect and its relationship with the state of Iran. It is the religious basis for what to us appears to be essentially political acts that will enable us to make sense of them. That religious basis might well also make us truly label them 'fanatical', but might also lead us to question the assumptions of irrationality and abnormality which are often made in Western analyses. That same religious basis also provides the ideological context which gives rise to the behavioural rules that facilitate the process of terrorism in the way which we have discussed earlier.

Examples of Shi'ite suicide attacks against American targets are well known. On 18 April 1983, at shortly after 1.00 pm, a van containing approximately 400 lbs of explosive was driven into the side of the United States Embassy in Beirut. It was then detonated by the driver, and some 60 people were killed, including the driver, and some 120 injured; the dead and injured were mostly American personnel. Some American observers have described this explosion as 'the single largest non-nuclear blast on earth since World War II'. Whilst this attack is often regarded as the first of a series of suicide bombings, it was in fact preceded by earlier suicide attacks on the Israeli Defence Forces. For example, on 13 April, 6 Israeli soldiers were killed by a suicide lorry bombing. Responsibility for the United States bombing was claimed by, amongst others, Al Jihad al-Ismali, an offshoot of the Lebanon Shi'ite Amal militia. In the terms which the terrorist might use to evaluate this incident, it was a spectacular success, in that a high security perimeter was breached and considerable damage was done, especially to key intelligence personnel thought to be attending a meeting there.

A further devastating attack followed against the United States Marine Headquarters in the Lebanon, with a simultaneous attack on the French Headquarters on 23 October 1983 which killed some 60 American and 59 French personnel. The drivers of both vehicles who detonated the explosives were killed. Both these bombings were again claimed by Al Jihad al-Ismali. Once more, it has to be said that from the terrorist perspective, these were very successful attacks, demonstrating precision in targeting, a capacity to penetrate high security areas, and an ability to co-ordinate and plan actions. Incidentally, they may also demonstrate the involvement of the intelligence services of other regional powers in the Middle East, notably Syria, for it is unlikely that Al Jihad al-Ismali (or whatever Shi'ite grouping that organisation stands as a front for) would have the capacity to find out sufficient details of the buildings and security arrangements necessary to penetrate the perimeters. Further attacks against American and Israeli personnel and installations subsequently took place during that year, and in the following year.

These attacks were undoubtedly successful, in that they reached their targets, caused considerable damage and, of course, received enormous publicity. Despite intense and sophisticated security provisions, the suicide bomber was able to penetrate the target area with apparent ease. An obvious moral that might be drawn from this is the inadequacy of technology-based security systems in the absence of adequate psychological understanding of both the attackers *and* security personnel. The bombers, after all, penetrated the compounds.

These attacks had a profound effect on American policy towards Lebanon, yet, as we have noted, they have not set the pattern for other terrorist activity in the Middle East. Within the broader context of contemporary terrorism, these attacks stand out as being unique, and in the long term of relatively little strategic significance. Deliberate self-destruction, where the terrorist's death is a necessary part of the act in detonating the bomb (as opposed to accidental death), is not a feature of terrorist activity. Only 9 per cent of terrorist bombing victims from 1977 to 1983 were thought to be terrorist bombers, for example,[8] and those terrorist deaths that did occur were largely thought to be the result of accidental explosions, rather than deliberate. In contemporary times, suicide attacks are very rare outside of the Middle East.

These acts of terrorism strike fear into most observers, and are to most of us beyond comprehension. To the Western observer, such acts can readily be described as 'fanatical'. The often violent and extreme rhetoric of the participants and the organisations they belong to increase our concern, and seems to the Western ear extreme, bizarre and abnormal.

Viewed from the standpoint of Shi'ite culture and its Islamic context, however, such acts of destruction do not seem so pathogenic and fanatical, and have a clear and appropriate cultural, historical and religious context as martyrdom, with historical precedents in the acts of the 'Assassins'.[9] They gain their meaning and overall logic from the concept of 'Jihad', or Holy War. This is sometimes described as the 'sixth pillar' of Islam, and has a special meaning in Shi'a religious observance.

The Assassins (also known as Ismailis-Nizari) were a Shi'a Islamic community who were evident in strength in the period 1090-1275; they still exist in a much modified form in the contemporary world. They shared many of the attributes of contemporary terrorist groups, in that their actions had explicit political aspirations (in the sense that politics and religion in Islam are intimately entwined); they even foreshadowed the contemporary international terrorist movements, by having little regard for national boundaries. Their aspiration was to unite and reconstitute Islam into one community through their actions, principally the death of orthodox or political leaders who refuse to heed the warnings of the Assassins, hindered the spread of the 'new' Islam, or '. . . acting in ways that demonstrated complicity in Islam's corruption'.[10] In their method of killing, the Assassins exposed themselves to capture and death, for they were often trusted members of the household of the person assassinated. In so exposing themselves, the Assassins can best be described in their own terms as accepting martyrdom, where their own lives, and those of their victims, 'atone' in some sense for human frailties and failures in promoting Islam.

That these themes are underlying intimate (if relatively infrequently expressed) qualities of Islam can be seen in the way in which Muslim countries outside of the Middle East have reacted to challenges to Muslim social order. Dale,[11] for example, has discussed in a historical context the nature and extent of suicidal violence in Muslim countries in and around the Indian Ocean when faced with European colonial expansion. He describes the forces that lead to suicidal attacks on the colonial powers in terms similar to those of Rapoport,[12] emphasising the qualities of martyrdom. In contrast to analyses of contemporary Islamic terrorism, however, Dale stresses the element of 'despair' (with implicit notions of frustration) as a quality of the martyrdoms of his Asian examples. This does not appear to be a feature of contemporary Islamic activity, in any obvious sense, however.

The forces that gave rise to the Assassins and Muslim Asia's suicidal warfare remain and influence the Shi'ites today and indeed have a wider influence of Islamic thinking. Furthermore, as Taylor[13] notes, events we might refer to as terrorism (suicide bombings, kidnapping, random explosions in residential areas) are not only features of the present situation in Lebanon, but in some sense have been a part of the process of politics and diplomacy in the Middle East for many centuries. What the West might term 'terrorism' is used as an instrument of policy by States such as Iran to pursue its political ends against its enemies. Indeed, we can see in probably the most explicit way in this Islamic context the use of terrorism as a form of warfare, and in this context, parallel with Clausewitz's[14] notions of the relationship between war and politics are of course obvious. Terrorism is used in the Middle East in the furtherance of political objectives, especially by Iran, and this is apparent in the way that suicide attacks, for example, are not confined to use against the Western enemies of Iran, but are used also against its regional enemies. Unknown numbers of combatants (including children) have been killed in what were effectively suicide attacks, or attempts to clear minefields. In the absence of media attention, however, the Western audience is in the main unaware of the scale and effectiveness of these attacks.

In a sense, what we fear as fanaticism and label as terrorism is in its context part of the 'normal' process of political activity. Taking hostages, for example, has prominently featured as a political tool in the Middle East for a long time, as it has in historical times in Europe. Failure to recognise this and the social and religious context in which it occurs can lead to serious consequences, as the various attempts to negotiate with holders of Lebanese hostages over the period 1980-90 has shown. It has been seen repeatedly that approaches to groups holding hostages, using the same assumptions as those which might be used in the West, are met with either incredulity or disdain.

We can better understand the origins of what to us are suicide bombers (but to themselves, and their social context, are martyrs) if we consider a little of the context to Muslim, and especially Shi'ite thinking, and in so doing, try to identify areas where Western assumptions seem to be inappropriate. In doing this, we will begin to identify the rule-following contingencies that characterise militant Shi'ite Islam, placing it in the context of the discussion of violence offered in earlier chapters. Of course, in a sense, what we regard as Shi'ite terrorism might properly be termed 'fanatical' if we consider the religious roots of the term, for the suicide bombings which we find so difficult to understand have their origins in the kind of religious practice which characterises Islamic fundamentalism, and especially that branch termed Shi'iteism.[15] In doing this, we will also see how these forms of Shi'ite behaviour fit within the broader context of fanaticism as a particular feature of rule following. Our discussion is largely confined to Shi'a thinking, but it should be noted that there is a broader Islamic context to this.[16]

A characteristic of Shi'a religious practice has been an emphasis on legitimacy, which we in the West often seem to characterise as fundamentalism. This is evident as a desire to return to the religious and social practices described in the Qur'an and resisting the introduction of heretical practices, especially those of the West. Shi'a practice, therefore, has particularly drawn on distinctive literal interpretations of the law expressed by Qur'anic texts, themselves a form of ideological prescription in the sense used here. Associated with this has been the more general historical desire in Islam to see the creation of an Islamic State embodying the principles expressed in the Qur'an.[17] In this Islamic State, the distinction between the religious and secular would not exist; thus, whilst the notion of a written law derived from authority is of foremost importance, the notion of law outside of its religious context would have little meaning. Related to this, the distinction between politics and religion is also largely meaningless, and therefore the Western concept of democracy as a legislative process creating laws in such a State would be irrelevant. Because Islam is a 'social religion', in that it prescribes appropriateness of behaviour in a wide variety of everyday contexts, so even the intimate details of relationship become part of the social structure of the State. For example, this is particularly the case with respect to the relationships between men and women; the Qur'an devotes more to this issue than to any other area of life. Iran, as conceived after the defeat of the Shah in 1979, is an attempt at creating such a State, and it is in that context that we must seek to try to understand the Islamic terrorists. We should note in passing that the Shi'a are not the only fundamentalist grouping in contemporary Islam. Strong fundamentalist trends are evident in contemporary Sunni ideology, owing much to the Egyptian Muslim Brotherhood, and the writings of Sayyid Qutb. Whilst differing in their origins, and in some senses being bitterly opposed to each other, both Sunni and Shi'a fundamentalism have large elements in common. They can be contrasted with more secular approaches to Arab (as opposed to Muslim) nationalism.

Despite the overriding importance of the written law in Islamic thinking, there is a particular feature of Shi'ite history to which we must draw attention in order that we can develop some understanding of the distinctive martyrdom context of the suicide bomber, as distinct from the related, but broader, category of Islamic fundamentalist. In 680, two very important early figures in Shi'ite history, Hussein, the son of Ali (the cousin of the Prophet), and his wife Fatima (the daughter of the Prophet) were killed at a place called Karbala in what is now Iraq, in an attempt to overthrow the Caliphate. The conflict of which this was a part related to legitimacy and the nature of the leadership of the Islamic world, an issue which today still divides the Shi'a from other major Islamic sects. Both Hussein and Fatima, and their forces, were killed ruthlessly and only a sick boy survived.

Shi'ites regard Hussein's death not as a defeat, but as a martyrdom, which is given added significance by the Shi'ite stress on the legitimacy of descent of religious leadership from the Prophet through Ali. This martyrdom of the kin of the Prophet remains an important quality of religious life for the Shi'ite, and more particularly supports and sustains the distinctive notion of sacrifice and martyrdom for the Shi'a cause as a feature of Shi'ite religious practice.

In Shi'ite terms, this motif is evident both in the historical origins of groups such as the Assassins, and is equally evident in many walks of contemporary Shi'a life, seen in for example, the Arous ad-Damm, the Brides of Blood. These are a group of women who are dedicated to avenge the death of Hussein through their own martyrdom. The Arous ad-Damm are symbolically pure (they are all virgins), who aspire to martyrdom to atone for and avenge the death of Hussein at Karbala. They are referred to as daughters of Hussein, the Prince of Martyrs, and can expect after martyrdom '. . . husbands chosen for them from amongst "the most pious and shapely young men, free of all blemish."'[18] It is from the ranks of organisations of candidates for martyrdom such as this that the suicide bombers are drawn.

Taheri[19] describes the circumstances of one member of the Arous ad-Dammn, Sumayah Sa'ad. She joined the Party of Allah's Sayyedah Zaynab Brigade, a female Shi'ite commando group, in 1983 when she was 16. Sayyedah Zaynab was the daughter of Ali, and the religious and symbolic significance of this Brigade in the Shi'ite context is quite clear. Sumayah Sa'ad's Sh'ite family originally lived in Southern Lebanon, but later sought refuge in West Beirut. She volunteered for the attack on the United States Marine Headquarters in 1983, and was apparently trained to fulfil that mission; but she was withdrawn from it, and eventually killed herself by detonating a car she was driving, loaded with dynamite, into an Israeli military position in South Lebanon in 1985.

It is important to stress that suicide is not in any sense condoned by Islam, and the deaths caused by what to the Western observer is a suicide attack are certainly not condoned as suicide within Shi'ite practice. The relationship between these acts of martyrdom and suicide are a matter of concern for Shi'ite theologians in Lebanon, and Kramer,[20] in his discussion of this issue, identifies the moral logic used to justify them. Nor is Hussein, when he was killed at Karbala, regarded as necessarily having sought martyrdom, but rather was chosen for martyrdom by Allah because of his 'special merit'. Thus, members of groups such as the Arous ad-Damm indicate their willingness to become martyrs, but their choice 'for merit' depends upon the representatives of Allah on earth. In Iran, this was the Ayatollah Khomeini, who was also Head of State. Through his representatives, the mullahs, those to be honoured by martyrdom are chosen. Thus we can see that there is an intimate link between the practice of martyrdom in Iran (through, for example, what to us may appear as suicide bombing) and the 'official' structure of Islam. Given that little distinction between religion and the State is made in contemporary Iran, we can see how what amounts to a form of religious devotion can become an instrument of State policy. In a sense, therefore, we see in Shi'ite suicide attacks a form of State terrorism. There are obvious parallels to be drawn here with the activities of the Japanese Kamikaze pilots of World War II[21] and the Gurkha soldiers of the British Army. Islam is not alone amongst religions in facilitating, and even condoning, death for the cause of defence of religion. What is unusual in Islam is its all-embracing sense of interrelationship with social structures.

Many volunteers for martyrdom exist and are trained in Iran. They seek righteousness through suffering and ultimately martyrdom, a common enough religious motif not unique to Islam. These volunteers are in many ways the inheritors of the traditions of the Assassins and seeing these acts as a form of religious devotion, yielding religious merit, allows us to place into perspective the apparently bizarre acts of what (to the Western observer) appear to be suicide. It also enables us to make sense of what to many Westerners seem to be the strange features of the actions of these volunteers. For example, the driver of the truck which devastated the United States Embassy, Beirut, in April 1983 smiled at the Marine Guard of the Embassy Gate on his way into the compound. This was the *bassamat al-farah*, the 'smile of joy',[22] which is worn by martyrs at their time of martyrdom. Martyrdom, because of its promise of merit hereafter, is an act of joy, symbolised by this smile.

The notion of joy in martyrdom can also be seen in the videotape left behind after San'ah Muheidli, a seventeen-year-old girl, exploded a car she was driving in Southern Lebanon amongst an Israeli military convoy on 9 April 1985. She killed 2 soldiers, wounded 2 more, and killed herself. Before becoming a martyr, she completed, as is required, a will, which in her case took the form of the videotape. She entreats her mother to '. . . be merry, to let your joy explode as if it were my wedding day'.[23] Themes like these permeate many of the suicide attacks, and enables us to understand a little of the religious context to what to us seem to be essentially political acts. Indeed, in its context it is not particularly inappropriate, and in so far as in Shi'a Islam death in this form can yield benefits in the afterlife, then it might be seen as being of positive benefit.

The acts we have discussed above seem properly to belong to the category of political violence, and equally can appropriately be described as fanatical. We should note, however, that they are far from irrational once we understand the assumptions on which they are based. Whilst they are quite clearly suicides, they should be distinguished from those examples of suicide where there seems to be some underlying pathology.

We have noted that the terrorist suicide seems to be uniquely a feature of Islamic terrorism. We might briefly pause in our discussion, however, to consider whether the related principle of inevitable death as part of *warfare* (as distinct from terrorism) is so unusual. Taylor and Ryan[24] have drawn attention to the parallels that might be drawn between the self-sacrifice of soldiers which has characterised warfare in World Wars I and II and the Islamic suicide terrorist. It might be argued that the forces that allow the development of the suicide attacker might not be that dissimilar to those which might characterise army training and control during warfare. We will consider this issue in more detail later, but we might note that the apparent 'uniqueness' of Islamic terrorism in terms of the *processes* involved might not after all be so unique.

Themes around the idea of salvation and redemption which we have encountered in our earlier discussion (in Chapter 5) recur in the above. The redemptive qualities of the suicide bomber, and the relationship between the historical events at Karbala, the present struggles to sustain and purify contemporary Islam, the effectiveness of human agencies in attaining or at least hastening the achievement of the desired 'pure' state, and in particular its imminence of attainment all suggest the powerful contingency rule relationships governing such behaviour. The explicitly religious and millenarian context in which the Islamic terrorist victimises himself provides the context and substance of the ideological framework controlling his behaviour. In contrast, the immediate contingencies related to personal survival that might be expected to influence behaviour quite clearly become subservient to these broader forces.

In the above, we can see evidence of all the qualities we have discussed in Chapters 4, 5 and 6 as elements contributing to political violence (i.e. militancy, millenarian imminence and lack of public space). Shi'ite rhetoric is replete with *militant* references, extolling the faithful to violence and aggression against enemies. For example, at a memorial service for three Iranian Revolutionary Guards killed in Lebanon in August 1985, a high official of the radical Islamic Hezbollah, Sheik Sobhi Tofeili, said '. . . the names of the Mujahedeen heroes who knocked down the fortress of the infidels and blew up the American Embassy . . . are still unknown. . . . Their actions were for the sake of Islam. We must preserve their blood and let the world and history be aware that Islam is the one that destroyed Israel and America.' Whilst there are numerous contemporary examples of urging the faithful to be violent in the name of Islam, we should note that their religious authority, the Qur'an, expresses similar sentiments.

Not only is Shi'a rhetoric militant, it is also millenarian. Islam, like most religions, looks forward to a better state. But amongst contemporary Shi'a, especially in Iran, the sense of personal contribution to attainment of that better state, and its sense of *imminent* attainment, is much stronger than in other branches of Islam. The fall of the Shah, and the circumstances surrounding the rise to power of the Ayatollah Khomeini, seem to have been a critical factor, paralleling prophetic elements of Shi'a teaching.[25] In addition, the features that give rise to the notion of such imminent attainment also serve to severely limit and constrain the extent of discussion and speculation about the fundamental issues of Shi'a belief. We see, therefore, the condition for lack of *public space*, evident in constraints on plurality, speech and public objects. As far as can be seen in contemporary Iran, there is no 'space of appearance' in which political debate about the nature of Islam and its relationship with the State can take place. The primacy of Shi'ite views on Islam is taken for granted, as evidenced by the lack of tolerance for other religious views in Iran.

The religious basis of Shi'ite society, therefore, creates the conditions in which we would expect to find the expression of political violence. Given the emergent quality of imminence associated with the return of the Ayatollah Khomeini to Iran in 1979, we can see how the various forces of ideological rules, militancy, imminence, and lack of public space interacted to set the conditions to produce a particularly violent result. Its religious context also, of course, quite properly enables us to label such behaviour as fanatical. Indeed, that it also has a political focus is in this case in a sense almost accidental, in the light of the failure to distinguish between the religious and the secular in contemporary Iran (and also probably necessarily in all Shi'ite communities).

Our discussion so far has enabled us to introduce the notion of rule following in the context of self-victimisation. We have also considered the extent to which the factors we have identified as contributing to political violence characterise the particular social and religious context of the Shi'ite suicide bombers. We now turn to a more explicitly and overtly political form of self-victimisation, lacking the obvious characteristic religious basis of the Shi'ite.

The Hunger Strike

Suicide aimed at attaining a political goal is not confined to the Middle East. Politically motivated suicide can be seen in the West, sometimes within a form of Christian context and most typically associated with self-induced starvation, the hunger strike. The political suicide can occur within a variety of cultural contexts and further demonstrates that perhaps the critical element is not necessarily membership of a particular religious sect, such as Shi'ites, but related to more general phenomena of the kind discussed earlier. We will discuss at some length in the following examples of political hunger strikes, because as phenomena they have played an important role in contemporary extreme political activity. After that discussion, we will place it into the context of the conceptual positions discussed in earlier chapters.

We tend to think of the hunger strike primarily within a historical context, which if it exists at all in the contemporary world, is related to spectacular and essentially media events such as the Provisional IRA and INLA series of hunger strikes in 1980 and 1981. Yet as a form of political and personal protest, the hunger strike has a surprising contemporary popularity and, outside the dramatic media-orientated events of the early 1980s, has probably always had a relatively high, if largely unremarked, incidence. We can judge this from the following: during the two-year period from September 1986 to September 1988, Associated Press[26] reported a surprisingly large total of 223 hunger strikes. This is, in fact, probably an underestimate of the numbers, given that the event requires some prominence to be noted by a press agency. Indeed, it is impossible to judge how many go unreported. For example, a large number of the 223 hunger strikes reported by Associated Press took place within prisons. For such information to become public (and therefore reported), there has to be some measure of exchange of information between places such as prisons and the outside world. In many societies this cannot always be assumed.

The incidence of hunger strikes reported by Associated Press has a wide geographical distribution. Most occurred in Eastern Europe (23 per cent of the total), with the majority in the Soviet Union (which itself accounted for 13 per cent of the total, and were mainly undertaken by prisoners). Western Europe and Asia each had 21 per cent of the total, followed by the United States and Canada (8 per cent), South America (7 per cent) and South Africa and the Middle East (5 per cent). 34 per cent of the total involved only a single individual on hunger strike, 6 per cent two or three people, and 60 per cent groups of three or more people on hunger strike; slightly more than half the total (52 per cent) lasted less than seven days.

All of the hunger strikes reported by Associated Press involved some form of protest, although the circumstances described are very varied. Some were little more than 24 hour token protests, usually to draw attention to some political or environmental objective, or to protest against some event. These hunger strikes are most likely to be undertaken in groups. Some hunger strikes are wholly related to personal events and have no political context. These, no doubt, have significance for the individual involved, but often seem inappropriate events on which to base a potentially life-threatening protest. For example, in Los Angeles airport on 12 January 1988, a Dutch tourist lost his pet dog on a flight from Dallas, and embarked on a hunger strike at the TWA terminal in protest. He swore he would keep the hunger strike up until the dog was found. He later learned that his unfortunate dog had escaped from its cage, and had been killed in traffic. This protest clearly contrasts with the hunger strike of Mrs Anna-Lisa Stoican, who fasted for 40 days outside a Romanian Embassy in Sweden in 1987 in protest against the refusal of the Romanian authorities to allow her husband, a Romanian citizen, to join her.

Whilst the hunger strike is therefore surprisingly popular as a protest with life-threatening *potential*, very few extend to the point at which the individual's physical conditions merits cause for concern, and even fewer result in death. Of the total of 223 Associated Press reports, some four people on hunger strike are thought to have died; all of these were prisoners (three in the Soviet Union). It is not easy to tell from the reports, however, whether they died from starvation, infection or similar causes consequential on their physical debilitation, or some other cause.

The use of the hunger strike as a means of political protest seems to gain prominence (or at least attention) at particular times in different countries. There are presumably situational as well as cultural factors evident from time to time that make the hunger strike a peculiarly appropriate political tool. The nature and extent of media coverage may be one important factor. In British India in the 1930s and 1940s, for example, the movement for independence from Britain successfully used the media attention created by hunger strikes to pressure British withdrawal. Mahatma Gandhi, for example, went on 17 hunger strikes in his lifetime in his attempts to force the withdrawal of the British Raj. Similar tactics were extensively used in Burma. After the immediate focus of the struggle for independence passed, so the reported incidence of hunger strikes appears to have diminished. In contrast, Russian political protest has historically made much use of the hunger strike and continues to do so.

The hunger strike as a political weapon is not, however, confined to the East, nor to colonial regimes. Hunger strikes outside these contexts are, however, relatively rare. In Great Britain, for example, the suffragette hunger strikes were important landmarks in the struggle for women's rights in the early part of this century. However, as a means of protest, its use in Great Britain (excluding Irish-related hunger strikes) seems to have been largely confined to that issue and that period. This may seem rather surprising, because the suffragettes used the hunger strike as an effective political tool in an explicitly political way. Painful and degrading as it was, it had considerable success in drawing attention to the problem of women's suffrage. The suffragettes themselves regarded it not as an end in itself, but as an element in a broader political strategy, foreshadowing its later usage by Irish terrorists.

The political focus of the suffragettes' hunger strikes can be seen in the way in which they deliberately used legal processes to promote their demands. We can see from the following example how the normal judicial processes (of arrest and conviction for an offence) were used by the suffragettes to create the conditions for hunger strike.[27] Whilst leading a procession around the East End of London on 14 February 1914, Sylvia Pankhurst records:

'Some stones were solemnly thrown at the window of a bank. My stone missed, but someone else managed to send one through the glass. To make sure of imprisonment, I broke a window in the police station, and was convicted for this and the bank window. ... Zelie Emerson and I went to prison for six weeks on Friday, and began the hunger and thirst strike.'

The suffragettes deliberately created conditions for arrest and imprisonment, victimising themselves and thus setting the scene for undertaking a hunger strike whilst in prison. The conditions endured by the women were undoubtedly unpleasant and extreme, and the hunger strikes they undertook had the potential for serious physical harm and death. The longest term of hunger strike endured was by Olive Wharry, who fasted for thirty-one days; the longest term of hunger and water fasting was by Freda Graham, who went for fifteen days. However, the hunger strikes were not the only privations endured by the women protesters. A part of government policy in dealing with the hunger strikes was to force feed them. This involved forcing a tube into the stomach, and passing food and liquid down that tube. Those who were subjected to this describe it as not only painful, but profoundly degrading.

Sylvia Pankhurst graphically describes what happened whilst she was forcibly fed.[28]

'The door opened ... a crowd of warderesses filled the doorway.... I struggled but was overcome, there were six of them, all much bigger and stronger than I. They flung me on my back on the bed, and held me down firmly by shoulders and wrists, hips, knees and ankles. Then the doctors came in. Someone seized me by the head and thrust a sheet underneath my chin. My eyes were shut. I set my teeth and tightened my lips over them with all my strength. A man's hands were trying to force open my mouth; my breath was coming so fast that I thought I should suffocate. His fingers were striving to pull my lips apart – getting inside. I felt them and a steel instrument pressing round my gums, feeling for gaps in my teeth ... "Here's a gap," one of them said. "No, here is a better one. This long gap here!" A steel instrument pressed my gums, cutting into the flesh.'

This continued until the tube was forced down her throat, and food passed into the stomach. Twice a day for the period of her confinement this continued, greatly adding to the pain and physical distress.

Forcible feeding was clearly degrading to both prisoners and prison staff, but as far as the suffragettes were concerned, it served to give an additional dimension to the victimisation process. The self-victimisation of the hunger strike became additionally the victimisation of forced feeding. Recognising this, in an attempt to avoid the need for forced feeding, the Government introduced 'The Prisoner's Temporary Discharge for Ill-Health Bill' on 25 March 1913. Under the terms of this Bill, which soon became known as the 'Cat and Mouse' Act, prisoners on hunger strike were licensed out of prison for short terms, for the duration of which their sentence was temporarily suspended. Thus, if prisoners went on hunger strike, they were released, but when recovered were re-arrested and brought back to prison to serve the balance of their sentence. This, of course, led not to a reduction in the incidence of hunger strikes, but the development of serial hunger striking by the same person; provision for forcible feeding remained, however, and was in fact subsequently used.

As part of the broader political strategy of the suffragettes in their struggle for female suffrage, the hunger strike clearly played an important role, both as a means of protest, and as a rallying point and focus for dissent. Whether the tactic actually assisted in gaining female suffrage is another matter, but that is probably beside the point. As a means of enhancing propaganda, and focusing dissent, it was certainly successful. But outside the Irish hunger strikes discussed below, the hunger strike has never again occupied a major role in British politics.

Irish Hunger Strikes

Some of the most notable public and political hunger strikes of recent times in the Western world have taken place in Ireland. Many of the reasons for this may lie in the historical origins of Irish social, religious and political culture, which seem to particularly support the notion of fasting as protest. The term 'fasting' as distinct from hunger strike has religious overtones, and fasting frequently has a role in religious devotions. Such a form of religious devotion, however, may well contribute to legitimising its later use as hunger strikes, and certainly established a facilitating context for its development. Fasting has, in fact, been described as an 'ancient weapon'[29] in Ireland with origins in the Medieval Irish civil code. This code specified the circumstances in which a fast could be used to resolve a debt, or to achieve justice. A complainant fasted on the doorstep of the defendant; if the complainant died, the defendant was judged guilty and required to pay compensation. Such fasts (or hunger strikes) belong in a broader historical context. Foster[30] describes the significance of this practice in terms of the traditional system of checks and balances that enabled ancient, and somewhat anarchic, early Irish society to function. Fasting is, of course, a feature of some Christian religious observance and there is even some evidence of the quasi-'legal' form of fasting described above being imported into the mythology of the Celtic Church. Legends exist of St. Patrick, for example, undertaking hunger strikes against God to effect some result.

These practices provide a rich cultural and mythical basis for the development of the contemporary Irish hunger strike, the significant differences from contemporary times being the broader supportive context which offset the hunger strike against other techniques of social control. However, suggestive as this ancient background might be, there are, in fact, few accounts of hunger strikes in the period from the Middle Ages to the early twentieth century. Indeed, the hunger strike seems to have had little political role until the present century.

The rise of the contemporary political hunger strike in Ireland is largely associated with the struggle for Irish independence, and the subsequent civil war. Whilst Irish women were, in fact, involved in the hunger strikes of the suffragettes, the hunger strike as a political weapon in Ireland gained political currency during the Anglo-Irish War of Independence following the 1916 Easter Rising. In 1917, for example, prisoners in Dublin's Mountjoy Prison refused to eat after brutal treatment which followed their refusal to do prison work and wear prison clothes. The leader of this protest was Thomas Ashe, the former president of the Irish Republican Brotherhood. Ashe collapsed after forced feeding, and subsequently died.

In 1920, Terrence McSwiney, the Lord Mayor of Cork and commander of the local IRA Brigade, was the next notable hunger striker. McSwiney was convicted of membership of the IRA and was sentenced to 2 years' imprisonment. He was taken to Britain to serve his sentence, where he went on hunger strike along with 60 other prisoners. He died in 1921 after 74 days' fasting; Joseph Murphy, another hunger striker amongst the prisoners, died on the 76th day of fasting. McSwiney's hunger strike was probably the first to become the focus for explicit political activity, through deliberate efforts to use the hunger strike in a political context. In this sense it foreshadowed the use made of the 1980–81 hunger strikes by the Provisional IRA. Maximum publicity was sought by staging rallies, protest meetings and marches to government offices and the prison. It was probably the first occasion upon which the media were actively involved in the development of a hunger strike.

On the British withdrawal from Southern Ireland, and after the foundation of the Irish Free State, the political turmoil which resulted in the Irish Civil War involved further hunger strikes. There is some evidence that the hunger strike occurred on a wider scale than is conventionally reported. In any event, the first publicly reported hunger striker in the new Republic was James Lennon, TD (a member of the Irish Parliament) who was imprisoned at the Curragh in July 1922. Lennon sought political prisoner status (a common theme in later hunger strikes). The hunger strike was resolved without serious harm to Lennon when the Curragh was designated a political detention centre. The next notable hunger striker was Mary McSwiney, the oldest sister of Terrence McSwiney who died on hunger strike in 1921. She was arrested by the Irish Free State authorities, and held without charge in Mountjoy Prison. Her younger sister, Annie, was refused permission to visit Mary, and she also embarked on a hunger strike at the gates of the prison. On the 24th day of the hunger strike, Mary McSwiney was unconditionally released.

Mary McSwiney's hunger strike became the focus for enormous publicity, and played an important role in the early stages of the Civil War. Women kept nightly vigils at the prison, reciting the rosary (a form of Roman Catholic religious practice). The Irish Free State security forces reacted to these protests by firing over the heads of marchers and using water hoses, thereby, of course, greatly enhancing the publicity generated, and contributing to public sympathy. Prominent ex-patriate Irish figures called for Mary's release; in Australia, for example, the Irish born Archbishop Mannix encouraged all Roman Catholics to support the McSwiney hunger strike and to denounce the inhumanity of the Irish Free State Government. The outcry surrounding Mary McSwiney's hunger strike was enormous, although paradoxically it failed to gain much support from male Republican leaders within Ireland. Her eventual release was probably related to attempts by the Irish Free State Government to retain credibility. The Government executed four young Republicans at Kilmainan jail, Dublin, on the 17th of November, and Erskine Childers on the 24th; Mary McSwiney was released on the 27th. The moral of this to protesters may well have been, however, that the hunger strike was a weapon to which the Irish Free State Government was sensitive.

In March 1923 a Dr Con Murphy, who was a government employee for 37 years, had allied himself with Republicans at the start of the Civil War, and began a hunger strike when he was arrested. This attracted little attention, despite attempts to create publicity, and Murphy was released when he signed an undertaking that he would no longer be involved in anti-government activity. More significantly in 1923, six women began a hunger strike (including Mary McSwiney again) in Kilmainan jail, led by Nellie Ryan. When this ended, a resolution was passed by the Dail (Irish Parliament) that any future hunger strikers would be allowed to die.

In October 1923, perhaps to test this, a hunger strike began in Mountjoy Prison amongst Civil War prisoners opposed to the Anglo-

Irish Treaty of 1921. The strike spread to other prisons, and eventually involved some 8000 prisoners. The scale of this hunger strike suggests a degree of co-ordination (although this was denied at the time) and clearly it was intended as a serious challenge to the Irish Government. A residual 200 prisoners continued the strike, 2 of whom died. This hunger strike, although extensive, attracted relatively little public sympathy and comment. This may be because after the heights of the Mary McSwiney hunger strike, public opinion had become somewhat jaded; it might also reflect the increased confidence of the new Irish Government in resisting demands made upon it. Even the funerals of the hunger strikers who died (Denis Barry and Andrew Mallow) failed to generate the public disorder expected (and intended), and this seems to have had a demoralising effect on the remaining hunger strikers, leading to its eventual collapse. Few hunger strikes lasted beyond 40 days, and the hunger strike gradually faded away.

There was then a lapse in the reported incidence of hunger strikes during the 1930s until the 1940s, when perhaps because of the strains and tensions of World War II and the Republic of Ireland's ambivalent position with respect to it, political circumstances changed. In 1940, two IRA members, Tony D'Arcy and Jack McNeda, were allowed to die on hunger strike in Mountjoy Prison, Dublin, in a protest over prison conditions and in a demand for political prisoner status. After the war, in 1946, the then IRA Chief of Staff, Sean McCaughey, went on hunger strike in an attempt to gain prisoner of war status. He too was allowed to die.

Thereafter, there was another lapse in the reported incidence of hunger strikes in the Irish Republic until the 1970s, when there was a further spate of hunger strikes. In 1973, 40 IRA prisoners, led by Billy McKee, went on hunger strike, once more for prisoner of war status. After 37 days, 'special status' was granted, and the hunger strike ended with no deaths. Shortly after, in the same year, Sean MacStiofain went on hunger strike to protest against his arrest after being interviewed by the Irish State Broadcasting Company. This lasted for 57 days, after which it was discontinued by MacStiofain.

The focus for hunger strikes then moved from the Irish Republic to the United Kingdom. Shortly after the MacStiofain hunger strike in 1973, Dolores and Marion Price, two sisters convicted for a car bombing in London, began a hunger strike, demanding the right to serve their sentence in Ireland. Two men sentenced with them also went on hunger strike. Their fast was interrupted by forced feeding, and lasted more than 200 days, after which they were repatriated. This was followed by a series of hunger strikes by Michael Ganghan and Frank Stagg during the period 1974–76, in an unsuccessful attempt to gain political status. Both eventually died in English prisons.

Attention then moved to Northern Ireland. From 1976 onwards, there were a series of protests, including hunger strikes, over the issue of special category status of prisoners (a form of political status) awarded to prisoners convicted in Northern Ireland before 1976. Aside from the political 'status' this implies, the particular problem related to those convicted after 1976 who were treated as ordinary criminals resulting in a loss both of status and privileges. This protest took a variety of forms, which culminated in the serial hunger strikes of 1981 in which 10 hunger strikers died. It included a 'mass' hunger strike of 7 prisoners in 1980, which was abandoned after 53 days. In many ways, the series of deaths in 1981 represents the most explicit and developed use of the hunger strike as a political weapon, and to date seems to mark the apotheosis of the hunger strike. Interestingly, however, the 1980–81 hunger strikes were in many ways foreshadowed by the hunger strikes associated with the German Baader-Meinhof group. It is worth digressing somewhat from the Irish examples, therefore, to examine this German hunger strike in some detail, for it illuminates many of the processes involved in the political and personal features of the contemporary hunger strike.

The Baader-Meinhof Hunger Strike

In the late 1960s, West German radical groups became involved in a 'war' against 'capitalism and imperialism', which resulted in a number of bombings and deaths. A small group of sympathisers coalesced around Andreas Baader, an ex-student, and Ulrike Meinhof, a radical journalist. The Baader-Meinhof group, as they become known, were responsible for a number of bombings and arson attacks against Western military installations and forces and businesses.

Baader and Meinhof, and others of the group, were eventually captured and sentenced to life imprisonment. Whilst in prison, they orchestrated an elaborate campaign to continue what, in their terms, they saw as the challenge to the German State, through protests and terrorist incidents, to accusations of torture, and eventually hunger strikes and death. In a sense, they terrorised themselves to recreate and continue the process they had initiated in their bombing campaigns.[31] Horst Mahler, one of the terrorist group, highlighted the *political* and outward looking purpose of the hunger strike when he said that it was used '. . . as a whip against the Left to mobilise them . . .'.

A series of kidnappings, hostage takings, bombings and protests occurred, organised by members of the group not captured, in an attempt to force the release of Baader and other members of the group. When these failed, and the German authorities proved to be resistant to pressure of this form, the tactic of the hunger strike was developed. Gudrun Ensslin captures the essence of this, when she describes the hunger strikes as using their bodies '. . . as our ultimate weapon'. This threat of death failed to move the German authorities and, in using their bodies as the ultimate weapon, Andreas Baader, Gudrun Ensslin and Jan-Carle Raspe committed suicide.

The circumstances in which this occurred were intended to suggest that they had, in fact, been murdered by the prison authorities; this does not appear to be the case, although there still remains some doubt about the events. What is clear is that their deaths were, in an immediate sense, related to the failure of a hijacking of a Lufthansa aircraft, and the taking hostage of its 87 passengers. The Palestinian hijackers of the aircraft demanded the release of Baader and the others in return for the release of the aircraft passengers. The hijacking eventually terminated at Mogadishu. Here, during the course of the negotiations, the Captain of the aircraft was murdered, and the passengers placed in what appeared to be very real mortal danger. A German anti-terrorist squad successfully stormed the aircraft, releasing the passengers unharmed (although killing 3 of the 4 hijackers).

When news of this operation reached Stammheim prison, in which Baader and the others were held, on the night of 17 October 1977, it appears to have triggered a suicide pact. Using weapons hidden in their cells, Baader apparently fired two shots at the wall of his cell, arranged the empty shell cases around him, and killed himself by firing into the nape of his neck. Jan-Carl Raspe also used a hidden gun to shoot himself through the temple. Gudrun Ensslin hung herself from her cell window grating with a piece of loudspeaker wire, and Irmgaard Möller stabbed herself four times in the chest; she alone of the group survived. Controversy persists still as to whether the group did commit suicide, or were murdered by the prison authorities, although official investigations have firmly concluded in favour of suicide. Even though Irmgaard Möller survived, and supported the murder theory, she has, in fact, contributed little to clearing up the circumstances of her own injuries, let alone the deaths of the others.

The Baader-Meinhof hunger strikes resulted in death, but not through starvation. Thus they stand apart somewhat from the more typical hunger strikes already noted, in that they lack the temporal and media qualities of prolonged death. The Baader-Meinhof example does illustrate, however, the essentially *political* context in which the suicides took place, and the way in which the *process* of the hunger strike, and the eventual deaths, reflect essentially ideological political forces, rather than personal dynamics. The unresolved accusations of murder simply serve to emphasise more clearly the importance of the processes of self-victimisation and the shift in responsibility for the deaths, as referred to in the introduction to this chapter, which might even be seen as a further sophistication of the development of the political process.

Irish Hunger Strikes 1980-81

The most dramatic recent examples of politically motivated suicide can be seen in the series of hunger strikes held by Republican prisoners in Northern Ireland during 1980 and 1981 which resulted eventually in the deaths of 10 hunger strikers. Analyses of emotive contemporary events, especially when bound by current conflicts, present obvious difficulties. This applies particularly to these hunger strikes, and the events surrounding them have acquired in some circles in Ireland an almost ethereal quality, inspiring admiration or revulsion depending on political position.

The political focus of these hunger strikes, like much Republican terrorist activity in Ireland, ostensibly relates to the ideological aim of a united Ireland, and the removal of British control from the Province of Ulster. The immediate origins of these hunger strikes lay in the 'dirty protest', when post-1976 Republican prisoners protested against being treated as prisoners, rather than enjoying the special category political status of earlier prisoners. In protest at having to wear prison clothes, the prisoners refused all clothing, and this escalated through disputes over the circumstances in which washing and personal hygiene took place, to the point where prisoners deliberately fouled their cells. Some 1300–1400 prisoners took part in the 'dirty protest', out of a prison population of some 2500. This in itself seems to be an outstanding example of *self-victimisation*, which offers unrivalled propaganda opportunities for portrayal as *victimisation*, and was of course used as such. Associated with this campaign was a programme of selective murder of prison officers, which inevitably contributed to a further exacerbation of conditions within the prison, and raised community tensions.

This strategy proved to be ineffective in achieving the short term ends, but demonstrated the existence of a large pool of latent support for the terrorist groups. To tap that support further, and perhaps emulating the sentiments expressed by Gudrun Ensslin, the prisoners 'used their bodies ... as their ultimate weapon' by embarking on a hunger strike. Initially, this consisted of seven men undertaking a mass strike in 1980, which collapsed after 53 days. This was then followed by the more extensive and better planned staggered hunger strikes of 1981, during which 10 men died. Given the failure of the earlier hunger strikes, it was probably inevitable that the second series would result in the deaths of the participants. In contrast to much of the emotive and factional literature on these events, the process of these hunger strikes has been well reviewed by Beresford.[32]

In contrast to the hunger strikes discussed earlier, these hunger strikes, and the dirty protest which preceded them, were tightly controlled and organised by the leadership of the paramilitary groups involved. Illicit but effective communications between the prisoners, and between the prisoners and outside, were maintained throughout, which made possible the sensitive management of the associated political protests through various support groups, and limited the ability of the prison authorities to control or influence events. The importance of this was foreshadowed by the Baader-Meinhof hunger strikes, where again co-ordinated action was possible because of communication between prisoners.

The pressure under which the prisoners were placed during this period cannot be underestimated, but it must be stressed that, in any formal sense, all the hunger strikers were volunteers. What this might mean in the circumstances at that time, however, may be more complicated. In many ways, parallels can be drawn between the processes of volunteering for martyrdom shown by the Shi'ite terrorists and the prisoners in this case. As in the Shi'ite case, many indicated their willingness to take part in the hunger strike, and from this pool were chosen by the prisoners' leadership those who were to take part. The contexts which apply to both allow the use of the term 'volunteer', but of course at the same time qualifies its meaning. The rather naive discussion in psychological terms of the hunger strike offered by Irish Republican authors[33] should be seen in this light.

The pressures to which the prisoners exposed themselves were considerable. On top of the constraints of prison life, the dirty protest represented a period of self-victimisation which heightened tensions and probably created intense social and group forces which almost inevitably escalated to and led from the dirty protest self-victimisation to the more extreme acts of suicide through starvation. But perhaps one of the most potent elements, serving to focus and enhance the group processes which inevitably occur in such circumstances, was the sense of militant purpose and direction (reflecting the essentially millenarian ideology of Irish Republicanism) which the political intentions of the hunger strike gave to the participants and their leadership. As Taylor and Ryan[34] have noted, within a combative but constrained political community, '... what more positive and confirming militant expression can be envisaged than political suicide?'

These hunger strikes were an explicit element in the political programme of the Provisional IRA, as in the earlier Baader-Meinhof hunger strikes, where media images were associated with well-organised structured political protest activities which, in turn, fed into the strategy of the hunger strikers. The first hunger striker eventually to die, Bobby Sands, was a very clever choice around which to develop a political campaign. In contrast to many of the later hunger strikers, Sands readily fitted the stereotype of the idealist, in contrast to the 'hoodlum'. He appears to have been articulate, and was physically attractive. As part of the political campaign associated with the hunger strikes, he was elected as a member of the British Parliament for the Fermanagh–South Tyrone constituency whilst on hunger strike, attracting enormous publicity in the process. The political consequences of these hunger strikes were considerable, serving to politicise the Nationalist community in Northern Ireland in an unprecedented way. They became a focus for protest, a process enhanced by the way in which the hunger strikes were stage-managed so as to result in a regular series of deaths.

Paradoxically, the extreme organisations of these hunger strikes, and the degree of control which that seems to indicate, may well have served ultimately to diminish their effects. Perhaps the degree of organisation which they showed crossed the barrier of what Skinner referred to as the conditions in which we give credit to behaviour. Certainly, after the shock of the first deaths, suspicions began to arise, not only about the extent of explicit coercion involved in maintaining the steady stream of suicides but also the capacity of prisoners in such extraordinary circumstances to be said to have 'freely' chosen to participate. Certainly, some of the relatives of the hunger strikers appeared to take that view. The diminishing returns of the serial hunger strike is shown by the fact that whilst the name of the first hunger striker to die, Bobby Sands, is well remembered, relatively few people outside of the Nationalist community in Ireland know or remember the names of those who died later. As far as is known, there is no obvious evidence of psychopathology amongst that group of hunger strikers, and it would seem inappropriate to seek explanations of their actions in terms of mental illness.

What is it that makes the hunger strike so potent a political symbol in Ireland? Whilst hunger strikes have invariably been used as part of Irish nationalist protest, outside the Irish context the hunger strike does not seem to be related *per se* to extreme and militant nationalism. Similar contemporary extreme militant nationalist movements (such as the Basque terrorist group ETA, for example) do not use the hunger strike as a political tactic. In contrast, more explicitly political terrorist movements in Spain have. For example, two members of the rather mysterious Spanish terrorist group called GRAPO have died on hunger strike in Spanish jails. GRAPO is an extreme Maoist organisation thought to be responsible for the deaths of over 30 people in Spain. These hunger strikes were not, however, part of a clearly defined and orchestrated propaganda campaign. The most recent hunger striker to die, on 25 May 1990, was Jose Manuel Sevilliano Martin. He was one of a group of convicted GRAPO members protesting against the dispersal of the group to different Spanish jails.

To achieve some end, hunger strikes are not, of course, necessarily different from the examples described in this chapter illustrating the more general processes that might be involved in political self-victimisation. They are usually less dramatic, and rather more mundane. Furthermore, when they are successful, we probably don't invest them with such emotional significance. The hunger strike of Avis Naccache illustrates this. Naccache was an Iranian national convicted of participating in a bungled bombing attack. He undertook a 19 week hunger strike in 1990, in an apparent attempt to blackmail or otherwise persuade the French Government to release him to Iran. It would appear that he was successful in the pressure he put on the French Government, for he was released early from French custody in April 1990.

The orchestrated and serial political hunger strike does represent a more developed form from the simple hunger strike, and merits further investigation on the more general processes that might be involved in political self-victimisation. Indeed, it is that context (as is the case with Iranian terrorism) that is all important in establishing the *behavioural* (as opposed to personal) features of the hunger strikes.

Analyses of Irish nationalism are complex, obscure and controversial. Because nationalist aspirations impinge on contemporary events, there is a dynamic quality to the conceptual analyses that makes it very difficult to be objective. Nor is it the purpose of this chapter to undertake such an analysis (although a useful discussion of the process has been given by Townshend[35]). It is sufficient for our purposes to draw attention to the importance of the notion of 'sacrifice' and 'martyrdom' as personal action in Irish culture as a context for both legitimising and sustaining the idea of self-victimisation. Indeed, the importance of this motif can be seen in the proclamation of the Irish Republic by Patrick Pearse in 1916. It began: '. . . In the name of God and the dead generations from which she receives her old traditions of nationhood, Ireland, through us, summons her children to her flag and strikes for her freedom. . . .' In this, there are echoes of Robert Emmet's speech from the dock in 1803. '. . . Let no man write my epitaph. . . . When my country takes her place among the nations of earth, then, and not till then, let my epitaph be written.' Emmet set out to lead, and made preparations for, a rebellion which degenerated into a rather minor street disturbance, which nevertheless holds a more symbolic importance in the mythology of Irish nationalism than the events in themselves would appear to merit.

Historical and cultural legitimisation of death for the purpose of propagating an ideology, when combined with the cohesiveness of shared religious belief (in the case of Irish nationalism and Roman Catholicism) which is itself intimately linked with nationalist aspirations, might well create conditions like those described by Arendt[36] as lack of public space (as discussed in Chapter 4). As we have noted, lack of public space in Arendt's view is intimately linked with man's 'sense of reality'. Like all political suicides, the hunger strike above all seems directly to challenge what most of us see as 'reality'. This might be a useful way of coming to terms conceptually with the hunger strike.

Another related theme that may help conceptual analysis is the notion of martyrdom, which is frequently associated with a reversal of failure into victory. This in its turn relates to the Paradox of Morality referred to earlier. Toloyan[37] has discussed the notion of 'martyrdom as legitimacy' in the context of Armenian nationalism, and there are many parallels that can be drawn between the Armenian and Irish context, that support the notion of martyrdom as an essential feature of nationalist aspiration. For example, both countries share similar religious values, and both have a history of defeat or occupation, where legitimacy of historical leadership seems to be associated not with victory, but rather defeat, which becomes interpreted as martyrdom. The very beginnings of Irish nationalism illustrate this, in the suicide of Wolf Tone.[38] Tone (interestingly enough a Protestant) led a rebellion in Ireland against English rule in 1796, making use of French troops as the catalyst for rebellion. The adventure failed and Tone was eventually captured in 1798. He was sent to Dublin for trial, where he committed suicide in his cell. Like many other Irish nationalists, Tone is thought of in the context of having 'died for Ireland', and his death begins the depressing cycle of which the hunger strikers are a part and which we see still so clearly today. These general cultural forces, ill defined as they may be, set the context for the Irish hunger strikers just as much as the martyrdom of Hussein legitimises Shi'ite martyrdom.

Processes of Self-victimisation

We have characterised the hunger strike, and also the Shi'ite suicide bombings, as self-victimisation, and we have noted at length the paradoxical and disturbing social and political features of political suicide as self-victimisation. It seems to be both illogical and bizarre, raising spectres of mental illness and abnormality. Yet, as we have examined it in greater detail, whilst it may remain bizarre, it clearly appears less and less irrational and abnormal. Taylor[39] has extended this analysis to other examples of self-victimisation within a political context, such as Buddhist self-immolation and the Japanese Kamikaze pilots of World War II. Indeed, less visible forms of politically orientated self-victimisation in the contemporary world may be relatively widespread. Furthermore, there are grounds for proposing that examples of self-victimisation come in waves, suggesting an imitative factor at work.

In the above, we have attempted to place the hunger strike within its broad social context. How might we now begin, therefore, to understand it in psychological terms in an individual context? Expressing the problem more explicitly within a behavioural framework, if we assume behaviour is related to its consequences, how can self-victimisation be understood in these terms?

An initial point which must be made is the need to distinguish

between general facilitating conditions and the immediate circumstances that give rise to a particular act. In this chapter, we have
made reference to the general cultural and historical circumstances
that give rise to the notion of martyrdom as a legitimate element in
political life, using examples from both Islamic and Irish context. (We
should note that both Islam and Irish nationalism are examples –
other societies or religions could have provided the basis for our
discussions.) Cultural and historical circumstances undoubtedly
impinge on behaviour, setting the conditions in which particular
behaviours can emerge; they may be said to if not define, at least
contribute to, the behavioural repertoire of the individual. The *particular* circumstances which give rise to individual acts can be distinguished from these forces, however, and it is to these particular
circumstances we now turn.

One way of attempting to understand the particular conditions
which give rise to behaviour involved in self-victimisation is to begin
by considering the more general problem of self-injurious behaviour
outside of a political context. If it is possible to identify a framework in
which such behaviour can be understood, it may then be possible to
locate within that framework the special characteristics, if there are
any, of politically motivated self-victimisation. Such a framework is
provided by clinical studies of self-injury as an element of some
abnormal behaviour states. The study of self-injurious behaviour in a
clinical context has tended to focus on its incidence in children
although it is not confined to childhood, and a recent review[40] has
noted its incidence over a wide range of patient populations. Self-
injurious behaviour is a relatively rare but very distressing feature of
some retarded or psychotic states, but it can also occur in individuals
with no known pathology, although usually to a lesser degree. When it
occurs in a clinical context to an extent that requires attention, it is
often either a life-threatening activity, or one which has the potential
for profound physical damage if left unchecked.

It should be noted that self-injurious behaviour in the clinical
context is generally not thought to be associated with lethal intent. It
usually takes the form of dermal, occular or genital mutilation,
although other forms are noted (e.g. head banging). On the other
hand, whilst it is clearly different in focus from political self-injury, it
may well represent a model of *processes* on which we can draw in
furthering our knowledge of political suicide. There have been a
variety of different explanations offered for self-injurious behaviour
but, as reviewed by Ross,[41] self-injurious behaviour seems to be best

understood in terms of the consequences of the behaviour, and especially within the clinical context, attention in some form. Attention serves as a positive reinforcer, actually serving to increase the self-injurious behaviour. Given this view, some of the obvious actions taken to protect a self-injurious child (such as restraint for example), whilst intended to prevent its occurrence, actually serves to sustain its development further by providing increased attention, however that attention might be given.

We know that the intention behind a third party initiating some particular act in this sort of situation need not necessarily have much relationship with the *actual* events and controlling circumstances that develop. Thus, whilst the caretaker of a self-injurious child might be attempting to restrain and minimise the damage, the attention (for example) which inevitably follows from restraint may well serve to further reinforce and develop the self-injurious behaviour. In a sense, therefore, it may be that in some circumstances the balance of positive consequence of attention exceeds the negative consequence of self-injury and resultant pain. We see here what is essentially an analysis of self-injurious behaviour as a learned response to the controlling circumstances (or consequences) of the environment. The potency of the situation is enhanced in the case of a child, for example, by the very nature of self-injury which ensures a swift and energetic response on the part of responsible caretakers, thereby maximising reinforcing qualities despite pain.

A similar analysis, in terms not necessarily of attention, but other kinds of reinforcing consequences, might be equally applied to suicide as political self-victimisation. Political self-victimisation can result in considerable public and personal positive consequences, which may well outweigh other more negative outcomes. Thus publicity, media attention, sympathy of significant others, and increased esteem may be potent forces to sustain and enhance self-victimisation. Furthermore, where self-victimisation occurs within an imminent millenarian context, where personal action may contribute to the attainment of the millenarian ideal, we can see a very strong positive consequence to that action.

We have already noted in Chapter 4, however, that explanations of behaviour in terms of 'linear' accounts of behaviour and consequence, whilst they may be appropriate in some circumstances, do not necessarily characterise all. In particular, in the context of ideological behaviour, we have stressed the importance of behavioural control, not in terms of control of immediate consequences but in terms of rule following. This is a powerful explanatory tool to introduce here; part of the paradox of political suicide is the contrast between what might be assumed to be the most powerful immediate contingency available (continuance of life) and death. Powerful reinforcers like attention may help explain self-injurious behaviour (where a reinforcer like attention is more 'powerful' than a negative consequence of self-injury), but this seems to be a weak explanation of death. On the other hand, strong and powerful rule-governed control over behaviour is a much better way of expressing ideological (and of course in our terms fanatical) insensitivity to immediate events, augmenting powerful immediate contingencies.

Cerutti[42] has discussed some of the circumstances that can contribute to insensitivity of rule-governed behaviour to immediate contingencies, and this analysis seems particularly appropriate here. The distant contingencies which give rise to rule-governed behaviour inevitably imply a measure of insensitivity to immediate contingencies, mediated by qualities such as compliance. An added dimension to this may well be the social context in which such self-victimisation might occur, which may result in even greater enhancement of the reinforcing consequences of compliance with ideological defined rule following. Here we might see in a sense the intermingling of culture with personal circumstance. This social context might be apparent in at least two senses: the supportive powers of the group, and the way in which as a society we value behaviour where there seem to be '... visible reasons for behaving to the contrary'.[43] Paradoxically, the peculiarity of self-victimisation might also lie at a social level, in terms of broader assumptions about the social organisation of behaviour contrasting with the essentially personal dynamics of an individual act.[44]

The power of both compliance with ideological prescription of behaviour and of group forces in the control and shaping of behaviour cannot be underestimated. In the context of the aetiology of terrorist violence, this has been discussed in earlier chapters, and has been more extensively discussed by Taylor.[45] Within the context of this chapter, whilst death as the consequence of self-victimisation has a finality lacking in the clinical examples outlined above, nevertheless it may be located within the same broad conceptual framework. There can be no doubt that such behaviour is rare and extreme, and no doubt requires special conditions for it to occur – in this book we have identified these conditions as militant ideology, millenarianism and lack of public space. But given this, the paradox of personal death being seemingly of less importance in the balance of consequences than the propagation of a religious, political or ideological cause becomes more understandable.

'Suicide is, after all, the result of a particular behaviour, and that behaviour is ... susceptible to the kinds of forces that control all behaviour; and we know that these forces in the main are related to immediate situational variables. Allied to this there may well be special qualities appropriate to particular ideologies, especially if that ideology has a strongly developed sense of militancy, perhaps associated with messianism in some form. In these circumstances, what more positive and confirming militant expression can be envisaged than political suicide?'[46]

The social and ideological context in which these behaviours might take place remains all important. Whilst this context might be expressed in behavioural terms as a variety of group forces and rule-governed contingency relationships, a useful way of elaborating further on this in a political context is, perhaps, to return to Arendt's concept of public space.[47] She attributes a number of important negative properties to lack of 'public space', and in particular we have noted that she uses it as a concept to help to explain the capacity of people to inflict atrocities on others. It is of some interest to speculate here that as in conditions of mass society (characterised by Nazi Germany), the examples of self-victimisation which we have considered all occur in constrained and limited social circumstances such that in Arendt's terms, public space cannot develop. This seems obvious in the sense of the prisoners on hunger strike (in prison, lacking open access, and in the cases discussed here, subjecting themselves to an extreme process of self-victimisation through the dirty protest), but it might equally result from the lack of plurality which occurs when all share a common militant social, religious or ideological view, as in an extreme sectarian state, such as contemporary Iran.

Clearly related to this are the ways in which we allocate 'credit' for behaviour, as much to ourselves as by others. In this context, we might also note again the comments of Skinner referred to earlier. Social approval of behaviour (and perhaps self-approval) seems to be inversely related to the conspicuousness and visibility of the causes of behaviour. As Skinner notes, outside of pathological situations, where there seem to be reasons for behaving differently, we give maximum credit. This helps us to understand the paradoxical qualities of self-victimisation, and its social consequences. The following quotation seems to be particularly appropriate in the context of this chapter:

'. . . We may coerce soldiers into risking their lives, or pay them generously for doing so, and we may not admire them in either case, but to induce a man to risk his life when he does not 'have to' and when there are no obvious rewards, nothing seems available but admiration.'[48]

The martyr, the Islamic terrorist, and the hunger striker all share attributes of 'not having to' in the sense that they were not subject to explicit coercion by a formal contractual relationship to do what they did. That the *personal* context in which they lived effectively provided something similar to that coercion little diminishes the sense of apparent choice which we assume, and which above all seems to be the quality that leads to our admiration. When mixed with political purpose, this represents a very powerful force in which the self-victim, mediated by ideological commitment, can participate.

The processes that Skinner is referring to are clearly related to what social psychologists have termed *fundamental attribution errors*.[49] This refers in part to our persistent tendency, when we look at another's behaviour, to ignore the context in which behaviour takes place, and to seek explanations in terms of disposition rather than situational causes. We tend to see people behaving as they do because of the 'kind of person' they are, rather than because of the environmental determinants of that behaviour. It also relates to what has been termed *the actor-observer* effect; the tendency to attribute our own behaviour to external or situational factors, but that of others to internal causes. An interesting and relevant example of this latter error can be seen in a part of the transcript of the interrogation of Irmgard Möller at the Bundestag Commission of Inquiry into the deaths of the Baader-Meinhof group in Stammheim prison,[50] of which Möller was the sole survivor.

Member of the Commission: 'Suppose you are on hunger strike so long that you die, do you call that kind of thing suicide?'
Möller: 'Never.'
Member: 'Why not? What would you call it?'
Möller: 'It's obviously murder.'

Möller's response is a typical illustration of both the actor-observer error where the result of the individual's own actions are attributed to some, perhaps unspecified, external agency, and also an illustration of the essential qualities of political self-victimisation. Suicide through its political context becomes murder, a common enough motif in the process of the hunger strike. Additionally, in different circumstances, where ideological forces provide the context, a similar process results and the suicide becomes martyrdom, where external forces again determine and legitimise suicide behaviour. Thus we can see the development of qualities of 'martyrdom' where self-victimisation becomes victimisation. The external attribution processes also gives us some clues as to how the *political* power of these acts come to be expressed, for quite clearly, political aspiration requires an external, as opposed to personal, referencing.

It might be argued that the political recognition of the effectiveness of the processes we have discussed above is a contemporary phenomenon. Camus[51] seems to suggest this in his discussion of the relationship between suicide and murder, although the political force of the martyr has of course long been recognised. However, the profound political power of the juxtaposition of such fundamentally abhorrent acts as murder and self-victimisation cannot be denied, and it represents the crossing of an important and disturbing boundary in the conduct of our affairs.

'... the very first thing that cannot be denied is the right of others to live. Thus, the self-same notion which allowed us to think that murder was a matter of indifference now undermines its justification....'[52]

CHAPTER 8

Black Milk of the Dawn: the SS and the Concentration Camps

The SS as an organisation that embodied many of the qualities associated with the development of political violence is discussed. The forces acting upon two examples of the SS membership (the camp guard and Dr Joseph Mengele) are used to illustrate how behavioural processes might help our understanding of the horrific events of the concentration camps.

In contemporary life, the image and reality of the concentration camps remains enduringly powerful. Paradoxically, their fundamental and essential inhumanity serves to place them outside normal discourse. The images are perhaps so horrific that conceptually they are alien to most of us. Perhaps they are so horrible that we have to deny or ignore them. Yet the concentration camps existed and we ignore them at our peril.

It is a commonplace observation to note that the impetus for fullest expression of the concentration camp ethos emerged in a country, Germany, which has contributed more than most to what Europeans might regard as their cultural heritage. This same country pursued a programme of genocide with a vigour and energy that can quite properly be described as fanatical. The administrators and operatives of the concentration camps acted with a singlemindedness of purpose, guided by political and ideological structures, which embodied most of the attributes of fanaticism which we identified earlier. That same ideology created powerful rule-governed contingencies that, in many ways, typify the processes discussed in this book. This chapter will attempt to throw some light on the processes that allowed and facilitated those appalling events. Concentration camps, or their equivalent, are not of course unique to Germany; nor is their incidence solely an aberration of the 1930s and 40s. For example, the Pol Pot régime in Cambodia during the 1970s arguably created conditions which rivalled those which obtained in Nazi Germany, and there is ample evidence of similar atrocities being conducted elsewhere (the Soviet Union during Stalin's régime, for example).

The German concentration camps were all liberated in 1945, yet even now, discussion of the circumstances that surrounded life in the concentration camps remains difficult for the outside observer. For that observer, it is hard to view the events of the camps with any degree of objectivity. Some authors such as Arendt[1] even feel that the experiences in the camps can never be understood. She is critical of Kogon,[2] for example, because he attempts to achieve some psychological understanding of the events of the camps. Certainly, any discussions that seem to explain (and perhaps, in doing so, to reduce) the horrors of the camps must be viewed with great caution, and must in no way be taken to condone those events, even by implication. Nor should any explanation be taken to limit or constrain the enormity of the concentration camp experience on the inmates, or those family members who survived. What follows in this chapter must be understood in this light.

Whilst the Nazi Party provided the ideological and political framework for the concentration camps, the principal agency which practically managed and sustained the camps was the military formation, the SS (*Schutzstaffel*). In this chapter we will attempt to understand how members of this organisation came to commit the crimes they did. We will approach this by describing how individuals became members of the SS, and how that membership influenced their lives. Initially we will do this by describing the organisation and social context of the SS, moving on from that to identify and establish the psychological pressures that influenced individual members of the SS. This, in turn, may help us to better understand their actions, and will enable us to locate these actions within the context of ideological control as rule following.

The SS: a Paradox

The SS was a major military and social institution of the Third Reich, having an important and pervasive symbolic and physical presence. Its membership in 1939 was thought to be in the region of 250,000 which by 1945 reached 400,000 to 500,000. Its top figure of membership probably was in the region of 750,000.[3] It was, therefore, numerically important as a large well-trained and armed force. In addition, it was also a well-indoctrinated ideological tool, providing a secure and forceful facility to undertake political action. The SS, as we will note, undertook an array of security functions within the Third Reich, but for our purposes we should note that amongst other duties, it was the organisation which had principal responsibility for both the practical management and the conditions which obtained in the concentration camps. It was condemned by the International Military Tribunal at Nuremberg as a criminal organisation guilty of crimes against humanity.[4] It was therefore an organisation with a large membership, which, as we will see, was in many ways central to the expression of Nazi ideology.

There can be no doubt that both collectively and individually members of the SS committed the most appalling crimes; crimes of such barbarity and inhumanity that to the observer they defy understanding. Because of this, we are inclined to try to explain their actions either by reference to some form of extreme psychopathology, or with reference to moral imperatives. However we try to explain their actions, we tend to characterise the SS member as a bizarre caricature of all that is evil and abhorrent.

No doubt such caricatures existed. It is difficult not to regard the account of concentration camp life given by Alfred Balachowsky, a survivor of concentration camps Buchenwald and Dora as evidence of the veracity of this caricature.[5] He describes what appears to have been a trade in tattooed and other human skin at Buchenwald concentration camp. 'I saw SS men come out of Block 2, the Pathological Block, carrying tanned skins under their arms. I know from my comrades who worked in Pathological Block 2, that there were orders for skins: and these tanned skins were given as gifts to certain guards and to certain visitors, who used them to bind books.' The head of the camp at the time, SS Standartenführer Koch, had a preserved human head in his office, and a lampshade made from human skin.[6]

The following extract of the interrogation of Andreas Pfaffenberger by United States Army officials[7] gives a little more detail of these particular events in Buchenwald:

'In 1939, all prisoners with tattooing on them were ordered to report to the dispensary. No-one knew what the purpose was; but after the tattooed prisoners had been examined, the ones with the best and most artistic specimens were kept in the dispensary and then killed by injections administered by Karl Beigs, a criminal prisoner. The corpses were then turned over to the Pathological Department where the desired pieces of tattooed skin were detached from the bodies and treated. The finished products were turned over to SS Standartenführer Koch's wife, who had them fashioned into lamp shades and other ornamental household articles. I myself saw such tattooed skins with various designs and legends on them, such as 'Hänsel and Gretel', which one prisoner had on his knee, and the designs of ships from prisoners' chests. This work was done by a prisoner named Wernerbach.... There I also saw the shrunken heads of two young Poles who had been hanged for having relations with German girls. The heads were the size of a fist, and the hair and marks of the rope were still there.'

It is difficult to understand these repulsive events. Furthermore, that there was a 'trade' in ornamental human artifacts extending beyond the individuals immediately involved beggars belief. Whilst it might be that the individual who seems to have been principally concerned, Koch, was extreme and highly unusual, his actions were known to others, and if not condoned, certainly not publicly condemned at their outset. Other official SS personnel appear to have participated in the trade by placing orders for skin, and generally providing a market for it. The prisoners presumably had no option but to co-operate, but certainly the other camp supervisory SS personnel were in positions to object. They did not. In any event, this gruesome example takes its place alongside a catalogue of horrors that have rarely been equalled, either as individual acts of bestiality, or as organised and controlled activities.

Yet in spite of behaviour like this, one of the victims of the camps at Dachau and Buchenwald, Bruno Bettelheim, can also say of the people who supervised and perhaps condoned or tolerated such acts that they

'. . . were people who, under other circumstances, would be considered normal, ordinary persons. From my own experience I can vouch that many of the SS men who ruled the concentration, and a few years later also the extermination camps, were ordinary people, bent on making their career within the system . . ..'[8]

Similarly, Cohen emphasises that:

'I do not consider the camp SS as sadists . . . it seems possible that among the camp SS men there were sadists, but the latter did not put their seal on the camp SS . . ..'[9]

Indeed, as Arendt[10] notes, there are grounds for saying that systematic efforts were made by the SS authorities to identify and 'weed out' those members who derived physical pleasure from what they were doing.

The most striking quality of the Nazi supporters was their ordinariness, and the SS seemed to be no exception to this. The paradox of the SS lies in the apparent capacity of what might be regarded as otherwise unexceptional people to inflict and participate in the most appalling examples of human degradation. Yet it is in this paradoxical capacity that we can see the operation of the forces of fanaticism which we have described in this book. This capacity extended across a broad array of individuals, and wasn't simply confined to odd atypical members. It embraced many others, extending for example to professionals like medical doctors, who might be expected to have had a caring attitude towards people which would prohibit their involvement in such acts. Cohen[11] illustrates this when he quotes a section from the diary of Professor Dr. Hans Hermann Kremer, who on 29 August 1942 was ordered to go the Auschwitz concentration camp to deputise for a physician who was ill. This quotation is reproduced in part below, to illustrate the apparent ease with which Kremer is able to juxtapose the epicurean with descriptions of the most appalling horror, In the quotation, reference to '*Sonderaktion*' (special action) refers to spectacular mass atrocities, often performed before visitors. One form of *Sonderaktion* practised at Auschwitz was the burning of live prisoners, especially children.

September 2, 1942. First time present at a *Sonderaktion* at 3 hours in the morning. Compared with this, the Inferno by Dante seems to me as a comedy. Auschwitz is not called for nothing the 'camp of extermination' . . . .

September 5, 1942. This afternoon present at a *Sonderaktion* from the female concentration camp (*Musselmänner*). The most horror of horrors. Hschf. Thilo, doctor of the troops, is right when he told me this morning that we are at *anus mundi*. In the evening, at approximately 8.00 hours, again present at a *Sonderaktion* from the Netherlands. Men all want to take part in these actions because of the special rations they get then, consisting of a fifth litre of schnapps, 5 cigarettes, 100 grms sausage and bread. Today and tomorrow on duty.

September 6, 1942. Today, Sunday, excellent lunch: tomato soup, half a hen with potatoes and red cabbage (20 g: fat), sweets and marvellous vanilla ice . . . in the evening at 8.00 outside for a *Sonderaktion*.

September 20, 1942. Listened to a concert of the prisoners' band this afternoon in bright sunshine. Bandmaster: conductor of the Warschauer Staatsoper, 80 musicians. For lunch we had pork, for dinner baked tench.

September 23, 1942. Last night present at 6th and 7th *Sonderaktion*. In the morning, Obergruppenführer Pohl arrived with his staff in the house of the Waffen SS. . . . In the evening at 2000 hours, dinner with Obergruppenfüher Pohl in the leader house, a real banquet. We had baked pike, as much as we wanted, good coffee, excellent ale and rolls. . . .

Professor Kremer did not have to serve in Auschwitz, nor carry out the duties of camp doctor. There are many examples of people who refused to take part in activities of this kind. Cohen[12] describes the situation of another camp doctor, an SS Captain Hofter, who in attempting to give medical care to prisoners came into conflict with the Chief Physician of all concentration camps, SS Colonel Dr. Lolling. Hofter applied for transfer to the front, a request which was quickly agreed. There are a number of other examples which suggest that it was possible not to take part in work in the concentration camps, which leads to the inescapable conclusions that those who worked there in some sense wanted to, or at least saw the cost of transfer to be less desirable than remaining in the camps. Indeed, there are grounds for supposing that many members of the medical profession in Nazi Germany condoned and co-operated with Nazi actions.[13]

There is another sense in which we can see German officials' ambivalence to the horrors of the camps. It was recognised by the SS authorities that service in the camps or similar work in the field amongst the Einsatzgruppen, for example, and the horrific duties which that entailed, was a source of stress to the men, and that allowances should be made for that stress. Many official German documents presented to the International War Crimes Tribunal make reference to this and the potential for damage to SS members of some of the work which they did. SS Untersturmführer Dr Becker, for example, referring to the use of mobile gas vans used for the extermination of Jews, makes the following plea to his superiors:

'I should like to take this opportunity to bring the following to your attention: Several commands have had the unloading, after the application of gas, done by their own men. I brought to the attention of the commanders of these special detachments concerned the immense psychological injury and damage to their health which that work can have for those men, even if not immediately, at least later on.'

We can see quite clearly, therefore, that on the one hand, the SS were capable of the most barbaric and inhuman acts – they properly merited conviction for crimes against humanity. Yet the individual participants were, in the main, recognised by both their authorities and at least some of their victims as ordinary people, in some measure vulnerable, and in respects other than those associated with the atrocious activities in the camps and their duties therein, relatively normal. Haritos-Fatouros[14] has addressed a similar paradox in his analysis of the military tortures during the period of military dictatorship in Greece from 1967 to 1974. We can seek the resolution of this paradox both in terms of the nature of the SS organisation, and in terms of the action of ideological control arising from membership of that organisation, as the processes we have identified which give rise to and sustain political fanaticism as rule following. Indeed, what we have referred to above as the paradox of the SS is clearly not limited to the particular organisation of the SS. We can suggest that it is shared by many organisations where distant rule-following control substitutes for more local immediate contingency control. The extreme example of the SS merely serves to make this more clear. We can begin to see how this might occur by considering the development of the SS organisation.

The Origins and Development of the SS

The origins of the SS lie in the efforts of the National Socialist Party to achieve political power in Germany during the 1920s. Its earliest existence seems to have been in the '*Stosstruppe Hitler*' (Shock Troops) in 1923, but this grouping was quickly disbanded, to reappear in 1925 initially as a 'Headquarters Guards' (*Stabswache*) which was later in the same year extended and renamed the *Schutzstaffel* (Protection Echelon). Its primary function was to provide a personal bodyguard for Hitler, and to act in some measure as a personal police force. The active role of the SS was largely eclipsed in 1926 with the reinstatement of the SA (*Sturm-Abteilung* – Storm Detachment), but it reemerged in importance after 1929, when Heinrich Himmler was appointed *Reichsführer SS*. From a membership of 280 in 1929, it grew in size to over 50,000 by 1933.

In essence, the SS developed as an élite force, unquestionably loyal to Hitler, and '. . . intended for security duties as opposed to the offensive mission of the SA'.[15] Those security duties extended beyond the person of the Führer, however, to include the internal security of the Reich. In this respect, it should be noted that in practice, if not in name, the internal police systems within the Third Reich eventually also came within the broader control of the SS. In 1936, Himmler was appointed by a decree of Hitler '*Reichsführer SS und Chef der Deutschen Polizei*' in circumstances which Buchheim[16] has argued effectively led to a merger in command of the Police forces of the Reich and the SS.

Thus, the SS grew from essentially a Party cadre, to the effective security organ of the Reich, and in the process, effectively enshrined Nazi Party objectives in the law enforcement and security objectives of the Reich.

To achieve the organisational ends envisaged for it, various branches of the SS developed, reflecting specialist focusing on particular aspects of security duties. Whilst the organisational structure of the SS shows clear evidence of dynamic functional development, in general, four major branches can be identified (although these branches did not necessarily all exist at any given time; nor were the boundaries between branches necessarily always clear cut). The first branch we can identify, the *Allgemeine* (General) *SS*, was described by the International Military Tribunal[17] as '... the common basis, the main stem, out of which the other branches grew. It was composed of all members of the SS who did not belong to any of the special branches.' Its members could include part-time volunteers, who have been described as '... voluntary political soldiers'.[18] In its early years, membership of the *Allgemeine SS* was not particularly demanding, requiring limited attendance at events, participation in sports, and some ideological preparation. Indeed, it was possible to become an 'Honorary Member' (*Fördernde Mitglied*) who simply undertook to pay a monthly subscription which was left to the individual's own discretion. For this, '... (i)n return he was entitled to wear the Honorary Members' badge and, more important still, was left in peace'.[19]

The second branch of the SS which we can identify was the *Waffen* (Armed) *SS*.

'The armed SS originated out of the thought: to create for the Führer a selected, long-service troop for the fulfilment of special missions. It should make it possible for members of the General SS, as well as for volunteers who fulfil the special requirements of the SS, to fight in the battle for the realisation of the Nationalist Socialist idea with weapon in hand in unified groups partly within the framework of the Army.'[20]

Thus, this branch of the SS was analogous to, and clearly in many ways complementary to, the Army. The term *Waffen SS* did not come into use until 1939. In origin, it emerged from the *Verfügungstruppe* (Special Service Troops) and the *Totenkopfverbände* (Death's-Head Units). The latter eventually emerged as the third branch of the SS, with the *Verfügungstruppe* constituting the *Waffen SS*.

The *Totenkopfverbände* are described by D'Alquen[21] as '... one part of the garrisoned SS'. It was made up of volunteers from the *Allgemeine*

SS, who were specifically recruited from 1933 to guard concentration camps. Its members were originally mainly ex-soldiers, and their previous military service counted towards the 12-year service obligation of membership of the *Totenkopfverbände*. The fourth branch of the SS, which focused on security, was the SD (*Sicherheitsdienst*). In origin, an ideological internal security branch, the functions of the SD developed under its chief Heydrich into a sophisticated espionage and secret police organisation.

Coherent and forceful arguments were presented at the International War Crimes Military Tribunal to establish that the SS as a whole was guilty of war crimes, and that all the various branches of the SS shared some part in the collective guilt of the organisation. This is an important issue, for arguments have sometimes been presented to, in some sense, distinguish the *Waffen SS* from other branches of the SS, on the grounds that it was under military command in the field. This seems to be an oversimplification. There was a long history of disputes between the *Wehrmacht* (the Conventional Armed Forces) and the SS over their military role. This resulted, amongst other things, in the SS being unable to seek members through press advertisement, the result of restrictions resulting from the *Wehrmacht*; indeed, because of this, applicants for membership to the SS were largely drawn from National Socialist organisations, such as the Hitler Youth (*Hitler Jugend*). Buchheim[22] discusses this issue at length, and concludes that the *Waffen SS* were outside of both the National Socialist Party and the State. They were part of '... the Führer authority sphere and part of the Führer Executive'. Furthermore, in organisational terms, after 1940 the term *Waffen SS* included all SS formations, including the Concentration Camp Inspectorate and Concentration Camp Organisation. There can be little doubt that all branches of the SS seem to have either taken part in some way or had knowledge of atrocities.

The focus of the discussion here, however, is not so much the general activity of the SS, but its role in the creation of the conditions that existed in the concentration camps. Whilst the *Totenkopfverbände* in origin were recruited for concentration camp duty, on the outbreak of the War, members of the *Allgemeine SS* replaced them, and undertook concentration camp guard duty. Because members of the *Totenkopfverbände* generally had previous military service, they constituted a useful supplement to the *Verfügungstruppe*, and in time became a part of them for the remaining duration of the war.

Becoming an SS Member

Membership of the SS was voluntary and in a sense competitive, and a selection procedure ensured the appropriateness of recruits. This rule changed in 1944 when men began to be drafted into the *Waffen SS* to make up numbers, because of the very heavy losses on the Eastern Front. The fundamental principle of selection was what Himmler described as 'Blood and Élite'. Racial 'purity', as judged by physique, ancestry, and freedom from hereditary disease was matched by personal and family ideological purity. As time passed, the dispute over recruitment between the *Wehrmacht* and the SS referred to above resulted in the membership of the SS being largely drawn from ideological committed National Socialist organisations, primarily the Hitler Youth, thus confirming and enhancing the ideological 'purity' of the organisation. However, this has to be understood in the context of the explicitly ideological function of organisations like the Hitler Youth, where eventual membership of, and status in, the principal organs of the Nazi Party were valued and presented to members as appropriate desirable ambitions. Within this context, membership of the SS might well have represented the fulfilment of ambitions for volunteers from the Hitler Youth.

Indeed, the Hitler Youth itself had within it a form of self-policing organisation, the *Streifendienst*, which served as a direct vehicle for recruitment into the SS. In an agreement between Himmler and the leader of the Hitler Youth in 1938, this is made quite clear:

> '... Since the *Streifendienst* in the Hitler Youth has to perform tasks similar to those which the SS perform for the whole movement, it is organised as a special unit for the purposes of securing recruits for the General (*Allgemein*) SS. However, as much as possible, recruits for the SS Special Troops, for the SS Death's-Head Units (*Totenkopfverbände*), and for the officer-candidate schools, should also be taken from these formations.... The selection of *Streifendienst* members is made according to the principles of racial selection of the *Schutzstaffel* (SS). The competent officials of the SS, primary unit leaders, race authorities, and SS physicians, will be consulted for the admissions test....'[23]

Within the context of National Socialism, the SS regarded themselves, and were regarded in general by others, as an élite force, whose function was actively to progress, in practical terms, the ideological objectives of National Socialism. Its élite qualities was expressed in terms of loyalty, obedience, courage, truthfulness, honesty, comradeship, responsibility, industry and abstention.[24] These qualities were supposed to be evident in their dealings with their own 'racial' groups;

their attitudes to other racial groups was very different, however, and well expressed by Himmler in 1943:

> 'One fundamental rule must be absolutely observed by the SS man: we must be honest, decent, faithful and friendly to those who are of our own blood and to nobody else. What happens to a Russian, to a Czech, does not interest me in the slightest.... Whether other nations live in prosperity or starve to death interest me only in so far as we need them as slaves for our culture: otherwise I am not interested.'[25]

At least until the exigencies of war forced change to procedures, there existed therefore a direct route of entry from the Hitler Youth (and other similar organisations) and the SS. That route was both premised on, and clearly emphasised, particular ideological qualities. We might see the function of such youth organisations, therefore, almost as a process of distillation, focusing and developing Nazi ideology. In effect, such youth movements created powerful conditions for the development of a special form of political socialisation.[26] That form of socialisation had, as a fundamental quality, millenarianism.[27] The ritual, the imagery, the very bases of the ideological indoctrination given to young members emphasised the qualities of millenarianism referred to in Chapter 5. Given this, the militant Nazi ideology and the profoundly enclosed and controlling nature of the Nazi régime, we can clearly see the foundation of a process establishing the distant rule-governed contingencies which subsequently shaped and facilitated the events of the concentration camps. In a sense, all education serves to establish future rule-governed contingencies of the form we have referred to here. The difference in this case, however, is the totality and consistency of the control established. The processes that facilitate the development of fanaticism in this context inevitably follow from such control.

The Concentration Camps

The development of the power of the SS in the Nazi State and the development of the concentration camp system were intimately related. The concentration camps (*Konzentrationslager*) were a sophisticated element of the Nazi programme of social control initiated, controlled, and dependent upon the SS. Their social and intimidatory influence greatly exceeded their actual size, which was itself of considerable capacity. The contemporary view of them is in terms of the extermination programmes of the later part of World War II; however, their existence and development paralleled the development of the Nazi Party, and the Nazi State, and the camps occupied a variety of political and economic roles. However, they were also the embodiment of Nazi ideology, and in a sense operationalised in a most compelling way the behavioural consequences of its ideological prescriptions and the more general processes of militancy, millenarianism and lack of public space. Indeed, they were the inevitable expression of the forces we have described in this book, and their development parallels in many ways the developing control of the ideological factors of imminent millenarianism, lack of public space and militancy.

In the very beginnings of the Nazi State, the concentration camps were principally conceived of as instruments of social control, although they in fact had considerable autonomy from both the Nazi Party and the State. The earliest concentration camps grew out of the secret locations used by the SA and the SS for holding their enemies. These early secret prisons were used to keep prisoners of the SS and SA out of the normal prison system, and retain them under their own control. They were largely quasi-legal autonomous punishment camps established in association with local Nazi Party officials. For example, Dachau was an early SS camp affiliated with *SS-Gruppen Süd* and *Ost*. As the Nazi Party developed its power, the concentration camp model developed, to the extent that during 1933–34 each SS region had associated with it a concentration camp. The staff which ran the early camps were often those who were poorly equipped to undertake other SS or SA duties, and the camps were a suitable location to dump not only prisoners, but unsuitable SS members. At this stage, the camps were purely instruments of punishment, and were used as such by both the SS and SA for service punishments, as well as for interning civilians.

From 1934 onwards, efforts were made to systematise and regularise the activities of the camps. After the SA purge of 1935, the camps as a whole came under the general direction of the SS, and were staffed by SS officers for guard and other duties. Administrative control of the camps fell either to the SS, or to the Gestapo (*Geheimes Staats-Polizeiamt*, State Secret Police Office), effectively removing the camps from local SS control. However, despite these administrative moves, some camps still remained under direct local SS control, which illustrates the complex nature of the camp structure, even at this relatively early date in the development of the Nazi State. Dachau, for example, remained under direct SS control. Furthermore, the Dachau complex included not only the concentration camp, but the general SS training camp, a supply camp, a police headquarters and the 'assembly point' for Austrian refugees. In terms of personnel involved as guards, however, in 1935 distinctions began to be made between those SS who undertook administrative duties within the camps (largely older members) and those that undertook guard duties and supervision of work details (young volunteers). This distinction paved the way for the establishment of the *Totenkopfverbände* (Death's-Head Units) in 1936.

Life for prisoners in the early camps was uniformly brutal, and the régimes were orientated towards punishment. Corruption amongst the guards was endemic, which paradoxically gave prisoners some slight opportunity for relief if they or their relatives could take advantage of it. In order to address some of these problems, in 1936 a series of reforms were initiated to improve the control over the guards and to improve the ideological position of the *Totenkopfverbände*. The result of these changes were to increase the degree of military training for the guards, and as far as the prisoners were concerned, to brutalise further conditions, so that even more intense punishment became the norm for breaches in camp discipline. At this time, plans were also laid for the closure of older camps, and for building camps at potentially more advantageous economic and political locations; the camp at Sachsenhausen, for example, was one such camp, opened in 1936.

Around this time as well, bureaucratic changes were set in motion to enmesh the camps into broader Nazi economic aspirations. From the very beginning at Dachau, workshops had been established to produce equipment for the SS. These workshops were subsequently extended to other camps, and as military planning began to develop in 1936 for German expansion, and ultimately war, the concentration camps became more clearly enmeshed within the Reich's economic planning. After the 1936 Olympic Games, programmes for rounding up potential slave labour for use in the concentration camps began. Groups of the so-called 'work-shy' and 'antisocial', such as professional criminals, pacifists, and various religious groups, were drawn into the camp system as workers to contribute to the Reich's economic development. Along with this, there was an increase in the size of the *Totenkopfverbände* to accommodate the increasing demands of prisoner management. At this time in 1937, the 'modern' concentration camp at Buchenwald was opened.

Contemporary commentary and analysis of the concentration camp system tends (quite rightly) to emphasise the horror and the moral degeneracy of the extermination programmes. We should not forget, however, that in many ways death in the concentration camps was a largely incidental event, secondary to other considerations, which often were associated with economic exploitation or deliberate neglect. It can be argued that this is even the case for the later explicit extermination camps; certainly from 1936–37 onwards, the economic potential of the concentration camps began to be realised and developed. Economic factors became more and more important determinants of such things as location of the camps (near to quarries, for example), the development of satellite camps (providing workers for local industries, etc.), and so on. These developments gained renewed impetus with the onset of the war and German occupation of the European countries.

As the war progressed, quasi-legal camps became established (echoing the original development of the concentration camps) in the occupied territories as collecting points for people who were rounded up by the SS and the local police; these camps were guarded by SS personnel. The camps at Auschwitz, Stutthof and Lubin, for example, began in this period. These camps were administered largely by personnel from the older camps, as were later camps established in 1940 and 1941 at Natzweiler, Neuengamme and Gross Rosen. These administrators were frequently of very poor quality, and the resultant incompetence undoubtedly contributed to the increasing brutality of the concentration camp régimes. In addition, the *Totenkopfverbände* cadres ceased to be used as guards, and guard duties were undertaken by others, many of whom were not even SS members (some 35,000 people appear to have acted as guards, of whom 10,000 were not SS[28]). Those that were SS members were often rejects from other units, or later in the war were wounded and incapable of occupying effective fighting roles. This undoubtedly contributed to the development of a brutal ethos in local régimes, into which were fitted new recruits to the ranks of the guards. Movement of personnel between camps merely served to reinforce these features.

As the war developed, however, economic forces began to be felt increasingly in the camps, as demands for more and more production were made. It can be argued that the mutually contradictory forces of increased brutality and economic production themselves further contributed to the development of degrading and truly inhuman conditions. On the other hand, even with their relative limited efficiency achievements of the production processes coupled with the undoubted efficiency in mass extermination reveals in them a frightening degree of co-ordination, competence and organisational flexibility. Adolph

Eichmann perhaps personifies the efficient bureaucrat who both developed and served the system.

Indeed, whilst we tend to focus on the brutality of the camps, the administrators of the camps and the system they served were themselves much more interested in the fulfilment of administrative, bureaucratic and economic goals. Adolf Eichmann, for example,[29] readily fits into the mould of an ideologically committed, efficient if narrow and unthinking administrator, rather than a raving psychopath. In the later concentration camps, labour was exploited for a variety of purposes, especially in construction-related areas such as the production of building stone, and newer camps were located to maximise their economic potential. Other areas of economic activity included such things as the production and distribution of food, clothing and furniture. These were often done in association with quasi-State companies, which drew on Party and State funds, and also private funds from the German banks and other institutions. Membership of the boards of directors of these companies included private citizens as well as senior SS officers. They provided opportunities for enrichment for their members on an enormous scale, and undoubtedly set the scene for the subsequent economic exploitation of prisoners not only through their labour, but also through their deaths and the attempts at the commercial use of their bodies and personal possessions.

Indeed, economic forces (both State and personal) for exploitation in Nazi Germany can also help to explain a number of other features of the Nazi régime. The most oppressed group of all, the Jews, offered unrivalled opportunities for exploitation and, arguably, from 1933 this economic exploitation provided the driving force behind the persecution of the Jews. That such persecution had in Nazi thinking an ideological basis merely legitimised lucrative opportunities for both the State and private individuals to expropriate Jewish wealth. Subsequent persecution of occupied peoples can be seen in a similar light. As the German State developed, so did the personal exploitation of Jews and other victimised groups become more and more organised and associated with the concentration camp system. By 1941, the productive potential of the concentration camps was being increasingly realised, which undoubtedly played a role in sustaining the German war effort. The labour needs of the German economy began increasingly to be met by the establishment of numerous satellite camps near factories, and prisoners' labour was bought and sold on a commercial basis.

The International Military Tribunal at Nuremberg[30] heard details of the scale of the programme of mass enslavement which supported German industrial production. It was estimated that some 4,795,000 people were involved in labour programmes. The conditions under which they were kept were appalling; poor food, lack of rudimentary hygiene, and physical abuse was the norm. One notable organisation which was intimately involved in the use of concentration camp labour was the German industrial company Krupps. In an affidavit submitted to the International Military Tribunal by Dr Willhelm Jäger, details are given of the conditions endured by foreign workers in the Krupps factory at Essen in 1942 to 1944. Eight satellite camps were established to service this factory. These camps were grossly overcrowded, with prisoners enduring great privation whilst being forced to work. Food was inadequate, sickness endemic, and the work régime brutal. The poorness of the conditions reveals one of the tensions evident in the concentration camp régime; the pressure to contribute to economic objectives, and the desire to eliminate and exterminate 'undesirable' elements, especially Jews. That these conflicting objectives were apparent to German planners, and gave rise to critical comment, can be seen in a document presented to the International Military Tribunal[31] where complaints are made about the economic consequences of extermination policies.

However, we should also note in relation to the above some caution. Whilst economic objectives undoubtedly played an important role in the development of the concentration camp system, some authors believe that the economic contribution of the camps has been exaggerated. Arendt,[32] for example, notes that the organisation of the camps was not particularly well suited to economic achievements. In her view, they did largely serve to finance their own supervisory apparatus, but little more. Camp buildings, and so forth, were almost always constructed by inmates, but the *quality* of the work was notoriously low. Kogon says of work in the camps:[33]

> '. . . A large part of the work extracted in the concentration camps was useless; either it was superfluous or it was so miserably planned that it had to be done over two or three times. Buildings often had to be begun several times because the foundations kept caving in. . . .'

As a resource behind the supply of the SS, however, the camps occupied an important position, contributing not only to the political independence of the SS, but its economic independence as well, reducing its dependency on other agencies.

Conditions in the Camps

Although the camps shared a common overall objective, and were staffed by a broadly homogeneous group (the *Totenkopfverbände*, and later other SS members), the various camps differed in their régimes. One obvious fundamental difference was between the extermination camps and the work camps, but even within these broad categories of camps, there were differences in régimes. Bettelheim[34] identifies three basic types of camps: *'re-education' or punishment camps*, where a brutal régime was developed to primarily intimidate and punish, *slave labour camps* which housed essentially expendable but temporarily useful workers, and *death camps* which were established to effect the 'Final Solution of the Jewish Problem' – their extermination. Not all the functions that this division implies were confined to particular camps, and particular camp conditions were more pragmatic than such a division would imply. Jews, for example, when shipped to death camps would nevertheless undergo a form of selection procedure to separate out those capable of work from those who were thought incapable; the latter would be killed immediately, the former would be worked for some time before being killed. Similarly, the death rate in both punishment camps and slave labour camps was very high; indeed, for many, their only release was death. Also, to confuse the issue further, the different kinds of camps might well be located in the same facility (at Auschwitz, for example).

Between camps, individual régimes could result in differences for inmates. In Dachau, for example, Bettelheim[35] notes that official punishment (as distinct from random abuse) was always directed at the individual. There was even a semblance of due process involved (a distant echo of a legal framework), in that before punishment was inflicted, there was a hearing before a commissioned SS officer. A camp doctor also inspected the prisoner before punishment (a flogging, for example). This seems to have been effectively an empty procedure, but at least it suggests some degree of order. In contrast, in Buchenwald, transgression by individual prisoners resulted not in individually monitored punishment, but some form of group punishment, where the working group collectively suffered for an individual member's transgressions. Rousset[36] similarly describes differences in régimes between, for example, Buchenwald and Neuengamme. This suggests that a difference in individual camp 'ethos' could be identified, presumably related to personnel, which was quite independent of the overall objectives of the concentration camp programmes.

For the inmates of the camps as they experienced conditions, however, these differences were to a large extent irrelevant. The conditions were uniformly appalling, degrading and inhuman. There is an enormous literature of survivors of the camps, and it is unnecessary to describe the particular indignities and horrors suffered by inmates here. Indeed, survival from the camps seems to demand for survivors the expression of their experiences, and many angry and moving accounts are available.

Our concern here, however, is not so much with the conditions inflicted on the inmates, but the circumstances that allowed the expression of those conditions. The furtherance and propagation of those conditions were not actions which spontaneously occurred. They were developed and maintained by both the organisational structure which sustained the camps, and the individual camp officers and guards. The zeal and vigour with which the duties of the camp officials were discharged seems truly to merit the term fanatical, in that it probably illustrates in a fashion unrivalled in the contemporary world the attributes of fanaticism which we identified in Chapter 2.

The Camp Staff

The camps were planned exercises in control and death. As such, they operated because of, and by, human agencies. The vigour with which the policies were implemented, and the ingenuity shown in the execution of these policies, seems appropriately termed fanatical. Who, then, implemented and controlled these policies? What kind of people were they? Can we come to terms with understanding their extraordinary and repulsive behaviour?

We can identify two broad categories of officials involved in running the camps: the senior staff, and the guards themselves. Both in different ways created the conditions in which inmates in the camps existed. Of those two categories of officials, detailed information is only available on the former – the senior staff. Indeed, such information that is available on them tends to relate to the more notorious of the senior staff, rather than the mundane. Furthermore, much of this information comes from the War Crimes Tribunal, and as such it is often not particularly orientated towards psychological or behavioural analysis. Nevertheless, some examination of that material as it pertains to one individual may serve as an example that will enable us to develop insights into the general activity of that group.

We should also note that a third group of individuals was involved in the detailed management of the camps, drawn from the ranks of the prisoners themselves. Much of the detail of such aspects as organisation of work duties and maintenance of discipline was undertaken by chosen and trusted senior prisoners. These prisoners, called Kapos, were often in the camps for committing criminal offences, rather than for racial, social or political reasons. Within limited parameters, the Kapos were given wide powers over prisoners under the direction of the guards. In return, they enjoyed status and somewhat improved conditions. Their activities largely lacked the broad political context of the camp officials, and their conduct seems more appropriate to analyses of sheer brutality rather than political violence. We will not be particularly concerned with them here, for the factors leading to their complicity in concentration camp violence are somewhat tangential to the focus of this work. We should not forget, however, that the Kapos materially contributed to the degradation and inhumanity of the camps. What this means is that, in effect, a camp's political and racial inmates were further victimised by other non-political prisoners.

Dr Joseph Mengele

Joseph Mengele is in many ways a good example on which to base a discussion of the qualities of senior Nazi staff. He was the camp doctor at Auschwitz during the later part of World War II and he has become known in the demonology of the Nazi era as 'Doctor Death', or 'The Angel of Death', one of the most hated and reviled of all the Nazi war criminals. He undertook 'scientific' research in Auschwitz aimed at the ultimate production of a genetically superior race, using mainly (but not exclusively) twins as subjects. Amongst his routine camp tasks was the selection of those from the transports who would be immediately exterminated in the gas chambers, and those preserved for work. After the defeat of Germany, he was never captured, and his whereabouts are unknown. He has generally been reported as living in South America, where amongst a relatively large expatriate Nazi community he reputedly advised dictators and took part in the drug trade. Mengele is thought to have died in 1979 in Brazil, where his grave was later claimed to have been found.

We have already noted our tendency to explain extreme behaviour in terms of mental illness, and explanations of Mengele's activities are no exception to this. Indeed, examples of his activities can most comfortably be understood in terms of abnormality, for any alternative explanation may be simply too much to accept. Yet such analyses of Mengele that are available,[37] and the reminiscences of those who knew him, do not seem to support a view based on psychopathy. On the contrary, they present Mengele as a relatively normal, if rather intense, individual who, in another context, would probably have gone unremarked. As we examine this further, we are not seeking to domesticate and thereby reduce the appalling atrocities with which he was associated. But further examination does enable us to place into perspective the forces that led to, and sustained, Mengele's behaviour. Indeed, in many ways, Mengele will serve us as a case study in the development and attributes of the fanatic, illustrating the operation of the forces we have identified in this book.

Mengele was born on 16 March 1911, the child of a reasonably wealthy Bavarian industrialist. Early friends remember him as popular, enthusiastic, and friendly. He did quite well in school, and was generally regarded as intelligent and ambitious. This latter quality probably persisted throughout his career and may well be related to some of his subsequent actions. His family had Nazi connections; his father, for example, is thought to have entertained Hitler in 1930 and the family ethos seems to have been supportive of the Nazis. Certainly, the family business prospered under Nazi rule. In 1931, Mengele became involved with right wing nationalist organisations, and joined the SA in 1933, applying for Nazi Party membership in 1937, and SS membership in 1938. He had, therefore, a long, early and continuing association with the National Socialist Movement and a consistent exposure to Nazi ideology. The ideologically focused content referred to earlier, therefore, had opportunity to exert its influence over Mengele. All the evidence suggests that indeed it did.

Mengele was a promising medical student, who gained a higher degree in anthropology as well as medicine. It is of some significance to note that his Ph.D. title was 'Racial Morphological Research on the Lower Jaw Section of Four Racial Groups', foreshadowing his interest in the genetical bases of racial differences. After various internships, he worked in the Third Reich Institute of Heredity, Biology and Racial Purity in Frankfurt, under the direction of Professor Freiherr Otmar von Verschuer, where he published three papers concerned with physical characteristics and abnormality. These papers were interpreted from a view emphasising the role of heredity. Mengele's ideological disposition well suited the Institute; it was closely associated with Nazi scientific ideology, as Professor von Verschuer indicated in 1935 when he defined the role of the Institute as being '. . . responsible for ensuring that the care of genes and race, in which Germany is leading the world, has such a strong basis that it will withstand any attacks from outside'.[38]

Mengele's work, emphasising the genetic and racial bases of behaviour, was supportive of Nazi ideology, and as we have noted, there is evidence that he encountered, and became sympathetic to, these ideologies relatively early in his academic career. We should note, however, that such views were not so unusual then, even outside of Nazi Germany. In Germany, at that time, the scientific establishment, and indeed the academic world generally, was more inclined to accept explanations of behaviour (and its physical correlates) in genetic and racial terms than contemporary workers would be. We should not underemphasise the extent to which Nazi ideology was accepted in German academic circles. Indeed, National Socialism commanded great support amongst some German intellectuals,[39] the more so after the exodus of Jewish and radical intellectuals in the early stages of Nazi rule.

The extent of Nazi ideological support and complicity in the actions of the Nazi State amongst official and academic circles was considerable, the extent of which remains even now largely unacknowledged.[40] Mengele was not by any means alone as a medical doctor in participating in the extermination programme, although he may have been unusual in his *direct* involvement. Distinguished German medical scientists, many of whom remained in their academic posts after the war, appear to have lent their wholehearted support to the Nazi eugenic programme, for example. This support seems to have been particularly evident in the German psychiatric establishment and extended, for example, to participation in the processes leading to the extermination of mental hospital patients. The following quotation from a report by a psychiatrist, Professor K Kleist in 1938, on the mental hospital at Herborn, reveals in its apparent concern for humane conditions the nature of care given at Herborn. '. . . As long as there is no law for the destruction of lives unworthy to be lived, those who are beyond cure have the right to humane treatment which assures their continued existence. The expenditure on these unfortunates should not fall below an acceptable minimum level. . . .'[41] The institution at Herborn killed mental patients through starvation and illness as a matter of policy.

The Nazi euthanasia programme was officially condoned in September 1939, and in October of that year in excess of 283,000 questionnaires were distributed to evaluate the extent and identity of incurable inmates in mental hospitals. These were completed by 9 Professors of Psychiatry and some 39 other Doctors of Medicine with psychiatric backgrounds as expert evaluators. The doctors received as payment between 5 and 10 pfennigs for completion of each questionnaire. Using this process of expert participation, at least 75,000 patients were identified for extermination. Müller-Hill notes that there is no record of any protests from psychiatrists, either collectively or individually, against this procedure. The development of procedures for the efficient extermination of mental hospital patients parallel those of the concentration camps, and indeed, camp facilities were used to 'process' some hospital inmates. We can see from the above that the medical ethos and establishment of the time would have found little difficulty in accommodating to Mengele's activities.

Contemporaries of Mengele suggest that, like many others, he wholeheartedly subscribed to Nazi ideologies. He accepted the Nazi doctrine of Nordic superiority and he became a vehement and extreme anti-semite. Later friends of Mengele describe him as being '. . . fully convinced that the annihilation of the Jews (was) a provision for the recovery of the world and Germany'.[42] The emphasis on hereditary factors of abnormalities which characterised his scientific work was consistent with, and no doubt intimately related to, Nazi ideology. We can, therefore, reasonably assume, in the terms in which we have discussed in Chapter 4, an extreme degree of ideological control over Mengele's behaviour.

Mengele's early education had all the hallmarks of success and he appeared to have aspirations towards an academic career. In July 1938 the University of Frankfurt awarded him his medical degree. By then, Mengele was regarded as a well placed up and coming researcher, who could indeed clearly anticipate an academic career. However, with the onset of the war, Mengele redirected his aspirations, and served in the armed forces as an SS member. During 1938–39 he served six months with a mountain light infantry regiment, followed by a year in the reserve medical corps. He then spent the next three years in the *Waffen SS*, serving mainly in Eastern Europe, including the Russian front. During service on the Russian front, he was wounded, and declared unfit for further combat. In all he received 5 decorations, including the Iron Cross First Class and Second Class. He would appear to have been a brave and successful soldier, with a commendation to the effect that he '. . . acquitted himself brilliantly in the face of the enemy . . .'.[43]

With injury marking the end of his military career, Mengele turned again to his academic interests. He seems to have explicitly asked to be sent to Auschwitz in order that he could continue his research. He was assigned as camp doctor, with the rank of *Hauptsturmführer*, to Birkenau, a female subcamp in the Auschwitz complex. Professor Verschuer, his old professor, continued to support Mengele and may well have been instrumental in helping Mengele to obtain his position in Auschwitz. He certainly appears to have been instrumental in convincing the German Research Society (*Deutsche Forschungsgemeinschaft*) to provide him with financial support to begin his research in Auschwitz. As far as can be judged, Mengele saw this move as a means of continuing the work he had already undertaken before his military experience. The camps offered unrivalled opportunities of access to human 'specimens' under circumstances in which he could effectively conduct whatever experiments he wished. It seems reasonable therefore to assume that Mengele went to Auschwitz explicitly to develop further his concept of scientific knowledge, and that his subsequent actions were directed primarily by that objective. Cruel as it may seem to his victims, the indignities and suffering he inflicted seem to have little to do with anything other than the satisfaction of his ambitions expressed through his concept of scientific knowledge allied with his ideological commitments.

In Auschwitz, Mengele was something of an oddity. As we have already noted, the camps in general were not staffed by officers of the highest intellect or military attainment; yet Mengele had a distinguished war *and* academic record. Reports suggest that he was extremely proud of his war record, wearing his medals, etc. His undoubted competence was brought to bear on his duties in Birkenau, which combined with his ideological perspective made him an enthusiastic and energetic camp doctor as well as researcher. His duties in the camp involved him in controlling and supervising such medical attention as was offered to the prisoners by inmate doctors; but his most public and notable duties were to select, from newly arrived prisoners, those who were to be sent to the gas chambers and those who were to be used for labour. Mengele brought to this task what has been described as zealousness; his energy and enthusiasm for his task made him stand out amongst the other doctors with whom he shared this duty. He was described as an elegant figure at the ramps where newly arrived prisoners were selected, well dressed and holding a riding crop as he enthusiastically performed his duties.

In this work, Mengele quite literally had the power of life and death at his disposal and he seems to have discharged that power vigorously. Dr Miklos Nyiszli, a prisoner pathologist who worked with Mengele, described the truly awful circumstances of the arrival of Jewish prisoners at the camp, and the extent of the power of the prison doctor who made the selection:

> 'Any person who entered the gates of the KZ (*Konzentrationslager* – concentration camp) was a candidate for death. He whose destiny had directed him into the left-hand column was transformed by the gas chamber into a corpse within an hour. Less fortunate was he whom adversity had singled out for the right-hand column. He was still a candidate for death but with this difference – that for three months, or as long as he could endure, he had to submit to all the horrors that the KZ had to offer, till he dropped from utter exhaustion.'[44]

In undertaking this task of selection, ex-prisoners described Mengele as having the image of '. . . a gentle and cultured man'. One inmate recalls him as '. . . a nice looking man . . . who looked at the bodies and the faces for just a couple of seconds . . . and said *Links* (left), *Rechts* (right), *Rechts . . . Links*, etc . . .'.

Perhaps one reason why Mengele was so enthusiastic in the selection of prisoners was that it offered him the opportunity to identify the twins who formed his principal research material. Twins have long been recognised as providing opportunities for research into genetic make-up, especially identical twins (monozygotic), who, because they originate from the same divided fertilised ovum, share precisely the same genetic endowments. The effects of interventions of various kinds to one twin, when compared to the other, uniquely offers the opportunity for investigating the role of genetic endowment. From the hundreds of thousands of prisoners brought to Auschwitz, Mengele identified probably in excess of 175 sets of twins. Most of these were children, although adults were included. This is more than any previous scientist has ever been able to accumulate together. Furthermore, he did this in circumstances where they were under his complete control, and where he could undertake whatever experimental interventions he wished. A fundamental flaw, however, in the whole structure of the research programme that Mengele constructed was the inevitable uncertainty about whether the twins selected were monozygotic or dizygotic (twins born together from two *different* fertilised ovums). Only monozygotic twins share the same genetic endowment; dizygotic twins have no more common genetic backgrounds than ordinary siblings. Mengele had no way of knowing what kind of twins he had; furthermore, he appears to have shown no interest or concern with this issue, a fundamental flaw in his research strategy. Not only, therefore, was Mengele's research barbaric and inhuman, it was also bad science.

Mengele's twins lived in a capricious and uncertain world, but endured few of the privations of concentration camp life. They lived in special blocks, ate reasonable food, and were often permitted to keep their own clothes. The reason for this seems to not lie with any charitable intentions, however; the twins were only of value to Mengele if they remained healthy. As might be expected in the case of laboratory animals used for experiments, conditions were arranged so that they did remain healthy. Mengele undertook careful and detailed observation and measurements of his twins, often together. His measurements were methodical and precise and there are reports of some twins being examined twice a week for a period of five months.

He also undertook experiments on them, occasionally involving the investigation of drug action. Sometimes these investigations inflicted intense pain on the children, causing them to lose consciousness, or die. On death, their bodies, as in life, were subjected to meticulous investigation to analyse the effects of hereditary influences. The appalling barbarity of Mengele's science is illustrated by Lifton,[45] who reports a deposition given in 1945 by a prisoner in Birkenau, Dr Miklos Nyiszli, who was Mengele's pathologist:

> 'In the work room next to the dissecting room, 14 gypsy twins were waiting . . . and crying bitterly. Dr Mengele didn't say a word to us, and prepared a 10 cc and 5 cc syringe. From a box he took evipan, and from another box he took chloroform, which was in 20 cubic-centimetre glass containers, and put these on the operating table. After that, the first twin was brought in . . . a 14 year old girl. Dr Mengele ordered me to undress the girl and put her on the dissecting table. Then he injected the evipan into her right arm intravenously. After the child had fallen asleep, he felt for the left ventricle of the heart and injected 10 cc of chloroform. After one little twitch, the child was dead, whereupon Dr Mengele had it taken into the corpse chamber. In this manner, all 14 twins were killed during the night.'

Mengele's intention in his work seems to have been to further support the Nazi ideological assumptions about the role of race and heredity. As far as can be seen, Mengele was not without emotions or feelings. Inmates talk of his kindness, and describe him as being '. . . as gentle as a father'. He played with the child twins, and showed every sign of affection to them. Some of the children called him 'Uncle Pepe', and indeed, in later life, some even found it difficult to believe what he had done. 'For us, he was like a papa, like a mamma' they are reported as saying.

Yet this affection was limited by other factors and it is these limitations that identify Mengele's fanatical qualities. Lifton[46] describes an incident involving two 7 or 8 year old twin boys, who were of interest because they had symptoms in their joints which were thought at the time to be indicative of a genetic basis to tuberculosis. These boys were great favourites of Mengele, and had been treated very well. Mengele was convinced that the boys had tuberculosis, whereas other doctors thought not. This gave rise at one time to a heated argument, during the course of which Mengele left the room. About an hour later, he returned, and said 'You are right. There is nothing.' To satisfy the argument, he had apparently gone to the boys, shot them in the neck, and, whilst they were still warm, dissected them.

Can Mengele's actions be described other than in terms of evil and horror? Is it possible to understand this depraved person? His actions are so far beyond the arena of the science he claimed to serve that we almost have to search for explanations in terms of abnormality, because to do otherwise admits of the potential in others to do as Mengele did. Yet the fanatical excesses of Mengele make little sense outside of the expression of his ideological and scientific aspirations. He treated his work in Auschwitz as a scientist does the world over. He read papers at scientific meetings (one in 1944 was entitled 'Examples of the Work in Anthropological and Hereditary Biology in the concentration camp'). On his escape from the concentration camp in 1945 at the end of the war, he appears to have taken at least some of his scientific data with him.[47] This would have been at some potential risk to himself were he ever discovered with it, and presumably indicates its value to him.

Indeed, the image of the sadistic voyeur does not seem to be sustained by the inmates he worked with. Mengele's victims report his apparent detachment from the events around him, and he seems to have taken no pleasure from watching or inflicting suffering. His role seems to have been primarily that of the observer, the scientist, rather than the malevolent sadist. His detachment seems to have extended to the camp surrounds as well as to his view of his own work. Dr Martina Puzyna, a Polish inmate, who in her former life had been an anthropologist and who, whilst an inmate, worked for Mengele, describes[48] Mengele's lack of regard for the immediate circumstances around him, standing transfixed by music, whilst work details carried the day's dead past him:

> 'Every day people died at work because they were so weak. Mengele was standing there, saying nothing, his head in his hands, eyes down, just listening. He was completely rooted to the spot, utterly oblivious of this march of the dead right next to him. There were the bodies and there was Mengele, just enraptured by the music. . . .'

This is not to say that Mengele did not, from time to time, indulge in excesses that were barbaric and sadistic. Given the extreme and ultimate power he possessed, the circumstances in which he possessed it, and the particular Nazi ideological commitments, it would be surprising that he did not. The important point to make is that such excesses do not properly *characterise* Mengele's actions. We see in Mengele the expression of Cohen's comment quoted at the beginning of this chapter: '. . . I do not consider the camp SS as sadists . . . it seems possible that among the camp SS men there were sadists, but the latter did not put their seal on the camp SS. . . .'[49] Mengele certainly showed no guilt or concern for his victims, but it seems wrong to describe him as a sadist. Sadism implies some sort of interest in the plight of the victim; Mengele appears simply not to have cared what happened, outside the demands and priorities of his job, his ideology, and his pseudo-science.

Nothing can condone Mengele's actions. Yet we can begin to see some of the circumstances that allowed them to occur. His absorption in a scientific purpose which to him, and those who shared his views, would materially contribute to the ultimate Nazi objectives; his enthusiastic and wholesale ideological commitment, which both supported, directed and complemented his considerable capabilities and energy; all these came to fruition in an environment that facilitated their expression in ways which would be impossible in other circumstances.

We can also see in Mengele how the various elements that we have argued earlier contribute to the development of violent fanaticism come to bear. Ideological priorities played a very prominent role in determining Mengele's actions in two senses – as a Nazi, and as a scientist. As a Nazi, ideology (including its millenarian qualities) seems to have controlled his view on racial issues and his views about the relationship of the German State to others. Its power can be judged by the extent of his commitment to the Nazi ideal, first by fighting in the SS and later by serving in his capacity as camp doctor. Scientific ideology, expressed as the attainment of knowledge, seems to have played an equally powerful role in his life, from his early education to the point at which Germany lost the war. We can only speculate about the additive power such forces might have when they are so clearly supportive of each other, as in Mengele's case.

Both ideological elements shaped and determined Mengele's actions as examples of the rule-following behaviour. His science (or rather pseudo-science) appears to have informed and controlled his relations with camp inmates. His Nazi ideology appears to have enabled the expression and fulfilment of his scientific inquisitiveness on the camp inmates as essentially expendable experimental material. We can see clearly in these two ideological elements the bases of rule-following contingencies. The qualities of rule following are evidenced in the way in which more distant but clearly articulated ideological objectives overruled what might be thought to have been pressing local contingencies related to suffering. There is no evidence to suppose that Mengele was incapable of appreciating the suffering that he was involved in – merely that he was indifferent to it, or saw it as a means towards the attainment of some greater end. Perhaps the messianic conviction of Nazi ideology, the sense of salvation related to the fulfilment of the extermination programme of the Jews, and the imminent attainment through victory in war of the millennial Reich and its ideological priorities, contributed to this indifference; or perhaps it simply legitimised the process by the ultimate desirability and attainment of those ideological objectives.

The fundamental agreement of Mengele with Nazi aspirations and the homogeneity of his world inevitably resulted in a failure to reflect upon it. What Arendt has termed a lack of public space may simply be another way of expressing the controls exercised over people like Mengele by rule-governed contingencies at the expense of those of his immediate environment. As we have noted, when powerful rule-governed forces exclude the influence of immediate circumstances (what Cerutti[50] has termed the insensitivity of rule-governed behaviour to its immediate consequences), the capacity to reflect upon circumstances will inevitably be lost, diminishing 'the space of appearance'[51] that so descriptively characterises Arendt's view on public space.

This same insensitivity is of course one of the principal attributes on which we might draw to categorise Mengele as a fanatic. Many of the attributes we described in Chapter 2 as those of fanaticism readily apply to Mengele – focusing, personalised view of the world, insensitivity, loss of critical judgement, certainty, and disdain/dismissal.

Therefore, through the operation of powerful rule-governed contingencies (expressed as ideology) we can see how Mengele both became a fanatic and sustained his fanatical views.

Mengele was in many ways a leader in the expression of Nazi pseudo-science. His scientific aspirations matched the ideological needs of the time. Can explanations in terms of ideological qualities of rule following, millenarianism, and lack of public space like that offered for Mengele help our understanding of the excesses committed by lesser functionaries of the Nazi system – the concentration camp guard, for example? Furthermore, can it throw any light on the broader problems of German support for the Nazi movement?

The Concentration Camp Guard

In contrast to the senior figures in the camp hierarchies, the guards who actually undertook supervisory duties with prisoners have received relatively little attention. They were the most numerous official group in the camps, and perhaps because they were not in executive roles, they can more readily avoid the accusations of criminality by claiming that they acted under orders, in ways in which the camp leadership cannot. This is a flimsy argument, however, even if accepted; the passivity and compliance it implies in régimes as barbaric as those of the camps must in any civilised context be regarded as unbelievable. Furthermore, what we know of camp conditions is that the guards rarely if ever intervened to ameliorate conditions for the prisoners; rather they through their actions added to the horrors inflicted on prisoners, or simply ignored them (which in some ways is even worse).

The extreme horrors committed by Mengele should not detract from the routine horror of camp life, supervised by ordinary members of the SS. As we have noted, the early camps were managed and administered by the *Totenkopfverbände* (Death's-Head Units), although later, after 1939, other SS members became involved (and also members of the *Wehrmacht*). Early membership of the *Totenkopfverbände* attracted rather less able individuals; ex-soldiers, miscreants, those who did not fit in with the general structure of the Nazi movement, yet retained the Nazi ideology. Merkl[52] gives some information on these earlier SS members, based on a series of autobiographical statements of pre-1933 SS and SA members, collected by Theodore Abel through an essay competition. These autobiographical statements as empirical evidence suffer from some methodological flaws, but nevertheless offer a rich and probably unique account of the qualities of early SS members.

Merkl developed a typology of attitudes of respondents, based on the statements in the autobiographical essays. Given the earlier discussion about the role of ideology in determining the actions of men like Mengele, Merkl's observations have particular relevance. He reports on the political motivation evident in the early attitudes of the SA and SS – 39.9 per cent were 'politically militarised' (marked by an urge to march and fight), 10.3 per cent were 'fully politicised' (highly ideologically and politically aware), 12.8 per cent were 'hostile militants' (heavy engagement in violence, and hostility to certain groups and society), 4.3 per cent were primarily authoritarian in motivation, and the remaining 33.7 per cent were pre-political or otherwise essentially 'non-political' in outlook. Thus, some two-thirds of the group were politically extreme, and ideologically or otherwise enthusiastically committed to Nazi ideals and aspirations. This contrasts with an approximate total of one-third showing similar motivations in decisions to join the Nazi Party (derived from the same source). Another striking quality which emerges from the Abel data is the evidence extent of millenarian thinking present amongst his respondents.[53] Thus the early membership of the SS seems to have been more politically extreme and influenced by ideology than members of the Nazi Party as such.

These results provide something of the background which enables us to evaluate the importance of ideology in the activities of the SS. If we see the excesses of the concentration camps as the ultimate fulfilment of the militant, messianic and essentially imminent Nazi ideology, materially contributing to its attainment, we can begin to appreciate the forces of control over the behaviour of individual SS members. These powerful contingencies, explicitly inculcated through indoctrination, created the distant rule-governed contingencies which shaped and controlled behaviour.

Many of the Abel sample seemed to have had disturbed family backgrounds of some kind, although it would be quite inappropriate to overstress the importance of these issues. Similarly, many had experience of unemployment and social deprivation in some form. Again, however, the importance of this should not be overstressed. The incidence of unemployment during the Weimar Republic and the early Nazi era was high, as was the related social deprivation. It seems more reasonable to conclude that the ideological commitments of aspirant SS was more important than unemployment as a *primary* causal agent, although the secondary (and confirming) role of unemployment and the general social conditions of the time may well be very important.

Where did the ideological commitments that provide the evidence of rule-governed contingencies come from? The influence of the various youth movements cannot be underestimated here. We have already noted the importance of the Hitler Youth organisation in channelling SS members, serving as a recruiting ground and screening mechanism. The many attractive activities such movements were able to offer members was sufficient in itself to encourage membership, and they provided an almost perfect setting for the introduction of Nazi ideology. One indicator of the effectiveness of such ideological exposure can be seen in attitudes to Jews shown by SA and SS members in the Abel sample. Merkl judged that only slightly more than one-third of the SA/SS (37 per cent) showed no evidence of anti-semitic prejudice (compared with under one-third (30.2 per cent) amongst Nazi Party members).

Merkl also presents a number of brief autobiographical sketches of the later careers of the Abel sample. He looked for as many of the Abel respondents that could be found amongst later Nazi Party records in the Berlin Documents Centre. Because they concern lesser operatives in the concentration camp structure, these accounts lack the dramatic references which have preoccupied this chapter. The role of lower rank SS in the concentration camps received sparse, if any, reference in remaining official documents. What can be gleaned is that relatively few of the Abel sample achieved particular promotion or made special progress in the Nazi régime. Those that gravitated into what Merkl terms 'the enforcers of terror' were primarily those from blue collar worker or farm backgrounds; a sizeable minority appear to have lost their fathers before the age of 18 (33 per cent) and a similar number lost their jobs in the depression (38.6 per cent); expressed religious affiliations were rare (27.9 per cent), although this probably reflects the situation in the general public. Educational levels and attainments were generally relatively low. Merkl characterised his SS sample as follows:

'Callow youths with minimal education, who grew up without a father and without religious commitment; workers or farmers, with families in social decline or foundering in the Depression, they had no higher ambition than to subject some of their less fortunate contemporaries to the régime of terror.'

The parallels between this account and more contemporary accounts of individuals involved in the systematic brutalisation of prisoners is striking. Haritos-Fatouros,[54] for example, in his analysis of the conditions that produced the 'official' torturers in the Greek Army during the period of the Greek Military Dictatorship from 1967 to 1974, describes similar features. Like the typical SS guard, the Greek torturers were drawn largely from low socio-economic classes, often from rural or village backgrounds. Ideological commitment (in the case of the Greeks, violently anti-communist) was an important element in selection. Whilst not on the same scale as the SS, the military organisation the Greek soldiers entered deliberately created and developed an environment which legitimised and normalised brutality.

Yet we must note the comments referred to earlier in this chapter by Bettelheim. The SS '... were people who, under other circumstances, would be considered normal, ordinary persons. From my own experience I can vouch that many of the SS men who ruled the concentration camps, and a few years later the extermination camps also, were ordinary people, bent on making their career within the system. ....'[55] They may not have been the most impressive or desirable elements of society – but all the evidence suggests that they were essentially of that society, and not particularly different or aberrant examples of it. As Haritos-Fatouros[56] notes of the Greek torturers: '... to believe that only sadists can perform such violent acts is a fallacy and a comfortable rationalisation to ease our liberal sensibilities'. To understand the actions of the SS, we need to look not in terms of abnormal psychological states, but at the environmental and ideological framework in which it occurs.

The SS Fanatic

Is it so surprising that in the constrained society which Nazi Germany became, with its intense, controlled ideology, excesses occurred? Perhaps the surprising feature is not that they occurred, but that they occurred on such a scale, that not only were those involved aware of what was happening, but that the broader population *must* have been aware of events, and effectively condoned them, through inaction if not active support. Allen[57] gives some indication of the conditions associated with the rise to power of the Nazi Party in a single German town which helps to place in context the nature and extent of environmental control the Nazis were able to exercise over people's lives. Regrettably, Mengele in many ways simply illustrates the prevailing ethos of the time (albeit in an extreme way).

When we look at the particular position of the concentration camp inmates, they were not just offenders or social outcasts. Because of the extreme ideological control of the Nazi régime, as Arendt notes, they ceased to have value as human beings. It is this essentially ideological position, allied with its militant righteousness, millenarian certainty, sense of personal agency, and totality of social control that made the awful events possible. Mengele's experiments and pseudo-science, for example, merely illustrate this in an extreme way. The need to encourage what we have termed fanaticism was recognised by the Nazi Party leadership. A quotation from *Mein Kampf* explicitly illustrates this:

> 'The future of a movement is conditioned by the fanaticism, yes, the intolerance, with which its adherents uphold it as the sole correct movement, and push it past other formations of a similar sort.'[58]

The emphasis on faith, control and millenarian images which permeate Nazi propaganda serve to illustrate the ideological bases of its appeal, as well as the potency of its effectiveness.

In describing the conditions in the concentration camps, Arendt[59] captures this in the following:

> 'Forced labour as punishment is limited as to time and intensity. The convict retains his rights over his body; he is not absolutely tortured and he is not absolutely dominated. Banishment banishes only from one part of the world to another part of the world, also inhabited by human beings; it does not exclude from the human world altogether. Throughout history slavery has been an institution within a social order; slaves were not, like concentration camp inmates, withdrawn from the sight and hence the protection of their fellow men; as instruments of labour they had a definite price and as property a definite value. The concentration camp inmate has no price, because he can always be replaced and he belongs to no one. From the point of view of normal society he is absolutely superfluous. . . .'

Under such circumstances, where militancy, righteousness, personal agency and racial ideology have free reign, what we regard as humanity becomes constrained.

Lest we should feel that the awful events of Nazi Germany were so unique as to defy and negate rational argument, we might note that in other arenas of World War II, parallel activities involving mass extermination took place. Recent evidence[60] suggests that the Japanese authorities were as heavily involved in the use of humans as experimental material as was Mengele. Japanese society at that time had many elements that might be thought to mirror Nazi social control, although stemming from different origins. We lack the focus of an effective War Crimes Tribunal to organise and collate the evidence, and the Japanese activities do not appear to have the racial focus that was a quality of Nazi ideology. Yet there do seem to be convincing grounds to support allegations of the use of civilian prisoners and Allied prisoners of war, in evaluating the effectiveness of various techniques of chemical warfare, which shows the same disregard for conventional humanitarian limits to behaviour. Perhaps the SS fanatic is not so aberrant and unlawful an individual as we would like to imagine when powerful ideological rule-governed contingencies gain control.

CHAPTER 9

The Normality of Excess

The broader application of the views developed in the book are discussed in relation to obedience, and more general issues of political violence.

'... we are back in the untenable position from which we tried to escape. In practice this line of reasoning tells us at one and the same time that killing is permissible and that it is not permissible. It abandons us in contradiction, with no grounds for forbidding murder or for justifying it, menacing and exposed to menace, driven by an entire world intoxicated with nihilism, and yet lost in loneliness, with knives in our hands and a lump in our throats.'

Albert Camus – The Rebel

An underlying, if largely unspoken, theme of this book is the ordinariness of explanations of fanatical political violence. Ordinariness may seem a strange word to use in the context of the brutal and unpleasant acts with which we have been concerned. We are referring, however, to the ordinariness of the process and forces that produce these behaviours, rather than the behaviours themselves. Explanations that take refuge in concepts like abnormality and psychopathology seem inappropriate ways of understanding these acts in general, even if they might be useful in some individual circumstances. Absence of pathology may not be the same as normality, of course, and the behaviours we have been concerned with are far from normal in any accepted sense. But, as we have noted, the forces which result in the expression of fanatical violence are in the main those forces that act upon the everyday lives of us all, even if the behaviour which results from them is far from normal. As suggested here, the issue resolves itself both around the notion of behavioural rule following and behavioural processes implied by some of those rules.

The implications of this for the regulation of our social affairs are very worrying. It might mean, for example, that the comfort we might take in distancing ourselves from the dreadful events we have discussed is largely illusory. There seem to be little or no grounds for supposing that the Nazi guard, or the Islamic freedom fighter, is *constitutionally* different from the Western liberal who feels such horror at the extreme violence they hear of from the media. The origins of the fanatical violence that horrifies us seem to lie in situational rather than constitutional factors. And if this is so, might we all be similarly affected given the right circumstances?

The examples we have used have of course referred to extreme social settings. Perhaps fortunately, such social circumstances are relatively rare. Nazi and Islamic examples relate to large social movements, the hunger strikes relate to more micro-environments, but both are equally unusual. Can the kinds of forces we have identified have effects in more normal social settings? In such situations, do they result in what we might term fanatical violence in the same way? Are the circumstances we have considered in extreme social settings (and therefore relatively obvious) also examples of situations that can occur more generally? These questions naturally follow from the extreme examples we have considered so far. In earlier chapters, examples have been given which reflect on this more general point, but in this final chapter we will explore some of this further. What we will now consider is the disturbing way in which fanatically violent behaviour might occur in circumstances which, at least at face value, appear to be less socially aberrant. Forces such as ideological commitment and lack of public space may well be more apparent than millenarian expectation, and perhaps we may need to amend our 'equation' of violence referred to earlier when considering more normal social situations. The general thrust of the analysis seems to remain, however.

Obedience

When we consider examples of fanatical political violence, we almost invariably find the individual concerned involved in a group of some form. This follows from the points we have noted earlier that groups are ubiquitous features of political life as forums for social and political interaction. In this sense, groups provide the context in which political activities might develop, rather than being primary forces in themselves – although again, as we have noted earlier, we can identify forces operating within groups which themselves affect group behaviour and decision making. Where a group shares a common ideological commitment, group forces themselves may become very powerful determinants of political behaviour, complementing and interacting with ideological processes. We can perhaps see group forces as providing supportive contingencies to rule-governed ideological behaviour.

Within this broad context of forces, derived from both ideological influence and membership of a group, the notion of authority and obedience is relevant. In a sense, ideology provides an 'authority' which the ideologically committed 'obey' – this is perhaps the clearest expression of ideological control as rule following that we might identify. Islam illustrates this. The term 'Islam' can be translated into English as 'submission' or 'obedience' to the law, as expressed in the Qur'an. 'Muslim' can be translated as 'that person or thing that obeys Allah's law'. Not for nothing are Muslims (and Christians) called the people of The Book. Furthermore, we also know that within any group, leadership, either informal or formal, is a critical variable in determining the nature and direction group influences might have. It might even be argued that in the most idealistic democratic group, influence, if not explicit leadership, plays a part in group decision making. Maintaining the 'party line', for example, expresses this where, of course, the 'leader' often interprets the appropriate behavioural response from a broad ideological position. Thus, in two senses, we might say that the ideologically committed are subject to the actions of authority, obey that authority, and therefore demonstrate obedience. This is through explicit injunctions derived from the ideological authority, and through group influence (directly or indirectly). The notion of obedience, therefore, is a necessary and critical element in our analysis.

In the context of fanatical political behaviour, the issue of obedience becomes even more important. Obedience in both the senses used above is often presented as the justification for violent acts. Progressing the inevitable victory of the Third Reich over international Jewry, for example, provided, in one sense, the overall authority for the individual SS member to obey his military authorities and contribute to the extermination programmes of the concentration camps. The terrorist similarly obeys not only the broader ideological prescriptions associated with his particular cause, but also obeys his own leadership in carrying out a particular attack. Overall ideological facilitation, therefore, sets the scene for obedience.

This latter point is often lost when considering violent political acts, like terrorist incidents, where we tend to focus on the broader justification, rather than on the events as they impinge on, and are experienced by, the individual terrorist. The scale of organisation involved in the activities of the Provisional IRA, for example, means that there is considerable specialisation of function of members in the conduct of their activities. When a particular target for attack has been selected, the logistics of moving weapons, explosives and other equipment without detection may present quite complex organisational problems, perhaps taking weeks to achieve. The individual terrorist who actually undertakes the bombing will probably have had little or nothing to do with the preliminaries associated with the attack. The person who plants the bomb, or actually conducts an ambush will be detailed in advance to take part in an attack, but only when he is practically on his way will he be told what the job is. In a very obvious sense, he obeys the instructions of his leadership in undertaking an attack. Those involved in the dangerous (but non-combative) activity of moving weapons, bombs, and equipment may know nothing of the eventual target. All, however, are part of the process of terrorism. This reality of individual terrorist behaviour, of course, contrasts starkly with the rhetoric of terrorist justification, with its frequent emphasis on personal responsibility and notions of freedom. The 'machine' metaphor (as in 'military machine') so often used to characterise the workings of State security activity applies just as readily to the realities of terrorist behaviour.

We can make a distinction relevant to the above between ideological justification and the factors that control individual behaviour. This is clearly similar to the distinction suggested in Chapter 1, between 'becoming' involved in some particular class of activities (becoming a terrorist, for example) and the circumstances that obtain at the time of a particular event. In this sense (as a factor in the control of individual behaviour), we can see that obedience is a very important element to consider in the expression of fanatical political violence of this kind. The very rationality of most political violence that we describe as fanatical betrays a high degree of planning and forethought: and because planning implies structure, and above all control, it also betrays an obedience relationship. Of clear relevance here are the particular factors associated with qualities of leadership (briefly described in Chapter 5), a topic related to, but beyond the scope of, this book.

Thus in the developmental process of fanaticism which we discussed in Chapter 3, the notion of obedience may well be important. However, tracing the role of obedience in the sense of relevance to us in examples of fanatical political violence is much more difficult than suggesting the processes. Most political groups of the kind of concern to us are difficult if not impossible to observe. Furthermore, the mix of potential pressures to which an individual is exposed is clearly very complex, and teasing out the various influences may be very difficult, if not impossible. However, there is one form of group which is common to most societies, and where obedience is an *explicit* element in the functions of the group. We are referring, of course, to the military. In the military, we can see, in a very exaggerated way, the influence of obedience as an element of behavioural control. Considering the extremes to which this might lead (one very obvious example being State terrorism) will help us discuss the role of obedience in the expression of more general forms of what we have termed fanatical violence.

It is important to note, of course, that the military differ in many ways from the kind of political ideological groups we are concerned with here. Generally speaking, the Western armed forces lack the explicit ideological commitment expressed in political terms we might associate with the small subversive cell. More importantly, they are the *legitimate* agency for the expression of *controlled, lawful* and *predictable* violence by the State. The fact of legitimacy, although often ignored or denied, quite clearly distinguishes an army from a terrorist group, at least within a democratic society. But there are circumstances where, for our purposes, we can usefully draw parallels between the activities of clandestine political fanatics and organised armed forces, particularly in situations where the constraint which limit the expression of violence in the military have been either impaired or are not operative.

In any given situation, a complex array of forces will doubtlessly operate. But in what now follows, we can at the very least see shadows of the forces and processes we have discussed earlier. Obedience to orders was the most prominent defence theme in the trial of Nazi war criminals at Nuremberg. The nature of World War II, and the difficulties of establishing, in detail, information about particular events from our perspective, limit the utility of pursuing in detail the notion of authority and obedience in that context. We will instead, draw upon a more recent and well-documented example to develop our analysis – the events that surrounded the killing of civilians by United States Army personnel at the village of My Lai 4 on 16 March 1968 during the war in Vietnam. This incident was not unique, nor is reference to it here a reflection on conditions in the United States Army at that time. The availability of reliable evidence simply makes it more accessible than others.

My Lai

The events that occurred at the village of My Lai 4 are unusually well documented, despite (or perhaps because of) attempts made in the immediate aftermath to cover them up. We can discern in those events an array of forces operating – in considering them, we will concentrate on only one perspective of events, as it impinges on and illustrates our discussion. The events, and their aftermath, at My Lai 4, however, go beyond the concerns of this book and contain a number of important themes which reflect on a range of contemporary issues.

The attack by Charlie Company on the village of My Lai 4 was part of a United States Army search and destroy mission undertaken against the 48th Vietcong Battalion. As such, it was a relatively minor action in the war in Vietnam, and were it not for the extent of events that happened and the eventual publicity they achieved, it would probably have passed into history along with many such operations, remembered only by the participants. That it did not, was probably the result of the presence of a photographer at the scene, Ronald Haerberle, who created a visual record of the events, and the concern of a soldier who had not even been at My Lai, Ronald Ridenhour, who heard of the events through friends and acquaintances that had been present. Ridenhour effectively 'broke' the story to the public through a series of letters he wrote; these letters, and Ridenhour's own activities, brought My Lai to the attention of Seymour Hersh, an investigative journalist, who eventually uncovered and published the events. It appears that from the beginning, the United States military authorities were in fact aware of the events of My Lai, but seem initially to have attempted to cover them up.

Charlie Company, as an infantry unit, was unremarkable. Up to the attack on My Lai, its members had achieved little by way of military success. The actions they had been involved in were limited, and frequently incomplete. They had suffered casualties from booby traps and mines rather than in action. The incident at My Lai (for in the scale of the Vietnam war, My Lai was a very minor military incident) was intended to inflict casualties on a major Vietcong formation which was thought to be operating in the area. For the men of Charlie Company, this was an important mission, for it appeared to offer them the opportunity of making the effective contribution they had so far failed to make. The attack was scheduled to take place at 0700 hrs, when it was assumed that the civilian population of the village would be away at market. Any persons left in the village after that time, therefore, were to be regarded as Vietcong. This was the first of a number of intelligence assumptions which proved to be wrong. The village was, in fact, full of old men, women and children. This erroneous assumption, although a critical variable that contributed to the scale of subsequent deaths, was not, of course, anything to do with Charlie Company. Charlie Company was airlifted by helicopter into the village at the scheduled time, and despite the fact that only non-combatants were there, began an orgy of killing, rape and torture of the villagers. In its own terms, the attack (but not the subsequent events) could probably be justified, even if the intelligence information and assumptions on which it was based were flawed. There appeared to be a high probability that the village was frequented by Vietcong, and indeed, in the initial stages of the attack, three apparent Vietcong fled the village, and were pursued and killed by helicopter gun ships; three weapons were eventually reported as recovered from the village, probably from these escaping Vietcong. But from 0800 hours, there is no evidence of even the most limited opposition to the American troops from any source.

After the initial stages of the attack on the village, the second platoon of Charlie Company to the north began '. . . to systematically ransack the hamlet and slaughter the people, kill the livestock and destroy the crops. Men poured rifle and machine gun fire into huts without knowing – or seemingly to care – who was inside.'[1] This pattern was indiscriminately carried out throughout the village. But the killings in My Lai were not simply the result of unnecessarily excessive and insensitive battle tactics. Many of the events had no military necessity at all. Vietnamese survivors described scenes of horror: for example, a baby trying to open its dead mother's blouse was shot and then slashed by a bayonet; a thirteen year old girl was raped before being killed. In total, somewhere in the region of 500 people were thought to have been killed.

Not all the deaths were in the heat of this unopposed action. There are accounts of mass executions of villagers that are reminiscent of the activities of the *Einsatzgruppen* in World War II. Some 75 villagers, mainly women and children, were gathered together at a drainage ditch. Several groups of villagers were executed in the ditch, and Spec-4 Charles Hall later testified that the villagers were '... just scattered all over the ground ... some in piles and some scattered out 20, 25 metres perhaps up the ditch.... They were very old people, very young children, and mothers.... There was blood all over them.'[2] Another witness, Pfc. Gregory Olsen, said of the victims: '... the majority were women and children, some babies ... some appeared to be dead, others followed me with their eyes as I walked across the ditch'.[3] This was stopped only by a warrant officer in an observation helicopter, CWO Hugh Thompson, landing and placing himself between the villagers and the members of Charlie Company. Indeed, Thompson's men were ordered to train their guns on the members of Charlie Company and to open fire if they fired on the villagers.

It seems unreasonable to seek explanations of the killings at My Lai in terms of some special qualities of the personnel in Charlie Company. From all the evidence available, Charlie Company was no different from other infantry units serving in the American forces in Vietnam at that time. They were aged between 18 and 21; somewhat less than half the Company were black, a few Mexican-American and the rest white. Most had volunteered for the draft, and their educational attainments, although limited, were comparable with those generally obtaining in similar companies.[4] There are no grounds for supposing that they were anything other than representative of infantrymen at that time, a conclusion also reached by the United States Army in its investigation of the Company. Yet they nearly all, in some measure, indulged in horrors which, even by the standards of the Vietnam war, were excessive and extreme, and furthermore, grossly atypical of the actions of other United States Army units involved in similar operations.

The reactions of the United States Military Authorities to the killings at My Lai 4 when they became public was to place on trial the commander of the First Platoon of Charlie Company, Lt. William Calley. Whilst almost all members of the Company had indulged in acts of gross barbarity, only Calley appeared to have deliberately organised the killings of groups of civilians rounded up for that purpose, as opposed to random shootings, or shootings which occurred as part of a fast moving sequence of events. Calley was charged with murder under the Uniform Code of Military Justice,

Article 118. He was originally charged with 109 killings, which were later reduced to 102. He was eventually convicted in 1971 of 22 killings, and received a life sentence. This was later reduced to 20 years, and then to 10. He was eventually released after serving only 3 years, all of which were served under house arrest, rather than in prison.

In warfare, killing the enemy is, of course, a part of a soldier's duty. In the kind of war conducted in Vietnam, the enemy appeared to be as frequently a civilian as a uniformed soldier. Thus it could be argued that the deaths of armed civilians (and those who are inescapably within the area of a legitimate military target) was a regrettable but inevitable, and in the circumstances 'reasonable', element of a war of the kind conducted in Vietnam. Indeed, it is in the very nature of such wars that the notion of combatant and non-combatant is explicitly blurred, both in terms of the political rhetoric of a war of liberation ('people's uprising'), and as a military strategy. The degree of coercion involved in people bearing arms does not diminish the general point. What is not 'reasonable', nor permissible in any context, was the organised element of killing that took place unrelated in any sense to combat, and it was in the organisation of the mass killings that it became possible to identify Calley. Equally, of course, it would be appropriate to assert that the rapes and torture which took place were also wholly inexcusable and unlawful. The difficulty for the United States Military Authorities in laying charges against individuals for these acts was one of identification of perpetrator, rather than principle.

Calley's defence in his trial was essentially that he was ordered to do what he did. Establishing the precise truth of this defence proved very difficult, and in any event it is not particularly relevant to our discussion. What is relevant is that the soldier generally speaking has a duty to obey a lawful order. Indeed, by failing to obey such an order, he renders himself liable for prosecution which, in some circumstances, might even lead to a sentence of death. There is also a general presumption that a soldier will obey an order, and in American Military law '... an order requiring the performance of a military duty may be inferred to be legal'.[5] However, there are limits on the duty of an individual to obey, where '... an act performed manifestly beyond the scope of authority, or pursuant to an order that a man of ordinary sense and understanding would know to be illegal ... is not excusable'.[6]

In trying to understand the events at My Lai, the behavioural forces acting upon the individual soldiers are probably much more important than the legal context of the orders they were given. It is not our purpose here to rehearse Calley's trial, nor to discuss at length the details of the orders Calley received, or those he passed on to his subordinates. Regardless of the legality of the events at My Lai, a group of otherwise perfectly normal soldiers engaged in a series of horrific acts. Although they occurred in the context of a 'legitimate' war, they are reminiscent of the acts of violence in the extreme settings discussed in earlier chapters, which we have characterised as fanatical. How then can we understand these appalling events?

The circumstances in which the events occurred are clearly very complex, and at first sight they do not seem related to the idea of ideological control over politically violent behaviour that we have emphasised throughout this book. We can say this in the sense that, for example, it would be quite unreasonable to assume that the individual members of Charlie Company were under the explicit ideological political control which is frequently assumed for members of a terrorist group. (Although we have noted earlier, however, that this assumption is probably erroneous, or at the least subject to qualification, as far as the individual terrorist is concerned.) The justification for, and the ultimate war aims of, the conflict in Vietnam were a matter of limited concern in any meaningful sense for these soldiers. In a personal sense, the events at My Lai were undoubtedly violent but, in the context used here, they do not appear to have been ideological acts in the political arena for the participants. They may, of course, be interpreted and located within an ideological framework, but that is a rather different matter from ascribing ideological motivations and control to the individuals concerned. We might assume that this will always be the case where behaviour falls outside of an explicitly political framework. However, even if this is so, it does not necessarily follow that the analysis presented here is inappropriate. The behavioural processes we have identified undoubtedly take their structure and potency from what we have characterised as ideological rule following, and this is most obviously identifiable in an explicitly political or religious context. But rule following does not only come from political or religious ideology, and other circumstances can be identified where contingencies involving explicit rule following are developed. The military offer one such example, where a disciplined environment and obedience to orders might be thought to substitute *military* for political ideology in providing rule-governed contingencies.[7] The theme common to both is obedience in the sense we have used it here.

Given this, forces similar to those we have described earlier in this book can be identified as operative in the events at My Lai, and we might certainly describe the actions of Charlie Company as fanatical, in the sense in which we have used the term here. The villagers died simply because they were the Vietnamese enemy, defined as such by those in charge of Charlie Company. In the context of that particular action, the Vietnamese villagers acquired distinctive, and in a behavioural sense, militarily ideological defined attributes.

We can see in the soldiers many of the qualities of fanaticism previously described. Most obviously the soldiers' behaviour showed a striking degree of what we earlier termed 'insensitivity', and 'loss of critical judgement'. It appears to have been under unusual and abnormal control during the action. Throughout the incident, the limits that normally apply to excessive behaviour were clearly lost as evidenced by the extreme assaults and killings. Indeed, the degree of insensitivity of the soldiers' behaviour *during* the action, and the extent to which their behaviour lacked normal social constraints, is illustrated by an event which happened after the action. By about 1100, the assault against the village was over, and the soldiers took their lunch break. During lunch, two young girls emerged from their hiding places and returned to the village. An hour before, the girls would have been ruthlessly hunted down and probably assaulted, raped or shot. Now, they were invited by the soldiers to share their food in a friendly way, suggesting that the soldiers had almost totally dissociated their earlier actions from the present. This shows, in a most dramatic fashion, the insensitivity and tolerance of incompatibility which is so striking a feature of fanaticism, but in this case bounded by the situational control of military action. It is, of course, during action that military ideology gains full expression and exercises its strongest control.

The members of C Company were quite clearly controlled by rules, which we could express as a form of ideology (although we might not normally express it as such, and this need not imply explicit political content) which obviously emphasised militancy by its very nature. These rules took the very explicit form of orders, based on both situational appropriateness and on a considerable past history of training. The structure of military institutions and command, in contrast to civilian life, support and sustain rule following to an extraordinary degree, which is even further enhanced in the particular circumstances of action. That rule following (or ideology), also by its nature and by the circumstances in which the soldiers found themselves, seriously limited public space in the sense in which we have used the concept here. The soldiers in Charlie Company, in common with other soldiers, had a duty of obedience based not only on military law, but also on training and past experience. In this context, debate and discussion of the kind related to the notion of public space, especially during action, is clearly inappropriate. These circumstances established the context that made possible the excesses of My Lai, where obeying orders merely sets the conditions for murder and violence. The sense of unreality Arendt describes in her accounts of the effects of lack of public space forcibly applies to this situation, and is of course illustrated in the example above, where the girls were offered lunch after the massacre.

In terms of this analysis, we can identify in the circumstances surrounding the events at My Lai both rule following that might be characterised as militant ideology, and lack of public space in the situation as it impinged on the members of Charlie Company. These are reflections on the military environment in the extreme circumstances of warfare. This established the facilitating context to the distortion to social constraints on violence when authority (in a broad sense of authority, or in this narrower situation of this example the command structure in general, and Lt. Calley in particular) requires obedience for deviant acts. The role of the leader in this kind of micro-social environment, as the interpreter of ideology and the source of authority, is clearly of critical importance in this example.

In behavioural terms, we can describe the contingencies that affected the men of Charlie Company in terms very similar to those we have described in our earlier discussion. Whilst the all-embracing control exercised by political or religious qualities which we have encountered earlier are lacking in this situation, we should recall that the conditions as experienced by soldiers in combat may be close to that all-embracing state. Obedience is required in circumstances of extreme and life-threatening danger, paralleling in many ways the fundamental circumstances of religious belief. The contingency rules[7] operating in this situation are 'easy to follow',[8] a quality which is enhanced by the particular circumstances of Charlie Company's weaknesses and leadership. It is even possible to speculate that 'redemption' in the sense used in Chapter 5 was attainable through success in the mission at My Lai, conferring the quality of personal agency so necessary to facilitate the expression of extreme violence.

The above is of course a *post hoc* explanation of events, rather than an empirical exploration of the circumstances surrounding Charlie Company's behaviour at My Lai. Given the circumstances, it is difficult to see how it could be otherwise. For our purposes, it does, however, serve to extend the discussion into other areas, and whilst perhaps not providing a complete explanation, may help us to focus better on analyses of analogous situations. The proposed explanation gains some force by drawing on explanatory tools which themselves have received empirical verification elsewhere. In one sense, the general account offered becomes all the more credible given the general duplicity surrounding reporting of events in Vietnam at that time, where official comment, almost to the very end, suggested that victory was imminent, and the Vietcong were consistently losing the battle. As Donovan[9] says, '. . . it was an article of faith that American military action inevitably resulted in success', something Charlie Company had been conspicuous in not attaining. The pressures on the soldiers and their leaders were, therefore, considerable, and it is not too difficult to see that the circumstances and contingencies as they impinged on the individuals involved became analogous to those described in earlier parts of this book.

In the absence of the necessary detailed information, extension of this discussion to more explicit related examples, such as State terrorism, is difficult. However, it is possible to see from the above how the processes described here might apply. The complexity of situations should not deter efforts at systematic analysis, however conditional such analyses might be.

*   *   *

A Drawing Together: Political Violence

This book has proposed a complex interaction of behavioural forces to account for fanatical political violence. In the way in which it has been used here, the term 'fanatical' qualifies political violence in the sense of drawing our attention to both its perseverative qualities, and its insensitivity to the circumstances that appear to control normal behaviour. It does not, however, suggest a process separate from that which might result in other forms of political behaviour. This is an important point to emphasise, for it implies that, given the right circumstances, what we fear as political violence might become evident in a wide variety of settings where a militant ideology emerges with qualities of imminent millenarian expectation and/or lack of public space. The most obvious expression of this which we can see in contemporary society takes the form of what we refer to as political terrorism. This is but one example: there is no necessary reason why the analysis need be confined to terrorism. The discussion of My Lai might offer one avenue to pursue further; there are no doubt many others.

An explicitly behavioural account of political violence has been developed here, using the concept of reinforcement as the critical environmental feature that shapes and controls our behaviour. It has developed that concept through the idea of rule-governed behaviour, generally equating ideology with behavioural control by political or religious behavioural rules. By doing this, it has offered a way of understanding the unquestionably complex behaviours we refer to as political violence by using concepts that have proven their utility in other areas. Of course there is an enormous array of possible reasons why the behaviour of people comes under what we have termed ideological control. The discussion in this book has not analysed these reasons exhaustively, although some general approaches to analysis have been suggested, principally in terms of social psychological processes of group membership. Given ideological control over an individual's behaviour, however, what we have proposed are a series of features of ideology (militancy, millenarianism and lack of public space) that increase the likelihood of political violence – collectively or individually they 'set the scene' for violent behaviour to become a feature of that particular political ideology. Those features may be evident in terms of broad ideological themes affecting large numbers of people, or may be the result of discrete micro-environments affecting only those immediately concerned. The factors as we have identified them probably relate to process, not scale, although of course this remains to be seen.

Whilst they may be critical factors in setting the scene for violence, the relationship between militancy, millenarianism and lack of public space remains unclear. Are all three factors necessary, or is some combination (given other features such as leadership) the critical issue? Are there other factors which occurring with one or all facilitate the occurrence of violence? Indeed, all three may be aspects of the same essence, in that collectively they necessarily occur when a particular kind of ideology develops. Equally, however, it seems perfectly possible to have a millenarian ideology that lacks militancy, and similarly it seems to be possible to have a society lacking in public space (through oppressive control) which lacks a sense of millenarian expectation. It might indeed be argued that the latter characterised the position in Eastern Europe before the Gorbachev reforms. Indeed, one way of developing a behavioural analysis of the changes in Eastern Europe during 1989 and 1990 might be in terms of the development of a millenarian sense of imminence. The resultant violence in Romania, for example, might be explained in terms of the coming together of the ideological qualities we have identified here; this is at least as tenable a suggestion as others that have been offered.

Where then does this leave us? The account presented gives a way of looking at violent political behaviour. It offers, therefore, a means of analysis and a way of structuring the problem. It would be difficult to envisage an empirical verification of the issues raised, and the analysis presented is largely *post hoc*. This is probably necessarily so, for the scale of events we have addressed are such that they clearly cannot be amenable to anything other than observation as they unfold. On the other hand, observations need structure to be meaningful, and the account presented here offers one such structure from which to describe events. The utility of the account will presumably stand or fall by its ability to both enhance understanding, and predict future change.

Given that the account offered helps our understanding, does this understanding have any particular consequence in a world where the effects of fanatical political violence are all too apparent? We can answer this in a number of ways. Placing the explanation of fanatical political violence in the broader context of explanations of other less obviously worrying behaviour is itself a matter of some importance. It means that such insights that we have into how we control other behaviour may apply equally to the situations where fanatically violent political behaviour occurs. In particular, it points our attention to the circumstances in which political violence takes place, rather than deflecting our interest either to essentially inaccessible processes within the individual, or to equally inaccessible social forces. In doing this, it may not tell us what to do, but it does tell us how to find out what to do. In particular, it gives at least a rationale for *empirical* explorations of the reinforcement and rule-governed contingencies related to violent political behaviour.

At the micro-level, we might see this taking effect in terms of increasing use of descriptive accounts of politically violent incidents, such as terrorist attacks. We know very little, for example, about the processes that lead to the choice of terrorist targets, in the sense of identification of a class of particular targets, the selection of a particular target from other potential targets, and the execution of a particular ambush, bombing, or other act. If we approach this analysis from the perspective suggested in this book, we might expect to see an increase in empirical explorations of these aspects of terrorist behaviour, related both to utility for the terrorist, the environmental context in which the behaviour occurs, and the broader relationship of terrorist behaviour to ideological rules. A further important issue here would be efforts systematically to describe and identify developmental qualities *within* politically violent groups. Changes in organisational influence, for example, might be one relevant dimension to explore. If pursued, this might have the virtue of offering greater predictive capacity for the security forces who have to deal with political violence, and also increase our conceptual understanding of particular ideological qualities that result in violence.

A related focus for further development may lie in the comparative study of politically violent groups. The academic literature is strangely limited in this important area, where most work focuses on descriptions of individual groups of national concern; perhaps this is a function of funding. The approach presented in this book develops from a single integrated behavioural theme, and a virtue of this is that it allows comparison to be made between widely different situations within a single conceptual framework. In doing this, it offers points of reference from which common explorations can develop.

Moving away from a research agenda, we might alternatively explore the utility of this approach in very broad terms by addressing matters of public policy. We might argue, for example, that political solutions to volatile social problems which have a relationship with one or other of the ideological qualities of imminence, lack of public space or militancy may affect the potential of these solutions for generating, or limiting, violence.

We can explore an example of how this might apply by examining some recent events in Northern Ireland. The present situation in Northern Ireland is an example of a profoundly intractable political problem, where a long history of intermittent social unrest, compounded with two decades of terrorist violence and reciprocal violence from the security forces, has produced a political environment which is both sensitive to political change and where such change is readily expressed in terms of violence. A long list of failed political initiatives to contain the violence and perhaps bring some measure of peace to the Province has been tried, and has failed universally. The latest initiative at the time of writing is the Anglo-Irish Agreement, signed between the Republic of Ireland and the British Government in 1985. Amongst many other things, one effect of this aggreement is that it gives the Irish Republic a consultative role in the affairs of Northern Ireland, and by doing so, in a sense it legitimises claims by the Republic to sovereignty over Northern Ireland. Recent assertions of the constitutionality of claims to sovereignty over Northern Ireland by the Irish Republic add further legitimacy to this.

The background to the implementation of the Anglo-Irish Agreement is of course complex. However, at the level at which broad political forces might impinge on the individual, it might be argued that by introducing a new role for the Irish Republic in Northern Ireland, it enhances the distant prospect of Irish unity. It even offers a mechanism whereby that might come about, by asserting that unity by consent would be acceptable to both the Irish Government and the British Government. This is presumably meant as encouragement for those in the Province who wish to seek a solution to the problem by peaceful means, facilitating the development of such measures as constitutional initiatives and power sharing, in contrast to the violent approach associated with terrorist groups such as the Provisional IRA. It might equally be argued, however, that these elements of the agreement also introduce and enhance a sense of imminent attainment. The goal of Irish unity is legitimised, and also made not only more attainable by the Agreement, but given for the first time in recent years a focus and end point. On the basis of the arguments presented in this book, it might be expected that there will therefore be an increase in violence, despite the aspiration of the Agreement to reduce the need for violence by Nationalists. The ideologies of the Nationalist movements in Ireland are frankly millenarian and militant, and the terrorist groups themselves are profoundly coercive with their own members and the communities in which they operate. Furthermore, rightly or wrongly, Northern Ireland is perceived by many of its nationalist inhabitants as being a coercive state (and perhaps because it is so perceived, it is so experienced), embodying many of the qualities of lack of public space. Into this potent ideological mixture, the Anglo-Irish Agreement introduced, or increased, a sense of imminence into the situation, and we might therefore anticipate increasing levels of political violence.

This has, in fact, occurred. In the Reports of the Chief Constable of the RUC from 1986 to 1989 details are given of the incidence of terrorist crime within Northern Ireland. If 1985, the year of the signing of the Anglo-Irish Agreement, is taken as a base point, the percentage incidence of terrorist crime rose over 1885 by 36 per cent in 1986, the year after the signing, 118 per cent in 1987 and remained at this high level in 1988 (105 per cent over the 1985 base level) and 1989 (103 per cent over the 1985 base level). Additionally, in the period since the signing of the Agreement there has been a major Provisional IRA offensive on the British mainland and against British targets in Europe. These are the highest levels of sustained violence this decade.

It may, of course, be wrong to make too much of this. The Anglo-Irish Agreement, by offering a route for constitutional nationalists to express their views, might be thought to offer a challenge to the terrorist organisations. Increased violence might be argued to be a product of this challenge, rather than the processes described here. If this is so, it is not clear what mechanism we might draw on to explain this increase, and as an explanation it seems rather unconvincing. It is also the case that this period coincides with increased availability to the Provisional IRA of explosives and weapons. This became apparent after a ship the *Eksund* was seized off the French coast in 1987 with a substantial cargo of weapons and explosives from Libya. Three other equally substantial cargos are thought to have entered Ireland before that. Whilst the arrival of those cargos more or less coincides with the increased violence, the time delay in utilising such munitions reduces the plausibility of that explanation. However, regardless of these alternative explanations, we can see that, by thinking in terms of the broader behavioural consequences of political initiatives such as the Anglo-Irish Agreement, we might gain new insights into their appropriateness.

Broad political processes of the kind introduced above are difficult to analyse in behavioural terms in any meaningful way. They refer to states and processes that are simply not of the same order as those events that impinge on our everyday lives. Yet there may be merit in examining them from the perspective of the kinds of forces outlined previously. Broad social conditions do impinge on behaviour, and we do need to develop means of understanding how this occurs.

Perhaps an easier approach, however, might be to develop more limited analyses in terms of effects upon political groups or individuals. In a sense, this brings us back to the more micro-analyses described earlier. To do this, of course, we need to gain some appreciation of the inner dynamics of the political group, something which is very difficult to attain without inadvertently contributing to the process under investigation. In the case of some political groups, like terrorist groups for example, detailed observation, perhaps involving membership, would of course present considerable moral and ethical problems, as well as the more obvious difficulty of illegality. One way of approaching this in the case of a political terrorist group, however, is in terms of analyses of terrorist communications. Such communications can offer some insights into the internal forces at work in terrorist activity.

Cordes,[10] in her analysis of terrorist communications, illustrates the utility of an analysis of terrorist communications, by presenting a content analysis of accessible communications. This makes it possible to infer the kind of contingency rules operative in the terrorist organisations she has studied. An interesting example of the value of this approach can be seen in the terrorists' use of what she describes as *autopropaganda*. Autopropaganda refers to the use of propaganda to persuade the members and supporters of a terrorist group of the value of its actions, in contrast to *propaganda* aimed at persuading others of the purpose of terrorist actions. A surprisingly large amount of terrorist communications are aimed at sustaining the terrorist group and its supporters, rather than persuading others. In a sense, such autopropaganda effectively reinforces the behaviour of group members and supporters, sustaining and enhancing the group qualities associated with ideological control. Maintaining the organisational integrity of an ideologically defined group is, of course, a major problem when it comes into conflict with authority. Amongst other things, autopropaganda might be thought to serve that purpose.

Cordes' analysis, and indeed the analysis presented in this book, is consistent with the recent renewed interest in the organisational features of political terrorist groups.[11] What Crenshaw characterises as organisational processes within the terrorist group used by the leader to ensure compliance and survival of the group fit readily into our analysis. What we have described as rule-following ideological forces are the background and facilitating context from which the group dynamics to which Crenshaw refers gain their meaning and direction. This short discussion also serves to bring us back to our behavioural focus, and enables us to relate the relatively focused psychological analysis presented in this book to broader social analyses.

*   *   *

Final Comments

There seems to be little likelihood that fanatical political violence will diminish in the coming years. Its character may well change, and in so far as it might impinge on the West, it may increasingly become evident in the actions of small groups of committed individuals energetically pursuing the goals which to themselves are all absorbing. The past can exercise no monopoly over the development of militant ideologies, and we can no doubt look forward to at least variants, if not original developments, on the themes of political violence we have experienced.

The forces we have identified in this book impinge on us all. We are all, in some measure, controlled by rule-governed contingencies. The fanatic, however, is exposed to, and controlled by, a more coherent and systematic set of contingencies than most of us. When this is expressed in a political context, we encounter forces of enormous power that, as we have seen, are very difficult to control. We urgently need to better understand these forces, and develop means of controlling them. To fail to do so might mean that we become engulfed in ever-increasing civil insurgences, fuelled by violent political fanatics, that may strike at the very heart of our civilisation, eroding liberties as a response to their depredations. There are encouraging signs that, at a conceptual level, we are beginning to understand political violence better; there seems to be little evidence as yet that such understanding is informing the political process.

Chapter Notes

Preface
1. Taylor, M *The Terrorist* (Brassey's Defence Publishers, London, 1988).
2. Mills, CW *The Sociological Imagination* (Oxford University Press, New York, 1959).
3. Penguin Books, 1973.
4. Trans. A Bower (Penguin Books, Harmondsworth, 1971).

Chapter 1   Fanaticism and Extreme Behaviour: an Introduction
1. See Taylor, M *The Terrorist* (Brassey's Defence Publishers, London, 1988) for a discussion of this (especially Chapter 4, 'Terrorism and Mental Health', p. 73).
2. Speech to the United Nations General Assembly, 1972, by the Indonesian Representative.
3. For a useful and comprehensive account of ways of categorising aggression, and a discussion of some of the conceptual issues involved, see Hinde, RA and Groebel, J The Problem of Aggression (in Groebel J and Hinde, RA (Eds.) *Aggression and War, Their Biological and Social Bases* (Cambridge University Press, Cambridge, 1989), p. 3.
4. The discussion here is largely concerned with instrumental violence. This is appropriate, given the political context of this book, but it should be noted that there are other forms of violence that can be identified. One useful classification of violence identifies five kinds; instrumental, emotional, felonious, bizarre and dysocial (Tinklenburg, JR and Ochberg, FM Patterns of Violence: a California Sample. In Hamburg, DA and Trudeau, MB (Eds.) *Biobehavioural Aspects of Aggression*, Liss, New York, 1981). As in all similar taxonomies, there is a considerable degree of overlap between the categories.
5. For example, Gurr, TR *Why Men Rebel* (Princeton, New Jersey, 1970).
6. For example, Muller, EN The Psychology of Political Protest and Violence. In Gurr, TR (Ed.) *Handbook of Political Conflict: Theory and Research* (Free Press, New York, 1983).
7. Thompson, JLP Deprivation, Resources and the Moral Dimension: A Time-Series Analysis of Collective Violence in Northern Ireland, 1922–1985. Paper presented to HF Guggenheim Conference on Terrorism and Public Policy, Santa Fe, 1987.
8. Taylor, M *The Terrorist* (Brassey's Defence Publishers, London, 1988) p. 33.
9. An example of this is Muller, EN Income Inequality, Régime Repressiveness and Political Violence. *Amer. Sociol. Rev.* 1985, **50**, 47.

10. An example of this is Snow, DE, Burke Rochford, E, Worden, SK and Benford, RD Frame Alignment Processes, Micromobilization and Movement Participation. *Amer. Sociol. Rev.* 1986, **51**, 464.

11. For a discussion of some of the terminological and definitional issues in this area, see Hinde, RA and Groebel, J The Problem of Aggression. In Groebel, J and Hinde RA (Eds.) *Aggression and War, Their Biological and Social Bases* (Cambridge University Press, Cambridge, 1989), p. 3.

12. Baron, RA and Byrne, D *Social Psychology. Understanding Human Interaction* (Allyn and Bacon, Newton, Mass. 1984), p. 325.

13. *Ibid.*

14. Bittner, E *The Functions of the Police in Modern Society.* (National Institute for Mental Health, Washington, D.C., 1970).

15. Rudin, J *Fanaticism. A Psychological Analysis* (Trans. E Reinecke and PC Bailey) (Univ. Notre Dame Press, Notre Dame, London, 1969).

16. Milgram, S The Social Meaning of Fanaticism *et cetera*, 1977, **34**, 58.

17. Clausewitz, C von *On War* (Trans. JJ Graham) (Penguin Books, Harmondsworth, 1968).

18. Milgram, S The Social Meaning of Fanaticism *et cetera*, 1977, **34**, 58.

19. See Skinner BF *Science and Human Behavior* (Free Press, New York, 1953) and Skinner, BF *Beyond Freedom and Dignity* (Knopf, New York, 1971) for a fuller discussion of these issues. See also Mead, GH *Mind, Self and Society* (University of Chicago Press, Chicago, 1934) and Baldwin, JD Mead and Skinner: Agency and Determinism, *Behaviorism*, 1988, **16**, 109, for a related account from a slightly different perspective.

20. Taylor, M *The Terrorist* (Brassey's Defence Publishers, London, 1988).

21. Cornish, DB and Clarke, RV *The Reasoning Criminal. Rational Choice Perspectives on Offending* (Springer-Verlag, New York, 1986).

22. Nee, C and Taylor, M Residential Burglary in the Republic of Ireland: a Situational Perspective. *Howard Journal*, 1988, **27**, 105.

23. Moscovici, S *The Age of the Crowd* (Cambridge University Press, Cambridge, 1985) and Graumann, CF and Moscovici, S *Changing Conceptions of Crowd Mind and Behavior* (Springer-Verlag, New York, 1986) discuss this issue at length.

24. Moscovici, S *The Age of the Crowd* (Cambridge University Press, Cambridge, 1985).

Chapter 2   The Concept of Political Fanaticism

1. A useful general discussion of the role of rules in social organisation can be found in Malott, RW Rule Governed Behavior and Behavioral Anthropology. *The Behavior Analyst*, 1988, **11**, 181.

2. Milgram, S The Social Meaning of Fanaticism *et cetera*, 1977, **34**, 58.

3. A readily accessible account of the Flagellant Movement can be found in Ziegler, P *The Black Death* (Penguin Books, Harmondsworth, 1984).

4. Reported in an interview with Vincent Brown in *The Sunday Tribune*, Dublin, 28 June 1990.

5. Arendt, H *Eichmann in Jerusalem. A Report on the Banality of Evil* (Penguin Books, Harmondsworth, 1977) p. 49.

6. Kellen, K *Terrorists – What are they like? How Some Terrorists Describe their World and Actions* (Rand Corporation, Santa Monica, 1979).

7. *Saint John*, 15, 13.
8. Skinner, BF *Contingencies of Reinforcement: a Theoretical Analysis* (Appleton-Century-Crofts, New York, 1969).
9. Fest, S *The Face of the Third Reich* (Weidenfeld and Nicholson, London, 1970) p. 185.
10. *Ibid.*
11. *German Resistance to National Socialism* (Press and Information Office of the Federal Government, Bonn, undated).
12. Quoted in Arendt, H *Eichmann in Jerusalem. A Report on the Banality of Evil* (Penguin Books, Harmondsworth, 1977), p. 101.
13. Quoted in Fest, S *The Face of the Third Reich* (Weidenfeld and Nicholson, London, 1970), p. 121.
14. Cited in Cordes, B When Terrorists do the Talking: Reflections on Terrorist Literature. In Rapoport DC (Ed.) *Inside Terrorist Organisations* (Frank Cass and Co., London, 1988).
15. Rudin, J *Fanaticism. A Psychological Analysis* (Trans. E Reinecke and PC Bailey) (Univ. Notre Dame Press, Notre Dame, London, 1969).

Chapter 3   The Psychological Context

1. Rudin, J *Fanaticism. A Psychological Analysis* (Trans. E Reinecke and PC Bailey) (Univ. Notre Dame Press, Notre Dame, London, 1969).
2. *Diagnostic and Statistical Manual of Mental Disorder* (3rd edition) (American Psychiatric Association, Washington, DC, 1980).
3. Rosenhan, DL and Seligman, MEP *Abnormal Psychology* (2nd edition) (WW Norton and Co., New York, 1989). There are differences in approach by other authors, but Rosenhan and Seligman capture the essential issues involved which, despite differences in emphasis, are shared by most authors in this area.
4. Taylor, M *The Terrorist* (Brassey's Defence Publishers, London, 1988), chapter 5, p. 94.
5. For a similar discussion of erroneous beliefs about more general issues related to aggression, see Goldstein, JH Beliefs about Human Aggression. In Groebel, J and Hinde, RA (Eds.) *Aggression and War, Their Biological and Social Bases* (Cambridge University Press, Cambridge, 1989), p. 10.
6. Masters, B *Killing for Company* (Jonathan Cape, London, 1985) discusses the trial of Nielson, and in particular presents the evidence used in court to judge the nature of Nielson's mental state (chapter 9, p. 200).
7. Watzlawick, P The Pathologies of Perfectionism *et cetera*, 1977, **34**, 12.
8. Rosenhan, DL and Seligman, MEP *Abnormal Psychology* (2nd edition) (WW Norton and Co., New York, 1989), p. 7.
9. Cleckley, H *The Mask of Sanity* (CV Mosby Co., St. Louis, 1976).
10. Hare, RD Criminal Psychopaths. In Yuille, JC (Ed.) *Police Selection and Training* (Martinus Nijhoff, Dordrecht, 1986), p. 187.
11. Rosenhan, DL and Seligman, MEP *Abnormal Psychology* (2nd edition) (WW Norton and Co., New York, 1989), p. 7.
12. Baron, RA and Byrne, D *Social Psychology. Understanding Human Interaction* (Allyn and Bacon, Newton, Mass., 1984), p. 170.
13. Although a considerable literature exists in this area, the original work by

Adorno, T, Frenkel-Brunswick, E, Levinson, D and Sanford, RN *The Authoritarian Personality* (Harper, New York, 1950) remains the principal reference.

14. This issue is discussed at length in Brockner, J and Rubin, JZ *Entrapment in Escalating Conflicts* (Springer-Verlag, New York, 1985).

15. *Ibid.*

16. Hewitt, C Terrorism and Public Opinion: A Five Country Comparison. *Terrorism and Political Violence*, 1990, **2**, 145. Hewitt quotes an opinion poll published in *Fortnight*, April 1988, which reported only a five per cent decline in those saying they sympathised with Provisional IRA after the Enniskillen bombing. This should be understood in the context of widespread *public* expressions of revulsion in both Northern Ireland and the Republic of Ireland after the bombing. For example, Books of Condolence were available for signature in several of the larger cities in the Republic of Ireland which gave opportunities for expression of that revulsion. They were widely supported. Hewitt's comments illustrate, however, the ambivalence felt towards terrorist activity in Ireland by some sections of the nationalist community. A more sophisticated understanding of the various audiences involved, and their different levels of engagement with terrorism, is necessary to begin to appreciate these complex issues.

17. Myers, DG Polarizing Effects of Social Interaction. In Brandstatter, H, Davis, JH and Stocker-Kreichgauer, G (Eds.) *Group Decision Processes* (Academic Press, London, 1983).

18. Janis, IL *Groupthink* (2nd edition) (Houghton-Mifflin, Boston, 1982).

19. Cornish, DB and Clarke, RV *The Reasoning Criminal. Rational Choice Perspectives on Offending* (Springer-Verlag, New York, 1986). This approach has much in common with rational choice analyses of political violence although there are differences of emphasis [See also Leites, N and Wolfe, C *Rebellion and Authority* (Rand Corporation, Santa Monica, 1970); Denardo, J *Power in Numbers: the Political Strategy of Protest and Rebellion* (Princeton University Press, Princeton, 1984); Mason, T Individual Participation in Collective Racial Violence and Terror: A Rational Choice Synthesis. *Amer. Pol. Sci. Rev.* 1984, **78**, 1040].

20. Taylor, M *The Terrorist* (Brassey's Defence Publishers, London, 1988), chapter 5, p. 94.

Chapter 4 Political Behaviour and its Ideological Context

1. Billig, M, Condor, S, Edwards, D, Gane, M, Middleton, D and Radley, A *Ideological Dilemmas. A Social Psychology of Everyday Thinking* (Sage Publications, London, 1988).

2. *Concise Oxford Dictionary* (6th edition) (Oxford University Press, Oxford, 1978).

3. This is referred to in Billig, M *Ideology and Social Psychology* (Blackwell, Oxford, 1982), p. 7.

4. *Ibid.*

5. Rokeach, M *Belief, Attitude and Values* (Jossey-Bass, San Francisco, 1968).

6. *Ibid.* pp. 123–124.

7. Camus, Albert (Trans. A Bower) *The Rebel* (Penguin Books, Harmondsworth, 1971).

8. Festinger, L, Ricken, HW and Schachter, S *When Prophecy Fails* (Univ. Minnesota Press, St. Paul, 1956).

9. Eysenck, HJ *The Psychology of Politics* (Routledge and Kegan Paul, London, 1954).

10. *Ibid.*
11. Bird, C *Social Psychology* (Appleton Century, New York, 1940).
12. Tomkins, SS Left and Right: a Basic Dimension of Ideology and Personality. In White, RW (Ed.) *The Study of Lives* (Atherton, New York, 1963).
13. See Stone, WP and Schaffner, PE *The Psychology of Politics* (Free Press, New York, 1988) chapter 4 for a general review of this.
14. Post, JM Hostilité, conformité, fraternité: The group dynamics of terrorist behavior. *Int. J. Psychotherap.* 1986, **36**, 211.
15. Camus, Albert (Trans. A Bower) *The Rebel* (Penguin Books, Harmondsworth, 1971).
16. Adorno, TW, Frenkel-Brunswick, E, Levinson, D and Sanford, RN *The Authoritarian Personality* (Harper and Row, New York, 1950).
17. Baron, RA and Byrne, D *Social Psychology. Understanding Human Interaction* (Allyn and Bacon, Newton, Mass. 1983), p. 531.
18. Davies, JC The Roots of Political Behaviour. In Herman, MG (Ed.) *Political Psychology* (Jossey-Bass, San Francisco, 1986), p. 39.
19. Davies, JC The Roots of Political Behaviour. In Herman, MG (Ed.) *Political Psychology* (Jossey-Bass, San Francisco, 1986). For a further discussion of the influence of Freudian thinking, see also Cocks, G Contributions of Psychohistory to Understanding Politics. In Herman, MG (Ed.) *Political Psychology* (Jossey-Bass, San Francisco, 1986), p. 139.
20. Lasswell, HD *Psychopathology and Politics* (Univ. Chicago Press, Chicago, 1931).
21. Adorno, TW, Frenkel-Brunswick, E, Levinson, D and Sanford, RN *The Authoritarian Personality* (Harper and Row, New York, 1950).
22. Ray, JJ Cognitive Styles as a Predictor of Authoritarianism, Conservatism and Racism: A Fantasy in Many Movements. *Political Psychology*, 1988, **9**, 303.
23. Eysenck, HJ *The Psychology of Politics* (Routledge and Kegan Paul, London, 1954).
24. *Ibid.*
25. Eysenck, HJ *The Structure of Human Personality* (Wiley, London, 1953).
26. Post, JM, Hostilité, conformité, fraternité: The group dynamics of terrorist behaviour. *Int. J. Psychotherap.* 1986, **36**, 211.
27. For example, see Christie, R Review of the Psychology of Politics, by HJ Eysenck. *Amer. J. Psychol.* 1955, **68**, 702, and Rokeach, M and Hanley, C Eysenck's Tendermindedness Dimension: A Critique. *Psychol. Bull.* 1956, **53**, 169.
28. Kellen, K *Terrorists – What are they like? How Some Terrorists Describe their World and Actions* (Rand Corporation, Santa Monica, 1979).
29. *Ibid.*
30. Taylor, M and Ryan, H Fanaticism, Political Suicide and Terrorism. *Terrorism*, 1988, **11**, 91.
31. This issue is discussed at length in Taylor, M *The Terrorist* (Brassey's Defence Publishers, London, 1988), p. 146.
32. Skinner, BF *Contingencies of Reinforcement* (Appleton-Century-Crofts, New York, 1968) introduces the term 'rule-following' in chapter 6, p. 133. Notes 6.1 to 6.4 are especially useful (pp. 157–171).
33. After Malott, RW Rule Governed Behavior and Behavioral Anthropology. *The Behavior Analyst*, 1988, **11**, 181–200.

34. There are relationships between the concept of behavioural rules and more traditional forms of cognitive psychology. These are coherently explored in Reese, HW Rules and Rule Governance: Cognitive and Behavioral Issues. In Hayes, SC (Ed.) *Rule-Governed Behavior. Cognition, Contingencies and Instructional Control* (Plenum Press, New York, 1989), p. 3.

35. Skinner, BF The Behavior of the Listener. In Hayes, SC (Ed.) *Rule-Governed Behavior. Cognition, Contingencies and Instructional Control* (Plenum Press, New York, 1989), p. 85.

36. Skinner, BF *Contingencies of Reinforcement* (Appleton-Century-Crofts, New York, 1968), p. 140.

37. The issues we have raised here relate to a complex area of behaviour analysis, and more technical details of this approach can be found in, for example, Skinner, BF *Contingencies of Reinforcement* (Appleton-Century-Crofts, New York, 1969); Malott, RW Rule Governed Behavior and Behavioral Anthropology. *The Behavior Analyst*, 1988, **11**, 181–200; Schlinger, H and Blakeley, E Function Altering Effects of Contingency-Specifying Stimuli. *The Behavior Analyst*, 1987, **10**, 27–40; Blakely, E and Schlinger, H Rules: Function-Altering Contingency-Specifying Stimuli. *The Behavior Analyst,* 1987, **10**, 183–188; Vaughan, M Rule-governed Behavior and Higher Mental Processes. In Modgil, S and Modgil, C (Eds.) *BF Skinner: Consensus and Controversy* (Falmer Press, New York, 1987); and Hayes, SC (Ed.) *Rule-Governed Behavior. Cognition, Contingencies and Instructional Control* (Plenum Press, New York, 1989).

38. Hayes, SC (Ed.) *Rule-Governed Behavior. Cognition, Contingencies and Instructional Control* (Plenum Press, New York, 1989). Whilst not explored in detail here, the notion of behavioural rules fits readily into the rational-choice paradigm, Cornish, DB and Clarke, RV *The Reasoning Criminal. Rational Choice Perspectives on Offending* (Springer-Verlag, New York, 1986), and also see for example Leites, N and Wolfe, C *Rebellion and Authority* (Rand Corporation, Santa Monica, 1970); Denardo, J *Power in Numbers: the Political Strategy of Protest and Rebellion* (Princeton University Press, Princeton, 1984); Mason, T Individual Participation in Collective Racial Violence and Terror: A Rational Choice Synthesis. *Amer. Pol. Sci. Rev.* 1984, **78**, 1040.

39. Malott, RW Rule Governed Behavior and Behavioral Anthropology. *The Behavior Analyst*, 1988, **11**, 181–200.

40. Cerutti, DT Discrimination Theory of Rule-Governed Behavior. *J. Exp. Anal. Behav.* 1989, **51**, 259.

41. Rhodes, JM *The Hitler Movement: A Modern Millenarian Revolution* (Hoover Institution Press, Stanford, 1980), pp. 14–15.

42. Dietrich, DJ National Renewal, Anti-Semitism, and Political Continuity: A Psychological Assessment. *Political Psychology*, 1988, **9**, 385.

43. Staats, A *Social Behaviorism* (Dorsey Press, Homewood, Ill, 1975).

44. Cerutti, DT Discrimination Theory of Rule-Governed Behavior. *J. Exp. Anal. Behav.* 1989, **51**, 259.

45. Skinner, BF *Contingencies of Reinforcement* (Appleton-Century-Crofts, New York, 1968), p. 169.

46. Allen, WS *The Nazi Seizure of Power* (Revised Edition) (Penguin Books, Harmondsworth, 1989).

47. Malott, RW Rule Governed Behavior and Behavioral Anthropology. *The Behavior Analyst*, 1988, **11**, 181–200.
48. Glenn, SS Contingencies and Metacontingencies: Towards a Synthesis of Behavioural Analysis and Cultural Materialism. *The Behavior Analyst*, 1988, **11**, 161.
49. Harris, M *Cultural Anthropology* (Harper and Row, New York, 1983).
50. See for example Schachter, S *The Psychology of Affiliation* (Stanford University Press, Stanford, 1959).
51. Taylor, M *The Terrorist* (Brassey's Defence Publishers, London, 1988).

Chapter 5   Millenarian Motifs
1. After Rhodes, JM *The Hitler Movement: A Modern Millenarian Revolution* (Hoover Institution Press, Stanford, 1980), pp. 29–30.
2. This is discussed in Harrison, JFC Millennium and Utopia. In Alexander, P and Gill, R *Utopias* (Duckworth, London, 1984), pp. 61–66.
3. See Rhodes, JM *The Hitler Movement: A Modern Millenarian Revolution* (Hoover Institution Press, Stanford, 1980), for an extensive discussion of millenarian influences in Nazi ideology.
4. Davies, JC The History of Utopia: the Chronology of Nowhere. In Alexander, P and Gill, R *Utopias* (Duckworth, London, 1984), pp. 1–17.
5. Morrison, A Uses of Utopia. In Alexander, P and Gill, R (Eds.) *Utopias* (Duckworth, London, 1984), pp. 139–151.
6. *Ibid*. p. 139.
7. Kinkade, K *A Walden Two Experiment* (William Morrow, New York, 1973) discusses the rationale and development of the community that was created in the image of Walden Two (see Note 8 following for origin).
8. Skinner, BF *Walden Two* (Macmillan Paperback, New York, 1948).
9. Lukes, S Marxism and Utopianism. In Alexander, P and Gill, R (Eds.) *Utopias* (Duckworth, London, 1984), pp. 153–167.
10. Lenin, VI The State and Revolution (1917). In VI Lenin *Collected Works* Vol. 25 (Lawrence and Wishart, London, 1960).
11. Rhodes, JM *The Hitler Movement: A Modern Millenarian Revolution* (Hoover Institution Press, Stanford, 1980).
12. Rapoport has published a series of important papers discussing the relationship between Millenarianism and violence. One relevant paper is Rapoport, DC Why Does Religious Messianism Produce Terror? In Wilkinson, P and Stewart, AM (Eds.) *Contemporary Research on Terrorism* (Aberdeen University Press, Aberdeen, 1987). Other papers are referred to in these footnotes as appropriate.
13. *Ibid*.
14. Qutb, S *Milestones* (International Islamic Federation of Student Organizations, Holy Koran Publishing House, Beirut and Damascus, 1978).
15. *Ibid*, p.7.
16. *Ibid*, p.8.
17. *Ibid*, p.9.
18. Sivan, E *Radical Islam. Medieval Theology and Modern Politics* (Yale University Press, New Haven, 1985), p. 27.
19. Qutb, S *Milestones* (International Islamic Federation of Student Organizations, Holy Koran Publishing House, Beirut and Damascus, 1978), p. 63.
20. *Ibid*, pp. 93 et seq.

21. The activities of the plotters, and the statement of the group's ideological aims written by Faraj, 'The Neglected Duty', are discussed in detail by Jansen, JJG *The Neglected Duty* (Macmillan, New York, 1986).

22. Burridge, K *New Heaven, New Earth. A Study of Millenarian Activities* (Blackwell, London, 1971).

23. See also the further Biblical reference in *2 Peter* 3:13 '. . . according to his promise, look for new heavens and a new earth, wherein dwelleth righteousness'.

24. Cordes, B *When Terrorists Do the Talking: Reflections on Terrorist Literature* (Rand Corporation, Santa Monica, 1987).

25. Hayes, SC, Zettle, RD and Rosenfarb, I Rule Following. In Hayes, SC (Ed.) *Rule-Governed Behavior. Cognition, Contingencies and Instructional Control* (Plenum Press, New York, 1989), pp. 202–211.

26. *Ibid*, p. 203.

27. *Ibid*, p. 206.

28. *Ibid*, p. 206

29. For a broad discussion of these issues, see the following: Lewis, B *The Assassins* (Octagon Books, New York, 1968); Rapoport, DC Fear and Trembling: Terrorism in Three Religious Traditions. *Amer. Pol. Sci. Rev.* 1984, **78**, 658; Rapoport, DC Messianism and Terror. *The Center Magazine*, 1986, Jan/Feb. 30–39.

30. An important and provocative discussion of this general issue can be found in Rapoport, DC Some Observations on Religion and Violence. Paper presented to XIIth World Congress of Sociology, Madrid, Spain, 1990.

31. Burridge, K *New Heaven, New Earth. A Study of Millenarian Activities* (Blackwell, London, 1971).

32. Cohn, N *The Pursuit of the Millennium. Revolutionary Millenarians and Mystical Anarchists of the Middle Ages* (Palladin, London, 1970).

33. Harrison, JFC *The Second Coming. Popular Millenarianism 1780–1850* (Routledge and Kegan Paul, London, 1984), pp. 7–10.

34. Burridge, K *New Heaven, New Earth. A Study of Millenarian Activities* (Blackwell, London, 1971), pp. 4–8.

35. See Morris, J *The Nobility of Failure: Tragic Heroes in the History of Japan* (Secker and Warburg, London, 1975), for a discussion of this and related matters.

36. The most coherent and systematic account of Skinner's thinking in this area can be found in Skinner, BF *Beyond Freedom and Dignity* (Penguin Books, Harmondsworth, 1971).

37. Skinner, BF *Walden Two* (Macmillan Paperback, New York, 1948).

38. Burridge, K *New Heaven, New Earth. A Study of Millenarian Activities* (Blackwell, London, 1971), p. 5.

39. This issue is discussed at length in Skinner, BF *Walden Two* (Macmillan Paperback, New York, 1948), and Skinner, BF *Beyond Freedom and Dignity* (Penguin Books, Harmondsworth, 1971).

40. The history of the Rappite movement is discussed by Taylor, A *A Vision of Harmony* (Clarendon Press, Oxford, 1987).

41. *Ibid*, p. 33.

42. The psychological bases of leadership are a major area of psychological investigation, although studies of political leadership are relatively poorly developed. As noted in the text, these issues are not discussed to any great extent in this work, but for a short review of the *political* application of much of this research, see

Herman, MG Ingredients of Leadership. In Herman MG, *Political Psychology* (Jossey-Bass, San Francisco, 1986). This paper stresses the need to understand the leader, the individuals and groups who are led, the nature of the relationship between the leader and followers, and the social context. Herman emphasises the complex interactive qualities of leadership, and cautions against simple analysis in terms of single dimension factors such as qualities of leaders.

43. See for a discussion of factors related to mass action and crowd behaviour Moscovici, S *The Age of the Crowd* (Cambridge University Press, Cambridge, 1985), and Graumann, CF and Moscovici, S *Changing Conceptions of Crowd Mind and Behaviour* (Springer-Verlag, New York, 1986). Much of this is based upon the earlier writings of Le Bon (Le Bon, G *The Crowd* (Ernst Benn, London, 1952)).

44. Rhodes, RH *The Hitler Movement: A Modern Millenarian Revolution* (Hoover Institution Press, Stanford, 1980).

45. Le Bon, G *The Crowd* (Ernst Benn, London, 1952). A discussion of the influence of Le Bon on Hitler and Goebbels can be found in Moscovici, S *The Age of the Crowd* (Cambridge University Press, Cambridge, 1985), pp. 64 and 146. Moscovici suggests that Hitler modelled much of his book *Mein Kampf* on Le Bon. He also suggests that Goebbels had a detailed knowledge of the techniques of mass influence described by Le Bon. (A quotation used by Moscovici from the secret diary of one of Goebbels' assistants reads 'Goebbels thinks that since the Frenchman Le Bon nobody has understood the masses as well as he does' [p. 64].)

46. Cohn, N *The Pursuit of the Millennium. Revolutionary Millenarians and Mystical Anarchists of the Middle Ages* (Palladin, London, 1970).

47. Harrison, JFC *The Second Coming. Popular Millenarianism 1780–1850* (Routledge and Kegan Paul, London, 1984), chapter 1.

48. For discussions of this, see Burridge, K *New Heaven, New Earth. A Study of Millenarian Activities* (Blackwell, London, 1971); Lidz, RW, Lidz, T and Burton-Bradley, BG Culture, Personality and Social Structure. Cargo Cultism – a Psychosocial Study of Melanesian Millenarianism. *J. Nerv. Ment. Dis.* 1973, **157**, 370; and Wilson, B *Magic and the Millennium* (Heinemann Books, London, 1973).

49. Lidz, RW, Lidz, T and Burton-Bradley, BG Culture, Personality and Social Structure. Cargo Cultism – a Psychosocial Study of Melanesian Millenarianism. *J. Nerv. Ment. Dis.* 1973, **157**, 370. For a more general discussion of the social context of Tangu, see Burridge, K *Tangu Traditions* (Clarendon Press, Oxford, 1969).

50. Lidz, RW, Lidz T and Burton-Bradley, BG Culture, Personality and Social Structure. Cargo Cultism – a Psychosocial Study of Melanesian Millenarianism. *J. Nerv. Ment. Dis.* 1970, **157**, 370.

51. Burridge, K *New Heaven, New Earth. A Study of Millenarian Activities* (Blackwell, London, 1971).

52. *Ibid*, pp. 64–69.

53. Lidz, RW, Lidz, T and Burton-Bradley, BG Culture, Personality and Social Structure. Cargo Cultism – a Psychosocial Study of Melanesian Millenarianism. *J. Nerv. Ment. Dis.* 1973, **157**, 370.

54. Burridge, K *New Heaven, New Earth. A Study of Millenarian Activities* (Blackwell, London, 1971), p. 65.

55. Malott, RW Rule Governed Behavior and Behavioral Anthropology. *The Behavior Analyst*, 1988, **11**, 181–200. This is one of the few works to discuss the broader

application of behavioural principles to social processes relevant to our discussion.

56. Lidz, RW, Lidz, T and Burton-Bradley, BG Culture, Personality and Social Structure. Cargo Cultism – a Psychosocial Study of Melanesian Millenarianism. *J. Nerv. Ment. Dis.* 1973, **157**, 370.

57. For a discussion of this see Rhodes, JM *The Hitler Movement: A Modern Millenarian Revolution* (Hoover Institution Press, Stanford, 1980).

58. This quotation is given in Cordes, B *When Terrorists Do the Talking: Reflections on Terrorist Literature* (Rand Corporation, Santa Monica, 1987).

59. Malott, RW Rule Governed Behavior and Behavioral Anthropology. *The Behavior Analyst* 1988, **11**, 181–200.

60. A discussion relevant to this issue can be found in Rapoport, DC Messianism and Terror. *The Center Magazine*, 1986, Jan/Feb. 30–39.

61. Hayes, SC, Zettle, RD and Rosenfarb, I Rule Following. In Hayes, SC (Ed.) *Rule-Governed Behavior. Cognition, Contingencies and Instructional Control* (Plenum Press, New York, 1989). See pp. 202–211.

62. Rapoport, DC Messianism and Terror. *The Center Magazine*, 1986, Jan/Feb. 30–39.

63. *Ibid.*

64. As discussed earlier and described in Taylor, A *A Vision of Harmony* (Clarendon Press, Oxford, 1987).

65. Popper, KR *Conjectures and Refutations* (Routledge and Kegan Paul, London, 1963), chapter 18, pp. 355–363.

66. Malott, RW Rule Governed Behavior and Behavioral Anthropology. *The Behavior Analyst* 1988, **11**, 181-200.

67. A most compelling account of the complex of issues involved in the relationship of police work to the use of violence can be found in Bittner, E *The Functions of the Police in Modern Society* (National Institute for Mental Health, Washington, DC, 1970).

Chapter 6   The Totality of Ideology: Public Space

1. Arendt, H *The Human Condition* (University of Chicago Press, Chicago, 1958), p. 208.

2. *Ibid*, chapter 2 and chapter 5. See also discussion in Parekh, B *Hannah Arendt and the Search for a New Political Philosophy* (Macmillan Press, London, 1981), chapter 4.

3. Parekh, B *Hannah Arendt and the Search for a New Political Philosophy* (Macmillan Press, London, 1981), chapter 4.

4. Arendt, H The Concentration Camp. *Partisan Review*, 1948, July, 743.

5. Arendt, H *The Origins of Totalitarianism* (André Deutsch, London, 1951).

6. Arendt, H *Eichmann in Jerusalem* (Penguin Books, Harmondsworth, 1977).

7. For an example of the psychodynamic literature associated with Arendt, see Alford, CF The Organisation of Evil. *Political Psychology*, 1990, **11**, 5.

8. Arendt, H The Concentration Camp. *Partisan Review*, 1948, July, 743.

9. Parekh, B *Hannah Arendt and the Search for a New Political Philosophy* (Macmillan Press, London, 1981), pp. 92–3.

10. Arendt, H The Concentration Camp. *Partisan Review*, 1948, July, 743.

11. *Ibid.*

12. Skinner, BF *Beyond Freedom and Dignity* (Penguin Books, Harmondsworth, 1971).

13. Burridge, K *New Heaven, New Earth. A Study of Millenarian Activities* (Blackwell, London, 1971).

14. For example, see Whorf, BL Science and Linguistics. In Carroll, JB (Ed.) *Language, Thought and Reality: Selected Writings of Benjamin Lee Whorf* (MIT Press, Cambridge, Mass., 1956).

15. Parekh, B *Hannah Arendt and the Search for a New Political Philosophy* (Macmillan Press, London, 1981), p. 95.

16. *Ibid.*

17. Le Bon, G *The Crowd* (Ernst Benn, London, 1952).

18. See for example Moscovici, S *The Age of the Crowd* (Cambridge University Press, Cambridge, 1985), and Graumann, CF and Moscovici, S *Changing Conceptions of Crowd Mind and Behavior* (Springer-Verlag, New York, 1986).

19. Arendt, H *Eichmann in Jerusalem.* (Penguin Books, Harmondsworth, 1977), p. 49.

20. *Ibid.*

21. For a discussion of the sense of legal due process in areas subjected to paramilitary control, see Morrissey, M and Pease, K The Black Criminal Justice System in West Belfast. *The Howard Journal*, 1982, **xxi**, 159, and Taylor, M *The Terrorist* (Brassey's Defence Publishers, London, 1988).

22. Parekh, B *Hannah Arendt and the Search for a New Political Philosophy* (Macmillan Press, London, 1981). See earlier discussion in Chapter 3 on psychological traps.

23. For an extensive discussion, see Janis, IL *Groupthink* (2nd edition) (Houghton-Mifflin, Boston, 1982).

24. This is discussed in Foa, UG Resource Theory of Social Exchanges. In Thibault, JS, Spence, J and Carlson, R (Eds.) *Contemporary Topics in Social Psychology* (General Learning Press, Morristown, N.J., 1976).

25. Parekh, B *Hannah Arendt and the Search for a New Political Philosophy* (Macmillan Press, London, 1981).

26. For example, for a discussion of these issues see Asch, SE Effects of Group Pressure upon the Modification and Distortion of Judgement. In Guetzkow, H (Ed.) *Groups, Leadership and Men* (Carnegie, Pittsburgh, 1951); Crutchfield, RA Conformity and Character. *American Psychologist*, 1955, **10**, 191; and Allen, VL and Wilder, DA Impact of Group Consensus and Social Support on Stimulus Meaning: Mediation of Conformity by Cognitive Restructuring. *J. Pers. Soc. Psychol.* 1980, **39**, 1116.

27. For example, see Milgram, S *Obedience to Authority* (Harper, New York, 1974) and Milgram, S Some Conditions of Obedience and Disobedience to Authority. *Human Relations*, 1965, **18**, 57.

28. Haritos-Fatouros, M The Official Torturer: A Learning Model for Obedience to the Authority of Violence. *J. App. Soc. Psychol.* 1988, **18**, 1107.

29. Crenshaw, M Theories of Terrorism: Instrumental and Organisational Approaches. In Rapoport, DC (Ed.) *Inside Terrorist Organisations* (Frank Cass and Co., London, 1988), pp. 13–31. This paper raises very important issues about the nature of terrorist action. Despite some confusion about the nature of 'instrumentality' (at least in a psychological sense), by emphasising the importance of organisational pressures the paper draws our attention to a frequently neglected factor in determining the behaviour of terrorists.

30. Cordes, B *When Terrorists Do the Talking: Reflections on Terrorist Literature* (Rand Corporation, Santa Monica, 1987).
31. For a discussion of these procedures, see Lovaas, OI A Program for the Establishment of Speech in Psychotic Children. In Wing, JK (Ed.) *Early Childhood Autism* (Pergamon, New York, 1966), and Lovaas, OI *Behavioral Treatment of Autistic Children* (General Learning Press, Morristown, N.J., 1973).
32. Arendt, H *The Human Condition* (University of Chicago Press, Chicago, 1958), p. 208.
33. See discussion in Chapter 5, and Taylor, A *A Vision of Harmony* (Clarendon Press, Oxford, 1987).
34. Crenshaw, M Theories of Terrorism: Instrumental and Organisational Approaches. In Rapoport, DC (Ed.) *Inside Terrorist Organisations* (Frank Cass and Co., London, 1988), pp. 13–31 and Note 29 above.

Chapter 7 Self-Victimisation – A Terrible Strength

1. Camus, Albert (Trans. A Bower) *The Rebel* (Penguin Books, Harmondsworth, 1971).
2. Stern, SL and Mendels, J Affective Disorders. In Kazdin, AE, Bellack, AS and Hersen, M (Eds.) *New Perspectives in Abnormal Psychology* (Oxford University Press, New York, 1980), pp. 202–226.
3. Skinner, BF *Science and Human Behavior* (Free Press, New York, 1973) (Peregrine Edition, 1988), p. 50.
4. This was an important theme in Nazi ideology, for example. See Rhodes, JM *The Hitler Movement: A Modern Millenarian Revolution* (Hoover Institution Press, Stanford, 1980), p. 151 for a discussion of this.
5. Toloyan, K Martyrdom as Legitimacy: Terrorism, Religion and Symbolic Appropriation in the Armenian Diaspora. In Wilkinson, P and Stewart, AM (Eds.) *Contemporary Research on Terrorism* (Aberdeen University Press, Aberdeen, 1987), pp. 89–103.
6. Taylor, M *The Terrorist* (Brassey's Defence Publishers, London, 1988), p. 99.
7. Begin, M *The Revolt – Story of the Irgun* (Schuman, New York, 1951).
8. *Terrorist Bombings* (U.S. Department of State, Office for Combating Terrorism, 1983).
9. See for example Lewis, B *The Assassins* (Octagon Books, New York. 1968) and Rapoport, DC Fear and Trembling: Terrorism in Three Religious Traditions. *Amer. Pol. Sci. Rev.* 1984, **78**, 658.
10. Rapoport DC Fear and Trembling: Terrorism in Three Religious Traditions. *Amer. Pol. Sci. Rev.* 1984, **78**, 658.
11. Dale, SF Religious Suicide in Islamic Asia. *J. Conflict Resolution* 1988, **32**, 37.
12. Rapoport, DC Fear and Trembling: Terrorism in Three Religious Traditions. *Amer. Pol. Sci. Rev.* 1984, **78**, 658.
13. Taylor, M *The Terrorist* (Brassey's Defence Publishers, London, 1988). More detailed commentaries on the contemporary situation in Islam with respect to violence can be found in Sivan, E *Radical Islam. Medieval Theology and Modern Politics* (Yale University Press, New Haven, 1985) and Jansen, JJG *The Neglected Duty. The Creed of Sadat's Assassins and Islamic Resurgence in the Middle East* (Macmillan, New York, 1986).

14. Clausewitz, C. von *On War* (Trans. Graham, JJ) (Penguin Books, Harmonds-worth, 1968).

15. For a general discussion, see Lewis, B *The Assassins* (Octagon Books, New York, 1968); Rapoport, DC Fear and Trembling: Terrorism in Three Religious Tradi-tions. *Amer. Pol. Sci. Rev.* 1984, **78**, 658; and Rapoport, DC Messianism and Terror. *The Center Magazine*, 1986, Jan/Feb. 30–39.

16. See especially Sivan, E *Radical Islam. Medieval Theology and Modern Politics* (Yale University Press, New Haven, 1985) and Jansen, JJG *The Neglected Duty. The Creed of Sadat's Assassins and Islamic Resurgence in the Middle East* (Macmillan, New York, 1986).

17. See Kramer, M The Moral Logic of Hizballah. In Reich, W (Ed.) *Origins of Terrorism: Psychologies, Ideologies, Theologies, States of Mind* (Cambridge University Press, Cambridge, 1990), p. 132 for a brief discussion of the aspirations of Hizballah in this regard with respect to Lebanon.

18. Quoted from a taped sermon by Ayatollah Muhammed Aqda'i in Beirut on 25 March 1986 by Taheri, A *Holy Terror. The Inside Story of Islamic Terrorism* (Century Hutchinson, London, 1987), p. 116. Taheri is not always thought to be reliable, and many commentators discount his views. Disagreements about the detail of his work does not invalidate the more general points, however, which are generally well documented.

19. *Ibid*, pp. 116–117.

20. Kramer, M The Moral Logic of Hizballah. In Reich, W (Ed.) *Origins of Terrorism: Psychologies, Ideologies, Theologies, States of Mind* (Cambridge University Press, Cambridge, 1990), pp. 142–149.

21. Taylor, M *The Terrorist* (Brassey's Defence Publishers, London, 1988) discusses in this context the Japanese Kamikaze (pp. 112–116) and also the self immolation of anti-Vietnam war protestors (pp. 105–106).

22. Taheri, A *A Holy Terror. The Inside Story of Islamic Terrorism* (Century Hutchinson, London, 1987), p. 123.

23. *Ibid*, p.117.

24. Taylor, M and Ryan, H Fanaticism. Political Suicide and Terrorism. *Terrorism* 1988, **11**, 91.

25. We noted earlier in Chapter 5 the widely held view in some Iranian quarters that the Ayatollah Khomeini was the long awaited Mahdi, the re-embodiment of the infant son of the Eleventh Iman, Mohammed el Muntazar, the Twelfth Iman of the Line of Ali, who went into occulation in 837.

26. The following statistics were obtained from the Associated Press material on the Profile Information System data base, using as key word 'hunger strike'.

27. Pankhurst, ES *The Suffragette Movement. An Intimate Account of Persons and Ideals* (Virago, London, 1977), p. 439.

28. *Ibid*, p. 443.

29. Beresford, D *Ten Men Dead* (Grafton Books, London, 1987), p. 14. This book is an account of the hunger strikes from their political point of view. Because of this, it lacks the objectivity of a more reasoned account. On the other hand, it contains valuable material and seems to be generally reliable in the factual material presented.

30. Foster, RF *Modern Ireland 1600-1972* (Allen Lane, The Penguin Press, Harmonds-worth, 1988), p. 11. This book, along with Lee, JJ *Ireland 1912-1985: Politics and*

Society (Cambridge University Press, Cambridge, 1989), provide accurate and relevant accounts of the historical background to the present situation in the Republic of Ireland and Northern Ireland.

31. A discussion of the Baader-Meinhof Group in general, and in particular an account of the events whilst they were imprisoned, can be found in Aust, S *The Baader-Meinhof Group. The Inside Story of a Phenomenon* (Trans. A Bell) (Bodley Head, London, 1987).

32. Beresford, D *Ten Men Dead* (Grafton Books, London, 1987).

33. Authors such as Smyth (Smyth, J Unintentional Mobilization: The Effects of the 1980–1981 Hunger Strikes in Ireland. *Political Communication and Persuasion*, 1987, **4**, 179, and Smyth, J Stretching the Boundaries: The Control of Dissent in Northern Ireland. *Terrorism*, 1988, **11**, 289) illustrate this. For more sophisticated and contrasting views see for example Jeffrey, K Security Policy in Northern Ireland: Some Reflections on the Management of Violence. *Terrorism and Political Violence*, 1990, **2**, 21, and Macfarlane, L The Right to Self-Determination in Ireland and the Justification of IRA Violence. *Terrorism and Political Violence* 1990, **2**, 35.

34. Taylor, M and Ryan H Fanaticism, Political Suicide and Terrorism. *Terrorism* 1988, **11**, 91.

35. Townshend, C The Process of Irish Politics. In O'Sullivan, N *Terrorism, Ideology and Revolution* (Westview Press, Boulder, Co., 1986).

36. Arendt, H *The Human Condition* (University of Chicago Press, Chicago, 1958), as discussed in Chapter 4.

37. Toloyan, K Martyrdom as Legitimacy: Terrorism, Religion and Symbolic Appropriation in the Armenian Diaspora. In Wilkinson, P and Stewart, AM (Eds.) *Contemporary Research on Terrorism* (Aberdeen University Press, Aberdeen, 1987), pp. 89–103.

38. An interesting account of Tone's life can be found in Elliott, M *Wolf Tone: Prophet of Irish Independence* (Yale University Press, New Haven, 1989).

39. Taylor, M *The Terrorist* (Brassey's Defence Publishers, London, 1988),

40. Feldman, MD The Challenge of Self-Mutilation: A Review. *Comprehensive Psychiatry*, 1988, **29**, 252.

41. Ross, AO *Child Behavior Therapy. Principles, Procedures and Empirical Basis* (John Wiley and Sons, New York, 1981).

42. Cerutti, DT Discrimination Theory of Rule-Governed Behavior. *J. Exp. Anal. Behav.* 1989, **51**, 259.

43. See Chapter 3; Skinner, BF *Science and Human Behavior* (Free Press, New York, 1973) cited above (Note 2) for a discussion of this.

44. Taylor, M and Ryan, H Fanaticism, Political Suicide and Terrorism. *Terrorism* 1988, **11**, 91.

45. Taylor, M *The Terrorist* (Brassey's Defence Publishers, London, 1988).

46. Taylor, M and Ryan, H Fanaticism, Political Suicide and Terrorism. *Terrorism* 1988, **11**, 91.

47. Arendt, H *The Human Condition* (University of Chicago Press, Chicago, 1958) and discussion in Chapter 6.

48. Skinner, BF *Science and Human Behavior* (Free Press, New York, 1973), p. 57.

49. Baron, RA and Byrne, D *Social Psychology. Understanding Human Interaction* (Allyn and Bacon, Newton, Mass., 1984), p. 64.

50. Quoted by Aust, S *The Baader-Meinhof Group. The Inside Story of a Phenomenon* (Trans. Anthea Bell) (Bodley Head, London, 1987), pp. 543–544.

51. Camus, Albert (Trans. A Bower) *The Rebel* (Penguin Books, Harmondsworth, 1971).

52. *Ibid.*

Chapter 8   Black Milk of the Dawn: the SS and the Concentration Camps

1. Such as Arendt, H The Concentration Camp. *Partisan Review*, 1948, July, 743.

2. Kogon, E *The Theory and Practice of Hell* (Secker and Warburg, London, 1952).

3. International War Crimes Tribunal, 1947, Vol. 4.

4. International Military Tribunal, Nuremberg, 1947.

5. International War Crimes Tribunal, 1947, Vol. 5.

6. International War Crimes Tribunal, 1947, Vol. 6.

7. International War Crimes Tribunal, 1947, Vol. 3.

8. Bettelheim, B *Surviving the Holocaust* (Fontana Paperbacks, London, 1986), pp. 9–10.

9. Cohen, E *Human Behavior in the Concentration Camp* (Trans. MH Braaksma) (Norton, New York, 1953).

10. Arendt, H *Eichmann in Jerusalem* (Penguin Books, Harmondsworth, 1977). (See Postscript).

11. Cohen, E *Human Behavior in the Concentration Camp* (Trans. MH Braaksma) (Norton, New York, 1953).

12. *Ibid.*

13. This is discussed at length by Müller-Hill, B *Murderous Science. Elimination by Scientific Selection of Jews, Gypsies and Others, Germany 1933–1945* (Trans. GR Fraser) (Oxford University Press, Oxford, 1988).

14. Haritos-Fatouros, M The Official Torturer: A Learning Model for Obedience to the Authority of Violence. *J. App. Soc. Psychol.* 1988, **18**, 1107.

15. Buchheim, H The SS – Instruments of Domination. In Krausnick, H, Buchheim, H, Broszat, M and Jacobsen, H (Eds.) *The Anatomy of the SS State* (Trans. R Barry, M Jackson and D Long) (Collins, London, 1968), p. 143.

16. *Ibid.* pp. 157–166, 203–254.

17. International Military Tribunal, 1947, Vol. 4.

18. Cohen, E *Human Behavior in the Concentration Camp* (Trans. MH Braaksma) (Norton, New York, 1953).

19. Buchheim, H The SS – Instruments of Domination. In Krausnick, H, Buchheim, H, Broszat, M and Jacobsen, H (Eds.) *The Anatomy of the SS State* (Trans. R Barry, M Jackson and D Long) (Collins, London, 1968), p. 255.

20. International War Crimes Tribunal, 1947, Vol. 4.

21. d'Alquen, G *Die SS, Geschichte, Aufgabe, Organisation. Bearbeitet im Auftrage des Reichsführer SS von SS-Standartenführer Günter d'Alquen.* Schriften der Hochschule für Politik. II. Der Organisatorische Aufbau des Dritten Reiches (Junker und Dünnhaupt, Berlin, 1939).

22. Buchheim, H The SS – Instruments of Domination. In Krausnick, H, Buchheim, H, Broszat, M and Jacobsen, H (Eds.) *The Anatomy of the SS State* (Trans. R Barry, M Jackson and D Long) (Collins, London, 1968), pp. 229–234, 264.

23. International War Crimes Tribunal, 1947, Vol. 5.

24. Cohen, E *Human Behavior in the Concentration Camp* (Trans. MH Braaksma) (Norton, New York, 1953).
25. International War Crimes Tribunal, 1947, Vol. 4.
26. For a useful discussion of this drawing on material from outside Nazi Germany, see Koon, TH *Believe, Obey, Fight. Political Socialization of Youth in Fascist Italy, 1922–1943* (University of North Carolina Press, Chapel Hill, 1985).
27. Rhodes, JM *The Hitler Movement: A Modern Millenarian Revolution* (Hoover Institution Press, Stanford, 1980).
28. Koehl, RL *The Black Corps. The Structure and Power Struggles of the Nazi SS* (University of Wisconsin Press, Madison, 1983), p. 167.
29. As discussed in Arendt, H *Eichmann in Jerusalem* (Penguin Books, Harmondsworth, 1977).
30. International Military Tribunal, Nuremberg, Vol. 3, pages 402 onwards.
31. *Ibid*, p. 563.
32. Arendt, H The Concentration Camp. *Partisan Review*, 1948, July, 743.
33. Quoted in Arendt, H The Concentration Camp. *Partisan Review*, 1948, July, 743.
34. Bettelheim, B *Surviving the Holocaust* (Fontana Paperbacks, London, 1986).
35. Bettelheim, B *The Informed Heart* (Peregrine Books, Harmondsworth, 1986).
36. Rousset, D *A World Apart* (Trans. Y Moyse and R Senhouse) (Secker and Warburg, London, 1951).
37. See for example Lifton, RJ Mengele. What Made this Man? *New York Times Magazine*, 21 July 1985, and Posner, GL and Ware, J *Mengele. The Complete Story* (Futura Publications, London, 1986).
38. Quoted by Posner, GL and Ware, J *Mengele. The Complete Story* (Futura Publications, London, 1986), pp. 11–12.
39. See Fest, JC *The Face of the Third Reich* (Penguin Books, Harmondsworth, 1970). See also Müller-Hill, B *Murderous Science. Elimination by Scientific Selection of Jews, Gypsies and Others, Germany 1933–1945* (Trans. GR Fraser) (Oxford University Press, Oxford, 1988).
40. Müller-Hill, B *Murderous Science. Elimination by Scientific Selection of Jews, Gypsies and Others, Germany 1933–1945* (Trans. GR Fraser) (Oxford University Press, Oxford, 1988).
41. *Ibid*, p. 39.
42. Lifton, RJ Mengele. What Made this Man? *New York Times Magazine*, 21 July 1985.
43. *Ibid*.
44. Quoted by Posner, GL and Ware J *Mengele. The Complete Story* (Futura Publications, London, 1986), p. 26.
45. Lifton, RJ Mengele. What Made this Man? *New York Times Magazine*, 21 July 1985.
46. *Ibid*.
47. Posner, GL and Ware, J *Mengele. The Complete Story* (Futura Publications, London, 1986), p. 61.
48. *Ibid*, p. 44.
49. Cohen, E *Human Behaviour in the Concentration Camp* (Trans. MH Braaksma) (Norton, New York, 1953).
50. Cerutti, DT Discrimination Theory of Rule-governed Behaviour. *J. Exp. Anal. Behav.* 1989, **51**, 259.

51. See earlier discussions in Chapter 6, and Parekh, B *Hannah Arendt and the Search for a New Political Philosophy* (Macmillan Press, London, 1981).

52. Merkl, PH *The Making of a Stormtrooper* (Princeton University Press, Princeton, N.J., 1980).

53. Rhodes, JM *The Hitler Movement: A Modern Millenarian Revolution* (Hoover Institution Press, Stanford, 1980), p. 27.

54. Haritos-Fatouros, M The Official Torturer: A Learning Model for Obedience to the Authority of Violence. *J. App. Soc. Psychol.* 1988, **18**, 1107.

55. Bettelheim, B *The Informed Heart* (Peregrine Books, Harmondsworth, 1986).

56. Haritos-Fatouros, M The Official Torturer: A Learning Model for Obedience to the Authority of Violence. *J. App. Soc. Psychol.* 1988, **18**, 1107.

57. Allen, WS *The Nazi Seizure of Power* (Revised Edition) (Penguin Books, Harmondsworth, 1989).

58. Quoted in Rhodes, JM *The Hitler Movement: A Modern Millenarian Revolution* (Hoover Institution Press, Stanford, 1980), p. 167.

59. Arendt, H The Concentration Camp. *Partisan Review*, 1948, July, 743.

60. For example, see Williams, P and Wallace, D *Unit 731* (Hodder and Stoughton, London, 1989).

Chapter 9   The Normality of Excess

1. Hersh, S *My Lai 4: A Report on the Massacre and its Aftermath* (Vintage Books, New York, 1970). For a more general discussion of obedience and violence, see Kelman, HC and Hamilton, VL *Crimes of Obedience. Towards a Social Psychology of Authority and Responsibility* (Yale University Press, New Haven and London, 1989).

2. Goldstein, J, Marshall, B and Schwartz, J (Eds.) *The Mai Lai Massacre and its Cover Up: Beyond the Reach of Law?* (Academic Press, New York, 1976).

3. *Ibid.*

4. Hersh, S *My Lai 4: A Report on the Massacre and its Aftermath* (Vintage Books, New York, 1970).

5. Manual for Courts Martial, United States, 1969. Par. 16, sub-par. d.

6. *Ibid.*

7. Malott, RW Rule Governed Behavior and Behavioral Anthropology. *The Behavior Analyst*, 1988, **11**, 181-200.

8. *Ibid.*

9. Donovan, D *Once a Warrior King. Memories of an Officer in Vietnam* (Corgi Books, London, 1987).

10. Cordes, B *When Terrorists Do the Talking: Reflections on Terrorist Literature* (Rand Corporation, Santa Monica, 1987).

11. Crenshaw, M Theories of Terrorism: Instrumental and Organizational Approaches. In Rapoport, DC (Ed.) *Inside Terrorist Organizations* (Frank Cass and Co., London, 1988).

Bibliography

Adorno, T, Frenkel-Brunswick, E, Levinson, D and Sanford, RN *The Authoritarian Personality* (Harper and Row, New York, 1950).

Alford, CF The Organisation of Evil. *Political Psychology*, 1990, **11**, 5.

Allen, VL and Wilder, DA Impact of Group Consensus and Social Support on Stimulus Meaning: Mediation of Conformity by Cognitive Restructuring. *J. Pers. Soc. Psychol.* 1980, **39**, 1116.

Allen, WS *The Nazi Seizure of Power* (Revised Edition) (Penguin Books, Harmondsworth, 1989).

d'Alquen, G *Die SS, Geschichte, Aufgabe, Organisation. Bearbeitet im Auftrage des Reichsführer SS von SS-Standartenführer Günter d'Alquen.* Schriften der Hochschule für Politik. II. Der Organisatorische Aufbau des Dritten Reiches (Junker und Dünnhaupt, Berlin, 1939).

Arendt, H The Concentration Camp. *Partisan Review*, 1948, July, 743.

Arendt, H *The Origins of Totalitarianism* (André Deutsch, London, 1951).

Arendt, H *The Human Condition* (University of Chicago Press, Chicago, 1958).

Arendt, H *Eichmann in Jerusalem. A Report on the Banality of Evil* (Penguin Books, Harmondsworth, 1977).

Asch, SE Effects of Group Pressure upon the Modification and Distortion of Judgement. In Guetzkow, H (Ed.) *Groups, Leadership and Men* (Carnegie, Pittsburgh, 1951).

Aust, S *The Baader-Meinhof Group. The Inside Story of a Phenomenon* (Trans. Anthea Bell) (Bodley Head, London, 1987).

Baldwin, JD Mead and Skinner: Agency and Determinism. *Behaviorism*, 1988, **16**, 109.

Baron, RA and Byrne, D *Social Psychology. Understanding Human Interaction* (Allyn and Bacon, Newton, Mass., 1984).

Begin, M *The Revolt – Story of the Irgun* (Schuman, New York, 1951).

Bettelheim, B *The Informed Heart* (Peregrine Books, Harmondsworth, 1986).

Bettelheim, B *Surviving the Holocaust* (Fontana Paperbacks, London, 1986).

Beresford, D *Ten Men Dead* (Grafton Books, London, 1987).

Billig, M *Ideology and Social Psychology* (Blackwell, Oxford, 1982).

Billig, M, Condor, S, Edwards, D, Gane, M, Middleton, D and Radley, A *Ideological Dilemmas. A Social Psychology of Everyday Thinking* (Sage Publications, London, 1988).

Bird, C *Social Psychology* (Appleton Century, New York, 1940).

Bittner, E *The Functions of the Police in Modern Society* (National Institute for Mental Health, Washington, D.C., 1970).

Blakely, E and Schlinger, H Rules: Function-Altering Contingency-Specifying Stimuli. *The Behavior Analyst*, 1987, **10**, 183–188.

Brown, V *The Sunday Tribune*, Dublin, 28 June 1990.

Brockner, J and Rubin, JZ *Entrapment in Escalating Conflicts* (Springer-Verlag, New York, 1985).

Buchheim, H The SS – Instruments of Domination. In Krausnick, H, Buchheim, H, Broszat, M and Jacobsen, H (Eds.) *The Anatomy of the SS State* (Trans. R Barry, M Jackson and D Long) (Collins, London, 1968).

Burridge, K *Tangu Traditions* (Clarendon Press, Oxford, 1969).

Burridge, K *New Heaven, New Earth. A Study of Millenarian Activities* (Blackwell, London, 1971).

Camus, Albert (Trans. A Bower) *The Rebel* (Penguin Books, Harmondsworth, 1971).

Cerutti, DT Discrimination Theory of Rule-Governed Behavior. *J. Exp. Anal. Behav.* 1989, **51**, 259.

Christie, R Review of the Psychology of Politics, by HJ Eysenck. *Amer. J. Psychol.* 1955, **68**, 702.

Clausewitz, C von *On War* (Trans JJ Graham) (Penguin Books, Harmondsworth, 1968).

Cleckley, H. *The Mask of Sanity* (CV Mosby Co., St. Louis, 1976).

Cocks, G Contribution of Psychohistory to Understanding Politics. In Herman, MG (Ed.) *Political Psychology* (Jossey-Bass, San Francisco, 1986).

Cohen, E *Human Behavior in the Concentration Camp* (Trans. MH Braaksma) (Norton, New York, 1953).

Cohn, N *The Pursuit of the Millennium. Revolutionary Millenarians and Mystical Anarchists of the Middle Ages* (Palladin, London, 1970).

Cordes, B *When Terrorists Do the Talking: Reflections on Terrorist Literature* (Rand Corporation, Santa Monica, 1987).

Cordes, B When Terrorists do the Talking: Reflections on Terrorist Literature. In Rapoport, DC (Ed.) *Inside Terrorist Organisations* (Frank Cass and Co., London, 1988).

Cornish, DB and Clarke RV *The Reasoning Criminal. Rational Choice Perspectives on Offending* (Springer-Verlag, New York, 1986).

Crenshaw, M Theories of Terrorism: Instrumental and Organisation Approaches. In Rapoport, DC (Ed.) *Inside Terrorist Organisations* (Frank Cass and Co., London, 1988).

Crutchfield, RA Conformity and Character. *American Psychologist*, 1955, **10**, 191.

Dale, SF Religious Suicide in Islamic Asia. *J. Conflict Resolution*, 1988, **32**, 37.

Davies, JC The History of Utopia: the Chronology of Nowhere. In Alexander, P and Gill, R (Eds.) *Utopias* (Duckworth, London, 1984).

Davies, JC The Roots of Political Behavior. In Herman, MG (Ed.) *Political Psychology* (Jossey-Bass, San Francisco, 1986).

Denardo, J *Power in Numbers: the Political Strategy of Protest and Rebellion* (Princeton University Press, Princeton, 1984).

Diagnostic and Statistical Manual of Mental Disorder (3rd Edition) (American Psychiatric Association, Washington, D.C. 1980).

Dietrich, DJ National Renewal, Anti-Semitism, and Political Continuity: A Psychological Assessment. *Political Psychology*, 1988, **9**, 385.

Donovan, D *Once a Warrior King. Memories of an Officer in Vietnam* (Corgi Books, London, 1987).

Elliott, M *Wolf Tone: Prophet of Irish Independence* (Yale University Press, New Haven, 1989).

Eysenck, HJ *The Structure of Human Personality* (Wiley, London, 1953).

Eysenck, HJ *The Psychology of Politics* (Routledge and Kegan Paul, London, 1954).

Federal Government, Bonn *German Resistance to National Socialism.* Press and Information Office. Undated.

Feldman, MD The Challenge of Self-Mutilation: A Review. *Comprehensive Psychiatry*, 1988, **29**, 252.

Fest, JC *The Face of the Third Reich* (Weidenfeld and Nicholson, London, 1970).

Festinger, L, Ricken, HW and Schachter, S *When Prophecy Fails* (Univ. Minnesota Press, St. Paul, 1956).

Foa, UG Resource Theory of Social Exchanges. In Thibault, JS, Spence, J and Carlson, R (Eds.) *Contemporary Topics in Social Psychology* (General Learning Press, Morristown, N.J., 1976).

Foster RF *Modern Ireland 1600–1972* (Allen Lane, The Penguin Press, Harmondsworth, 1988).

Glenn, SS Contingencies and Metacontingencies: Towards a Synthesis of Behavioral Analysis and Cultural Materialism. *The Behavior Analyst*, 1988, **11**, 161.

Goldstein, J, Marshall, B and Schwartz, J (Eds.) *The Mai Lai Massacre and its Cover Up: Beyond the Reach of Law?* (Academic Press, New York, 1976).

Goldstein, JH Beliefs about Human Aggression. In Groebel, J and Hinde, RA (Eds.) *Aggression and War, Their Biological and Social Bases* (Cambridge University Press, Cambridge, 1989).

Graumann, CF and Moscovici, S *Changing Conceptions of Crowd Mind and Behavior* (Springer-Verlag, New York, 1986).

Gurr, TR *Why Men Rebel* (Princeton, New Jersey, 1970).

Hare, RD Criminal Psychopaths. In Yuille, JC (Ed.) *Police Selection and Training* (Martinus Nijhoff, Dordrecht, 1986).

Haritos-Fatouros, M The Official Torturer: A Learning Model for Obedience to the Authority of Violence. *J. App. Soc. Psychol.* 1988, **18**, 1107.

Harris, M *Cultural Anthropology* (Harper and Row, New York, 1983).

Harrison, JFC Millennium and Utopia. In Alexander, P and Gill, R (Eds.) *Utopias* (Duckworth, London, 1984).

Harrison, JFC *The Second Coming. Popular Millenarianism 1780–1850* (Routledge and Kegan Paul, London, 1984).

Hayes, SC (Ed.) *Rule-Governed Behavior. Cognition, Contingencies and Instructional Control* (Plenum Press, New York, 1989).

Hayes, SC, Zettle, RD and Rosenfarb, I Rule Following. In Hayes, SC (Ed.) *Rule-Governed Behavior. Cognition, Contingencies and Instructional Control* (Plenum Press, New York, 1989).

Herman, MG Ingredients of Leadership. In Herman, MG *Political Psychology* (Jossey-Bass, San Francisco, 1986).

Hersh, S *My Lai 4: A Report on the Massacre and its Aftermath* (Vintage Books, New York, 1970).

Hewitt, C Terrorism and Public Opinion: A Five Country Comparison. *Terrorism and Political Violence*, 1990, **2**, 145.

Hinde, RA and Groebel, J The Problem of Aggression. In Groebel J and Hinde RA (Eds.) *Aggression and War, Their Biological and Social Bases* (Cambridge University Press, Cambridge, 1989).

International Military Tribunal. *Proceedings of the International Military Tribunal, Nuremburg*. Official Text in the English language. Nuremberg, 1947. Volumes I – XII.

Janis, IL *Groupthink* (2nd edition) (Houghton-Mifflin, Boston, 1982).

Jansen, JJG *The Neglected Duty. The Creed of Sadat's Assassins and Islamic Resurgence in the Middle East* (Macmillan, New York, 1986).

Jeffrey, K Security Policy in Northern Ireland: Some Reflections on the Management of Violence. *Terrorism and Political Violence*, 1990, **2**, 21.

Kellen, K *Terrorists – What are they like? How Some Terrorists Describe their World and Actions* (Rand Corporation, Santa Monica, 1979).

Kelman, HC and Hamilton, VC *Crimes of Obedience. Towards a Social Psychology of Obedience and Violence* (Yale University Press, New Haven and London, 1989).

Kinkade, K *A Walden Two Experiment* (William Morrow, New York, 1973).

Koehl, RL *The Black Corps, The Structure and Power Struggles of the Nazi SS* (University of Wisconsin Press, Madison, 1983).

Kogon, E *The Theory and Practice of Hell* (Secker and Warburg, London, 1952).

Koon, TH *Believe, Obey, Fight. Political Socialization of Youth in Fascist Italy, 1922–1943*. (University of North Carolina Press, Chapel Hill, 1985).

Kramer, M The Moral Logic of Hizballah. In Reich, W (Ed.) *Origins of Terrorism: Psychologies, Ideologies, Theologies, States of Mind* (Cambridge University Press, Cambridge, 1990).

Lasswell, HD *Psychopathology and Politics* (Univ. Chicago Press, Chicago, 1931).

Le Bon, G *The Crowd* (Ernst Benn, London, 1952).

Lee, JJ *Ireland 1912–1985: Politics and Society* (Cambridge University Press, Cambridge, 1989).

Leites, N and Wolfe C *Rebellion and Authority* (Rand Corporation, Santa Barbara, 1970).

Lenin, VI The State and Revolution (1917). In VI Lenin *Collected Works* Vol. 25 (Lawrence and Wishart, London, 1960).

Lewis, B *The Assassins* (Octagon Books, New York, 1968).

Lidz, RW, Lidz T and Burton-Bradley, BG Culture, Personality and Social Structure. Cargo Cultism – a Psychosocial Study of Melanesian Millenarianism *J. Nerv. Ment. Dis.* 1973, **157**, 370.

Lifton, RJ Mengele. What Made this Man? *New York Times Magazine*, 21 July 1985.

Lovaas, OI A Program for the Establishment of Speech in Psychotic Children. In Wing, JK (Ed.) *Early Childhood Autism* (Pergamon, New York, 1966).

Lovaas, OI *Behavioral Treatment of Autistic Children* (General Learning Press, Morristown, N.J., 1973).

Lukes, S Marxism and Utopianism. In Alexander, P and Gill, R (Eds.) *Utopias* (Duckworth, London, 1984).

Macfarlane, L The Right to Self-Determination in Ireland and the Justification of IRA Violence. *Terrorism and Political Violence* 1990, **2**, 35.

Malott, RW Rule Governed Behavior and Behavioral Anthropology. *The Behavior Analyst*, 1988, **11**, 181–200.

Mason, T Individual Participation in Collective Racial Violence and Terror: A Rational Choice Synthesis. *Amer. Pol. Sci. Rev.* 1984, **78**, 1040.

Masters, B *Killing for Company* (Jonathan Cape, London, 1985).

Mead, GH *Mind, Self and Society* (University of Chicago Press, Chicago, 1934).

Merkl, PH *The Making of a Stormtrooper* (Princeton University Press, Princeton, N.J., 1980).

Milgram, S Some Conditions of Obedience and Disobedience to Authority. *Human Relations*, 1965, **18**, 57.

Milgram, S *Obedience to Authority* (Harper, New York, 1974).

Milgram, S The Social Meaning of Fanaticism *et cetera*, 1977, **34**, 58.

Morris, J *The Nobility of Failure: Tragic Heroes in the History of Japan* (Secker and Warburg, London, 1975).

Morrissey, M and Pease, K The Black Criminal Justice System in West Belfast. *The Howard Journal*, 1982, **xxi**, 159.

Morrison, A Uses of Utopia. In Alexander, P and Gill, R (Eds.) *Utopias* (Duckworth, London, 1984).

Moscovici, S *The Age of the Crowd* (Cambridge University Press, Cambridge, 1985).

Muller, EN The Psychology of Political Protest and Violence. In Gurr, TR (Ed.) *Handbook of Political Conflict: Theory and Research* (Free Press, New York, 1983).

Muller, EN Income Inequality, Regime Repressiveness and Political Violence. *Amer. Sociol. Rev.* 1985, **50**, 47.

Müller-Hill, B *Murderous Science. Elimination by Scientific Selection of Jews, Gypsies and Others, Germany 1933–1945* (Trans. GR Fraser) (Oxford University Press, Oxford, 1988).

Myers, DG Polarizing Effects of Social Interaction. In Brandstatter, H, Davis, JH and Stocker-Kreichgauer, G (Eds.) *Group Decision Processes* (Academic Press, London, 1983).

Nee, C and Taylor, M Residential Burglary in the Republic of Ireland: a Situational Perspective. *Howard Journal*, 1988, **27**, 105.

Pankhurst, ES *The Suffragette Movement. An Intimate Account of Persons and Ideals* (Virago, London, 1977).

Parekh, B *Hannah Arendt and the Search for a New Political Philosophy* (Macmillan Press, London, 1981).

Popper, KR *Conjectures and Refutations* (Routledge and Kegan Paul, London, 1963).

Posner, GL and Ware, J *Mengele. The Complete Story* (Futura Publications, London, 1986).

Post, JM Hostilité, conformité, fraternité: The group dynamics of terrorist behaviour. *Int. J. Psychotherap.* 1986, **36**, 211.

Qutb, S *Milestones* (International Islamic Federation of Student Organizations, Holy Koran Publishing House, Beirut and Damascus, 1978).

Rapoport, DC Fear and Trembling: Terrorism in Three Religious Traditions. *Amer. Pol. Sci. Rev.* 1984, **78**, 658.

Rapoport, DC Messianism and Terror. *The Center Magazine*, 1986, Jan/Feb. 30–39.

Rapoport, DC Why Does Religious Messianism Produce Terror? In Wilkinson, P and Stewart, AM (Eds.) *Contemporary Research on Terrorism* (Aberdeen University Press, Aberdeen, 1987).

Rapoport, DC Some Observations on Religion and Violence. Paper presented to XIIth World Congress of Sociology, Madrid, Spain, 1990.

Ray, JJ Cognitive Style as a Predictor of Authoritarianism, Conservatism and Racism: A Fantasy in Many Movements. *Political Psychology*, 1988, **9**, 303.

Reese, HW Rules and Rule Governance: Cognitive and Behavioral Issues. In Hayes, SC (Ed.) *Rule-Governed Behavior. Cognition, Contingencies and Instructional Control* (Plenum Press, New York, 1989).

Rhodes, JM *The Hitler Movement: A Modern Millenarian Revolution* (Hoover Institution Press, Stanford, 1980).

Rokeach, M *Belief, Attitude and Values* (Jossey-Bass, San Francisco, 1968).

Rokeach, M and Hanley, C Eysenck's Tendermindedness Dimension: A Critique. *Psychol. Bull.* 1956, **53**, 169.

Rosenhan, DL and Seligman, MEP *Abnormal Psychology* (2nd Edition) (WW Norton and Co., New York, 1989).

Ross, AO *Child Behaviour Therapy. Principles, Procedures and Empirical Basis* (John Wiley and Sons, New York, 1981).

Rousset, D *A World Apart* (Trans Y Moyse and R Senhouse) (Secker and Warburg, London, 1951).

Rudin, J *Fanaticism. A Psychological Analysis* (Trans E Reinecke and PC Bailey) (Univ. Notre Dame Press, Notre Dame, London, 1969).

Schachter, S *The Psychology of Affiliation* (Stanford University Press, Stanford, 1959).

Schlinger, H and Blakeley, E Function Altering Effects of Contingency-Specifying Stimuli. *The Behavior Analyst*, 1987, **10**, 27–40.

Sivan, E *Radical Islam. Medieval Theology and Modern Politics* (Yale University Press, New Haven, 1985).

Skinner, BF *Walden Two* (Macmillan Paperback, New York, 1948).

Skinner, BF *Science and Human Behavior* (Free Press, New York, 1953).

Skinner, BF *Contingencies of Reinforcement* (Appleton-Century-Crofts, New York, 1968).

Skinner, BF *Contingencies of Reinforcement: a theoretical analysis* (Appleton-Century-Crofts, New York, 1969).

Skinner, BF *Beyond Freedom and Dignity* (Knopf, New York, 1971, and Penguin Books, Harmondsworth, 1971).

Skinner, BF The Behavior of the Listener. In Hayes, SC (Ed.) *Rule-Governed Behavior. Cognition, Contingencies and Instructional Control* (Plenum Press, New York, 1989).

Smyth, J Unintentional Mobilization: The Effects of the 1980–1981 Hunger Strikes in Ireland. *Political Communication and Persuasion*, 1987, **4**, 179.

Smyth, J Stretching the Boundaries: The Control of Dissent in Northern Ireland. *Terrorism*, 1988, **11**, 289.

Snow, DE, Burke Rochford, E, Worden, SK and Benford, RD Frame Alignment Processes, Micromobilization and Movement Participation. *Amer. Sociol. Rev.* 1986, **51**, 464.

Staats, A *Social Behaviorism* (Dorsey Press, Homewood, Ill., 1975).

Stern, SL and Mendels, J Affective Disorders. In Kazdin, AE Bellack, AS and Hersen, M (Eds.) *New Perspectives in Abnormal Psychology* (Oxford University Press, New York, 1980).

Stone, WP and Schaffner, PE *The Psychology of Politics* (Free Press, New York, 1988).

Taheri, A *Holy Terror. The Inside Story of Islamic Terrorism* (Century Hutchinson, London, 1987).

Taylor, A *A Vision of Harmony* (Clarendon Press, Oxford, 1987).

Taylor, M *The Terrorist* (Brassey's Defence Publishers, London, 1988).

Taylor, M and Ryan, H Fanaticism, Political Suicide and Terrorism. *Terrorism*, 1988, **11**, 91.

Thompson, JLP Deprivation, Resources and the Moral Dimension: A Time-Series Analysis of Collective Violence in Northern Ireland, 1922–1985. Paper presented to HF Guggenheim Conference on Terrorism and Public Policy, Santa Fe, 1987.

Tinklenburg, JR and Ochberg, FM Patterns of Violence: a California Sample. In Hamburg, DA and Trudeau, MB (Eds.) *Biobehavioral Aspects of Aggression* (Liss, New York, 1981).

Toloyan, K Martyrdom as Legitimacy: Terrorism, Religion and Symbolic Appropriation in the Armenian Diaspora. In Wilkinson, P and Stewart, AM (Eds.) *Contemporary Research on Terrorism* (Aberdeen University Press, Aberdeen, 1987).

Tomkins, SS Left and Right: a Basic Dimension of Ideology and Personality. In White, RW (Ed.) *The Study of Lives* (Atherton, New York, 1963).

Townshend, C The Process of Irish Politics. In O'Sullivan, N (Ed.) *Terrorism, Ideology and Revolution* (Westview Press, Boulder, Co., 1986).

Vaughan, M Rule-governed Behavior and Higher Mental Processes. In Modgil, S and Modgil, C (Eds.) *BF Skinner: Consensus and Controversy* (Falmer Press, New York, 1987).

Watzlawick, P The Pathologies of Perfectionism *et cetera*, 1977, **34**, 12.

Williams P and Wallace, D *Unit 731* (Hodder and Stoughton, London, 1989).

Wilson, B *Magic and the Millennium* (Heinemann Books, London, 1973).

Whorf, BL Science and Linguistics. In Carroll, JB (Ed.) *Language, Thought and Reality: Selected Writings of Benjamin Lee Whorf* (MIT Press, Cambridge, Mass., 1956).

Ziegler, P *The Black Death* (Penguin Books, Harmondsworth, 1984).

Index